IMPORTANT:

 W9-AVN-972

HERE IS YOUR REGISTRATION CODE TO ACCESS
YOUR PREMIUM McGRAW-HILL ONLINE RESOURCES.

For key premium online resources you need THIS CODE to gain access. Once the code is entered, you will be able to use the Web resources for the length of your course.

If your course is using **WebCT** or **Blackboard**, you'll be able to use this code to access the McGraw-Hill content within your instructor's online course.

Access is provided if you have purchased a new book. If the registration code is missing from this book, the registration screen on our Website, and within your WebCT or Blackboard course, will tell you how to obtain your new code.

Registering for McGraw-Hill Online Resources

TO gain access to your McGraw-Hill web
resources simply follow the steps below:

1. USE YOUR WEB BROWSER TO GO TO: **http://www.mhhe.com/airasian5e**

2. CLICK ON **FIRST TIME USER**.

3. ENTER THE REGISTRATION CODE* PRINTED ON THE TEAR-OFF BOOKMARK ON THE RIGHT.

4. AFTER YOU HAVE ENTERED YOUR REGISTRATION CODE, CLICK **REGISTER**.

5. FOLLOW THE INSTRUCTIONS TO SET-UP YOUR PERSONAL UserID AND PASSWORD.

6. WRITE YOUR UserID AND PASSWORD DOWN FOR FUTURE REFERENCE.
   KEEP IT IN A SAFE PLACE.

TO GAIN ACCESS to the McGraw-Hill content in your instructor's **WebCT** or **Blackboard** course simply log in to the course with the UserID and Password provided by your instructor. Enter the registration code exactly as it appears in the box to the right when prompted by the system. You will only need to use the code the first time you click on McGraw-Hill content.

Thank you, and welcome
to your McGraw-Hill
online Resources!

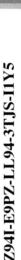

REGISTRATION CODE

Z94I-E9PZ-LL94-3TJS-I1Y5

* YOUR REGISTRATION CODE CAN BE USED ONLY ONCE TO ESTABLISH ACCESS. IT IS NOT TRANSFERABLE.

0-07-298853-3 T/A AIRASIAN: CLASSROOM ASSESSMENT, 5/E

CLASSROOM ASSESSMENT

FIFTH EDITION

CLASSROOM ASSESSMENT

CONCEPTS AND APPLICATIONS

PETER W. AIRASIAN

Boston College

Boston   Burr Ridge, IL   Dubuque, IA   Madison, WI   New York   San Francisco   St. Louis
Bangkok   Bogotá   Caracas   Kuala Lumpur   Lisbon   London   Madrid   Mexico City
Milan   Montreal   New Delhi   Santiago   Seoul   Singapore   Sydney   Taipei   Toronto

The *McGraw-Hill* Companies

Higher Education

CLASSROOM ASSESSMENT: KEY CONCEPTS AND APPLICATIONS, FIFTH EDITION

Published by McGraw-Hill, a business unit of The McGraw-Hill Companies, Inc., 1221 Avenue of the Americas, New York, NY 10020. Copyright © 2005, 2001, 1997, 1994, 1991 by The McGraw-Hill Companies, Inc. All rights reserved. No part of this publication may be reproduced or distributed in any form or by any means, or stored in a database or retrieval system, without the prior written consent of The McGraw-Hill Companies, Inc., including, but not limited to, in any network or other electronic storage or transmission, or broadcast for distance learning.

Some ancillaries, including electronic and print components, may not be available to customers outside the United States.

 This book is printed on acid-free paper.

1 2 3 4 5 6 7 8 9 0 QPF/QPF 0 9 8 7 6 5 4

ISBN 0-07-248869-7

Publisher: *Emily Barosse*
Sponsoring Editor: *David S. Patterson*
Senior Developmental Editor: *Cara Harvey*
Developmental Editors: *Beth Kaufman, Alan Venable*
Senior Marketing Manager: *Pamela S. Cooper*
Media Producer: *Shannon Gattens*
Project Manager: *Richard H. Hecker*
Senior Production Supervisor: *Jason Huls*
Senior Designer: *Violetta Diaz*
Media Project Manager: *Meghan Durko*
Associate Photo Research Coordinator: *Natalia C. Peschiera*
Photo Researcher: *Natalia Peschiera*
Cover Design: *Lisa Buckley*
Cover Images: © *Eric Fowke/Photo Edit;* © *Bob Daemmrich/The Image Works*
Typeface: *10/12 Valjovic*
Compositor: *Shepherd, Inc.*
Printer: *Quebecor World Fairfield Inc.*

Library Of Congress Cataloging-in-Publication Data

Airasian, Peter W.
    Classroom assessment : concepts and applications / Peter W. Airasian.—5th ed.
      p. cm.
    Includes bibliographical references and index.
    ISBN 0-07-248869-7 (softcover : alk. paper)
    1. Educational tests and measurements—United States. 2. Academic achievement—United States—Testing. 3. Education—United States—Evaluation. I. Title.

LB3051.A5627 2005
371.26'0973—dc22

2004049358

www.mhhe.com

*I dedicate this book
to Lynn and Greg, and
always, to Gwen.*

ABOUT THE AUTHOR

Peter W. Airasian is Professor of Education at Boston College, where he is Chair of the Department of Counseling, Developmental Psychology, and Research Methods. His main teaching responsibilities are instructing pre- and in-service teachers in classroom assessment. He received his PhD degree from the University of Chicago, with a concentration in assessment and evaluation. He is a former high school chemistry and biology teacher. He is coauthor of *Minimal Competency Testing* (1979), *School Effectiveness: A Reassessment of the Evidence* (1980), *The Effects of Standardized Testing* (1982), *Assessment in the Classroom* (1996), *Teacher Self-Evaluation Tool Kit* (2001), *Taxonomy for Learning, Teaching, & Assessing: A Revision of Bloom's Taxonomy of Educational Objectives* (2001), and *Educational Research: Competencies for Analysis and Applications* (2002), as well as many articles on classroom assessment and testing. He is past Chair of the American Educational Research Association's Special Interest Group on Classroom Assessment. Currently, he is studying the process classroom teachers use to assess themselves.

BRIEF CONTENTS

CONTENTS

CHAPTER 5

ASSESSMENT DURING INSTRUCTION   123

ASSESSMENT TASKS DURING INSTRUCTION   125

VALIDITY AND RELIABILITY IN INSTRUCTIONAL ASSESSMENT   130

IMPROVING ASSESSMENT DURING INSTRUCTION   133

QUESTIONING: PURPOSES AND STRATEGIES   135

ACCOMMODATIONS DURING INSTRUCTION   141

CHAPTER 6

OFFICIAL ASSESSMENTS   149

FORMATIVE AND SUMMATIVE ASSESSMENTS   150

THE LOGIC OF FORMAL ASSESSMENT   153

PLANNING AN OFFICIAL ASSESSMENT   154

PREPARING PUPILS FOR OFFICIAL ASSESSMENTS   162

CHAPTER 7
PAPER-AND-PENCIL TESTING   172

CHAPTER 8
IMPROVING PAPER-AND-PENCIL ASSESSMENTS   204

PREFACE

A Conceptual and Applied Approach

This is a textbook for students taking a first course in classroom assessment. As in previous editions, the goal of *Classroom Assessment: Concepts and Applications,* fifth edition, is to show how skilled assessment underlies a teacher's craft, driving decisions in planning and in the course of teaching itself. The text is organized to relate the principles of assessment to the natural progression of a teacher's work—from organizing the classroom as a social setting, to planning and conducting instruction based upon sound objectives, to the formal assessment of pupil learning, to grading students, and finally to interpreting standardized tests and statewide assessments. The goal is to show students that assessment is an ongoing part of teaching, not some esoteric activity divorced from the daily classroom routine.

The ability to construct and use classroom assessments is an essential educational skill for all teachers. Ongoing formal and informal classroom assessments provide teachers with the information they need to monitor and make decisions about their teaching and their students' learning. Increasingly, teachers must address not only their own traditional classroom assessments, but also those required by external sources of assessment such as statewide testing and standardized tests. This text covers the broad range of assessments that confront teachers both in their classrooms and beyond. Each type of assessment is presented with attention to both concepts and application, so students will understand the reasons and cautions that are inherent in the assessments they construct and interpret.

Proven Features and Content

This edition includes many of the features of prior editions.

Realistic Assessment: The focus throughout is on the realities of classrooms and how assessments can serve these realities.

Validity and Reliability: These central assessment concepts are introduced in the first chapter and then linked in later chapters to each specific type of assessment information. The validity and reliability issues of informal assessment, planning and delivering instruction, grading, using paper-and-pencil tests, performance assessments, and standardized testing are identified. Practical strategies to improve validity and reliability of varied assessment approaches are presented in each chapter.

Practical Guidelines: A significant portion of each chapter focuses on practical guidelines to follow and common errors to avoid when using the type of assessment being presented. The implications of ignoring the recommendations are also described.

Teacher Thinking: Throughout the text, excerpts from teachers about assessment add the wisdom of day-to-day practice to assessment situations.

Student-Friendly Writing Style: The text is written with a clear, friendly, and accessible style and is well integrated with examples and tables to thoroughly engage students.

New to the Fifth Edition

The fifth edition of *Classroom Assessment* has been expanded to include a number of helpful features.

Thinking About Teaching: Questions at the opening of each chapter prompt students to put chapter topics into the context of the classroom.

Case Studies: Accessible through the Online Learning Center, case studies bring chapter topics to life.

Key Assessment Tools: These boxes, at least two for each chapter, highlight practical resources and tools to use in the assessment process.

Assessment and Technology: These boxes highlight ways to use technology in assessment.

No Child Left Behind: New coverage of No Child Left Behind legislation and expanded coverage of high-stakes testing is provided.

Children with Special Needs: The assessment of children with special needs has been integrated into many chapters of this book.

Test Construction: Coverage of ways to construct student tests has been greatly expanded.

Online Learning Center. Located at www.mhhe.com/airasian5e, this center includes a student study guide with practice quizzes, case studies, Web links, and PowerWeb current news articles.

In addition to the above improvements, instructors who have used the fourth edition will notice that the coverage of educational objectives has been expanded to two chapters, and that performance assessment is now covered in one chapter instead of two.

McGraw-Hill's Primis Online
www.mhhe.com/primis/online

McGraw-Hill's Primis Online is an ideal solution for instructors looking for a briefer assessment text—whether to fit the need of a one-credit course or a course that covers several major topics. Through Primis Online you can choose the material you want to use from *Classroom Assessment* and, if you wish, mix and match materials from other McGraw-Hill texts. Create a custom text for consideration for your course, or order as many different books as you like. There is no cost to you, no obligation, and no minimum number of student copies per order.

Here's how it works:

1. Visit www.mhhe.com/primis/online and select "EDUCATION" from the discipline drop-down menu found on the blue bar to the left of your screen. You can also call us (1-800-962-9342) if you prefer to work over the phone.

2. Click on Airasian Classroom Assessment, 5/e, in the listing. Click on "Add" to select the chapters you wish to include in your custom printed textbook or eBook. To aid your decision making, you can "View" the complete text of the book online with a professor password. If you wish, add selections from other textbooks to address new topics outside the main book coverage.

3. Use the progress bar steps (located in the top blue bar) to step you through the book creation process. "Review" and rearrange the order of your selections, fill in and save your "Cover" information, and then fill in and save your shipping information to "Finish." Then submit your complimentary review copy to us.

4. Eight to 10 days later, visit your mailbox because we have mailed your actual printed book. Review your complimentary examination copy. Make changes online, by fax, or by phone.

5. If you want to adopt, give your bookstore the ISBN on your approved custom book so they can place an order for your custom version of *Classroom Assessment.* Your text will be on bookstore shelves in 4 to 6 weeks—designed and priced especially for your needs and for those of your students.

Supplements that Accompany Classroom Assessment

For the Instructor

Instructor's Manual: An updated and expanded instructor's manual is available on the Instructor's Resource CD-ROM.

Test Bank: An updated test bank, in Microsoft Word and as a computerized test bank, is available on the Instructor's Resource CD-ROM.

PowerPoint Slides: PowerPoint slides are now available on the Instructor's Resource CD-ROM and on the instructor's area of the Online Learning Center.

For the Student

Online Learning Center: The new Online Learning Center at www.mhhe.com/airasian5e includes practice quizzes (with feedback), a student study guide, case studies, examples of assessment tools, Web links, PowerWeb articles, and PowerWeb current news articles.

Acknowledgments

With appreciation for their efforts to improve this work, I acknowledge the following reviewers whose frank and detailed suggestions added much to this revision:

Linda Espey, Drake University

Jean Ann Foley, Northern Arizona University

Theresa Harris, Coppin State College

Mahnaz Moallem, University of North Carolina at Wilmington

Patricia Morrell, University of Portland

Bruce G. Rogers, University of Northern Iowa

Terry H. Stepka, Arkansas State University

Beth Kaufman of McGraw-Hill was exceptionally supportive in the development of this revision. Alan Venable and Cara Harvey provided suggestions that greatly improved the edition.

Damian Bebell, Miguel Ramos, James W. Cheng, and Dana Diaconu provided suggestions during the writing.

Peter W. Airasian
Boston College

CHAPTER 1

THE BREADTH OF CLASSROOM ASSESSMENT

KEY TOPICS

- *Purposes of Classroom Assessment*

- *Types of Assessment*

- *Assessment, Testing, Measurement, and Evaluation*

- *Three General Ways to Collect Data: Paper-and-Pencil, Observation, and Oral Questioning*

- *Standardized and Nonstandardized Assessments*

- *Good Assessments: Valid and Reliable*

- *Ethical Issues and Responsibilities*

CHAPTER OBJECTIVES

After reading this chapter, you will be able to:

♦ Define assessment, measurement, test, standardized, validity, reliability, and other basic terms
♦ Describe the various purposes of assessment
♦ Contrast the three main types of assessment and give examples of each
♦ Describe common methods of collecting assessment information
♦ Explain what validity and reliability are and how they influence the use of assessment information
♦ State examples of teachers' ethical responsibilities in collecting or using assessment information

THINKING ABOUT TEACHING

How do school teachers differ from other groups who are called teachers?

Assessment is the process of collecting, synthesizing, and interpreting information to aid in decision making. Assessment is a necessary part of classroom life.

Classroom assessment is the process of collecting, synthesizing, and interpreting information to aid in classroom decision making. This book explores a broad range of assessment strategies for classroom management, instruction, and planning. Chapter 1 lays out a general scheme of types of assessments and their uses that will be covered more deeply in later chapters. It explains how validity and reliability are the keys to effective assessment. It ends with some thoughts about ethical issues related to classroom assessment.

Every day in every classroom, teachers make decisions about their pupils, the success of their instruction, and the classroom climate. Today was a typical day in Ms. Lopez's classroom. In addition to meeting the school buses in the morning, readying the room for the day's activities, putting the work schedule on the chalkboard, reviewing her lesson plans, greeting pupils as they entered the classroom, taking attendance, distributing supplies, reminding pupils of next Saturday's school fair, and monitoring the lunchroom, Ms. Lopez also performed the following tasks.

♦ Assigned grades to her pupils' science tests on the planets
♦ Referred Aaron to the Special Education Department to be screened for poor gross motor skills
♦ Completed the monthly school progress report on each pupil in the class
♦ Moved Tamika from the middle to the high reading group
♦ Selected Rosa, not Sarah, to deliver a note to Mr. Brown, the school principal
♦ Decided on topics to cover in next Monday's math lesson
♦ Met with the special education teacher to review the accommodations Mauricio needed when taking a multiple-choice test

◆ Stopped the planned language lesson halfway through the period in order to review the previous day's lesson

◆ Placed pupils who were below the accepted cut-off scores on the statewide test in a special remedial group

◆ Rearranged the class seating plan to separate Jamar and Ramon and to move Claudia to the front of the room so she could see the chalkboard better

◆ Called on Kim twice even though her hand was not raised

◆ Studied the statewide writing standards to determine what topics to emphasize in instruction

◆ Switched social studies instruction from discussion to seatwork when the class became bored and unruly

◆ Previewed and selected a filmstrip on astronomy for next week's science unit

◆ Congratulated Manuela and Chad for their scores of 100 on long division with remainders

◆ Encouraged Jing to redraft his English composition to correct spelling and grammar errors

◆ Decided to construct her own test for the social studies unit rather than using the textbook test

◆ Sent Antonio to the school nurse when he complained of a headache

◆ Selected pupils to work together on a cooperative learning exercise in math

◆ Decided to allow her pupils two more days to complete their poetry portfolios

◆ Judged that Tabitha's constant interruptions and speaking out in class warranted a note to her parents about the problem

◆ Assigned homework in science and social studies, but not in math and language

◆ Checked with the school counselor regarding possible reasons for Miguel's increasingly inattentive class behavior

◆ Took part in a special education conference to determine whether Angelina's Individual Education Plan needed to be altered

◆ Paired Kim, a class isolate, with Aretha, a class leader, for the project in social studies

◆ Sent Ralph to the principal because he swore at a teacher and threatened a classmate

◆ Held a parent-teacher conference with Ivan's parents in which she told them that he was a capable student who could produce better work than he had thus far

◆ Consulted last year's standardized test scores to determine whether the class needed a review of the basic rules of capitalization

As you can see, Ms. Lopez's day in the classroom, like those of all teachers, was filled with situations in which she had to make decisions. Some of these decisions concerned individual pupils and some concerned the class as a whole. Some were about instructional matters, some about classroom climate, some about pupil personalities, and some about pupil learning. Some, like the decisions to change Tamika's reading group, were infrequently made decisions. Others, like planning topics for instruction, calling on pupils during class, and assigning grades to pupils, were made many times each day. All of Ms. Lopez's actions resulted from decisions she made, and all her decisions were based upon some type of evidence. Like other good teachers, she continually observes, monitors, and reviews pupil performances to obtain evidence for decision making. Taken together, these decisions serve to establish, organize, and monitor classroom qualities such as pupil learning, interpersonal relations, social adjustment, instructional content, and classroom climate.

Classroom decisions must be reflective and thoughtful, not impulsive and erratic. The decisions Ms. Lopez made were based upon many different kinds of evidence. How did Ms. Lopez know that the way to settle her bored and unruly social studies class was to switch from discussion to seatwork, when there were many other things she might have done to settle the class? What made her decide to move Tamika to the high reading group? Why did she think pairing Kim with Aretha for the social studies project was better than pairing Kim with someone else? Why did she feel that spending two extra days working on the poetry portfolio would be more useful than using the time to introduce some other topic? Why was Rosa, but not Sarah, trusted to deliver a note to Principal Brown? All of these choices were based upon information that helped Ms. Lopez choose a course of action when confronted by the need to make a decision. Think of all the possible sources of evidence Ms. Lopez might have used to help her make these decisions. Notice also that many of the decisions she made were fast paced, practically oriented, and focused on both instructional and social factors. Others involved more thoughtful, lengthy consideration.

PURPOSES OF CLASSROOM ASSESSMENT

Teachers assess for many purposes because they are required to make many decisions. If we review Ms. Lopez's decisions during her classroom day, we get a sense of the many purposes teachers have for assessment. The remainder of this text focuses on assessment concerns and strategies for the following purposes: establishing classroom equilibrium, planning and conducting instruction, placing students, providing feedback and incentives, diagnosing pupil problems and disabilities, and judging and grading academic learning and progress.

Establishing Classroom Equilibrium

One purpose of assessment is to establish and maintain the social equilibrium of the classroom. Classrooms are complex social settings in which people interact with one another in a multitude of ways. For classrooms to be positive social and learning environments, order, discipline, and cooperation must be present. Thus, helping pupils to learn well and maintaining order in the classroom are closely related; orderliness is needed if teaching and learning are to be successful. When Ms. Lopez selected Rosa instead of Sarah to deliver a note to Principal Brown, and when she changed the class seating plan to move Jamar and Ramon farther apart, she was making decisions to preserve classroom order and stability. That she allowed Antonio to go alone to the school nurse indicated her trust in him. On the other hand, Tabitha's constant interruptions and speaking out necessitated sending a note to her parents, and Ralph's swearing and fighting led to his being removed from the classroom. Ms. Lopez's efforts to make Kim a part of the classroom society by calling on her even though her hand was not raised was another attempt to create and maintain a viable social and learning environment.

An often overlooked purpose of assessment is to establish and maintain the classroom society.

Planning and Conducting Instruction

Many of the decisions that Ms. Lopez made were focused on planning and conducting classroom instruction. This should not be surprising, since instruction is a central classroom activity. The instructional decisions that Ms. Lopez made can be divided into two types: planning decisions and process, or teaching, decisions. When Ms. Lopez selected the topics to be included in tomorrow's lessons, previewed and selected the astronomy filmstrip for next week's science unit, decided to spend two extra days on the poetry portfolios, and assigned homework in one subject but not another, she was planning future instructional activities.

In addition to planning decisions, the actual process of teaching a class requires constant assessment and decision making. At two points during the day, Ms. Lopez altered her instruction in the middle of the lesson because her pupils were confused and unruly. Once she stopped her language lesson to review the prior day's lesson because pupil responses to her questions indicated that the class did not understand its content. Another time she switched her method of instruction from discussion to seatwork when the students became bored and unruly.

Assessment information is used to organize pupils into a functioning classroom society, plan and carry out instruction, and determine pupil learning. Assessment is much more than giving formal paper-and-pencil tests to students.

Placing Pupils

Classroom teachers make decisions also about the placements of their pupils. Whenever a teacher divides pupils into reading or math groups, organizes pupils into cooperative learning groups, pairs or groups pupils for class projects, or recommends that a particular pupil be placed with a particular teacher next year, assessments for placement purposes have taken place. Ms. Lopez made a placement decision when she moved Tamika from the middle reading group to the high reading group. She made another placement decision when she identified pupils who were below the cutoff score on the statewide basic skills test and placed them into a remedial group. Finally, when she paired Kim, the class isolate, with Aretha for the social studies project, she made another placement decision. Note that Ms. Lopez's placement decisions were made for both academic and social reasons.

Providing Feedback and Incentives

Young learners and their caregivers need feedback and encouragement. Observations and feedback intended to alter and improve students' learning while instruction is taking place are called **formative assessment.** To provide such feedback, teachers must constantly assess student learning and behavior. For example, Ms. Lopez used assessment information from Jing's first-draft book report to increase his incentive and suggest improvements. She held a parent-teacher conference with Ivan's parents to provide them information about his progress. In both examples of formative assessment, information about academic performance was used to provide feedback to pupils or parents about performance.

Diagnosing Pupil Problems and Disabilities

Much of the assessment data teachers gather is used to identify, understand, and remediate pupils' problems and learning difficulties. Teachers are always on the lookout for pupils who are having learning, emotional, or social problems in the classroom. Having identified such problems, the teacher can sometimes carry out the remedial activities or make accommodations, but at other times the pupil must be referred for more specialized diagnosis and remediation outside the classroom. Thus, Ms. Lopez set up her own in-class group for basic skill remediation, but she recommended that a specialist screen Aaron for his apparent gross motor skill deficiency. Referring Aaron to the Special Education Department for screening was another diagnostic decision. Chapter 3 will say much more about disabilities and accommodations.

Judging and Grading Academic Learning and Progress

The task of grading or making final judgments about students' learning at the end of instruction is termed **summative assessment.** A number of Ms. Lopez's decisions involved judging pupils' academic learning and progress. She assigned grades to her pupils' science tests, completed a monthly progress report on each pupil, decided to construct her own test for the social studies unit rather than use the test provided in her textbook, and determined whether Angelina's Individual Education Plan was still appropriate for her. Much of a teacher's time is spent collecting information that will be used to grade pupils or make final judgments about their academic progress.

TYPES OF ASSESSMENT

All of Ms. Lopez's decisions and all of the purposes of assessment just described can be grounded into three general types or areas of assessment based on purpose. Table 1.1 describes and compares these three assessment

TABLE 1.1   COMPARISON OF THREE TYPES OF CLASSROOM ASSESSMENTS

	Early Assessments	**Instructional**	**Official**
Purpose	Provide teacher with a quick perception and practical knowledge of pupils' characteristics	Plan instructional activities and monitor the progress of instruction	Carry out the bureaucratic aspects of teaching, such as grading, grouping, and placing
Timing	During the first week or two of school	Daily throughout the school year	Periodically during the school year
Evidence-gathering method	Largely informal observation	Formal observation and pupil papers for planning; informal observation for monitoring	Formal tests, papers, reports, quizzes, and assignments
Type of evidence gathered	Cognitive, affective, and psychomotor	Largely cognitive and affective	Mainly cognitive
Record keeping	Information kept in teacher's mind; few written records	Written lesson plans; monitoring information not written down	Formal records kept in teacher's mark book or school files

Teachers perform three types of assessment: early assessment, instructional assessment, and official (administrative).

Instructional assessments are used to help plan and deliver instruction.

types. Some classroom assessments help teachers carry out their official responsibilities as members of the school bureaucracy. Decisions such as grading, grouping, assessing progress, interpreting test results, conferencing with parents, identifying pupils for special needs placement, and making promotion recommendations are all part of the official responsibilities a teacher assumes as an employee of a school system. These are **official assessments.** Other assessments are used to plan and deliver instruction and include decisions about what will be taught, how and when it will be taught, what materials will be used, how a lesson is progressing, and what changes in planned activities must be made. These are **instructional**

TABLE 1.2 VARIED PERSPECTIVES AND USES OF CLASSROOM ASSESSMENTS

National and State Policy Makers
♦ Setting state and national standards
♦ No Child Left Behind
♦ Developing policies based on assessment
♦ Tracking the progress of national and state achievements
♦ Providing resources to improve learning
♦ Providing rewards or sanctions for pupil, school, and state achievements

School Administrators
♦ Identifying program strengths and weaknesses
♦ Using assessment to plan and improve instruction
♦ Monitoring classroom teachers
♦ Identifying instructional needs and programs
♦ Monitoring pupil achievements over time

Teachers
♦ Monitoring pupil progress
♦ Judging and altering classroom curriculum
♦ Identifying pupils with special needs
♦ Motivating pupils to do well
♦ Placing pupils in groups
♦ Providing feedback to teachers and pupils

Parents
♦ Judging pupil strengths and weaknesses
♦ Monitoring pupil progress
♦ Meeting with teachers to discuss pupils' classroom performance
♦ Judging teacher quality

assessments. A third kind of assessment is used by teachers early in the school year to learn about their pupils' social, academic, and behavioral characteristics and needs so as to enhance instruction, communication, and cooperation in the classroom. These **early assessments** allow teachers to set up and maintain an effective classroom society. Succeeding chapters will describe these three general types of assessment in greater detail.

Teachers study their students in the first weeks of school so that they can organize their classrooms into social and learning communities.

Another way to think about types of assessments is to consider the differing perspectives of teachers and other groups with important stakes in education. See Table 1.2.

ASSESSMENT, TESTING, MEASUREMENT, AND EVALUATION

This book is about the process teachers use to properly gather, evaluate, and use information in classroom decision making. As you work your way through it, be sure to keep in mind that **assessment** is a broad process of collecting, synthesizing and interpreting information in which *testing, measurement, and evaluation* play contributing parts.

When people hear the word assessment, they often think right away of tests. A **test** is a formal, systematic, usually paper-and-pencil procedure used to gather information about pupils' performance. While paper-and-pencil tests are one important tool for gathering assessment information, the preceding list of Ms. Lopez's decisions makes clear that there are many other information-gathering tools, including projects and portfolios. Shortly, we'll say more about written tests, as well as techniques of observations and oral questioning. Later chapters will cover these options in greater detail.

A test is a formal, systematic, usually paper-and-pencil procedure for gathering information.

Measurement is the process of quantifying or assigning a number to performance. The most common example of measurement in the classroom is when a teacher scores a quiz or test. Scoring produces a numerical description of performance: Jackie got 17 out of 20 items correct on the biology test; Dennis got a score of 65 percent on his math test; Rhonda's score on the creative essay was 85 percent. In each example, a numerical score is used to represent the individual's performance.

Measurement is the process of quantifying or assigning a number to performance.

Once assessment information is collected, teachers use it to make decisions or judgments about pupils, instruction, or classroom climate. **Evaluation** is the process of making judgments about what is good or desirable as in, for example, judging the quality of pupils' essays or the desirability of a particular instructional activity. Evaluation occurs after assessment information has been collected, synthesized, and thought about because this is when the teacher is in a position to make informed judgments.

Evaluation is the process of judging the quality or value of a performance or a course of action.

olc

**CHAPTER CASE
STUDY**

Visit the text OLC
to read the case
of Gina Shrader, a
student teacher
who learns about
the complexities of
a typical teaching
day as she
observes a second
grade teacher and
her class.

www.mhhe.com/
airasian5e

*In classrooms, teachers
constantly assess their
pupils, and pupils assess
the teacher, instruction,
and each other.*

Imagine a teacher at the start of the year who wants *assess* the mathematics readiness of her pupils in order to decide where to start instruction. Notice that the reason for assessing is that a decision must be made. First, the teacher gives a grade-appropriate paper-and-pencil *test* of mathematics readiness. The pupil's scores on the test provides a *measurement* of their math readiness. Of course the teacher uses other forms of assessment to determine readiness. She talks to the pupils about math, watches them while they do math exercises, and checks prior grades and test scores in their school record files. The teacher then thinks about all the assessment information she has collected. She *evaluates,* or makes a judgment about, the pupils' current stage of readiness in math. Her final decision, based on her assessment and evaluation, is to recommend a review of last year's math before beginning this year's topics.

While the focus of this book is teacher-centered classroom assessment, it is important to note that other types of assessment also go on in classrooms. Just as teachers constantly assess their pupils, instruction, and classroom climate, so too do pupils constantly assess their teacher, instruction, and classroom climate. Just as teachers want to know whether pupils are motivated, hardworking, academically able, and adjusted to the culture of the classroom, so too do pupils want to know if the teacher is fair, gives hard tests, enforces rigid discipline, can be swayed by a "sob story," and likes them as individuals (Jackson, 1990). Moreover, in all classrooms, pupils are being constantly assessed by their peers. The classroom is a public place and it does not take most pupils long to learn where they stand, both in the teacher's eyes and in the academic, athletic, and social pecking orders established by their peers. Assessment in the classroom is as likely to come from classmates as from the teacher. As you know from your school experience, you probably do judge teachers and other students.

THREE GENERAL WAYS TO COLLECT DATA: PAPER-AND-PENCIL, OBSERVATION, AND ORAL QUESTIONING

*Teachers gather most of
their assessment
information using
paper-and-pencil
techniques, observation
techniques, and oral
questioning techniques.*

Teachers rely on three primary methods to gather assessment information for classroom decisions: paper-and-pencil techniques, observation techniques, and oral questioning techniques.

In addition to the following sources, helpful supplementary information can be obtained from the pupils' prior teachers, school staff, and parents. Teachers routinely consult previous teachers to corroborate or reinforce current observations. Parents frequently volunteer information and respond to teacher queries. While useful, each of these supplementary sources of infor-mation has its limitations and should be treated with caution when making decisions.

Supplementary assessment information can be obtained from previous teachers, school staff, and parents.

Paper-and-Pencil Techniques

Paper-and-pencil techniques refer to assessment methods in which pupils write down their responses to questions or problems. When pupils take a multiple-choice test, complete a written homework assignment, construct a written report, draw a picture, write an essay, or fill in a worksheet, they are providing paper-and-pencil evidence to the teacher. Paper-and-pencil assessment techniques are of two general forms: selection and supply. Mul-tiple choice, true-false, and matching items are called **selection items,** or selected response items, because as the name implies, the pupil responds to each question by selecting an answer from choices provided. **Supply items,** or production items, require the pupil to construct a response to a question. The length of the response can vary substantially. For example, an essay question necessitates the pupil's construction of a lengthy, detailed response, while a short answer or "fill-in-the-blank" question may only require a word or phrase. Complex supply items, such as book reports, jour-nal entries, portfolios, science experiments, and class projects, are also com-monly referred to as **performance assessments.** Notice that a selection-type item provides the maximum degree of control for the question writer, since he or she specifies both the question and the answer choices. A supply-type item provides the question writer with control only over the item itself, since responsibility for constructing a response resides with the pupil.

Paper-and-pencil assessments involve pupils writing down their responses to questions or problems.

There are two forms of paper-and-pencil assessment: selection and supply.

Selection techniques require students to select an answer from choices that are provided; supply techniques require pupils to construct a response to a question or problem.

Observation Techniques

Observation is a second major method classroom teachers use to collect assessment data. As the term suggests, **observation** involves watching or listening to pupils carry out some activity (observation of process) or judg-ing a product a pupil has produced (observation of product). Teachers are made aware of such student behaviors as mispronouncing words in oral reading, interacting in groups, speaking out in class, bullying other pupils, losing concentration, having puzzled looks on their faces, patiently waiting their turn, raising their hands in class, dressing shabbily, and failing to sit still for more than three minutes through observation. When pupils submit a science fair project, produce a still-life drawing, set up laboratory equip-ment, or complete a project in shop class, the teacher observes and judges the product they have produced.

In most classrooms, the teacher's desk faces the pupils', and during instruction, the teacher faces the pupils. Because teachers and their classes

Observation techniques are applied to student activities and to student products.

are located in a confined space, facing and interacting with one another from one to six hours a day, teachers can observe a great deal of their pupils' behavior, appearance, and reactions.

Some teacher observations are formal and planned in advance while others are informal and spontaneous.

Some observations are formal and planned in advance, as when teachers assess pupils as they read aloud in reading group or present an oral report to the class. In such situations, the teacher wants to observe a particular set of pupil behaviors. For example, in reading aloud, the teacher might be watching and listening for clear pronunciation of words, changing voice tone to emphasize important points, periodic looking up from the book while reading, and so forth. Because such observations are planned, the teacher has time to prepare the pupils and identify in advance the particular behaviors that will be observed.

Other teacher observations are unplanned and informal, as when the teacher sees someone talking when they should be listening, notices the pained expression on a pupil's face when a classmate makes fun of his clothes, or observes the pupils fidgeting and looking out the window during a science lesson. Such spontaneous observations, based on what is often called "kid watching," reflect momentary unplanned happenings that the teacher observes, mentally records, and interprets. Both formal and informal teacher observations are important information-gathering techniques in classrooms.

Oral Questioning Techniques

Asking oral questions is the third major method teachers use to collect assessment data. "Why do you think the author ended her story that way?" "Explain to me in your own words what an improper fraction is." "Jack, did you call Ron a nasty name?" "Raise your hand if you can tell me why this answer is incorrect." "Who can summarize yesterday's discussion about the water cycle?" "Why don't you have your homework today?" These are all teacher-type questions used to assess pupils during and at the end of a lesson. Questioning students is very useful during instruction, when it can be used to review a prior topic, brainstorm a new one, find out how the lesson is being understood by pupils, and engage a student who is not paying attention. The teacher can gather the information he or she wants without the intrusiveness of some form of paper-and-pencil assessment. Oral examinations are used in subject areas such as foreign language, speech, and vocal music.

Oral questioning provides a great deal of formal and informal information about pupils. Questioning is especially useful during instruction.

The full range of data analysis methods is needed to gather all the information required for classroom assessment.

Paper-and-pencil, observation, and questioning techniques complement one another in the classroom. Imagine classroom decision making without being able to observe pupils' reactions, performances, answers to questions, and interactions. Now imagine what it would be like if no paper-and-pencil information could be obtained in classrooms, and imagine what it would be like if teachers could not ask oral questions of their students. Each type of information is needed to carry out the rich and meaningful assessments that occur in classrooms. As a result, it's important for teachers to master all of these evidence-gathering approaches.

STANDARDIZED AND NONSTANDARDIZED ASSESSMENTS

The information teachers collect and use in their classrooms comes from assessment procedures that are either standardized or nonstandardized. In both cases, most often they are administered in groups.

Standardized Assessments

Standardized assessment procedures are those administered, scored, and interpreted in the same way for all test takers, regardless of where or when they are assessed. Standardized assessments are meant to be administered in many schools across the nation. Standardized assessments are intended to be administered to pupils in many different classrooms, but always under identical conditions of administration, scoring, and interpretation. The main reason for standardizing assessment procedures is to ensure fair comparisons among pupils in different schools and states can be made.

Standardized assessments are intended to be administered, scored, and interpreted in the same way for all test takers.

The Scholastic Assessment Test (SAT) and the American College Testing Program Test (ACT) are examples of standardized tests. So are national achievement tests such as the Iowa Tests of Basic Skills and the Stanford, Metropolitan, California, and SRA Achievement tests. Regardless of where a pupil is taking the test, that pupil will be administered the same test, under the same conditions, with the same directions, and in the same amount of time as all other students who are taking the test at that time. Moreover, the results of the test will be scored and interpreted the same way for all test takers. When Ms. Lopez identified pupils below the cutoff score on the state-mandated basic skills test and consulted the previous year's test scores to determine if the class needed a review of capitalization rules, she was examining information from standardized assessment instruments.

Nonstandardized Assessments

Nonstandardized assessments are constructed for use in a single classroom with a single group of pupils. Most reflect the particular areas of instruction focused on in that single classroom.

Nonstandardized (teacher-made) assessments are developed for a single classroom with a single group of students and are not used for comparison with other groups.

When Ms. Lopez decided to construct her own test for the science unit and assigned grades to her pupils based upon the test, she was relying upon assessment information that was not standardized. Many of Ms. Lopez's unplanned observations of her students' behavior also are classified as non-standardized assessments. These fleeting, infrequently occurring, unpredictable, seldom repeated classroom observations represent a rich and important, though nonstandardized, form of assessment data. Teachers use these idiosyncratic observations to make decisions about individual pupils and the class as a group.

Standardization is important when pupils are compared across different locations and classrooms.

It is important to note that standardized assessments are not necessarily better than nonstandardized ones. Standardization is important when comparing pupils across many different classrooms and locations. If comparison beyond a single classroom is not desired, rigorous standardization is not needed, and indeed may be less appropriate for students in that classroom.

TECHNOLOGY AND ASSESSMENT

ERIC: Practical Assessment, Research, and Evaluation (http://PAREonline.net)

olc This large site has become a central source of Web-based assessment and evaluation information with numerous partnerships for the electronic dissemination of information, active websites, and pathfinders to help locate information. The site provides balanced information about educational assessment, evaluation, and research methods.

An excellent starting point for learning about available ERIC/AE resources is the Test Locator on the site.

People come to ERIC/AE looking for ideas, suggestions, and resources to help with real school-based problems. The focus of the site is practice-centered assessment information.

Administration in Groups

Administering group assessments saves time but provides less insight and information about individual pupils.

Virtually all group-administered assessments rely on paper-and-pencil tests, since these permit many pupils to work simultaneously on a task. When the task to be assessed involves oral reading, giving a speech, or assembling equipment, group-administered procedures are not useful.

Informal group assessment occurs often in the classroom, primarily through teacher observation. Thus, when Ms. Lopez watched the class become bored and unruly during a lesson, she was performing group assessment. Similarly, when her pupils had difficulty answering her questions during the language lesson, she stopped what she was doing to review the previous day's lesson. This is another example of informal, group-based assessment.

GOOD ASSESSMENTS: VALID AND RELIABLE

Whether assessment information helps produce good decisions depends on whether the assessment information is good.

Whether assessment information helps teachers to make *good* decisions depends upon whether the assessment information collected is itself good. The key ideas are validity and reliability. We begin our examination into the characteristics of good assessment information with an example.

Mr. Ferris has just finished a three-week math unit on computing long division problems with remainders. During the unit, he taught his pupils the computational steps involved in doing long division problems and the concept of a remainder. He gave and reviewed both homework problems and examples from the text, and he administered a few quizzes. Now, at the end of the unit, Mr. Ferris wants to gather assessment information to find out whether his pupils have learned to do computational problems involving long division with remainders. He wants to gather this information to help him make a decision about how well his pupils have learned from his instruction so that he can assign a grade to each pupil.

To gather the information needed, Mr. Ferris decides to give a test containing items similar in content, format, and difficulty to those he has been teaching. From the millions of possible long division with remainder problems, Mr. Ferris selects 10 that are representative of his teaching. Note that if he picks 10 items that cover different content or are much harder, easier, or presented in a different format than what he taught in class, the results of the test will *not* provide good decision-making information. To assess how well his students learned from his instruction, his test items must be similar in content, format, and difficulty.

Mr. Ferris recognizes this potential pitfall and avoids it by writing 10 items that are similar in content, difficulty, and format to the items taught and practiced in his classroom. He assembles the items into a test, administers the test during one class period, and scores the tests on a scale of 0 to 100. Mr. Ferris then has the assessment information he needs to make a decision about each pupil's grade.

Manuela and Joe each score 100 on the test and receive an A grade for the unit. Stuart scores 30 and receives a D grade. The grades are based upon Mr. Ferris's evaluation of the quality of their performance on the 10-item test. If Mr. Ferris is asked to interpret what Manuela's and Joe's A grades mean, he will likely say that "Manuela and Joe can do long division with remainder items very well." He will also likely say that Stuart's D is "indicative of his inability to do such items well."

In making these statements, Mr. Ferris illustrates the relationship between assessment data and resulting teacher decisions. He says Manuela and Joe "can do long division with remainder items very well." He does not say "Manuela and Joe can do the 10 items I included on my test very well." He judges and describes their performance in *general* terms rather than in terms of his specific 10-item test. Similarly, Stuart is judged in general rather than in test-specific terms. The logic that Mr. Ferris and all teachers use in making such judgments is that if a pupil can do well on the test items or performances that are actually assessed, the pupil is likely to do well on similar items and performances that are not assessed. If pupils do poorly on the 10 test items, it is likely that they also will do poorly on similar, unasked items. Hence, when asked to describe the performance of Manuela and Joe, he indicates that they do very well on long division with remainder problems in general.

Regardless of its other characteristics, the most important characteristics in determining the usefulness of assessment information are its validity and reliability.

The essence of classroom assessment is to look at some of a pupil's behavior and to use that information to make a generalization or prediction about the pupil's behavior in similar situations or on similar tasks.

Mr. Ferris's 10-item test illustrates a characteristic that is common to virtually all classroom assessments, regardless of whether they are formal or informal, paper-and-pencil, observational or oral, or standardized or non-standardized. The essence of classroom assessment is to look at a *sample* of a pupil's performance and use that sample to make a generalization or prediction about the pupil's performance on similar, unobserved tasks.

This process is not confined to assessments of pupils' learning. Teachers often form lasting impressions of their pupils' personalities or motivation based on a few brief observations made in the first week of school. They observe a small sample of the pupil's behavior and on the basis of this sample make general judgments such as "he is unmotivated," "she is a trouble-maker," and "they are hard workers." These are informal generalizations about pupils that teachers routinely make based on only a small sample of the pupil's school behavior.

What if the behavior sample the teacher collects is irrelevant or incomplete? What if the items on Mr. Ferris's test were not typical of his classroom instruction? What if the pupil has an "off day" or the teacher's impatience does not permit a pupil to show his or her "true" performance? If these things happen, then the decision made about the pupil is likely to be wrong and probably unfair.

Let's now consider a related, more scientifically precise term than fairness.

Validity

Validity is concerned with whether the information being gathered is relevant to the decision that needs to be made.

The single most important characteristic of good assessment is its ability to help the teacher make correct decisions. This characteristic is called **validity.** Assessment information is *valid* to the extent that it is *sufficient* for making a given decision. Without validity, assessment data will not lead to correct decisions. When a teacher asks, as all teachers should, "Am I collecting the right information for the decision I want to make?" she is asking about the validity of her assessments (Linn, 1997). For any decision, some forms of evidence are more valid than others. For example, it was more valid for Mr. Ferris to determine his pupils' achievement by giving a test that contained items similar to those he had been teaching than it would have been for him to ask pupils to write an essay about their feelings towards math. Similarly, it is more valid to determine pupils' motivation or ability by observing their classroom work over a period of time than it is to base such judgments on the performance of their older siblings or the section of the city they come from. These latter indicators are likely to be less valid for decision making than more direct classroom observation.

We shall have more to say about validity throughout this text. At this point it is sufficient to say three things about the validity of assessment information. First, validity is concerned with whether the information being gathered is really relevant and appropriate to make the desired decision. Second, validity is the most important characteristic that assessment

Invalid assessment information is of no use.

Key Assessment Tools 1.1

KEY ASPECTS OF ASSESSMENT VALIDITY

1. Validity is concerned with this general question: To what extent will this assessment information help me make an appropriate decision?

2. Validity refers to the decisions that are made from assessment information, not the assessment approach itself. It is not appropriate to say the assessment information is valid unless the decisions or groups it is valid for are identified. Assessment information valid for one decision or group of pupils is not necessarily valid for other decisions or groups.

3. Validity is a matter of degree; it does not exist on an all-or-nothing basis. Think of assessment validity in terms of categories: highly valid, moderately valid, and invalid.

4. Validity is always determined by a judgment made by the test user.

---

information can possess because, without it, the assessment information is of no use. Third, concerns about validity pertain to all classroom assessment, not just to those involving formal, paper-and-pencil techniques. Each of the many decisions Ms. Lopez made during the school day was based upon some type of assessment information. It is appropriate, therefore, to ask about the validity—that is, the appropriateness—of the assessment information behind each of Ms. Lopez's many daily decisions. Key Assessment Tools 1.1 identifies key concerns in the validity of assessments.

Validity (relevance to decision making) is just as applicable to informal teacher observations as it is to formally gathered paper-and-pencil information.

One other note of caution about validity should be mentioned at this point. Decisions that may affect a student's education in a major way should not be made simply on the basis of one result, even if the validity of a single assessment seems strong. It is always prudent to assess the student's ability or performance through several different means in order to enhance the overall rightness of a major decision (Moss, 2003).

Reliability

A second important characteristic of good assessments is its consistency, or **reliability.** Would the assessment results for this person or class be similar if they were gathered at some other time? If you weighed yourself on a scale, got off it, then weighed yourself again on the same scale, you would expect the two weights to be almost identical. If they weren't, you wouldn't trust the information provided by the scale. The information it provides you is not reliable. Similarly, if assessment information does not produce stable, consistent information, a teacher should exercise caution in using that information to make a decision about a pupil or the class.

Reliability refers to the stability or consistency of assessment information, i.e., whether it is typical of a pupil's behavior.

Think of a friend whom you consider to be unreliable. Is he sometimes punctual and sometimes late? When she tells you something or promises to do something, can you rely on what she says? A person who is unreliable is inconsistent. It is the same with assessment information; unreliable or inconsistent information does not help teachers make decisions that they can rely on.

Recall that Ms. Lopez observed Rose's class interruptions and Miguel's inattentive behavior over a period of time before deciding to take action. She did this to be sure that she was observing stable, consistent behavior from these students. Did they behave the same way at different times and under different circumstances? By observing them over a period of time, Ms. Lopez could have faith in the reliability of her observations. Similarly, Mr. Ferris included 10 long division with remainder questions on his test, not just one, so that he would obtain reliable information about his pupils' achievement. He can have more confidence about pupils' learning by assessing them on 10 items than on only one or two.

Since any single assessment provides only a limited sample of a pupil's behavior, no single assessment procedure or instrument can be expected to provide perfect, error-free information. All assessment information contains some unreliability or inconsistency due to such factors as ambiguous test items, interruptions during testing, differences in pupils' attention spans, clarity of assessment directions, pupils' luck in guessing items, changes in pupils' moods, mistakes in scoring (especially essay and observational assessments), and obtaining too small a sample of behavior to permit the pupil to show consistent, stable performance. Obviously, it is important to minimize the inconsistency. Key Assessment Tools 1.2 reviews key aspects of the reliability of assessment information.

All assessment information contains some error or inconsistency; thus validity and reliability are both a matter of degree and do not exist on an all-or-nothing basis.

One of the purposes of this text is to suggest methods that can help reduce the amount of unreliability in classroom assessments. If a teacher cannot rely upon the stability and consistency of the information gathered during an assessment, he or she must be careful not to base important decisions on that information. Thus, along with validity, which asks if the

---

Key Assessment Tools 1.2

KEY ASPECTS OF ASSESSMENT RELIABILITY

1. Reliability refers to the stability or consistency of assessment information and is concerned with this question: "How consistent or typical of the pupils' behavior is the assessment information I have gathered?"

2. Reliability is not concerned with the appropriateness of the assessment information collected, only with its consistency, stability, or typicality. Appropriateness of assessment information is a validity concern.

3. Reliability does not exist on an all-or-nothing basis, but in degrees: high, moderate, or low. Some types of assessment information are more reliable than others.

4. Reliability is a necessary but insufficient condition for validity. An assessment that provides inconsistent, atypical results cannot be relied upon to provide information useful for decision making.

assessment information being gathered is relevant to the decision to be made, the classroom teacher must also be concerned with reliability, which asks if the information obtained is consistent and stable.

Consider the following assertion regarding the relationship between validity and reliability. "Valid assessment must be reliable, but reliable assessment need not be valid." The first half of the statement is fairly straightforward. Valid decisions are not possible if the assessment data on which the decisions are based are not consistent. So, to have a valid assessment, there must be reliable information.

As to the second part of the statement, imagine the following scenario. Suppose you ask a pupil in your class how many brothers and sisters he has. He says six, and you ask him again. He says six. You repeat the question several times, and each time the pupil indicates six brothers and sisters. You have assessed the number of his brothers and sisters with consistency; the assessment information you have gathered from him is reliable. Suppose you then use this reliable information to make a decision about what reading group to place the pupil in: the more brothers and sisters, the higher the placement. Since the number of brothers and sisters has little relevance to the pupil's reading performance, a decision based on this information, no matter how reliable it is, is not valid. In short, assessments can be reliable, but not necessarily valid. Figure 1.1 depicts the relationship between validity and reliability through the metaphor of shots at an archery target. Succeeding chapters will explore the relationship between validity and reliability in greater detail and offer suggestions for improving the validity and reliability of classroom assessment.

FIGURE 1.1   *Interactions of Validity and Reliability.*

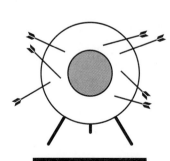  

Lack of validity and reliability	**Good reliability but poor validity**	**Good validity and reliability**
Arrows scattered about the target indicate poor validity and reliability	Reliability indicated by closely grouped arrows, but failure to reach target center shows lack of validity	Hits are closely grouped and centered on the bull's-eye, indicating the assessment is reliable and valid

ETHICAL ISSUES AND RESPONSIBILITIES

Teachers' assessments have important long- and short-term consequences for students; thus teachers have an ethical responsibility to make decisions using the most valid and reliable information possible.

Thus far we have presented a general technical introduction to classroom assessment. However, assessment is more than just a technical activity; it is a human activity that influences and affects many people, including pupils, parents, teachers, coaches, college admission counselors, and employers. Think about the different kinds and purposes of assessment described in this chapter, and then think about all the ways people can be affected by them. This will give you a sense of the human side of assessment.

Appendix A lists some national standards for teacher competence in assessment. Teaching is a profession that has both a knowledge base and a moral base. Like other professionals who have knowledge and expertise, their clients do not have and whose actions and judgments affect their clients in many ways, classroom teachers are responsible for conducting themselves in an ethical manner. This responsibility is particularly important in education, because pupils have no choice about whether they will or will not attend school. Also, compared to their teachers, pupils tend to be less experienced and more impressionable. Among the ethical standards that cut across all dimensions of teaching are the need to treat each pupil as an individual, to avoid physical or emotional abuse of pupils, to respect diversity, to be intellectually honest with pupils, to avoid favoritism and harassment, to provide a balanced perspective on issues raised in instruction, and to provide the best instruction possible for all pupils.

In simple terms, each of these ethical standards refers to some aspect of a teacher's fairness in dealing with his or her pupils. Clearly, gathering and interpreting valid and reliable data for decision making are fundamental to the fairness of teachers' assessments. Other aspects of fairness include: (1) informing students about teacher expectations and assessments before beginning teaching and assessment; (2) teaching pupils what they are to be tested on before assessment; (3) not making snap judgments and identifying pupils with emotional labels (e.g., disinterested, at-risk, slow learner) before you have spent time with them; (4) avoiding stereotyping pupils (e.g., "He's just a dumb jock," "Kids from that part of town are troublemakers," and "Pupils who dress that way have no interest in school"); (5) avoiding terms and examples that may be offensive to students of different gender, race, religion, culture, or nationality; (6) avoiding bias toward pupils with limited English or with different cultural experiences when providing instruction and constructing assessments (Holloway, 2003; Ben-Yosef, 2003). There are many dimensions to fairness in the classroom.

Ethical Issues and Assessment

In addition, there are ethical considerations specifically applicable to assessment. Classroom teachers are in a position to obtain a great deal of information about their pupils' academic, personal, social, and family backgrounds.

Beyond having access to such information, teachers use it to make decisions that can have important short- and long-term consequences for pupils. As another example, college entrance and future employment opportunities, not to mention pupil self-esteem, often hang in the balance of teachers' assessments decisions.

Clearly, there are responsibilities associated with the collection and use of assessment information. Teachers should always strive to obtain valid and reliable information before making important decisions that can influence pupils. Moreover, once assessment information is collected, teachers have a responsibility to protect its privacy, recognize its decision-making limitations, and never use it to demean or ridicule a pupil. See Appendix A for other important teacher competencies in the assessment of pupils.

Table 1.3 presents a list of ethical standards for teachers developed by the National Education Association. Table 1.4 is a list related specifically to

---

TABLE 1.3   ETHICAL STANDARDS FOR TEACHERS' RELATIONS WITH PUPILS

Commitment to the Student

The educator strives to help each student realize his or her potential as a worthy and effective member of society. The educator therefore works to stimulate the spirit of inquiry, the acquisition of knowledge and understanding, and the thoughtful formulation of worthy goals.

In fulfillment of the obligation to the student, the educator:

1. Shall not unreasonably restrain the student from independent action in the pursuit of learning.

2. Shall not unreasonably deny the student access to varying points of view.

3. Shall not deliberately suppress or distort subject matter relevant to the student's progress.

4. Shall make reasonable effort to protect the student from conditions harmful to learning or to health and safety.

5. Shall not intentionally expose the student to embarrassment or disparagement.

6. Shall not on the basis of race, color, creed, sex, national origin, marital status, political or religious beliefs, family, social or cultural background, or sexual orientation, unfairly:
   a. Exclude any student from participation in any program
   b. Deny benefits to any student
   c. Grant any advantage to any student

7. Shall not use professional relationships with students for private advantage.

8. Shall not disclose information about students obtained in the course of professional service, unless disclosure serves a compelling professional purpose or is required by law.

SOURCE: *NEA Handbook,* 1992–1993. Reprinted with permission of the National Education Association.

> ### TABLE 1.4   TEACHERS' ETHICAL RESPONSIBILITIES REGARDING ASSESSMENT
>
> ♦ Make fair and impartial decisions
> ♦ Construct and administer fair and clear assessments
> ♦ Motivate pupils to do their best
> ♦ Teach pupils the varied types of assessments
> ♦ Provide opportunities for pupils to practice test approaches
> ♦ Make reasonable accommodations for students with disabilities

assessment. Note the range of ethical concerns and responsibilities that accompany teaching.

Fairness in Accommodating Special Needs

As part of their ethical responsibilities, teachers should be alert to indications of disabilities that some students may have—and be ready to participate in an Individual Education Program (IEP), as described in Chapter 3, to see that these students obtain needed help. Both law and general fairness to students with special needs require six things in this regard (McMillan, 2000):

1. Proper training for those administering test of disabilities.
2. Assessment in the student's native language.
3. The identification of a student's specific needs, not just an overall judgment of ability.
4. Effective reflection of a student's ability or performance, in spite of any disability.
5. The use of multiple scores or assessments before an IEP decision is reached.
6. A multidisciplinary assessment team for assessing a suspected disability.

This chapter has indicated that classrooms are complex environments calling for teacher decision making in many areas. Within such an environment, teachers are not expected to be correct in every decision they make. That would be an unrealistic standard to hold anyone to, especially in fluid, decision-rich classroom settings where uncertainty abounds. However, teachers should be expected and are morally bound to provide defensible assessment evidence to support classroom decisions and actions. This is the least that can be expected in an environment where teacher actions have such vital consequences for pupils.

CHAPTER SUMMARY

olc

CHAPTER REVIEW

Visit Chapter 1 of the Online Learning Center at **www.mhhe.com/ airasian5e** to take chapter quizzes, link to related websites, read PowerWeb articles and news feed updates, and access study tools, including the case study referenced in the chapter.

♦ Every day in every classroom, teachers make decisions about their pupils, their instruction, and their classroom climate. Teachers collect and interpret various sources of evidence to help them evaluate and choose suitable courses of action.

♦ There are many purposes for classroom assessment: establishing classroom equilibrium, planning and conducting instruction, placing pupils, providing feedback and incentives, diagnosing pupil problems, and judging and grading academic learning and progress.

♦ All the purposes of assessment can be divided into three general categories: official assessments, such as grades, which teachers are expected to provide as part of their role in the school bureaucracy; instructional assessment, which includes both planning and delivering instruction to pupils; and early or beginning assessment, which occurs early in the school year and is used by teachers to get to know their pupils.

♦ Assessment is the general process of collecting, synthesizing, and interpreting information to aid teachers in their decision making. A test is a formal, usually paper-and-pencil way to gather information. Measurement is describing performance numerically. Evaluation is making judgments about what is good or desirable.

♦ Many forms of assessment evidence are used by teachers, including pencil-and-paper tests, observation, oral questioning, interviews, comments from prior teachers, and school record folders.

♦ Standardized assessments are intended to be administered, scored, and interpreted in the same way, no matter when or where they are given. These conditions are necessary because a primary purpose of standardized assessments is to compare the performance of pupils across different classrooms. Nonstandardized assessments are typically used by classroom teachers.

♦ The goodness of assessments is determined by their validity and reliability. Validity, the most important characteristic of assessments, is concerned with the collection of information that is most relevant for making the desired decision. Reliability is concerned with the consistency or typicality of the assessment information collected.

♦ Although assessment is thought of as a technical activity, there are ethical concerns associated with the assessment process. Since teachers' decisions can influence pupils' self-perception and life opportunities, when assessing, teachers must be aware of their many ethical responsibilities.

QUESTIONS FOR DISCUSSION

1. In what ways do the three general types of classroom assessment described in this chapter influence and interact with one another? For example, how do early assessments influence instructional assessments?

2. What kinds of learning are best assessed by observation? By other means?

3. Do teachers' ethical responsibilities to their pupils change as pupils get older? How? Are there some ethical responsibilities that remain constant across age levels?

ACTIVITIES

1. Interview a teacher about classroom decision making. Ask the teacher how he or she learns about students at the start of the school year: what characteristics are considered, on what basis are decisions about pupils made, and so forth?

2. Imagine you are a first-year teacher. School starts in three weeks. Discuss in small groups what you must do to prepare for its start. Select the three most important things and explain why.

REVIEW QUESTIONS

1. What are the three main types of classroom assessment? How do they differ in purpose, timing, and the types of information most likely to be used in carrying them out?

2. Explain the difference between standardized and nonstandardized assessments; supply and selection test items; and validity and reliability.

3. How would you explain the concept of validity to a fellow teacher? What examples would you use to make your point?

4. Why are validity and reliability important concerns in classroom assessments? Why is validity more important?

5. What are three ethical responsibilities a teacher has to her or his pupils? Give an example of how each responsibility might occur in a classroom.

REFERENCES

Ben-Yosef, E. (2003). Respecting students' cultural literacies. *Educational Leadership, 61* (2), 80–82.

Fenstermacher, G. D. (1990). Some moral considerations on teaching as a profession. In J. Goodlad, R. Soder, and K. Sirotnik (Eds.), *The moral dimensions of teaching* (pp. 130–151). San Francisco: Jossey-Bass.

Holloway, J. H. (2003). Managing culturally diverse classrooms. *Educational Leadership, 61* (1), 90–91.

Jackson, P. W. (1990). *Life in classrooms.* New York: Teachers College Press.

Linn, R. L. (1997). Evaluating the validity of assessments: The consequences of use. *Educational Measurement: Issues and Practices, 16* (2), 14–16.

McMillan, J. H. (2000). *Essential Assessment Concepts for Teachers and Administrators.* Thousand Oaks, CA: Corwin Press.

Moss, P. A. (2003). Reconceptualizing validity for the classroom. Educational Measurement: Issues and Practices, *22* (4), 13–25.

Strike, K. A. and Soltis, J. F. (1998). Thinking about education: *The ethics of teaching,* 3rd edition. New York: Teachers College Press.

CHAPTER 2

LEARNING ABOUT PUPILS: EARLY ASSESSMENT

KEY TOPICS

- *Gathering Information about Pupils*

- *Sources of Learning about Pupils*

- *Forming Pupil Descriptions*

- *Concerns about Ethics and Accuracy*

- *Improving Early Assessments*

- *Clues to Language Disabilities*

CHAPTER OBJECTIVES

After reading this chapter, you will be able to:

♦ Identify features of classrooms that make them social settings and explain the need for teacher early assessment
♦ Describe the sources of teacher assessments at the start of school
♦ Differentiate between cognitive, affective, and psychomotor behaviors
♦ Distinguish between formal and informal observations
♦ Identify weaknesses in the validity and reliability of early assessments and suggest ways to overcome them
♦ State potential effects of early assessments on pupils
♦ Explain strategies that can improve teacher early assessments
♦ Discuss early assessment for disabilities

THINKING ABOUT TEACHING

What can teachers do to have a smooth beginning of the school year? What are the three most important things for a teacher to do?

The first days of the school year are important for both teacher and pupils. They set the tone and lay the foundation for the rest of the year. For both teacher and pupils, these days are the one opportunity to make an initial impression. It is in these early days that a group of diverse individuals begins to come together to form a class. Although most teachers and pupils have been through the beginning of school many times before, uncertainties always accompany the start of a new school year. Each new group of pupils has its own special mix of backgrounds, abilities, interests, disabilities, needs, and personalities that make it unlike any other class the teacher has encountered.

The activities in the first few days of school set the stage for how well pupils will behave, attend, and learn during the school year. In the first days of school, teachers and pupils must get to know and understand one another.

In this chapter we explore questions that confront all teachers at the start of the school year: how to get to know new pupils, and what will the teacher need to know about them to provide an orderly, civil learning environment. To discover this information teachers ask and try to answer questions such as the following about their pupils:

♦ Will they get along well and be cooperative with each other?
♦ Are they academically ready for my curriculum?
♦ What intellectual, emotional, and physical strengths and weaknesses do they have?
♦ Do some students have disabilities that require classroom accommodations?
♦ Are there particularly disruptive pupils in the class?

If you were a teacher, what other questions would you add to this list and why?

GATHERING INFORMATION ABOUT PUPILS

In the early days of the school year teachers try to learn about each individual pupil and the class as a whole and to organize a classroom society that is characterized by communication, order, and learning (Garcia, 1994). It is very important to understand that a class is more than a group of pupils who happen to be in the same place at the same time.

A classroom is more than a group of students who happen to be in the same place at the same time. It is a society of people who communicate with each other, pursue common goals, and follow rules of order.

Certain basic realities apply, like those summarized in Table 2.1. A class is a society, a social system, made up of people who communicate with each other, pursue common and individual goals, and follow rules of order. For example, all classrooms have rules that govern such matters as who can visit the bathroom and when, how tardiness or lost homework will be treated, and how papers are distributed and collected. There also must be rules to govern the flow of communication in the classroom: "Don't talk when the teacher or another class member is talking"; "Raise your hand if you have a question"; "If you know the answer to a question don't blurt it out"; "If you don't know the answer to a question sit quietly and listen."

TABLE 2.1   THE BASIC REALITIES OF CLASSROOMS

1. The classroom is a social and cultural environment as well as an educational environment. The social and cultural dimensions influence greatly the educational dimension. Classrooms involve
   - ◆ persons interacting with persons
   - ◆ persons teaching persons
   - ◆ rules/order/communication/common goals

2. Each classroom culture differs in some ways from all others. There are few universals across all classrooms, except perhaps the teacher's moral responsibilities to pupils; teachers must make sense of their classroom cultures and use this sense to understand who the pupils are, where they are, and what they need.

3. Because of the uniqueness of every classroom culture, teacher judgment is a critical ingredient of successful classrooms. Life in classrooms is a series of judgments or decisions about pupils, curriculum, instruction, and learning; no one can or should make these judgments for the classroom teacher.

4. The teacher is both a participant and an observer in the classroom, which makes it difficult for the teacher to recognize his or her own contributions to classroom problems.

5. It is not reasonable to expect the classroom teacher to be correct in every judgment or decision he or she makes, especially since there is little codified knowledge to guide teachers' judgments and actions. However, it is reasonable to expect that classroom teachers can provide good and defensible grounds for their decisions and actions.

Pupils learn quickly that the fastest way to anger a teacher is not by doing poorly on a homework assignment or a test, but by doing such things as talking out of turn, pushing in line, laughing at the teacher, or engaging in some other breach of classroom etiquette.

Establishing a set of classroom rules and routines is one of the most important things a teacher can do to promote positive social and learning environments. Without rules and routines the classroom would be chaotic, making instruction and learning very difficult. Of course, classrooms are more than just social settings, they are also instructional settings in which teachers plan and deliver instruction and assess pupils. And finally, classrooms are places where one member, the teacher, has responsibility for other members, the pupils, thus making it a moral and ethical environment (McCaslin and Good, 1996). At the beginning of the school year the teacher must begin to set up this complex social, academic, and moral society.

Although all classrooms are simultaneously social, academic, and moral environments, the specific features of particular classrooms differ greatly from one another. For example, the academic and socioeconomic backgrounds of pupils, as well as their mix of personalities, learning styles, languages, special needs, and interests, differ from classroom to classroom (Ladson-Billings, 1994; Delpit, 1995). From one year to the next, a teacher cannot count on having similar groups of pupils. Because of such differences, planning and delivering instruction are context-bound activities; that is, the ways that teachers plan and teach are dependent upon the varied characteristics of their pupils. This means, of course, that the teacher must know about the characteristics of his or her pupils. Try to imagine planning and teaching a lesson for a group of pupils you know nothing about. What will interest the pupils? How long can they pay attention? What have they learned previously? What learning needs do they have? What accommodations must be met to help pupils with disabilities learn? Similarly, try to imagine how you would discipline students you did not know. What strategies might work with different pupils? Is a student acting out because she is bored, unable to follow the lesson, or testing the teacher? Teachers size up their pupils at the start of the school year to answer such questions in a process that we call "early assessment."

All teachers must learn about their pupils, although teachers will gather different information depending on the goals of schooling at different levels. At the elementary school level, curriculum goals include both academic and socialization outcomes. Elementary teachers were asked about the importance of socialization outcomes in their classrooms. Here are a few of their comments.

> Every spare minute I try to stress good citizenship and cooperation. If these issues arise during instruction, I stop the lesson and remind the students about good classroom behavior and cooperation. Even if a student just took someone's pencil, I would say, "Do you realize. . .?" I think that good citizenship, civility, and cooperation are as important as learning subject matter. Some of them don't get it at home.

TECHNOLOGY AND ASSESSMENT

WHAT TYPICAL YOUNG READERS REALLY ARE LIKE

Imagine yourself in your first week of teaching a class of eager first, second, or third graders. You are keenly aware that this is a crucial time in their lives, since children who do not read and write fluently by the end of third grade are likely never to catch up to their peers in these essential skills. Are the pupils in your class on track to reach this crucial milestone?

Some of your pupils surprise you with their high degree of skill. Others strike you as being much less fluent than you thought they should be. Are your faster students way ahead of the game? Are the slower ones really behind, or do the fast ones just make them seem so? Exactly what levels of skill should pupils in your class be showing?

To answer such questions, the Learning Research and Development Center at the University of Pittsburgh and the National Center on Education and the Economy (NCEE) have documented what pupils are actually like and what basic skills they should master, grade by grade. The extremely useful fruits of their labor are two sets of standards called Reading and Writing Grade by Grade: Primary Literacy Standards for Kindergarten through Third Grade, and Speaking and Writing for Preschool through Third Grade. In addition to describing performance expectations at each grade level, these publications come with a rich set of print examples and CD-ROM videos that show you normally progressing pupils reading, writing, listening, and speaking at each grade level. By watching the videos you can see, for example, the level of word decoding skills your pupils should display.

If you don't find these materials in your college education library, you can buy them from the website of the NCEE (www.ncee.org). As of this writing, similar products for the fourth and fifth grades were nearing publication.

I'm trying to make them good citizens in the classroom community and beyond, not only good learners. I make sure they know what is expected of them by the time they are out of the sixth grade, the difference between right and wrong.

In elementary schools, most pupils spend 5 to 6 hours a day in the same classroom with the same teacher and classmates. Often, much of the instruction is carried out in small groups, so that while one group is occupying the teacher's attention, other pupils must keep themselves busy and productive without constant teacher supervision. Thus, in elementary classrooms, a teacher's initial assessments tend to embrace pupils' academic capabilities and their general classroom behavior.

The goals of schooling at the high school level are predominantly academic and vocational. Pupils may already be grouped into tracks and most have already been socialized in appropriate school behavior. Instead of seeing 20 to 25 pupils for 6 hours a day as in the elementary school, high school teachers see 100 to 125 pupils in five different classes lasting about an hour each. While high school teachers are interested in their pupils' affective and personal characteristics, they do not "live" with their pupils in the same way that elementary teachers do. As a consequence, the learning done by high school teachers tends to focus on academic characteristics, work habits, behavior, subject matter interest, and attitude. Still, to suggest that high school teachers are not concerned with emotional and interest outcomes is to overstate the matter. One high school business teacher notes: "I try to prepare my students for life. I want them to know how to keyboard and balance ledgers, but I am equally concerned that they are respectful, honest, good citizens, and so forth." All teachers are concerned with their pupils' cognitive and affective characteristics, although the relative emphasis on these characteristics differs by grade level.

If early assessment is not done well, a disorganized, disruptive, unresponsive class results, one for which communication and learning are inhibited. Each of us can recall a particular classroom in which the social system was characterized by anarchy, where personal impulse replaced social consideration, and where teaching and learning were constantly undermined by failure to establish order.

While teachers do control many classroom features (e.g., rules and routines, methods of instruction, topics covered, and grading practices), there are some they do not control. Table 2.2 describes two teachers' classrooms. Imagine that these classrooms are at the same grade level. Notice that all of the characteristics listed in the table are those over which teachers normally have little control; of some the teacher may not even be aware until they suddenly pose a challenge; they are the "givens" that each teacher has to work with.

Teaching is a context-bound activity involving many things teachers cannot control, such as the characteristics of their students and the resources available to them.

TABLE 2.2   COMPARISON OF TWO CLASSROOM CONTEXTS

Classroom A	Classroom B
30 pupils	16 pupils
Pupils abilities clustering at three disparate levels	Fairly homogeneous pupil abilities
Several pupils with speech impairments and physical disabilities	A few pupils who crave attention while a few seem extremely shy
Range of socioeconomic backgrounds	Uniformly middle class
Parent pressures for multicultural learning	Parent pressures for high grades
Balanced gender mix	Predominantly boys
Separate art and music programs in another class	No separate art or music
Spacious, quiet room	Small room with noise from class next door
Nearly all pupils together for several years	Most pupils meeting each other for the first time
Individual pupil desks	Tables and chairs
Classroom aide available	No classroom aide

How might these various characteristics influence the way the two teachers maintain classroom order, organize activities for individuals, groups, or the class as a whole, or plan specific lessons? Which characteristics seem most advantageous to a teacher, and which seem disadvantageous? Are the teachers' "givens" likely to lead to identical teacher approaches? Thinking about these questions should give you some sense of how approaches to teaching are always dependent on both the students and the classroom "givens."

At the beginning of each year teachers must get to know their pupils so that they can organize them into a classroom learning community.

Early assessment is becoming more difficult for teachers. American teachers increasingly face learners varied in ability, class, race, culture, and language. Issues of poverty, disabilities, violence, abuse, teen pregnancy, and drugs confront too many of our students and impact their school performance and success (Wiseman, Cooner, & Knight, 1999). However, in spite of this difficult reality, teachers are expected to know and teach all their students. The information about pupils a teacher collects during the beginning days of school forms perceptions and expectations that will influence the way the teacher plans for, interacts with, and manages pupils and instruction. Some important pupil characteristics may not manifest themselves in the first few days of school; issues such as poverty, violence, abuse, and pregnancy may not be immediately apparent to a teacher, while issues of culture, language, and physical disabilities probably will be.

SOURCES OF LEARNING ABOUT PUPILS

The information teachers use to know their pupils can come from both formal and informal sources. Table 2.3 lists some common sources and kinds of information that teachers seek.

Teachers use a variety of information to size up their students, including personal observations, school records, comments from other teachers, and formal assessments.

For one example of informal sources, sit and listen in the teachers' room. Hear Ms. Robinson or Mr. Rutherford complain about Jim or Shaylah's continual inattentiveness or defiant behavior in class. Listen to Mr. Hobbs describe Marion's cooperation and insight. Hear Ms. Jeffry complain about Mike's interfering and demanding parents. One does not have to know Jim, Shaylah, Marion, or Mike personally to begin forming impressions of them as persons and pupils. Many pupils' reputations precede them into the classroom and teachers who have never set eyes on them often already have heard a great deal about their strengths and weaknesses.

Several teachers relate how the information they collected helped them with the early assessment of their pupils at the start of the school year.

> School records are kept in the office and are available on all pupils. I could look at these before the school year started to get information about my pupils' abilities, prior school performance, home situation, and learning problems.

> In my school, classes are assigned by level. Before classes start I know whether a class is high or low level.

TABLE 2.3 SOME COMMON EARLY ASSESSMENT SOURCES AND WHAT INFORMATION THEY MAY YIELD

What Pupils Say	What Pupils Do	What Pupils Write
Responses to questions	Early homework assignments	Early written homework assignments
Class discussion	In-class tasks	Early or prior journals
Interaction with others		Early or prior tests
Early oral reports		Prior portfolios
Potential Information	**Potential Information**	**Potential Information**
Attention span	Attention span	Organizational abilities
Oral fluency	Ability to complete work on time	Logicality
Politeness	Ability to follow directions	Neatness
Vocabulary	Level of performance	Penmanship
Ease of participation	Ability to get along with others	Level of performance
Anxiety		
Ability to respond to prompts		
Tendencies to talk out of turn in class		

Sometimes when I compare my class list with another teacher's, the other teacher may comment on a pupil, the sibling of the pupil, or the parents of the pupil. Susie's brother was a nice, quiet boy. Sam's sister was defiant and disruptive in class. Andy is the last of the eight Rooney children, thank goodness. Be careful, Mrs. Roberts is overly protective of Peter and very concerned about grades.

By the end of the first week of school I will know whether each child is going to work, care about school, get along with the other pupils, be responsible enough to relay messages for me, and have a pleasant personality. I know these things by observing the children in class. Whether a student volunteers an answer or comments willingly or if he needs to be called on to give an answer tells me about the pupil's type of personality. I watch how they get along with each other. The look of interest on their faces tells me about how hard they will work.

Thus, at the start of school, teachers have their antennae up, constantly listening and watching for information about their students. Sometimes their attention is drawn to things that seem, on the surface, to have little to do with the main task of the school: the way pupils dress, their posture and body language, pupil discussions in the hallways and cafeterias, and who they "hang around" with. By such means, by the end of the first or second week of school, most teachers have sized up their pupils and classes and can provide fairly detailed descriptions of pupil characteristics.

Two facts about this early information deserve attention. First, much of it comes from informal observations. As the "could" in the previous first teacher quote hints, most teachers do not rely heavily on tests or formal assessments when initially determining pupil characteristics. If they seek formal information, and many do not, they often go to the school record folders or administer subject matter pretests. Second, because this initial information is obtained largely by means of informal observations, teachers are exposed to only a small sample of each pupil's behavior.

Teachers rely heavily on informal observations when initially sizing up their students.

Two types of problems limit the validity and reliability of this style of early assessment based on personal observation and communication. First, because of the limits of the human mind and memory, teachers may "lose," or forget, important pieces of information about a student or class. If memory is faulty or incomplete, the appropriateness or validity of the personal communication information is lowered.

A second problem concerns the amount of information teachers obtain to learn about a student or class. Since teachers can observe any given pupil only part of the time, it is inevitable that their observations will be incomplete and limited. Personal communications are varied, often brief, and focused on a large number of pupils, thus increasing the possibility that insufficient information will be obtained to provide reliable interpretations about pupil characteristics. Teachers need to recognize the potential problems of selective memory and insufficient information.

FORMING PUPIL DESCRIPTIONS

On the basis of whatever degree of information they do collect, teachers synthesize their early assessments into general descriptions of pupils, like the following:

Jemella (a second grader) has had an exceptional beginning of school. She does her work very well and on time, raises her hand to answer questions, and seems to be enjoying school. This is not the case for many of the new second graders.

Joslyn (a fifth grader) walks into class each day with a worried and tired look on her face. Praising her work, or even the smallest positive action, will bring a smile to her face, though the impact is brief. She is inattentive, even during the exercises we do step-by-step as a class. She is shy, but sometimes will ask for help. But before she gives herself a chance, she will put her head down on her desk and close her eyes. I don't know why she lacks motivation so severely. Possibly it's a chemical imbalance or maybe problems at home. She will probably be this way all year.

Alfredo (an eighth grader) is a smooth talker, a Casanova. He is a nice dresser, a nice kid with a head on his shoulders. Unfortunately he is very unmotivated, most likely because of his background. He's street smart, loves attention, and has a good sense of humor. He is able to "dish it out" but can also take it. Alfredo is loud in class but not to the point of disruption; he knows where to draw the limit. If only he had some determination, the kid could go a long way.

Larinda (an eleventh grader) is athletic and good-natured. She flirts with the boys and sometimes with her teachers. She doesn't go beyond the bounds of good taste and is respectful in class. Her ability is average.

These are rich and detailed descriptions of pupils. Each includes many different pupil characteristics, relies heavily on informal information, and conveys a perception about many dimensions of pupil behavior and background. Notice that the teachers' descriptions include both academic and nonacademic factors. Notice also that they often make a prediction about how the pupil will perform during the school year. That teachers assess pupils is not in itself remarkable; people in any social system size each other up. What is important, however, is the speed at which teachers can form impressions about almost all the pupils in the class.

Assessments produce a set of perceptions and expectations that influence the manner in which the teacher plans for, instructs, and interacts with the pupils throughout the school year (Good & Brophy, 1997). This is, after all, the purpose of early assessment: to help the teacher get to know the pupils so he or she can organize them into a classroom society and know how to interact with, motivate, and teach them.

To get a sense of the use and importance of early assessment, imagine that it is the middle of January and you have been called in to substitute for the regular eighth grade teacher at Memorial Middle School. You have detailed plans for the subject matter you are to teach during the day. Just after the beginning bell rings and pupils are seated, a boy in the back of the room raises his hand and asks to go to his locker to get a book he has forgotten. Should you let him go? Can he be trusted to return after getting the book or will he wander the corridors for an hour? What is the classroom teacher's policy on forgotten books? A few minutes later two girls get up and start to leave the room. "We always go to the library to see Ms. Flanders for extra help at this time on Wednesday. We'll be back in about an hour." Do they? Will they? Shortly thereafter, two pupils start arguing over the last copy of a reference book. The argument grows louder and begins to disturb the class. How should you react? What strategy will pacify these particular pupils? The classroom teacher knows the answers to all these questions because she or he is a founding member of the classroom society. The teacher is the person who has sized up the pupils' characteristics and established the routines. As a substitute, you are an outsider, a stranger to this classroom society and thus do not know its workings, personalities, rules, and routines. Early assessments provide the classroom teacher with the kinds of practical, nitty-gritty knowledge needed to make a classroom function.

These early assessments provide teachers with the kinds of practical, nitty-gritty information needed in order to make a classroom function effectively.

Table 2.4 reviews the main characteristics of early assessment.

TABLE 2.4   CHARACTERISTICS OF EARLY ASSESSMENT

1. **Early assessment is done at the start of the school year.** Most teachers can describe the personal, social, and academic characteristics of each pupil and the class as a whole after the first two weeks of school.

2. **Early assessment is pupil-centered.** Pupils and their characteristics are the focus of assessment.

3. **Informal observation is used.** Much of the information about pupil behavior and performance is collected through spontaneous, informal observations.

4. **Observations are synthesized into perceptions.** Teachers put together their observations in idiosyncratic ways to form a generalized perception of pupils.

5. **Impressions are rarely written down.** Unlike test scores or grades, which are written down in rank books or report cards, the perceptions formed from early assessments are unwritten and selectively communicated.

6. **Observations are broad and diverse.** Teachers attend to a broad range of cognitive, affective, and psychomotor characteristics when they size up their pupils.

7. **Early impressions tend to become permanent.** Teachers are very confident about the accuracy of the assessments they do in the first days of school. Initial perceptions are very stable from the first week of school to the end of the school year.

Bear in mind that early assessments are simply a special case of a natural tendency to observe and make judgments about people on the basis of what is seen and heard about them in everyday interactions. These assessments facilitate "knowing" or "labeling" others so that it is no longer necessary to interact with them as if they were strangers; they help bring order into social situations, including schools. They provide a frame of reference within which social interaction and meaningful instruction can take place.

CONCERNS ABOUT ETHICS AND ACCURACY

Because early assessments form the basis for many important judgments made throughout the school year, teachers have an ethical responsibility to make them as valid and reliable as possible. However, an assessment process that is based upon quickly obtained, often incomplete evidence has the potential to produce incorrect, invalid, and unreliable decisions about pupils.

The General Problem

Consider four additional realities of the situation. First, teachers' initial impressions of their pupils tend to remain stable over time. Once a teacher forms an impression of a pupil, that impression is likely to stick, and teachers will act to maintain their pupil impressions, even in the face of contradictory evidence. Second, classroom teachers are fairly accurate in their beginning-of-the-year predictions of pupils' academic performance as measured by test scores, although, even the most accurate teacher is not correct about every pupil. However, teachers' accuracy when sizing up pupils' personalities, interests, emotions, motivation, self-concepts, and social adjustment is lower. Overall, teachers' perceptions of these emotional characteristics are less accurate than their academic perceptions, at least at the start of the school year.

Because initial early assessments have important consequences for pupils, teachers have an ethical responsibility to make them as valid and reliable as possible.

Third, early assessments not only influence the way teachers perceive, treat, and make decisions about pupils, they are often transmitted to pupils. Teachers often unknowingly and unintentionally communicate their assessments, such as with offhand comments that tell individuals and the class a great deal about the teacher's perceptions: "Oh Robert, can't you even remember what we just talked about?" "All right, Sarah, will you tell the rest of the class the answer it can't seem to come up with?" "Didn't Ruby read that paragraph with a lot of expression?" Sometimes perceptions are conveyed indirectly, as when a teacher waits patiently for one pupil to think through a problem but allows another only a few seconds; expresses encouragement and assurance to one pupil but says "at least try" to another; encourages one to "think" but another to "take a guess." Tone of voice, physical proximity, gestures, seating arrangements, and other signals all tell pupils how they are perceived in the classroom.

Teachers often communicate their assessments to pupils in unintended ways, and students may live up to these teacher perceptions.

Fourth, teachers' perceptions and expectations may even create a **self-fulfilling prophecy,** in which the expectations for a pupil lead the teacher to interact with that pupil in a particular manner (Good & Brophy, 1997). The pupil, in turn, observes the way the teacher interacts with him or her and begins to behave in the way or at the level the teacher expects, whether or not the original expectation is correct. Needless to say, it is the teacher's ethical responsibility to avoid this situation by making the assessments as fair and accurate as possible for all pupils, and not using them to demean or embarrass a pupil. This is especially so since the process happens so quickly, is often done unconsciously, and leaves no permanent record outside the teacher's head.

Thus far, we have seen that early assessments are largely based upon information that is gathered at the start of the school year, that teachers form these assessments relatively quickly, that they use them to "know" students, and that they remain fairly stable once formed. Early assessments determine perceptions and expectations, which in turn influence teachers' interactions with pupils. Because assessments can be so influential in setting expectations, influencing pupil-teacher interactions, and affecting pupils' performance and self-perceptions, it is important to examine more closely the dangers inherent in that process and the strategies teachers can use to improve their initial assessments.

The Problem in Terms of Validity and Reliability

In the previous section we mentioned the ethical need for teachers to make early assessments valid and reliable. Let's explore that theme more fully. As stated in Chapter 1, the two main criteria for good assessments are validity and reliability. Validity is concerned with the collection of *appropriate* evidence; that is, evidence that is related to the pupil characteristic under consideration: Does the evidence I have gathered tell me about the characteristic I wish to judge? Reliability pertains to collecting *enough* evidence to be relatively certain that the pupil's *typical* performance is being observed: Is the evidence gathered indicative of the pupil's typical or normal performance? Validity and reliability work hand in hand to ensure that the perceptions formed in assessment are appropriate and fair, leading to good decisions about pupils.

Threats to Validity

Observer prejudgment can stem from prior knowledge, first impressions, or personal prejudices, and often interferes with fair and valid assessments.

There are two main problems that occur during assessment that diminish the validity of the information teachers gather: prejudgment and logical error. **Prejudgment** occurs when a teacher's prior knowledge, first impressions, or personal prejudices and beliefs interfere with the ability to make a fair and valid assessment of a pupil. All of us have personal prejudices or beliefs; we prefer some things to others and some people to others. We have beliefs, interests, ideas, and expectations that differentiate us from others. However, when these likes, dislikes, beliefs, and prejudices interfere with our ability to make fair pupil assessments, there is a real problem.

Prejudging pupils results from three main sources. The first is *prior information,* information a teacher obtains before meeting a pupil. Information passed through the school grapevine or the performance of prior siblings often influences and prejudices a teacher's perceptions, even before the pupil enters the teacher's classroom: "Oh, you're Sarah's brother! I'm expecting you to do as well as she did when she was in my class."

The second is *initial impressions,* which tend to influence subsequent impressions. If the teacher judges a pupil upon how he is dressed on the first day of school or how she behaved in study hall last year, the teacher may unconsciously let this initial impression dictate subsequent observations and interpretations of the pupil's characteristics.

The third source of prejudging is teachers' *personal theories and beliefs* about particular kinds of pupils, which often lead to stereotyped perceptions. When teachers think "this pupil is from Oldtown, and kids from Oldtown are poor learners and discipline problems," or "girls do poorly in math," or "everyone knows that members of that group have no interest in school," or "he's just another dumb jock," they are expressing their personal theories or stereotypes of what they think certain people are like and how they behave. Being labeled with such stereotypes without a fair chance to show true characteristics can injure pupils and inhibit their learning.

This is especially so with regard to teachers' racial, cultural, disability, and language prejudices or stereotypes. While the variety of pupil languages, cultures, races, and disabilities represented in American classrooms is increasing, the variety of teachers who teach these students is not increasing as quickly. When making early assessments, teachers who are not familiar with pupils' cultures and languages often interpret what are really cultural *differences* as cultural *deficits* (Ladson-Billings, 1994: Delpit, 1995). Similarly, teachers' stereotypes or personal beliefs can produce invalid early assessments for students who are different from the teacher. For example, many Americans, including many teachers, believe that the majority of children of color are poor, live in large cities, come from single-family homes, and live on public assistance. How might a teacher who erroneously believes these misconceptions perceive a pupil of color on the first day of school? Do you think he or she might have some prejudgments or stereotypes that could influence initial perceptions of the pupil? The dangers of prejudgment are real and consequential. Teachers must strive to recognize their personal beliefs and stereotypes and judge each individual pupil on the basis of how he or she actually performs in class. Each pupil is entitled to be judged on his or her own merits, not on the basis of stereotypes and personal beliefs. This is a teacher's ethical responsibility.

Teachers should be careful not to interpret cultural differences as cultural deficits.

Many teachers recognize that prejudgments and stereotyping can invalidate early assessments, as the following statements indicate.

I don't like to hear anything about a student's behavior from past teachers. Every teacher is different, just like every student is different. A student may have a negative experience with one teacher, but a positive experience with another teacher. I prefer to make my own decision about every child.

I remember the time I stereotyped three of my female students as "Valley" girls—not too bright and mainly superficial—on the first day of class. This assessment came about due to their physical appearance and their shallow contributions in discussion. Yet when it came time for formal assessment, these three individuals ranked the highest in the class.

Logical error occurs when teachers select the wrong indicators to assess desired pupil characteristics, thereby invalidating their judgments. It is tempting to read a great deal into a single observation, especially at the start of the year when teachers want to quickly characterize each pupil in order to organize their classes. It would be convenient, for example, to read a whole series of inferences about motivation, attention span, interest in

olc
CHAPTER CASE STUDY
Visit the text OLC to read the case of Marsha Warren, an experienced third grade teacher who is overwhelmed by the problems created by her heterogeneous class.
(www.mhhe.com/ airasian5e)

the subject, self-concept, and leadership from a pupil's eager hand raising. Maybe all the interpretations will prove to be correct, but it is dangerous not to recognize the difference between what is directly observed and interpretations made from an observation. When observation of one characteristic (hand raising) is used to make inferences about other, unobserved characteristics (motivation, interest), the potential for logical errors and invalid assessment is great.

> A third grade teacher described Katie's first day in school in this way: "I knew right away that Katie was cooperative and a hard worker. She was the first child to complete her Summer Vacation essay, and instead of wasting her free time, she offered to get the dictionary and help the other children with their spelling." Are cooperative and hard working the only interpretations of Katie's behaviors? What are some others? If Shandella, not Katie, had done the same things, would Shandella have been judged in the same way?

Teachers should be careful not to mislabel students based on observations that do not justify the label.

To state the issue in another way, the labels teachers use to describe their pupils represent their interpretations of observed behaviors. Teachers do not directly observe characteristics such as motivation, intelligence, leadership, self-confidence, aggressiveness, anxiety, shyness, intolerance, and the like. Rather, teachers observe a pupil behaving in some way, interpret what the behavior signifies, and give the behavior a name. In most cases, it is the name given to the behavior that attaches to the pupil, not the specific behavior that prompted the name. Teachers remember that a pupil is a bully, self-confident, aggressive, aloof, motivated, or shy, but they rarely remember the specific observations that led them to label the pupils in that way. Because teachers' labels "stick" to pupils, it is important that the observations leading to a label are valid indicators of that label.

Threats to Reliability

Teachers should be careful not to form a permanent perception of pupils based on one or two observations that may not be typical behavior.

While validity is concerned with collecting information that is appropriate for determining a pupil's characteristics, reliability is concerned with collecting enough information to be sure that it represents typical pupil behavior. For example, was the teacher's observance of Katie's performance on that first day of school sufficient to conclude that she will be cooperative and a hard worker? Probably not. Why? Whether formal or informal, teachers' assessments are based upon samples of their pupils' behavior. These samples are used to determine pupils' more general behavior patterns. Thus, an important issue in teacher assessment is how well the observed samples represent pupils' general or typical behavior patterns. Reliable information captures consistent and stable pupil characteristics.

The nature of early assessment creates special reliability problems. As noted earlier, the spontaneity of many teacher-pupil interactions limit what teachers are able to see and what pupils are willing to show. Also, the time available to observe pupils often is brief, since attention must be distributed among many pupils and classroom activities, especially at the beginning of the school year. In short, the few initial samples of behavior that are observed under these circumstances may not provide reliable indicators of pupils' typical behavior.

Many teachers recognize this problem, as evidenced by the following statements:

> First impressions are so important. They can either make or break a child. It all depends on how much opportunity a particular teacher gives to a student to prove himself before passing a judgment.

> The first three days are very difficult. The students will not even present their normal classroom behaviors to you in the first three days. They are somewhat intimidated and uncomfortable; they don't know you. Even kids who are badly behaved in the first three days, they're just feeling you out, they're testing, trying to see how far they can get.

> Carol breaks up with her boyfriend a week before the beginning of school, leaving her depressed and unmotivated. Does her English teacher know the reason for Carol's behavior? Is her assessment of Carol after one day of school correct?

The implication of these comments is that teachers must be sure they observe sufficient samples of pupils' behavior before they solidify their initial perceptions and use them for decision making. There are times, such as the start of the school year, when pupils' behavior may not be indicative of their typical behavior. Typical behavior cannot be determined by observing a pupil just once, especially at a time when the pupil may feel uncomfortable in new surroundings. Key Assessment Tools 2.1 summarizes the threats to validity and reliability.

IMPROVING EARLY ASSESSMENTS

Following are some strategies that can be used to improve early assessments. While teachers will never be correct in all early assessments, it is their ethical responsibility to do everything possible to minimize errors and to revise judgments when initial impressions prove to be wrong.

How effective you can be in early assessment will always depend in part on having an orderly and supportive early classroom and school environment in which to observe your pupils and gather other data about them. In that spirit, Tables 2.5 and 2.6 (pp. 43–44) can be helpful.

1. *Be aware of early assessment and its effects on pupils.* Early assessment is such a natural part of the start of the school year that many teachers are unaware that they are doing it. They do not recognize the dangers of forming incorrect impressions of pupils. As a first step, then, it is important for teachers to be aware of this type of assessment

Key Assessment Tools 2.1

THREATS TO THE VALIDITY AND RELIABILITY OF EARLY ASSESSMENTS

Validity Threats

I. Observer prejudgments that prevent teachers from making an objective assessment of the pupils.

a. Prior information from school grapevine, siblings, or nonclassroom experiences

b. First impressions that influence subsequent impressions

c. Personal theories or attitudes that influence subsequent observation (e.g., girls can't do math or athletes have no interest in serious academic pursuits)

II. Logical errors that cause teachers to judge pupils based on the wrong characteristics (e.g., observe attention and judge learning; observe clothes and judge ability).

Reliability Threats

I. Inadequate behavior sampling in which too few observations prevent learning about pupils' typical behavior and characteristics.

a. Basing decisions about a pupil on a single piece of information.

b. Observing behaviors in one setting (e.g., the playground) and assuming behavior will be the same in another setting (e.g., the classroom).

---

and to be sensitive to the consequences of making incorrect judgments based on incomplete or invalid observations.

Teachers should treat initial impressions as hypotheses to be confirmed or corrected by later information.

2. *Treat initial impressions as hypotheses to be confirmed or corrected by subsequent observations and information.* First impressions should be considered tentative hypotheses that need to be confirmed or disproved by subsequent observation and information. Teachers should refrain from judging and labeling pupils on the basis of hearsay, a single brief observation, or a pupil's race, culture, gender, or language. They should also gather their own evidence about pupils and confirm first impressions with subsequent observations and information. They should not be afraid to change an incorrect first impression.

One way to make your observations more thorough, and less likely to be unconsciously selective, is to pick one pupil characteristic per day and structure classroom activities to permit all pupils in the class to demonstrate that characteristic.

3. *Use direct indicators to gather information about pupil characteristics.* To learn about pupils, teachers must interpret the pupil observations they gather. Some observations require less interpretation than

TABLE 2.5 A DISCIPLINE "DAILY DOZEN" FOR TEACHERS

1. *Be consistent.* When you reprimand an action one day and ignore it the next, children don't know what to expect. As a result, they'll try it again to see if they can "get away with it." They are also quick to see and resent the basic unfairness of inconsistency.

2. *Don't make idle threats.* If you decide that punishment is necessary, carry it out, or your word will mean nothing.

3. *Look for the reasons behind misbehavior.* It often stems from the lack of interest by your pupils in the curriculum or the teaching approach.

4. *Be sure that they know the rules.* If you expect your pupils to behave in a certain way, tell them so, and explain the reason why. A class discussion of these rules can be enlightening both to you and your class. You may discover that some of your rules have no real purpose.

5. *Check your own feelings about individual students.* Do you "play favorites"? It's hard to like sullen or rebellious students, easy to like the quiet conformists. But your dislike of the rebel incites more rebellion.

6. *Watch your tongue.* "The teacher's tongue, sharper than a two-edged sword, sometimes stabs children, leaving wounds that never heal," said R. L. Frye, supervisor of secondary education, Louisiana State Department of Education. A tongue lashing may end the disturbance— but at what cost?

7. *Don't make study a punishment.* The teacher who keeps pupils after school to study arithmetic or spelling, as a penalty for misbehavior, is saying: "Study is an unpleasant thing. There is no joy or satisfaction in it. It's so painful that I use it as a punishment." This hardly creates a thirst for learning in youngsters.

8. *Let them know that you like them.* Look for things to praise, especially in students who are discipline problems. Accept them as worthwhile in spite of their misbehavior. Disapprove the act certainly, but not the individual.

9. *Don't try to do the impossible.* Some students have emotional problems only a better-trained person can solve. When a youngster is a consistent troublemaker, and all your efforts to help him fail, the time has come to refer him to the ACT team or vice principal. There are limits to what a teacher can do in child study, diagnosis, and treatment.

10. *Control your temper.* Flying off the handle merely shows students that they've gotten through to you. When you "lose your cool" you lose your ability to solve the discipline problem sanely, rationally, thoughtfully.

11. *Don't be afraid to apologize if you've treated a pupil unjustly.* You will gain, not lose, the respect of the class for admitting your error.

12. *What you see as delinquent behavior may be normal behavior in a child's cultural background.* It may take time, patience, and tact to break the pattern.

SOURCE: Natick Middle School, Natick, Massachusetts. Used by permission.

> **TABLE 2.6　SUGGESTIONS FOR THE BEGINNING OF SCHOOL FOR NEW TEACHERS**
>
> 1. Create classroom plans for the first few days. Plan at least twice as much as you think you will need.
> 2. Find someone who "knows the ropes," likely an experienced teacher, who can serve as a mentor.
> 3. Watch your conversation in the faculty room.
> 4. Learn to use the school copying machine, scanner, computers, and so on.
> 5. Never, ever leave your class alone. Find someone to cover.

When making assessments, teachers should try to use information that requires minimum interpretation.

others. The closer the behavior observed is to the pupil characteristic a teacher wishes to describe, the more valid the resulting information is and the more confident the teacher can be about the pupil's true characteristic. For example, actually listening to a pupil read aloud provides more direct and valid evidence about a pupil's oral reading than the reading grades the pupil got from a prior teacher or the pupil's reported interest in reading.

In early assessments, teacher-pupil encounters are often brief, and the tendency is for the teacher to focus on superficial, indirect characteristics such as dress, facial expression, helpfulness, mood, or general appearance. Teachers then read into these superficial observations complex traits and personality factors like motivation, self-concept, trustworthiness, self-control, and interest. Such indirect generalizations are likely to be invalid. Thus, the moral is to focus evidence gathering on direct behaviors and indicators.

Because informal observations involve spontaneous behavior that may not be repeated, teachers should supplement their informal observations with more structured activities.

4. *Supplement informal observations with more formal, structured activities.* There is no rule that demands that only informal observations be used to assess pupils. In fact, complete reliance on informal observations means that the teacher does not have control over many of the behaviors that occur, especially in the first few days of school. Good teachers recognize this limitation and supplement their informal early observations with more structured activities. For example, they:

   ♦ Administer textbook review or diagnostic pretests to assess pupils' entering levels.
   ♦ Require pupils to keep a journal during the first week of school or write an essay on What I Did Last Summer to assess pupils' experiences, writing skills, and thought processes.
   ♦ Carry out group discussions or group projects to assess how pupils interact and work in groups.

◆ Let pupils read aloud to determine reading facility.

◆ Play classroom games based on spelling words, math facts, geographical knowledge, or current events to assess general knowledge, interest, and competitiveness.

◆ Use games related to listening skills to assess pupils' abilities to follow directions and process auditory information.

◆ Employ more formal observational instruments.

Some school systems collect samples of pupils' work into what are called **portfolios.** These portfolios often accompany the pupils as they progress from grade to grade and provide a new teacher with concrete examples of a pupil's work. Note that having actual samples of a pupil's work from previous years is quite different from the hearsay evidence teachers accumulate through the school grapevine. (Portfolios and other formal methods of assessing pupil performance are described more fully later, beginning in Chapter 6.) Formal assessments provide information about pupils' interests, styles, and academic performance that is not always obtainable from informal observations. Formal assessments also often require all pupils to perform the same behavior and thereby permit comparisons of desired characteristics among pupils.

Formal assessments that require students to perform the same behavior permit comparison among pupils.

5. *Observe long enough to be fairly certain of the pupil's typical behavior.* Reliable information is that which represents the *typical* behavior of a pupil. To obtain reliable data, the teacher must look for *patterns* of behavior, not single, one-time behaviors. The greater the consequences that an assessment is likely to have for pupils, the more the teacher should strive to gather reliable information. A good rule of thumb to follow is see it at least twice, thus making sure the behavior being observed is typical.

Reliable assessments usually require multiple observations in order to identify typical student behavior.

6. *Determine whether different kinds of information confirm each other.* Teachers can have more confidence in their pupil perceptions if they are based upon two or more kinds of supporting evidence. For example, are test scores supported by classroom performance? Are classroom observations of a pupil's needs consistent with those identified by last year's teacher and the pupil's parents? Do classroom behavior patterns persist in the lunchroom and on the playground?

Whenever possible, teachers should base their decisions on different kinds of information that support one another.

These questions suggest the use of multiple sources of information to corroborate the teacher's perception of a pupil. However, note that it is better if the present teacher forms his or her own impressions of the pupil *before* obtaining corroborative information from other sources. By doing this, the teacher avoid letting his or her perceptions be influenced or prejudiced by the perceptions of others.

CLUES TO LANGUAGE DISABILITIES

If your class includes bilingual students, you face a special challenge. For more than three decades, culturally and linguistically diverse students have tended to be overrepresented in some types of special education for disabilities and underrepresented in programs for gifted and talented students (Klingner & Artiles, 2003). In cases where a bilingual background may be the source of a learning difficulty, you may want to consult with a special education teacher to be sure that the student is appropriately placed. Regarding students in your class whose first language is English, your early assessment will also need to watch for language disabilities.

The higher the level of grade you are teaching, the more likely it should be that a pupil's weakness in some area has already been detected, and some alert has been passed on. In prior grades, a pupil's parents and teachers may already have created a formal plan called an Individual Education Plan, or IEP (described in Chapter 3), to accommodate a disability. But it is not uncommon for weaknesses to go unrecognized and unaddressed for longer than they should.

One hint of a weakness is avoidance, as when a kindergarten child avoids activities like coloring, drawing, writing letters, or tying shoes because of slow motor control development.

A language disability may not be recognized for the first few years of elementary school simply because it can take that long for the signs to be obvious that a pupil is not keeping up with his or her peers in reading or writing. Yet early clues may have been overlooked, and classroom teachers should be alert to them. Even if a disability is not severe enough to warrant a formal IEP, there may still be informal accommodations that can be made to help the pupil stay abreast.

To notice where pupils are weak or behind, of course, a teacher needs to be familiar with what is a normal behavior of level of skill at the pupil's grade level. A recent book called *Overcoming Dyslexia* (Shaywitz, 2003, 95–97) summarizes and discusses the basic normal accomplishments of readers at different grades. It also provides many tips that indicate what is likely to be slow or abnormal language skill development for a given age.

Apparently seeing letters reversed (e.g., saying "d" for "b") has long been regarded as a telltale sign of dyslexia, but many children who are not dyslexic also do this, and there are many other clearer indicators of problems. Most centrally, problems in learning to read and write are often presaged by problems in listening and speaking. A young dyslexic child is often less skilled than his or her peers at recognizing the sound structure of words and therefore less sensitive to rhymes. Familiarity with nursery rhymes at the preschool age is a strong indicator of later success in reading. By kindergarten, most children are able to judge whether two words rhyme, but dyslexic children may not.

As dyslexic children get older they may cover up a difficulty in retrieving a familiar word that they mean to say to name a relatively common object by substituting a vague word like "stuff." In this way, compared with language-normal children, a dyslexic child's ability to *think* may be far more in advance of his or her ability to *express* the thought. Dyslexic children may also be less able than others to produce a word that the teacher prompts them to say through clues or pictures. Dyslexic children who have learned to read to some extent can often *recognize* a correct word that they cannot be prompted to retrieve from memory.

While cultural differences do exist, most American children come to kindergarten able to recognize and name at least most of the individual letters of the alphabet in both lower- and uppercase. Delay in learning the names and sounds of letters is another indication of problems with learning to read and write. As children's reading skills mature, fluency is another sign of normally developing skills.

Another clue to the possibility of language learning problems in children is the language of their parents. Language deficits can be inherited, so children with language problems often have parents with similar problems who may still show difficulty reading and writing in their first language.

Where reading instruction does not emphasize and assess the learning of the sound codes of letters and phonemes, dyslexic pupils may use their ability to recognize the visual patterns of individual words to get as far as fourth or fifth grade without a fundamental problem being detected. By that point or earlier, however, the pupil is likely to be experiencing considerable stress, as the ability to read words based on the sound meaning of their letters becomes a more and more necessary skill.

Along with alertness to possible clues and the willingness to consult a learning specialist about pupils, teachers also need to keep in mind that many factors can make learning difficult for a child (see Table 2.7).

TABLE 2.7   FACTORS THAT CAN COMBINE TO MAKE LEARNING DIFFICULT

1. Intelligence
2. Sensory deficits
3. Activity level
4. Attention span
5. Brain injury or minimal brain dysfunction
6. Genetic factors
7. Maturational lag
8. Emotional factors
9. Environmental factors
10. Shortcoming in prior or current instruction
11. Dyslexia, math-learning disabilities, or other learning disabilities of unspecified origin

CHAPTER SUMMARY

olc

CHAPTER REVIEW

Visit Chapter 2 of the Online Learning Center at **www.mhhe.com/ airasian5e** to take chapter quizzes, link to related websites, read PowerWeb articles and news feed updates, and access study tools, including the case study referenced in the chapter.

♦ In the first few days of school teachers must learn about their pupils and organize them into a classroom society characterized by communication, order, and learning. This is part of the agenda of early assessment.

♦ Information for pupil descriptions comes from a variety of sources, including the school grapevine, comments by other teachers, school records, classroom discussion and observation, pupil comments, pretests, body language, and pupil dress, among others.

♦ Informal assessments are a natural part of social interactions. In classrooms they lead teachers to form and often communicate expectations to pupils. Moreover, teachers' first impressions of pupils tend to remain stable, although they are not always accurate. As a consequence, teachers must consider carefully when sizing up and labeling pupils at the start of the school year.

♦ Two main problems affect the validity of assessments: prejudgment and logical error. Prejudgments occur when a teacher's prior knowledge, first impression, or personal beliefs interfere with his or her ability to make a fair and objective assessment of a pupil. This is of special concern when teachers know little about the racial, cultural, handicapping, and language characteristics of their pupils. Teachers who are not familiar with pupils' varied cultures and languages often interpret what are really cultural differences as cultural deficits when they judge pupils who are different from themselves. Logical error occurs when teachers use the wrong kind of information to judge pupil characteristics, as, for example, when they judge interest by where a pupil sits in a class.

♦ Reliability is a special problem in early assessment because the process takes place so quickly and is based upon many fleeting observations; thus, it is difficult to assess pupils' typical or consistent performance. However, reliability is important in early assessments, and teachers should not label pupils based on only a few observations.

♦ Six suggestions for improving early assessments are (1) be aware of early assessments and their potential effects on students; (2) treat initial impressions as hypotheses to be confirmed or corrected by subsequent observation and information; (3) use direct, low inference indicators to gather information about pupil characteristics; (4) supplement informal observations with more formal, structured activities; (5) observe students long enough to be fairly certain of the pupil's typical behavior; and (6) determine whether different kinds of information confirm one another.

♦ Throughout all grades but especially in the elementary years, teachers can notice and act on clues about dyslexia and other learning disabilities.

QUESTIONS FOR DISCUSSION

1. How does the fact that a classroom is a social setting influence planning, teaching, grading, managing, and interacting with pupils?

2. What are the advantages and disadvantages of examining a pupil's school (cumulative) record folder before the start of class? Under what circumstances would you examine a pupil's record folder?

3. How much must teachers really know about a pupil's home and family background? What home and background information is absolutely essential for teachers to know? Why? What information does a teacher have no right to know about a pupil's home or background?

4. Why do teachers rely so heavily on informal observation when sizing up pupils? Should teachers use such observations to label pupils?

ACTIVITIES

1. Table 2.2 shows the resources available in two different classrooms. In small groups, compare the two classrooms. How do the resources in each classroom influence planning and instructing pupils? Give specific examples.

2. Interview a classroom teacher. Find out the answers to questions like the following: What information does the teacher have about pupils before the first day of class? What are the sources of that information? How much does the teacher rely upon the comments of other teachers when getting to know a new class? If the teacher could know only two specific characteristics of each pupil at the end of the first day of class, what would these be? Why? What information is most useful for managing pupils in the classroom? Add three questions of your own to this list. Why did you select those three questions?

REVIEW QUESTIONS

1. What factors make a classroom a social setting or society? How do these factors influence a teacher's assessment responsibilities?

2. What is early assessment? How is it done? How does it differ from other types of classroom assessments? What are three dangers that can reduce the validity and reliability of early assessment? What are three strategies a teacher can use to improve early assessments?

3. What are the main problems of validity and reliability in early assessment and assessments for planning and delivering instruction?

4. Why are early assessments important? What do they help teachers accomplish?

5. What are some differences between formal and informal observation?

6. What might be early signs of a reading disability?

REFERENCES

Delpit, L. (1995). *Other people's children: Cultural conflict in the classroom.* New York: The New Press.

Garcia, E. (1994). *Understanding and meeting the challenge of student cultural diversity.* Boston, MA: Houghton Mifflin.

Good, T. L., and Brophy, J. E. (1997). *Looking in classrooms.* New York: Longman.

Goodson, I. (1992). Studying teachers' lives: Problems and possibilities. In I. Goodson (Ed.), *Studying teachers' lives* (pp. 234-249). New York: Teachers College Press.

Klingner, J. A., Artiles, A. J. (2003). When should bilingual students be in special education? *Educational Leadership,* 61 (2), 66–71.

Ladson-Billings, G. (1994). *The dreamkeepers.* San Franciso: Jossey-Bass.

McCaslin, M., and Good, T. (1996). *Listening to students.* New York: Harper-Collins.

Shaywitz, S. (2003) *Overcoming Dyslexia: A New and Complete Science-Based Program for Reading Problems at Any Level.* New York: Alfred A. Knopf.

Solas, J. (1992). Investigating teacher and student thinking about the process of teaching and learning using autobiography and repertory grid. *Review of Educational Research 622,* 205–225.

Wiseman, D. L., Cooner, D. D., and Knight, S. L. (1999). *Becoming a teacher in a field-based setting.* Belmont, CA: Wadsworth.

LESSON PLANNING AND ASSESSMENT OBJECTIVES

KEY TOPICS

- *The Instructional Process*

- *Instructional Planning*

- *Three Levels of Teaching Objectives*

- *Three Domains of Objectives*

- *Stating and Constructing Objectives*

- *Lesson Plans*

- *Improving the Tie Between Planning and Assessment*

- *Planning, Disabilities, and Accommodations*

CHAPTER OBJECTIVES

After reading this chapter, you will be able to:

- ♦ Define curriculum, instruction, achievement, ability, educational objective, and other basic terms
- ♦ Describe the main considerations in planning lessons
- ♦ Write a lesson plan that communicates purpose, process, and assessment strategy
- ♦ State educational objectives, differentiate well-stated from poorly stated objectives, and distinguish between and write higher level and lower level educational objectives
- ♦ Cite common errors in planning instruction
- ♦ Compare features of assessment used for planning and delivering instruction
- ♦ Suggest ways to improve the validity and reliability of assessment during instruction
- ♦ Discuss accommodations for pupils with disabilities

THINKING ABOUT TEACHING

What is the role of planning in teaching? What kind of planning do teachers do?

Education is the process of helping to change students' knowledge and behavior in desired ways.

The purpose of schools is to educate pupils, but what does it mean to educate? Under what circumstances can a teacher claim credit for helping to educate a pupil? To **educate** means to help pupils change, to help them learn and do new things. When teachers have helped pupils to read, identify parts of speech in a sentence, use the scientific method, or write a cohesive paragraph, they have educated these students. Many experts describe education as a process intended to help pupils change in important and desirable ways. This view leads to a fundamental question all teachers have to ask themselves: what do I want my pupils to know or be able to do following instruction that they did not know or do at the start of instruction? Education is the process of fostering these important and desired pupil changes.

It is important to point out, however, that this view of education is not the only possible one. Thoughtful critics often suggest that education conceived solely as a process of preplanned pupil behavior change can lead to a preoccupation with narrow outcomes and afford the pupil virtually no role in the creation of his or her own educational program. Critics recognize the importance of a teacher's ability to artistically build upon a pupil's prior experience and to seek multiple, not necessarily predefined, outcomes from instruction. But despite the merits of alternative views, education for most teachers is conceived, practiced, and assessed with the primary function of helping to change learners in desired ways.

A **curriculum** describes the skills, performances, knowledge, and attitudes pupils are expected to learn in school. The curriculum contains statements of desired pupil learning and descriptions of the methods and materials that will be used to help pupils attain this. The methods and processes actually used to change pupils' behavior are called **instruction.** Lectures, discussions, worksheets, cooperative projects, and homework are but a few of the instructional techniques used to help pupils learn.

Pupils undergo many changes during their school years, and many sources beside the school contribute to these changes: maturation, peer groups, family, reading, and TV, among others. The term **achievement** is used to describe school-based learning, while terms like **ability** and **aptitude** are used to describe broader learning that stems from nonschool sources. Since the focus of schooling is to help pupils attain particular behaviors, understandings, and processes, almost all of the formal tests that pupils take in school are intended to assess their achievement. The Friday spelling test, the unit test on chemical equations, the math test on the Pythagorean theorem, the delivery of an oral speech, the autobiography, and midterm and final examinations all should focus on assessing pupil achievement—that is, what they have learned of the things that were taught in school.

Achievement refers to school-based learning, while ability and aptitude refer to broader learning acquired mostly through nonschool sources such as parents and peer groups.

The central concept in this chapter is that planning and assessment should be driven by a clear knowledge of desired objectives about what students will learn and master. Some have called this a backward approach to planning, inasmuch as it starts by defining the intended results (Wiggins & McTighe, 1998). Indeed it is; and in this case "backwardness" is a virtue.

THE INSTRUCTIONAL PROCESS

The instructional process comprises three basic steps. The first is *planning instruction,* which includes identifying desired pupil learning outcomes, selecting materials to foster these outcomes, and organizing learning experiences into a coherent, reinforcing sequence. The second step involves *delivering the planned instruction* to pupils, that is, teaching them. The third step involves determining whether or not pupils have learned or achieved the desired outcomes, or *assessing pupil outcomes.* Notice that to carry out the instructional process the three steps should be aligned with one another. That is, the planned instruction should be logically related to the actual instruction and the assessments should relate to the plans and instruction.

The instructional process involves three interdependent steps: planning, delivering, and assessing.

Figure 3.1 shows these three steps and the relationships between them. Notice that the diagram is presented as a triangle rather than as a straight

FIGURE 3.1
Steps in the
Instructional Process.

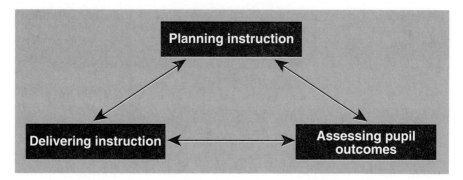

line. This indicates that the three steps are interrelated in a more complicated way than a simple one-two-three sequence. For example, in planning
instruction (step 1), the teacher considers the characteristics of pupils and
the resources and materials available to help attain desired changes (step 2).
Similarly, the information gained at the time of pupil assessment (step 3) is
useful in assessing the appropriateness of the learning experiences provided
pupils (step 2) and the suitability of intended pupil outcomes (step 1). Thus,
the three steps are interdependent pieces in the instructional process that
can be aligned in different orders.

All three steps in the
instructional process
involve assessment and
teacher decision
making.

All three steps in the instructional process involve teacher decision
making and assessment. Obviously step 3, assessing pupil outcomes,
involves the collection and synthesis of formal information about how
well pupils are learning or have learned. But the other two steps in the
instructional process are also dependent upon a teacher's assessment
activities. For example, a teacher's planning decisions incorporate information about pupil readiness, appropriate methods, available instructional resources, materials, pupil culture, language, and other important
characteristics obtained from early assessments. Similarly, during
instruction the teacher is constantly "reading" the class to obtain information to help make decisions about lesson pace, reinforcement, interest,
and comprehension. Thus, the entire instructional process, not just the
formal assessment step, depends upon decisions that rely on assessment
evidence of various kinds.

Teachers define their
own success and
rewards in terms of their
students' learning.

The processes of planning and providing instruction are important activities for classroom teachers. Not only do they occupy a substantial amount
of their time, but teachers define their teaching rewards in terms of their
pupils' instructional successes. Teachers like to work with pupils, make a
difference in their lives, and experience the joy of a pupil "getting it."
Teachers feel rewarded when they know that their instruction has reached
their pupils. Since the classroom is where pride in teaching is forged, it is
not surprising to find that teachers guard their classroom instructional time
jealously. They want few interruptions to distract them from their pupils,
teaching responsibilities, and rewards.

INSTRUCTIONAL PLANNING

The true rewards of teaching are identified in terms of the impact that the teachers' instruction and mentoring has upon pupils. Pride in teaching does not come from collecting lunch money, planning field trips, meeting the morning bus, and the thousand other semiadministrative tasks teachers perform. It comes from teachers' knowledge that they have taught pupils to do, think, or perform some things they otherwise would have been unable to do, think, or perform.

Teachers plan in order to modify the curriculum to fit the unique characteristics of their pupils and resources. To plan, teachers reflect on and integrate information about their pupils, the subject matter to be taught, the curriculum they are following, their own teaching experience, the resources available for instruction, the classroom environment, and other factors. Their reflection and integration of these factors leads to an instructional lesson plan. The plan helps teachers allocate instructional time, select appropriate activities, link individual lessons to the overall unit or curriculum, sequence activities to be presented to pupils, set the pace of instruction, select the homework to be assigned, and identify techniques to assess pupil learning.

Planning helps teachers in five basic ways:

1. By helping them feel comfortable about instruction and giving them a sense of understanding and ownership over the teaching they plan.
2. By establishing a sense of purpose and subject matter focus.
3. By affording the chance to review and become familiar with the subject matter before actually beginning to teach it.
4. By ensuring that there are ways in place to get instruction started, activities to pursue, and a framework to follow during the actual delivery of instruction.
5. By linking daily lessons to broader integrative goals, units, or curriculum topics.

Classrooms are complex environments that are informal rather than formal, ad hoc rather than linear, ambiguous rather than certain, process-oriented rather than product-oriented, and people-dominated rather than concept-dominated. The realities and strains of the classroom call for order and direction, especially when teachers are carrying out formal instruction. In such a world, some form of planning and organization is needed.

Planning instruction is a context-dependent activity that includes consideration of pupils, teacher, and instructional materials. A lesson that fails to take into account the needs and prior knowledge of the pupils or that poorly matches lesson aims to lesson instruction is doomed to failure. Similarly, a lesson that does not take into account the context in which it will be taught can also lead to difficulty.

Teachers have a great deal of control over many classroom features associated with lesson planning. For example, most teachers have control over the physical arrangement of the classroom, the rules and routines pupils must follow, the interactions with pupils, the kind of instruction planned and the nature of its delivery, and the methods used to assess and grade pupils. However, there are important features that teachers do not control. For example, most teachers have little control over the number and characteristics of the pupils in their classes, the size of their classroom, the quality of their instructional resources, and the state and district curriculum guidelines. In planning, teachers must arrange the factors they do control to compensate for the factors they do not.

Table 3.1 allows us an exercise similar to the one we did in Chapter 2, comparing two teachers' classroom situations. Once again, imagine that these classrooms are at the same grade level in the same school. Suppose the teachers are each planning a lesson on the same topic. Again, as in Table 2.2, teachers normally would have little control over these characteristics of their classrooms. How might these different classroom characteristics influence the ways these two teachers plan instruction? What features are especially influential in determining teaching plans? Which characteristics would be advantageous to a teacher and which ones might be disadvantageous? Do you think the teachers would construct identical instructional plans? In what ways might they differ? The following discussion examines in more detail how pupil and teacher characteristics as well as instructional resources can affect instructional planning.

TABLE 3.1   COMPARISON OF TWO CLASSROOM CONTEXTS

Classroom A	Classroom B
22 pupils	34 pupils
Range of pupil abilities	Mainly low-ability pupils
Strong pupil self-control	Poor pupil self-control
Good prerequisite skills	Range of prerequisite skills
Intense parental interest	Moderate parental interest
10-year-old textbooks	New textbooks
Mandated district curriculum	Teacher-selected instructional topics
Poor school library	Excellent school library
Small classroom size	Large classroom size
Individual pupil desks	Pupils sit at four-person tables
Little colleague support	Strong colleague support

Pupil Characteristics

Initial and extremely important considerations when planning instruction are the present status and needs of the pupils. What are they developmentally ready to learn? What topics have they mastered thus far in the subject area? How complex are the instructional materials they can handle? How well do they work in groups? What disabilities do they have and how are they accommodated? What is the range of pupils' culture and language in a given classroom? What are their learning styles? The answers to these questions provide needed and valuable information about what and how to teach. Note that teachers obtain much of the information to answer these questions from their early assessments.

Planning in elementary school classrooms generally is more complex than planning in high school classrooms because the range of pupil characteristics that must be considered is broader in lower grades. For example, in addition to content, the elementary teacher must take into account pupil readiness, behavior, and learning styles, as well as how a lesson will fit with other lessons to be given that day. The ebb and flow of elementary school activities from small-group instruction to seatwork to large-group instruction and back again make consideration of pupil characteristics such as independence, work habits, and attention span very important. When the teacher is working with one reading or math group, seatwork for pupils not in that group must accommodate their learning abilities and allow them to work independently and quietly.

Instructional planning tends to be more complex in elementary schools because students usually are more differentiated and because teachers must plan in many subject areas.

In addition, the elementary teacher often works with many different pupil groupings that use different instructional materials geared to the group level. Plans for each group differ according to the ability, prior achievement, needs, and socialization levels in the group. Further, most elementary school teachers are responsible for planning instruction in all subjects, not just one or two as is typical at the high school level. Planning is a complex and time-consuming task for these teachers.

At the start of the school year, most teachers begin instruction by reviewing subject matter concepts and skills normally mastered in the prior grade or course. The information gained in such a review provides the most direct evidence about pupils' readiness and needs. It is especially important to assess readiness and needs in those subjects that are sequentially organized, such as mathematics, foreign languages, and reading. The structure of these subjects is such that concepts and ideas build upon one another. For example, in order to do long division problems correctly, a fourth or fifth grader must be able to use the processes of addition, subtraction, regrouping, and multiplication. Thus, it would make little sense for a fifth grade teacher whose pupils did not understand regrouping and multiplication to teach only long division, even though it might be the normal focus of fifth grade mathematics instruction.

In other subjects, such as social studies and English, the content is not as sequential and interdependent as in math, reading, and foreign languages. The "expanding horizons" focus of elementary school social studies texts, for example, moves from homes and neighborhoods to communities to regions of America to U.S. history to world history. For the most part, each year's text and content is distinct from the prior or succeeding year's. In this case, the teacher has more discretion in planning what to stress.

It is obvious that pupil characteristics such as disability, readiness, independence, and self-control should be taken into account in planning instructional activities. To ignore these factors would be irrational. However, it is very important to recognize that much of the needed information comes to teachers from their initial early assessments. Consequently, it is crucial that teachers strive to make their initial assessments as valid and reliable as possible.

Teacher Characteristics

When planning instruction, teachers should take their own characteristics and knowledge into account along with their pupils' characteristics and the time and resources available.

Most beginning teachers do not take their own characteristics into account when planning instruction. However, subject matter knowledge, personality, and physical limitations are important factors in planning and delivering instruction. It is impossible for teachers to know everything about all the topics they teach. Nor can they be expected to keep abreast of all advances in subject matter knowledge or pedagogy. Consequently, the topics teachers choose to cover, the accuracy and up-to-dateness of their topical coverage, and their teaching methods all are influenced by their own knowledge limitations. Moreover, teachers' personalities often lead them to favor certain instructional techniques over others. While individual preferences are to be expected among teachers, it is important to understand that when carried to the extreme, they can result in an overly narrow repertoire of teaching methods. This has the potential to limit learning opportunities for those pupils who could learn better from other instructional techniques. Finally, since teaching is a rigorous, fatiguing activity, teachers should consider their own physical limitations when planning instruction. This caution is especially appropriate for beginning teachers, whose enthusiasm and lack of experience often lead them to overestimate what they can physically accomplish in the classroom. A common complaint heard from college students during their first full-time classroom practicum is how mentally and physically draining a day in the classroom can be.

Instructional Resources

The instructional resources available to a teacher influence not only the nature of instruction but also the learning outcomes that are possible. The term *resources* is used here in its broadest sense to include available supplies, equipment, space, aids or volunteers, texts, and time. Each of these resources influences the nature of instruction and therefore the pupil achievements that can be pursued.

A second grade teacher may wish to have his pupils construct felt pictures of book covers, but is unable to because the school cannot afford to provide the felt. A biology teacher may wish his or her class to learn about the internal organs of a frog by having each pupil perform a frog dissection. However, if the school has no biology laboratory and no dissecting equipment, the teacher must forgo this objective. In these and other ways, material resources matter.

Classroom aids or volunteers who read to pupils, work with small groups, or serve as "computer moms" during a unit on the computer can free the classroom teacher to plan and pursue enrichment activities that might not have been possible otherwise. Resources of all kinds are important to consider when planning instruction.

Another resource that greatly influences what is planned, taught, and learned in classrooms is the textbook. More than any other single resource, the textbook determines instructional plans in many classrooms. A large part of students' learning time and a large part of the teacher's instructional time are focused on textbook use.

The teacher's edition of most textbooks contains many resources to help teachers plan, deliver, and assess instruction. However, teachers should not abdicate their planning, teaching, and assessment decision-making responsibilities to the textbook. To do so reduces the classroom teacher from a professional decision maker to a mindless technician carrying out the instructional program and plans of others. It is incumbent upon all teachers to assess the status and needs of *their* pupils, the curriculum requirements of *their* state or community, and the resources available in *their* classrooms when planning instruction for their pupils. In the end, decisions about what to emphasize rest with the individual classroom teacher, who knows her pupils better than anyone else and who is in the best position to plan and carry out instruction that is suited to their needs. We will discuss textbooks in greater detail in Chapter 4.

To slavishly follow the lessons in a textbook is to abdicate instructional decision making.

A final important, though often overlooked, resource that greatly influences teacher planning is time. Because there is never enough time to teach pupils all the important skills and concepts in a subject area, teachers must carefully match their instructional time to their intended instructional outcomes. Each teacher's decisions about what content to stress or omit is based in part on the instructional time available. When a teacher skips a concept, unit, or chapter in a textbook, the teacher is saying, "All other things being equal, I prefer to spend my limited instructional time focusing on other topics and skills that are more important."

While teachers make decisions about the allocation or instructional time daily, it is often in the last few weeks of the school year that these decisions become most apparent. The end of the school year always seems to arrive before all the planned topics can be taught. At this point, explicit decisions

TABLE 3.2	AREAS TO CONSIDER WHEN PLANNING INSTRUCTION	
Pupil Characteristics	**Teacher Characteristics**	**Instructional Resources**
Prior knowledge	Content knowledge	State curriculum standards
Prerequisite skills and knowledge	Instructional method preferences	Time
Work habits, socialization	Assessment preferences	Textbook materials
Special learning needs	Physical limitations	Technology
Learning styles		Collegial and administrative support
Cultural/language differences		Other resources (space, aids, equipment)
Disabilities		

about how to allocate scarce time are made: "We must cover subtraction of fractions before the end of the year, but we can omit rate, time, and distance word problems." "If I don't finish parts of speech this year, next year's teacher will be upset. I'll take the time from the poetry unit to work on parts of speech." Time is a limited resource that has important consequences for planning instruction. Table 3.2 summarizes pupil, teacher, and instructional resources and considerations.

THREE LEVELS OF TEACHING OBJECTIVES

In our everyday activities, objectives help us focus on what's important; they remind us of what we want to accomplish. Objectives in teaching describe the kinds of content and processes teachers hope their pupils will learn from instruction.

Other names for objectives are learning targets, educational objectives, instructional objectives, behavioral objectives, pupil outcomes, and curriculum objectives, among others. Whatever they are called, objectives are important in developing lesson plans. Teachers cannot help pupils meet their objectives if they do not know what their objectives are. Similarly, if teachers don't identify their objectives, instruction and assessment will be purposeless.

Objectives are particularly crucial in teaching because teaching is an intentional and normative act. Teaching is intentional because teachers teach for a purpose; they want pupils to learn something as a result of teaching. Teaching is also normative because what teachers teach is viewed by them as being worthwhile for their pupils to learn. In fact, it would be unethical for teachers to teach things that they did not believe were beneficial to pupils.

Because teaching is both intentional and normative, it always is based on objectives. Normative teaching is concerned with selecting objectives that are worthwhile for pupils to learn. Intentional teaching is concerned with issues of how teachers will teach their objectives—what learning environments they will create and what methods they will use to help pupils learn the intended objectives. Although teachers' objectives may sometimes be implicit and fuzzy, it is best that objectives be explicit, clear, and measurable.

Objectives can range from very general to very specific. Compare the following two objectives: "The pupil can add three one-digit numbers," and "The pupil will become mathematically literate." Clearly the former is more specific than the latter. Notice how different instructional time, learning activities, and range of assessments would be needed for the two objectives. Because objectives vary widely in specificity, a more limited framework for discussing objectives is commonly used. Three levels of abstraction represent degrees of objective specificity: global, educational, and instructional (Krathwohl and Payne, 1971). Note that regardless of the type or specificity of an objective, its focus should always be on *pupil* learning and performance.

There are three general levels of objectives: global, educational, and instructional, ranging from most broad to least broad.

Global objectives, often called "goals," are broad, complex pupil learning outcomes that require substantial time and instruction to accomplish. They are very general, encompassing a large number of more specific objectives. Examples include:

◆ The pupil will become a lifelong learner.
◆ The pupil will become mathematically literate.
◆ Pupils will learn to use their minds well, so that they may be prepared for responsible citizenship, further learning, and productive employment in our nation's economy.

Because they are broadly inclusive, global objectives are rarely used in classroom assessment unless they are broken down into more narrow objectives. Global objectives mainly provide a rallying cry that reflects what is important in education policy. The breadth encompassed in global objectives makes them difficult for teachers to use in planning classroom instruction. Narrower objectives are needed to meet classroom needs.

Educational objectives represent a middle level of abstraction. Here are several examples:

♦ The pupil can interpret different types of social data.
♦ The pupil can correctly solve addition problems containing two digits.
♦ The pupil distinguishes between facts and hypotheses.
♦ The pupil can read Spanish poetry aloud.

A number of guidelines can improve planning instruction including: knowing pupil's needs and strengths; being sure that the textbook includes all the important topics to be taught, including both lower-level and higher-level objectives; planning activities that fit pupil's needs and readiness; aligning objectives, instruction, and assessment; and being aware of one's own limits.

Educational objectives are more specific than global objectives. They are sufficiently narrow to help teachers plan and focus teaching, and sufficiently broad to indicate the richness of the objective and to suggest a range of possible student outcomes associated with the objective.

Instructional objectives are the least abstract and most specific type of objective. Examples of instructional objectives include:

♦ The pupil can correctly punctuate sentences.
♦ Given five problems requiring the pupil to find the lowest common denominator of a fraction, the pupil can solve at least four of five.
♦ The pupil can list the names of the first five U.S. presidents.

Instructional objectives focus teaching on relatively narrow topics of learning in a content area. These concrete objectives are used in planning daily lessons.

Increasingly, pupils with disabilities are placed in general education classrooms. Because teachers must accommodate many pupils with disabilities in the classroom, they should be aware of the legal issues related to these pupils and some of the common accommodations used in classrooms.

Table 3.3 illustrates the difference in degree of breadth among the three types of objectives and compares their purposes, scopes, and time frames. The distinctions among these three levels of objectives are far more than semantic. The level at which an objective is stated influences its use in planning, instructing, and assessing. For example, the perspectives of teachers planning instruction and assessment for a global objective such as "The pupil will become mathematically literate" are quite different from those of teachers planning instruction and assessment for an instructional objective such as "The pupil will write common fractions in their lowest terms." Thus, the level at which an objective is stated—global, educational, or instructional—has an impact on the manner in which processes such as planning, instructing, and assessing will be structured and carried out.

THREE DOMAINS OF OBJECTIVES

Classroom assessments cover cognitive, affective, and psychomotor behaviors.

By this point it should be clear that objectives are logically and closely tied to instruction and assessment. In addition to differing in terms of level, classroom objectives (and their related instruction and assessments) differ in terms of three general types of human behavior: the cognitive, affective, and psychomotor domains.

TABLE 3.3   COMPARING THE THREE LEVELS OF TEACHING OBJECTIVES

Level of Objective	Global	Educational	Instructional
Scope	Broad	Intermediate	Narrow
Time to accomplish	One or more years	Weeks or months	Hours or days
Function	Provide vision	Develop curriculum, plan instruction, define suitable assessments	Plan teaching activities, learning experiences, and assessment exercises
Examples of breadth	The pupil will acquire competency of worldwide geography	The pupil will gain knowledge of devices and symbols in maps and charts	Given a map or chart, the pupil will correctly define 6 of the 8 representational devices and symbols on it
	The pupil will be aware of the roles of civics and government in the United States	The pupil will interpret various types of social data	The pupil can interpret bar graphs describing population density
	The pupil will know how to repair a variety of home problems	The pupil will use appropriate procedures to find solutions to electrical problems in the home	Given a home repair problem dealing with a malfunctioning lamp, the pupil will repair it

---

The Cognitive Domain

The most commonly taught and assessed educational objectives are those in the cognitive domain. The **cognitive domain** includes intellectual activities such as memorizing, interpreting, applying, problem solving, reasoning, analyzing, and thinking critically. Virtually all the tests that pupils take in school are intended to measure one or more of these cognitive activities. Teachers' instruction is usually focused on helping pupils attain cognitive mastery of some content or subject area. A weekly spelling test, a unit test in history, a worksheet on proper use of *lie* and *lay,* an essay on supply and demand, and an oral recitation of a poem all require cognitive behaviors. The Scholastic Assessment Test (SAT), the ACT, the written part of a state driver's test, an ability test, and standardized achievement tests such as the Iowa Test of Basic Skills and the Stanford, Metropolitan, SRA, and California Achievement tests also are intended to assess pupils' cognitive behaviors.

In Chapter 1, Ms. Lopez was relying primarily upon cognitive information about her pupils when she made the following decisions: assigned grades, moved Tamika from the middle to the high reading group, planned

Cognitive assessments involve intellectual activities such as memorizing, interpreting, applying, problem solving, reasoning, analyzing, and thinking critically.

instruction, identified pupils for remedial work in basic skills, graded pupils' American government projects, and consulted last year's standardized test scores to find out whether she needed to review the rules of capitalization for the class. In each case, Ms. Lopez was assessing her pupils' thinking, reasoning, memory, or general intellectual behaviors.

Bloom's Taxonomy

The many cognitive processes have been organized into six general categories. This organization is presented in the *Taxonomy of Educational Objectives: Book 1, Cognitive Domain* (Bloom et al., 1956). Commonly referred to as Bloom's Taxonomy, or the Cognitive Taxonomy, it is widely used by teachers to describe and state cognitive objectives (see Appendix B).

A taxonomy is a system of classification. Bloom's cognitive taxonomy is organized into six levels, with each successive level representing a more complex type of cognitive process. Starting with the simplest and moving to the most complex, the six cognitive taxonomic processes are knowledge, comprehension, application, analysis, synthesis, and evaluation (see Table 3.4). It is important to note that in Bloom's Taxonomy "knowledge" refers only to memorizing and remembering information. It does *not* include other kinds of cognitive processes. The table provides some action verbs indicative of each cognitive process of Bloom's Taxonomy, and the general description of each process. Below are sample objectives derived from Bloom's Taxonomy with the taxonomic category shown in parentheses.

The pupils can identify the correct punctuation marks in a writing assignment. (knowledge; remember)

The pupils can integrate the information from the science experiment into a lab report. (synthesis; organize into a whole)

The pupils can punctuate correctly in a writing task. (application; solve a problem)

The pupils can translate French sentences into English. (comprehension; state in your own words)

The pupils can distinguish facts from opinions in eight newspaper editorials. (analysis; categorize)

The pupils can categorize paintings by their historical periods. (analysis; identify relationships)

The pupils can judge the quality of varied persuasive essays. (evaluation; judge the quality)

The pupils can add previously unseen proper fractions. (application; solve a new problem)

TABLE 3.4 TYPES OF COGNITIVE PROCESS IDENTIFIED IN BLOOM'S TAXONOMY

Taxonomy Level	Related Verbs	General Description
1. Knowledge	Remember, recall, identify, recognize	Memorizing facts
2. Comprehension	Translate, rephrase, restate, interpret, describe, explain	Explaining in one's own words
3. Application	Apply, execute, solve, implement	Solving new problems
4. Analysis	Break down, categorize, distinguish, compare	Breaking into parts and identifying relationships
5. Synthesis	Integrate, organize, relate, combine, construct, design	Combining elements into a whole
6. Evaluation	Judge, assess, value, appraise	Judging quality or worth

In recent years, besides Bloom's taxonomy, other systems of cognitive-related objectives have been developed. A prominent one is a revision of Bloom's taxonomy by Anderson and others (Anderson, 2001). Another is *Designing a New Taxonomy of Educational Objectives,* by Marzano and others (Marzano, 1993). Although these taxonomies have extended the reach of objectives, Bloom's taxonomy remains the most used in assessment.

Although cognitive taxonomies can differ in the particular levels or categories they include, their most important function is to remind teachers of the distinction between higher and lower level thinking behaviors. In general, any cognitive behavior that involves more than rote memorization or recall is considered to be a **higher level cognitive behavior.** Thus, the knowledge level of Bloom's Taxonomy represents **lower level cognitive behavior,** since the focus is upon memorization and recall. All succeeding levels in these taxonomies represent higher level behaviors that call for pupils to carry out thinking and reasoning processes more complex than memorization. There is a growing emphasis in classroom instruction and assessment to focus upon teaching pupils higher order thinking skills (HOTS) that go beyond rote memorization.

Lower level cognitive behaviors involve rote memorization and recall; cognitive behaviors that involve more than rote memorization or recall are termed higher level cognitive behaviors.

The Affective Domain

A second behavior domain is the affective domain. The **affective domain** involves feelings, attitudes, interests, preferences, values, and emotions. Emotional stability, motivation, trustworthiness, self-control, and personality

Affective assessments involve feelings, attitudes, interests, preferences, values, and emotions.

Teachers rarely make formal affective assessments but are constantly making them informally.

are all examples of affective characteristics. Although affective behaviors are rarely assessed formally in schools and classrooms, teachers constantly assess affective behaviors informally, especially when sizing up pupils. Teachers need to know who can be trusted to work unsupervised and who cannot, who can maintain self-control when the teacher has to leave the classroom and who cannot, who needs to be encouraged to speak in class and who does not, who is interested in science but not in social studies, and who needs to be prodded to start class work and who does not. Most classroom teachers can describe their pupils' affective characteristics based on their informal observations and interactions with the pupils.

Ms. Lopez was relying mainly upon her assessment of pupils' affective behaviors when she selected Rosa, not Sarah, to deliver a note to the school principal; when she changed the class seating plan to separate Jamar and Ramon, who were unable to control themselves when seated together; when she switched instruction from discussion to seatwork to avoid unruliness; and when she selected pupils to work together on a cooperative assignment.

In contrast to the cognitive domain, there is no single, widely accepted taxonomy of affective behaviors, although the taxonomy prepared by Krathwohl and associates (Krathwohl, Bloom, & Masia, 1964) is the most commonly referred to and used. In general, affective taxonomies are all based upon the degree of a person's involvement in an activity or idea. The lower levels of affective taxonomies contain low-involvement behaviors such as paying attention, while the higher levels contain high-involvement behavior characterized by strong interest, commitment, and valuing.

The Psychomotor Domain

Psychomotor assessments involve physical and manipulative behaviors.

Psychomotor assessments are particularly important with very young or some special-needs students.

A third behavior domain is the psychomotor domain. The **psychomotor domain** includes physical and manipulative activities. Shooting a basketball, setting up laboratory equipment, building a bookcase, typing, holding a pencil, buttoning a jacket, brushing teeth, and playing a musical instrument are examples of activities that involve psychomotor behaviors. Although psychomotor behaviors are present and important at all levels of schooling, they are especially stressed in the preschool and elementary grades, where tasks like holding a pencil, opening a locker, and buttoning or zippering clothing are important to master. (How would you like to button the jackets of 24 pupils?) Similarly, with certain special-needs pupils, a major part of education involves so-called "self-help" skills such as getting dressed, attending to personal hygiene, and preparing food, all of which are psychomotor accomplishments.

There are a number of psychomotor behavior domain taxonomies (Hannah & Michaels, 1977; Harrow, 1972). Like the affective domain, however, no single taxonomy has become widely accepted and used by the majority of teachers and schools. The organization of psychomotor taxonomies typically ranges from a pupil showing a readiness to perform a psychomotor task, to the pupil using trial and error to learn a task, to the pupil actually carrying out the task on his or her own.

Ms. Lopez was concerned with her pupils' psychomotor behavior when she moved Claudia to the front of the room so that she could see the chalkboard better, sent Antonio to the school nurse because he felt ill, and referred Aaron to the special-education department because he continued to exhibit poor gross motor skills. In each case, Ms. Lopez's decision was based upon assessment evidence that pertained to some aspect of a pupil's physical or motor behavior.

As noted previously, early assessments encompass the cognitive, affective, and psychomotor domains because teachers are interested in knowing about their pupils' intellectual, attitudinal, and physical characteristics. Notice, however, that different assessment approaches characterize the different behavior domains. For example, the cognitive domain is most likely to be assessed using paper-and-pencil tests or various kinds of oral questioning. Behaviors in the affective domain are most likely to be assessed by observation or questionnaires: for example, which subject do you prefer, English or chemistry? Do you believe that teachers should be accountable for their pupils' learning? Psychomotor behaviors are generally assessed by observing pupils carrying out the desired physical activity.

STATING AND CONSTRUCTING OBJECTIVES

There many ways to state objectives, but not all of them convey clearly what pupils are to learn from instruction. Ensuring clarity requires being aware of what makes an objective statement complete.

Essential Elements of the Statement

Consider the following three objectives:

1. Pupils will learn to use their minds well, so that they may be prepared for responsible citizenship, further learning, and productive employment in our nation's economy.
2. The pupil can read Spanish-language poetry.
3. The pupil can correctly punctuate sentences.

Although they represent a global, educational, and instructional objective, respectively, these objectives have common characteristics. First, all are stated in terms or what the pupil is to learn from instruction. Objectives describe *pupil learning,* not teacher learning or the activities teacher or pupils engage in during instruction. Instructional activities are not objectives, although activities are an important aspect of lesson planning and must be described. Second, each objective contains two parts: some content for pupils to learn and a process to show their learning. The content in the three objectives above are, respectively, "citizenship," "Spanish-language poetry," and "sentences." The cognitive processes are "develop," "read," and "punctuate." Another way to think about an objective's content and process is in terms of nouns and verbs. The content is the noun and the process is the verb. Thus, at a minimum, an objective is stated in terms of the content (noun) and process (verb) the pupil is expected to learn. Third, notice that the nouns and verbs differ from one objective to another because different subject matters, grade levels, and teaching styles require different objectives.

Objectives such as those shown above are widely used to guide teachers' planning, instruction, and assessment. For example, the objective "The pupils can categorize paintings by their historical periods" is focused on analysis (categorize) by identifying relationships. Or, the objective "The pupil can explain in his or her own words the meaning of a second-year-level French paragraph" is focused on comprehension (explain). Note that the verbs in the objectives we have examined (e.g., summarize, add, remember, categorize, explain) are *not* labeled using Bloom's generic taxonomy names (e.g., knowledge, comprehension, analysis). Instead, they are described using narrower, more specific verbs. These more specific and observable cognitive verbs are preferred over the generic taxonomy names because they more clearly indicate the particular process (verb) the pupils will be expected to carry out. Table 3.5 provides a number of these more *precise verbs* to use in stating clear objectives for each category of Bloom's Taxonomy.

Forming Complete Statements

Examine the sample objectives in Table 3.6 and consider their usefulness in helping a teacher plan and guide instruction and assessment. Remember, the intent of an objective is to clearly identify what pupils are to learn in order to (1) communicate to others the purpose of instruction, (2) to help teachers select appropriate instructional methods and materials, and (3) to help plan assessments that will indicate whether or not pupils have learned what they were taught.

In Table 3.6, objectives 1, 2, and 3 all have the same deficiency. Each describes a body of content that will be covered in instruction, but each omits information about what the pupils will be expected to do with that content. Will they be expected to identify causes of the war, match generals to battles, cite strengths and weaknesses of the two sides, or explain in their own words why Gettysburg was the turning point of the war? What should pupils know or understand about American government and the laws of motion? Without including information about what pupils are to know or do about the Civil War, American government, or laws of motion, it is hard to select appropriate instructional materials, activities, and assess-

TABLE 3.5   EXAMPLES OF TERMS USED TO WRITE EDUCATIONAL OBJECTIVES FOR EACH CATEGORY OF BLOOM'S TAXONOMY

Knowledge	Comprehension	Application	Analysis	Synthesis	Evaluation
count	classify	compute	break down	arrange	appraise
define	compare	construct	diagram	combine	conclude
identify	contrast	demonstrate	differentiate	compile	criticize
label	convert	illustrate	discriminate	create	critique
list	discuss	solve	outline	design	grade
match	distinguish		separate	formulate	judge
name	estimate		subdivide	generalize	recommend
quote	explain			generate	support
recite	generalize			group	
repeat	give examples			integrate	
reproduce	infer			organize	
select	interpret			relate	
state	paraphrase			summarize	
	rewrite				
	summarize				
	translate				

TABLE 3.6   SAMPLE STATEMENTS OF POOR EDUCATIONAL OBJECTIVES

1. The Civil War
2. American government
3. The laws of motion
4. Analyze
5. Understand
6. Appreciate
7. Worthy use of leisure time
8. Pursue lifelong learning
9. Become a good citizen

ment techniques. For example, it will make a difference in instruction and assessment if pupils have to match generals to battles (teach recall and assess with a matching item) or explain in their own words why Gettysburg was the turning point of the war (teach interpretation and assess with an open-ended question). Clarity and consistency between what is taught and what is assessed is necessary for valid assessment results.

olc
CHAPTER CASE STUDY

Visit the text OLC to read the case of Therese Carmen, a first grade teacher in her second year of teaching. Therese is presented with a new districtwide science curriculum that she finds unteachable.

www.mhhe.com/ airasian5e

Well-written educational objectives should clearly specify what students are to learn and how they are to demonstrate that learning.

Objectives 4, 5, and 6—analyze, understand, and appreciate—provide no reference to content matter. These statements prompt the question: analyze, understand, and appreciate what? Just as a content description by itself lacks clarity because it does not include a desired pupil performance, so too does a behavior by itself lack clarity if there is no reference to a targeted body of content.

There is an additional problem in objectives 4, 5, and 6. Words like *analyze, understand,* and *appreciate* are themselves nonspecific. They can be interpreted in many different ways and hence do not clearly convey what pupils will learn. For example, one teacher might interpret the objective "understanding the basic features of a society" to mean the pupils will be able to explain the features in their own words. Another teacher might interpret the same objective to mean the pupils will give a real-life example of the social features studied. A third teacher might want pupils to distinguish between correct and incorrect applications of features. Although each teacher taught "understanding the basic features of society," each would teach and assess completely different outcomes. Such misunderstandings can be avoided if teachers describe their educational objectives in terms of the actual behaviors they expect their pupils to perform after instruction. For example, pupils can explain features in their own words, give real-life examples of the features, or distinguish correct from incorrect applications of the features. This level of specificity distinguishes clearly the different interpretations of *understand.*

In stating educational objectives, it is better to clearly describe the behavior the pupil will perform than to use more general, ambiguous terms that are open to many different interpretations. Thus, it is better to say *explains* the importance of conserving natural resources than to say *realizes* the importance of conserving natural resources; better to say *translates* Spanish sentences into English than to say *understands* Spanish sentences; better to say can *differentiate* subjects and predicates than to say *knows* about subjects and predicates; better to say *states* three differences between good and bad art than to say *appreciates* art. In each example, the first statement describes a pupil behavior that can be observed, instructed, and assessed, while the second uses less clear, unobservable, and ambiguous terms. Clear descriptions foster alignment among objectives, instruction, and assessment, thus producing valid assessment results.

Objectives 7, 8, and 9 are too general and complicated to be achieved by pupils in a single subject area or grade level. They are, as noted previously, goals. Not only do these outcomes take years to develop, but their generality provides the classroom teacher with little guidance regarding the activities and materials that could be used to attain them. Broad goals such as these must be narrowed by the classroom teacher before they can be used to instruct and assess pupils.

Some Good Examples of Objectives

In summary thus far, the basic requirements for well-stated educational objectives are that they (1) describe a pupil behavior that should result from instruction; (2) state the behavior in terms that can be observed and assessed; and (3) indicate the content on which the behavior will be performed. A simple model for preparing educational objectives is "the pupils can" (observable behavior) (content). Here are examples of appropriately stated educational objectives.

◆ The pupils can list three causes of the Civil War.

◆ The pupils can solve word problems requiring the sum of two numbers.

◆ The pupils can write a correctly formatted and punctuated business letter.

◆ The pupils can translate a French paragraph into English.

◆ The pupils can count to 20 aloud.

◆ The pupils can list three differences between the climates of Canada and Mexico.

◆ The pupils can write balanced chemical equations.

◆ The pupils can state the main idea of short stories.

◆ The pupils can explain the water cycle in their own words.

Notice how these objectives help focus the intended student learning and thus help the teacher identify suitable instructional activities, materials, and assessments.

Other information can be added to elaborate an objective. For example, some teachers wish to include information in their objectives about the conditions of pupil performance and about how well the pupil must perform the objective in order to master it. Such extended objectives would be written as follows:

◆ Given 10 word problems requiring the sum of two numbers, the pupils can solve at least 8 correctly.

◆ Given a diagram of the water cycle, the pupils can explain in their own words what the water cycle is with fewer than two errors.

◆ Given a French paragraph of less than 20 lines and a dictionary, the pupils can translate the paragraph into English in 5 minutes with fewer than six errors.

Extended objectives provide more details about the conditions under which the behavior must be performed and the level of performance the pupil must show. Extended objectives take more time to prepare than their

Extended objectives provide additional details about the conditions under which pupils must demonstrate their learning and the level of performance they must show.

Key Assessment Tools 3.1

CRITERIA FOR SUCCESSFUL OBJECTIVES

1. Be sure the objectives have clear answers.
2. Be sure the objectives represent important aspects of a lesson or chapter.
3. Be sure the objectives center on a verb that specifies pupil performance.
4. Be sure that the objective can be fulfilled in a reasonable amount of time.

---

simpler counterparts and are sometimes difficult to state prior to the start of instruction. Consequently, the simpler model suffices in most instructional situations. Key Assessment Tools 3.1 is a brief reminder of criteria for successful objectives.

Questions Often Asked about Educational Objectives

1. *Is it necessary to write down objectives?* Beginning teachers and students in a teaching practicum usually are required to write lesson objectives. Even if you are an experienced teacher, listing your objectives reminds you to focus on what pupils are expected to get out of instruction, not just what your teaching activities will be. Annual assessment of existing objectives is an important part of any teacher's classroom assessment responsibilities, because each year pupils and curriculum change.

2. *What are higher-level objectives?* Cognitive behaviors can be divided into lower-level ones such as memorizing and remembering and higher-level ones requiring more complex thinking behaviors. Higher-level behaviors, or higher order thinking skills (HOTS), include activities such as analyzing information, applying information and rules to solve new problems, comparing and contrasting objects or ideas, and synthesizing disparate pieces of information into a single, organized idea. In the following examples, the lower-level objective calls only for memorization, while the higher-level objective calls for a more complex behavior.

Higher-level objectives include cognitive activities such as analysis, application, synthesis, and evaluation. These take longer to teach and evaluate than lower-level objectives involving rote memorization.

Lower level: The pupil can write a definition of each vocabulary word.

Higher level: The pupil can write sentences using each vocabulary word correctly.

Lower level: The pupil can match quotes from a short story to the characters who said them.

Higher level: The pupil can contrast the motives of the protagonist and the antagonist in a short story.

Lower level: The pupil can write the formula for the Pythagorean theorem.

Higher level: The pupil can use the Pythagorean theorem to solve new word problems involving the length of ladders needed by the fire department.

All teachers should be aware of the difference between lower- and higher-level thinking skills and should strive to incorporate some higher-level objectives in their plans and instruction.

3. *How many objectives should I state in a subject area?* The answer to this question depends in part upon the time frame being considered and the specificity of the objectives: the longer the period of instruction and the more specific the objectives, the more objectives that can be stated with expectation for pupils to attain. In general, there may be many instructional objectives and fewer educational objectives. Also, higher-level objectives usually take longer to teach and learn, so fewer of them can be taught in a given instructional period; it takes longer to teach pupils to interpret graphs than to memorize a formula. Teachers who have hundreds of objectives for the year's instruction either are expecting too much of themselves and their pupils or are stating their objectives too narrowly. On the other hand, teachers who have only five objectives for the school year are either underestimating their pupils or stating their objectives much too broadly.

4. *Are there any cautions I should keep in mind regarding objectives?* Objectives are usually stated before instruction actually begins and are meant to guide both instruction and assessment. However, objectives are not meant to be followed slavishly when circumstances suggest the need for adjustments. Because objectives are written before instruction starts and because it is difficult to anticipate the flow of classroom activities during instruction, teachers must exercise discretion regarding how closely they will follow the objectives they stated prior to the start of actual instruction.

Because educational objectives are written before instruction begins, teachers must be ready to deviate from them when necessary.

LESSON PLANS

Key Assessment Tools 3.2 shows the components of a lesson plan. Once relevant information about the pupils, the teacher, and the instructional resources is identified, the teacher's task is to synthesize it into a set of instructional plans. When planning, teachers try to visualize themselves teaching, mentally viewing and rehearsing the learning activities they contemplate using in the classroom. This mental dress rehearsal provides instructional direction for both pupils and teacher.

> **Key Assessment Tools 3.2**
>
> ## COMPONENTS OF A LESSON PLAN
>
> **Educational objectives**—also called "targets" by some: Description of the things pupils are to learn from instruction: what pupils should be able to do after instruction (e.g., the pupils can write a summary of a story, the pupils can differentiate adverbs from adjectives in a given passage).
>
> **Materials:** Description of the resources, materials, and apparatus needed to carry out the lesson (e.g., overhead projector, clay, map of the United States, Bunsen burners, video on the civil rights movement).
>
> **Teaching activities and strategies:** Description of the things that will take place during instruction; often includes factors such as determining pupil readiness, identifying how the lesson will start, reviewing prior lessons, providing advanced organizers, specific instructional techniques to be used (e.g., discussion, lecture, silent reading, demonstrations, seatwork, game, cooperative activities) sequence of techniques, providing pupils practice, and ending the lesson.
>
> **Assessment:** Description of how pupil learning from the lesson will be assessed (e.g., homework assignment, oral questions, writing an essay).

Many Instructional Approaches

There are many different instructional approaches that teachers can and do use when planning instruction, such as Madeline Hunter's lesson design cycle model (Hunter, 1982), cooperative learning models (Slavin, 2003), and more recently, the work of Howard Gardner on multiple intelligence (Gardner, 1995). Gardner's approach divides intellectual or thinking abilities into seven distinct kinds of intelligence:

1. Linguistic (using words)
2. Logical/mathematical (using reasoning)
3. Spatial (using images and pictures)
4. Musical (using rhythms)
5. Interpersonal (using interpersonal interactions)
6. Intrapersonal (using meditation or planning)
7. Body/kinesthetic (using physical activities)

Different methods of instruction lead to different forms of instruction and assessment. Teachers must be able to teach pupils in more than one way.

Employing Gardner's approach to multiple intelligence—or any other approach to learning—has implications for classroom instruction. For example, Gardner would argue that his approach demands that teachers teach a broader range of outcomes using a broader range of styles that engage pupils in different multiple intelligences. While simultaneously implementing the seven multiple intelligences in classrooms may be very difficult, Gardner's theory reminds teachers that there is more than one

---

TECHNOLOGY AND ASSESSMENT

RESOURCES ON LESSON PLANNING

olc Visit the Web links section in Chapter 3 of the Online Learning Center (www.mhhe.com/airasian5e) to read the following very helpful Web resources on lesson planning.

THE LESSON PLANS PAGE

◆ This site provides more than 1,000 lesson plans developed by classroom teachers. You begin by selecting a subject area (math, science, language arts, computers, social studies, art, physical education and health, or multidisciplinary), followed by a specific level (grades PreK–1, 2–3, 4–5, 6–7, junior/high school, or multiple). The site is free of charge and is also searchable by topic. However, I reiterate one major caution: These lesson plans were developed by teachers for use in their classrooms, not yours. Please make sure you take the time to scrutinize the objectives, content, materials, and activities, and adapt them to meet your individual needs.

AskERIC LESSON PLANS

◆ ERIC, the Educational Resources Information Center, also maintains a database of lesson plans developed by classroom teachers. Once again, please make sure that you take the time to closely examine all aspects of the lesson plan and adapt them to meet your individual needs. The database is searchable by topic and grade level. Also included is a link to AskERIC's "Write-a-Lesson Plan Guide," which provides some very useful planning advice, as well as more links to lesson plan websites.

CREATING LESSON PLANS

◆ This site of the ERIC Clearinghouse on Teaching and Teacher Education contains an extensive collection of lesson plans for every subject, ideas to help manage and access information for the classroom, and extensive K–12 educational resources.

---

way for all pupils to learn and be assessed. How might instruction and assessment based on a cooperative learning approach differ from instruction and assessment in a multiple-intelligence approach? Different methods often lead to different instructional strategies and different outcomes (Wiggins & McTighe, 1998).

Writing a Plan

A common misconception, especially on the part of preservice teachers, is that there is only one way to develop a daily lesson plan. But there is no single way (i.e., one "correct" format) to write a lesson plan. The format of a lesson plan is largely determined by the purpose of the lesson. In some instances, it may be more appropriate to focus on your behavior as well as that of the students; other times, you may decide that the focus of the lesson should be entirely on what the students will be doing. The detailed format of a lesson plan is not something that can be determined by someone who is not familiar with your classroom and teaching style. You must find a format that works for you and your style of planning and teaching.

Even though they are detailed, lesson plans are not written in stone and do allow for flexibility. Lesson plans can appear rigid if they are developed, and ultimately followed, as if they were scripts. Remember that lesson plans are guides; their purpose is to *direct* your instruction, not *dictate* your instruction. They are meant to provide direction, while at the same time allowing you to act as a professional, making appropriate decisions and adjustments as you proceed through a lesson.

The key is always that the lesson plan is written in conscious awareness of the teaching objective.

IMPROVING THE TIE BETWEEN PLANNING AND ASSESSMENT

In planning instruction, there are a few common guidelines that teachers can follow to strengthen the effectiveness of their planning.

1. *Perform complete early assessments of pupils' needs and characteristics.* Because the purpose of instruction is to help pupils do things they were unable to do before instruction, planning responsive lessons requires that the needs and characteristics of pupils be taken into consideration. Knowledge of pupils' readiness, abilities, and attention spans helps the classroom teacher determine how long lessons should be, whether they should involve whole-class or small-group activities, and whether they should be teacher-led or pupil-directed. The more valid and reliable pupil and class early assessments are, the more appropriate the lesson plans are likely to be.

2. *Use early assessment information when planning.* A teacher may have done an exceptional job with the early assessment of pupils, but if the teacher does not use that information when planning lessons, it is useless. Planning involves fitting instruction to pupil needs and characteristics, and it is the teacher's responsibility to plan accordingly.

3. *Do not rely entirely and uncritically on textbooks and their accompanying aids when planning.* As we have seen, the teacher's edition of textbooks can provide much of the information needed to plan, carry out, and assess instruction, but usually not all. It is important to match the suitability of textbook plans and assessments with pupil characteristics and needs. Teacher's guides should be assessed, adapted, and supplemented to provide the best possible instruction to each teacher's class.

4. *Include a combination of lower-level and higher-level objectives.* The instructional activities offered in most teacher's editions are heavily weighted toward whole-class practices such as recitation, teacher presentation, and seatwork. Such practices normally emphasize lower-level objectives. It is important, therefore, that lesson plans and activities (whether textbook or teacher-made) include *both* lower- and higher-level objectives.

5. *Include a wide range of instructional activities and strategies to fit your pupils' instructional needs.* Teachers who use the same strategy (e.g., lecture, seatwork, or board work) every day with little change or variety create two problems. First, they risk boring pupils and reducing their motivation to attend to the repetitive activity. Second, by limiting their teaching repertoire to a single or very few strategies, they may not be reaching pupils whose learning styles, handicaps, or language backgrounds are best suited to some other method (e.g., small-group instruction, learning games, hands-on materials). It is important to include varied teaching strategies and activities in lesson plans.

6. *Match educational objectives with teaching strategies and planned assessments.* Objectives describe the desired results of instruction. Teaching strategies and activities represent the means to achieve those results. Assessment is a measure of the success of the objectives and instruction. To reach the desired ends, the means must be relevant and appropriate. Without pupil ends clearly in mind, it is difficult to judge the adequacy of an instructional plan or the quality of an assessment. Figure 3.2 shows the relationship between statements of ends (objectives) and statements of means (teaching activities).

7. *Recognize one's own knowledge and pedagogical limitations and preferences.* Teachers assess many things when planning instruction, but they often neglect an assessment of themselves. Content knowledge

---

Means: Read a short story silently.
End: The pupils can summarize a short story in their own words.

Means: Show a film about computers.
End: The pupils can differentiate between computer hardware and software.

Means: Discuss the organization of the periodic table.
End: The pupils can plan an element in its periodic group when given a description of the element's properties.

FIGURE 3.2
Examples of Instructional Means and Ends.

Key Assessment Tools 3.3

GUIDELINES IN PLANNING INSTRUCTION

♦ Perform complete early assessments of pupils' needs and characteristics.

♦ Use early assessment information when planning.

♦ Do not rely entirely and uncritically on textbooks and their accompanying aids when planning.

♦ Include a combination of lower-level and higher-level objectives.

♦ Include a wide range of instructional activities and strategies to fit your pupils' instructional needs.

♦ Match educational objectives with teaching strategies, activities, and planned assessments.

♦ Recognize one's own knowledge and pedagogical limitations and planned preferences.

♦ Include assessment strategies in instructional plans.

limitations may lead a teacher to omit an important topic, teach it in a perfunctory or superficial manner, or provide pupils with incorrect information. Likewise, preferences for one or two teaching methods may deprive pupils of exposure to other methods or activities that would enhance their learning. When a teacher's knowledge limitations and pedagogical preferences outweigh pupil considerations in determining what is or is not done in classrooms, serious questions must be raised about the adequacy of the teacher's instructional plans.

8. *Include assessment strategies in instructional plans.* The object of planning and conducting instruction is to help pupils learn new content and behaviors. Consequently, lesson plans should include some formal measure or measures to determine whether pupils have learned the desired objectives and to identify areas of misunderstanding or confusion. While informal assessments about pupil enthusiasm and participation can be useful, they are not substitutes for more formal assessments such as follow-up seatwork, homework, quizzes, or oral questioning. Key Assessment Tools 3.3 summarizes the guidelines to follow in planning lessons.

PLANNING, DISABILITIES, AND ACCOMMODATIONS

Initially it may seem odd to introduce pupil disabilities and accommodations in a chapter focused on objectives and planning instruction. On reflection, however, it is not really odd at all. Pupil disabilities and particularly pupil accommodations are very important aspects that must be addressed in a teacher's instructional planning.

In recent years there has been increasing emphasis on integrating pupils with disabilities into regular classrooms. Prior "pull out" programs that educated pupils with disabilities in classrooms separate from the majority of pupils are diminishing with the growing emphasis on inclusion of special pupils with their nondisabled peers (Ferguson, 1995). Increased inclusion has placed greater responsibility and challenge on the classroom teacher, who is often charged with educating pupils with varied disabilities (Hoy and Gregg, 1994; Roach, 1995). In this section we will examine laws that define how pupils with disabilities must be diagnosed, the IEP process by which their learning is planned, and other broad accommodation issues. Later chapters will say more about accommodations during instruction, testing, and other forms of assessment.

Legal Issues

Figure 3.3 summarizes recent federal legislation related to teaching children with disabilities. The enactment of the Education for All Handicapped Children Act of 1975 mandated that free public education be provided for *all* school-age children, including those with disabilities, many of whom had been excluded from a free public education. This act also prescribed assessment procedures and practices for pupils identified as having special needs. The Individuals with Disabilities Education Act of 1990 (IDEA) extended the rights of pupils with disabilities by requiring a free and appropriate education for preschool pupils with disabilities. This act called for the placement of pupils with disabilities in the least restrictive environment, requiring that, to the maximum degree possible, pupils with disabilities should be educated in classrooms with pupils who do not have disabilities. Section 504 of the Vocational Rehabilitation Act of 1973 reinforced and expanded protection of pupils with disabilities by broadening the definition of what constitutes a disability. These acts have substantially increased classroom teachers' responsibilities for identifying, instructing, and assessing pupils with disabilities (*Phi Delta Kappan,* 1995). Figure 3.4 describes the major provisions of IDEA. More wide-ranging discussion of legal issues in educating such pupils can be found in Ordover and Boundy (1991), Rothstein (2000), and Overton (1996).

The law requires school systems and teachers to identify and assess all children who have disabilities or are at risk of having their learning impaired because of some cognitive, affective, or psychomotor disability. The range of conditions that qualify as disabilities is large, spanning from physical disabilities and hearing or visual impairments to emotional disorders, learning disorders, and speech impairments. Although the manner of identifying such pupils varies greatly, the classroom teacher is a primary source, especially in the preschool, elementary, and middle school grades. These teachers spend a great deal of time each day with a small group of pupils and thus are in an advantageous position to observe and identify

FIGURE 3.3　*History of the Federal Laws for the Education of Learners Who Are Exceptional.*

1973　Vocational Rehabilitation Act (VRA)
(Public Law 93–112, Section 504)
- ◆ Defines "handicapped person"
- ◆ Defines "appropriate education"
- ◆ Prohibits discrimination against students with disabilities in federally funded programs

1974　Educational Amendments Act (Public Law 93–380)
- ◆ Grants federal funds to states for programming for exceptional learners
- ◆ Provides the first federal funding of state programs for students who are gifted and talented
- ◆ Grants students and families the right of due process in special education placement

1975　Education for All Handicapped Children Act (EAHCA) (Public Law 94–142, Part B)
- ◆ Requires states to provide a free and appropriate public education for children with disabilities (ages 5 to 18)
- ◆ Requires individualized education plans (IEPs)
- ◆ First defined "least restrictive environment"

1986　Education of the Handicapped Act Amendments (Public Law 99–457)
- ◆ Requires states to extend free and appropriate education to children with disabilities (ages 3 to 5)
- ◆ Establishes early intervention programs for infants and toddlers with disabilities (ages birth to 2 years)

1990　Americans with Disabilities Act (ADA) (Public Law 101–336)
- ◆ Prohibits discrimination against people with disabilities in the private sector
- ◆ Protects equal opportunity to employment and public services, accommodations, transportation, and telecommunications
- ◆ Defines "disability" to include people with AIDS

1990　Individuals with Disabilities Education Act (IDEA) (Public Law 101–476)
- ◆ Renames and replaces P. L. EAHCA
- ◆ Establishes "people first" language for referring to people with disabilities
- ◆ Extends special education services to include social work and rehabilitation services
- ◆ Extends provisions for due process and confidentiality for students and parents
- ◆ Adds two new categories of disability: autism and traumatic brain injury
- ◆ Requires states to provide bilingual education programs for students with disabilities
- ◆ Requires states to educate students with disabilities for transition to employment, and to provide transition services

1997　Individuals with Disabilities Education Act (IDEA) (Public Law 105–17)
- ◆ Requires that all students with disabilities must continue to receive services, even if they have been expelled from school
- ◆ Allows states to extend their use of the developmental delay category for students through age 9
- ◆ Requires schools to assume greater responsibility for ensuring that students with disabilities have access to the general education curriculum
- ◆ Allows special education staff who are working in the mainstream to assist general education students when needed
- ◆ Requires a general education teacher to be a member of the IEP team
- ◆ Requires students with disabilities to take part in state- and districtwide assessments

SOURCE: Vaughn, S., Bos, C., Schumm, J. (2003). *Teaching Exceptional, Diverse, and At-Risk Students in the General Education Classroom,* 3rd edition. Boston, MA: Allyn & Bacon.

Free and Appropriate Public Education

All children are entitled to a free and appropriate public education, regardless of the nature or severity of their disability.

Nondiscriminatory Assessment

Requires planning to ensure that tests, evaluation materials, and procedures for evaluating and placing children with disabilities will be selected and administered so as not to be culturally or racially discriminatory.

Development of an Individual Education Plan (IEP)

Requires the development of a written IEP for each child with a disability that will include a statement of current levels of educational achievement, annual and short-term goals, specific educational services to be provided, dates of initiation and duration of services, and criteria for evaluating the degree to which the objectives are achieved.

Due Process

Requires an opportunity to present complaints with respect to any matter relating to the identification, evaluation, or educational placement of a child. Specific due process procedures include: (a) written notification to parents before evaluation, (b) written notification when initiating or refusing to initiate a change in educational placement, (c) an opportunity to obtain an independent evaluation of the child, and (d) an opportunity for an impartial due process hearing.

Privacy and Records

Requires that educational and psychological records pertaining to a child remain confidential except to those individuals who are directly involved in a child's education and who have a specific reason for reviewing the records. Further, the law provides an opportunity for the parents or guardian of a child with a disability to examine all relevant records with respect to the identification, evaluation, and educational placement of the child.

Least Restrictive Environment

Requires to the maximum extent appropriate that children with disabilities be educated with children who are not disabled in as normal an environment as possible.

Related Services

Requires that support services (e.g., psychological, audiology, occupational theory, music therapy) be available to assist the child with a disability to benefit from special education.

SOURCE: Adapted from Individuals with Disabilities Education Act, P. L. 101–476.

FIGURE 3.4
Major Provisions of the Individuals with Disabilities Education Act.

pupils' strengths, weaknesses, needs, and potential disabilities. One of the teacher's official assessment responsibilities is to identify pupils suspected of having a special learning need or disability.

The law requires formal assessment of a pupil who has been identified as likely to have a disability that impacts his or her learning. The assessment helps determine whether the pupil does have special needs, what the needs are, and how they may best be addressed in instruction. Referrals for such pupil assessments can come from teachers, parents, counselors, physicians, and others. The composition of the assessment team that reviews a referred pupil varies, but it is usually made up of some or all of the following individuals: one or more special education teachers, the pupil's classroom teacher(s), specialists in areas of the pupil's perceived needs, parents, child advocates, counselors, and a social worker. The assessment conference must be carried out according to the following procedures and guidelines:

♦ A parent must have written notice, in nontechnical language and in the parent's native language, that a school system proposes to conduct an assessment. Prior notice is needed for a "preplacement" assessment to determine whether a child needs special education, as well as subsequent assessments.

♦ Parental consent must be obtained before pupils are assessed.

♦ Assessments must not be racially or culturally discriminatory.

♦ Assessments must be in the pupil's native language.

♦ No single test or procedure can be the basis for deciding that the pupil has a disability and requires help through instructional accommodations.

♦ Assessments must be conducted by a multidisciplinary team, including at least one teacher knowledgeable about the pupil's area of disability; the assessment must include all areas related to the pupil's disability including health, vision, hearing, emotional status, and so forth.

♦ The assessments used must have proven validity applicable to the decision to be made.

♦ Formal tests and assessments of the pupil must be administered by trained individuals.

♦ A written report must be presented after the assessment process is complete.

Although these procedures say little about the role of the classroom teacher, it is often the teacher who identifies a pupil's disability. Common areas of disability such as oral expression, listening comprehension, written expression, reading fluency, comprehension, and attention deficit are best identified by the classroom teacher. If an assessment is conducted, the teacher will provide important information about a pupil's classroom performance and behavior at the assessment conference.

If a pupil is identified as having a disability, the results of the assessment conference will be used to develop appropriate educational objectives, instructional approaches, and assessment methods for the pupil. Here again, the classroom teacher's recommendations are important in deciding how and what the pupil will be taught and assessed. Because the emphasis in assessment and instruction is on the individual pupil, not the identified disability, each assessed pupil is treated as an individual and the most suitable educational arrangement for that pupil is the primary focus. Two pupils with the same disability may have different objectives, instruction, and assessment strategies.

The specific educational plan developed for a pupil is called an **Individual Educational Plan** (IEP), and must include information about the pupil's present level of educational performance, annual goals and short-term objectives, prescribed educational services, degree of inclusion in regular education programs, and assessment criteria for determining achievement of the goals and objectives. An example of a complete IEP form is shown in Appendix C. In essence, the IEP defines a pupil's special needs and the ways that the teacher must modify objectives, instructional strategies, and assessment methods to best suit the pupil's needs and learning style. Key Assessment Tools 3.4 lists the required parts of an IEP. Examination of these parts shows how a pupil's IEP relates to the planning, instruction, and assessment of the pupil. Once the IEP is developed and agreed upon, it may not be unilaterally changed by school personnel or the classroom teacher.

Decisions about pupils' disabilities and accommodations focus on placing pupils in the least restrictive environment, which enables them to be educated in the most normal environment their disabilities allow. The overriding purpose of referral, IEP development, and placement in the least restrictive environment is to ensure that pupils receive an education appropriate for their needs. Figure 3.5 lists six levels of educational service, with level I the least restrictive.

Disabilities and Accommodations

In 1997, the National Academy of Science reported that 5 million pupils are eligible for assistance under IDEA. That is about 10 percent of the school pupils in the United States. Four areas account for the major portion of pupil disabilities: disabilities related to speech and language; mental retardation; severe emotional problems; and specific learning problems such as learning disabilities, physical limitations, attention deficits, and behavioral problems. The range of pupil disabilities is wide. Since each

Key Assessment Tools 3.4

REQUIRED CONTENTS OF AN INDIVIDUAL EDUCATION PLAN

1. A statement of the child's present levels of educational performance, including academic achievement, social adaptations, prevocational and vocational skills, psychomotor skills, and self-help skills.

2. A statement of annual goals which describes the educational performance to be achieved by the end of the school year under the child's individualized education program.

3. A statement of short-term instructional objectives, which must be measurable intermediate steps between the present level of educational performance and the annual goals.

4. A statement of specific educational services needed by the child (determined without regard to the availability of services), including a description of

   a. all special education and related services which are needed to meet the unique needs of the child, including the type of physical education program in which the child will participate, and

   b. any special instructional media and materials which are needed.

5. The date when those services will begin and length of time the services will be given.

6. A description of the extent to which the child will participate in regular education programs.

7. A justification of the type of educational placement that the child will have.

8. A list of the individuals who are responsible for implementation of the Individual Education Plan.

9. Objective criteria, evaluation procedures, and schedules of determining, on at least an annual basis, whether the short-term instructional objectives are being achieved.

Source: Federal Register, 41(252), p. 5692.

type of disability can range from mild to severe, the range of appropriate accommodations is even wider.

Some classroom disabilities are treated with medication. The widespread use of Ritalin to combat attention deficit disorder (ADD) is the classic example. Other disabilities are so severe that they require intense one-on-one interactions between a special needs teacher and the pupil. Many of these pupils are taught in special classrooms to meet their needs. In other cases, pupils with disabilities may split their time between a special education classroom and a regular classroom. Finally, many pupils with disabilities spend their whole day in a regular classroom, some with an aide and some without an aide (*Phi Delta Kappan,* 1995).

FIGURE 3.5   *Continuum of Educational Services for Students with Disabilities from Least to Most Restrictive.*

Least restrictive

Level I   General education classroom with consultation from specialists:
Student functions academically and socially in general education classroom full time. Specialists provide consultation.

Level II   General education classroom; cooperative teaching or co-teaching:
Special education teacher and classroom teacher co-plan and co-teach for part of school day. For the entire school day, student is included in general classroom, where support services are provided.

Level III   Part-time placement in special education classroom:
Student is placed in the general education classroom for part of the school day and in the special education classroom, usually the resource room, for a certain number of hours daily.

Level IV   Full-time special education classroom in a general education school:
Student is educated in a special education classroom housed in a general education school. This arrangement—being educated in the special education room so students have contact with general education peers only during nonacademic periods—may include part-time involvement with general education students for activities such as physical education and lunch.

Level V   Special school:
Student is provided special education services in a special education school.

Most restrictive

Level VI   Residential school, treatment center, or homebound instruction:
Student is provided special education services at home, or resides in a school or treatment center in which education is provided.

CHAPTER SUMMARY

◆ Education is the process of helping pupils acquire new skills and behaviors. A curriculum is the statement of the things pupils are expected to learn in school or in a course. Instruction includes the methods used to help pupils acquire the desired skills and behaviors. Changes in pupils brought about through formal instruction are called achievements.

◆ The instructional process is comprised of three steps: identifying desirable ways for pupils to learn, selecting materials and providing experiences to help pupils learn, and assessing whether pupils have learned. All three of these steps require teacher decision making and therefore involve assessment.

olc

CHAPTER REVIEW

Visit Chapter 3 of the Online Learning Center at **www.mhhe.com/ airasian5e** to take chapter quizzes, link to related websites, read PowerWeb articles and news feed updates, and access study tools, including the case study referenced in the chapter.

♦ Planning instruction involves teachers understanding and modifying the curriculum and instruction to fit the needs and characteristics of their pupils. Planning helps teachers reduce anxiety and uncertainty about their instruction, review and become familiar with the subject matter before teaching, select ways to get the lessons started, and integrate lessons into units.

♦ Planning is dependent upon the context in which instruction takes place and must take into account both the classroom characteristics teachers control (e.g., arrangement of the classroom, methods of instruction, or strategies for assessment) and those they do not (e.g., pupil characteristics, classroom size, or instructional resources).

♦ Four basic elements that teachers should include in their lesson plans are educational objectives, materials needed, teaching strategies and activities, and assessment procedures. Lesson plans should be written down in advance of instruction.

♦ Objectives are statements that describe what pupils are expected to learn from instruction and a process by which they will demonstrate that learning. Objectives have three general levels of abstraction—global, educational, and instructional—that range from broad to moderate to narrow. Classroom teaching relies primarily upon educational and instructional objectives.

♦ Objectives fall into three domains: cognitive, affective, and psychomotor. Bloom's Taxonomy describes important cognitive processes: knowledge, comprehension, application, analysis, synthesis, and evaluation.

♦ Higher-level educational objectives require pupils to do more than just memorize facts and rules. Higher-level objectives involve behaviors that require application, analysis, synthesis, or evaluation of content and ideas.

♦ Although educational objectives are useful in planning instruction, the fact that they are stated before instruction begins means that they may need to be amended once instruction is under way. It is appropriate to make such adjustments based on pupil readiness.

♦ Lesson planning can be improved by avoiding the following mistakes: not knowing pupils' learning needs and characteristics; ignoring pupil needs and characteristics in planning; relying uncritically on the textbook and its accompanying aids; emphasizing only lower-level educational objectives in plans; using a narrow range of instructional strategies and activities; ignoring the relationship between objectives and teaching activities; failing to recognize one's own weaknesses in content and teaching strategy; and omitting assessment from plans.

♦ An important part of planning instruction is to take into account pupil disabilities and their accommodations.

♦ Pupils who are identified as having a disability may be given an Individual Education Plan (IEP) that defines the services and accommodations that pupils should receive.

QUESTIONS FOR DISCUSSION

1. What pupil characteristics are most important to take into account when planning instruction? How realistic is it to expect a teacher to plan instruction that takes into account the important needs of all the pupils?

2. Which subject areas are most difficult to plan for? Why?

3. What would be the characteristics of a class that would be easy to plan for? What would be the characteristics of a difficult-to-plan-for group?

4. Why do you think that many teachers describe stating objectives as "backward planning"? Is "backward planning" useful? Why?

5. What differentiates a well-stated objective from one that is poorly stated?

6. What are the most common disabilities that pupils have? How might they influence planning, instruction, and assessment?

ACTIVITIES

1. Ask a teacher to show and discuss with you a lesson plan that he or she has used. Report on the teacher's objectives and how the plan took various resources and conditions into account, as well as how closely the plan was actually followed when the lesson was taught.

2. Develop a lesson plan in a topic of your choice. Include the four components of lesson plans discussed in the chapter.

3. In a small group, choose an imaginary pupil with a certain disability in a certain grade. To each student in the group assign the role of teacher, parent, a school administrator, and possibly a special resources member of the school staff. Go over the IEP form in Appendix C together, each taking your respective role. Fill out as much of the form as you can. (You may want to consult the accommodations information in Chapter 5 as well.)

REVIEW QUESTIONS

1. Explain the differences among education, achievement, instruction, and curriculum.

2. What three steps form the educational process?

3. What are the differences between Bloom's six cognitive processes and the three types of content knowledge?

4. What defines a good objective?

5. What are common errors made in planning instruction and how can they be overcome?

6. How do objectives influence decisions about instruction and assessment?

7. What are important guidelines for planning instruction?
8. What role does a classroom teacher play in identifying disabilities?
9. What role does the teacher play in the creation of an IEP?

REFERENCES

Anderson, L. W., et al. (2001). *A taxonomy for learning, teaching, and assessing: A revision of Bloom's taxonomy of educational objectives.* New York: Longman.

Bloom, B. S., et al. (1956). *Taxonomy of educational objectives: Handbook I: Cognitive Domain.* New York: McKay Publishing.

Ferguson, D. L. (1995). The real challenge of inclusion. *Phi Delta Kappan, 77,* 281–287.

Gardner, H. (1995). Reflections of multiple intelligences: Myths and messages. *Phi Delta Kappan.* Nov., 200–207.

Hannah, L. S., and Michaels, J. U. (1977). *A comprehensive framework for instructional objectives: A guide to systematic planning and evaluation.* Reading, MA: Addison-Wesley.

Harrow, A. H. (1972). *A taxonomy of the psychomotor domain.* New York: David McKay.

Hoy, C., & Gregg, N. (1994). *Assessment: The special educator's role.* Pacific Grove, CA: Brooks/Cole.

Hunter, M. (1982). *Mastery learning.* El Segundo, CA: TIP Publications.

Krathwohl, D. R., Bloom, B. S., and Masia, B. B. (1964). *Taxonomy of educational objectives: Handbook II: affective domain.* New York: Longman.

Krathwohl, D. R., & Payne, D. A. (1971). Defining and assessing educational objectives. *Educational Measurement.* R. L. Thorndike. Washington, D.C., American Council on Education: 17–41.

Marzano, R. C., Pickering, D., and McTighe, J. (1993). *Assessing student outcomes: Performance assessment using the dimension of learning model.* Alexandria, VA: Association for Supervision and Curriculum Development.

Ordover, E. L., & Boundy, K. B. (1991). *Educational rights of children with disabilities.* Cambridge, MA: Center for Law and Education.

Overton, T. (2000). *Assessment in special education: An applied approach,* 3rd edition. New York: Merrill.

Phi Delta Kappan (1995). Race, Testing and I.Q., 77(4), 265–328.

Roach, V. (1995). Supporting inclusion. *Phi Delta Kappan, 77,* 295–299.

Rothstein, L. F. (2000). *Special education law,* 3rd edition. New York: Longman.

Slavin, R. (2003). *Educational psychology: theory and practice,* 7th edition. Boston, MA: Allyn and Bacon.

Wiggins, G., & McTighe, J. (1998). *Understanding by design.* Alexandria, VA: Association for Supervision and Curriculum Development.

OTHER SOURCES OF EDUCATIONAL OBJECTIVES AND ASSESSMENTS

KEY TOPICS

- *Textbooks Objectives and Assessments*

- *Statewide Assessments*

- *Implications of High-Stakes Testing*

- *No Child Left Behind*

CHAPTER OBJECTIVES

After reading this chapter, you will be able to:

- ♦ Explain how textbook and related materials can be useful in a teacher's classroom objectives and assessments
- ♦ Describe what is going on in most states with regard to statewide standards and testing
- ♦ Explain how statewide standards and assessments are constructed
- ♦ Discuss some implications for teachers of high-stakes testing
- ♦ Summarize the intention of No Child Left Behind, as well as some possible problems with it

THINKING ABOUT TEACHING

How should teachers with pupils of different abilities prepare the pupils for high-stakes testing?

Chapter 3 introduced the principle that lesson planning and assessment should be driven by the teachers' objectives for the instruction of their pupils. In this chapter we continue that discussion by examining two main outside sources of objectives and related assessments. One important source is textbooks, whose contents and supplemental materials can both complicate and assist a classroom teacher's efforts, depending on how well they match the teacher's aims.

A second class of sources includes statewide educational standards and assessments and federal programs such as No Child Left Behind. As concerns about the performance of pupils, teachers, schools, and (increasingly) administrators have grown at a public policy level, these often-called "high-stakes" mandates are becoming more influential over all levels of schooling.

TEXTBOOK OBJECTIVES AND ASSESSMENTS

Modern textbooks and their accompanying teacher aids provide a great deal of information to help teachers plan, deliver, and assess their instruction. The richest and most used source of information is the teacher's edition of the textbook. Figure 4.1 illustrates the range of resources found in most teacher's editions of textbooks. While not every textbook or instructional package provides every one of the resources listed in the figure, most provide a majority of them and many provide more. At the very least, one can count on finding objectives, teaching suggestions, instructional activities, and assessment instruments. If you have never seen a teacher's edition of a textbook or the resources that accompany it, visit your curriculum library or a local school to examine some. Review a number of teacher's editions and compare the objectives and resources provided for the teacher's planning, teaching, and assess-

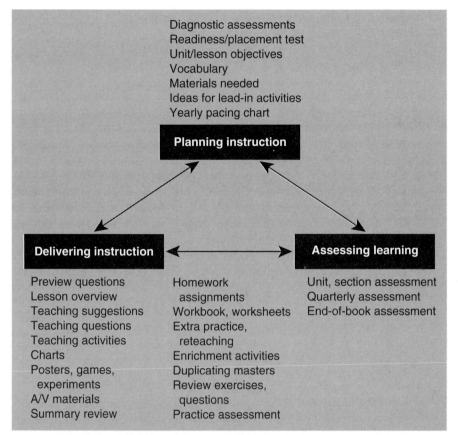

FIGURE 4.1
Common Instructional Resources in Teacher's Editions of Textbooks.

ment. Pay special attention to the introductory sections of the teacher's edition, which describe the resources and materials provided.

Evaluating Textbook Objectives and Lesson Plans

The objectives and other resources that accompany textbooks can be very useful to the classroom teacher—so useful that a teacher might be tempted to rely exclusively upon them. To do so, however, is to abdicate one's decision-making responsibilities, which require a teacher to carefully assess the adequacy of the textbook objectives and other materials in terms of pupil needs and resources. Two recent critics of textbooks assert that many textbooks are too long and at the same time superficial and poorly organized for constructing effective classroom objectives. Another limitation they note of basing instructional objectives solely on a textbook is that it tends to steer students toward accepting one authority and one point of view (Daniels & Zemelman, 2004).

Regardless of the merits of an individual textbook, textbook authors cannot tailor objectives, plans, and assessments to each varied user. They

Textbook objectives and questions can be useful to teachers in planning instruction, but they are not a substitute for the teacher's own careful planning of objectives, instruction, and assessment.

cannot take the status, needs, readiness, and resources of all teachers and classes into account when stating objectives, so they offer objectives and materials that they think most teachers would agree with and accept. It is the responsibility of all classroom teachers to assess the suitability of the textbook objectives and materials for their own particular situation. Blindly following the suggestions in the teacher's textbook can undermine the teacher's responsibility to determine objectives and instructional activities that are well matched to the needs of pupils.

Teachers should screen textbook objectives using three criteria: (1) Are the objectives and text materials clearly stated? (2) Are they suitable for pupils in this particular classroom? (3) Do they exhaust the kinds of objectives and activities these pupils should be exposed to? If the text material appears useful after these criteria have been applied, a teacher may use the text to help focus instruction and assess pupil learning.

The first criterion examines the way objectives and lesson plans are stated. Do they contain a clear description of the process and content knowledge the pupils will learn and the instructional activities that enhance learning? Most, though not all, textbook objectives do provide a clear description of the desired process and content. In the event that the author's objectives are vague and ambiguous, the teacher must define these terms, recognizing that his or her definition may differ from the author's and thus may not be reflected in the instructional suggestions and materials that accompany the text.

The second criterion examines appropriateness for the particular pupils in a teacher's class. When teachers develop their own objectives and plans, they take into account the status, needs, and readiness of the pupils. To not do so is to risk irrelevant instruction. Textbook authors, however, can only state a single set of objectives and plans for all the classes and pupils who will use the book. Often, these objectives and plans are more suitable for some classes than for others. Consequently, teachers must ask "Do my pupils have the prerequisites needed to master the textbook objectives? Can they be taught these objectives in a reasonable amount of time? Will the lesson activities interest them? Do the lesson activities pertain to all the important objectives in the unit?"

The final criterion examines completeness. Do the textbook objectives exhaust the important outcomes pupils should learn? Lesson plans in textbooks tend to emphasize structured, didactic methods in which the teacher either tells pupils things or elicits brief replies to teacher questions. Lessons using such objectives are easier to devise and present than less structured, more complex ones. Relatively few textbook objectives call for synthesis or analysis of ideas, themes, or topics. Although teachers commonly omit topics from a text when teaching, they rarely introduce new topics that are not in the text. If teachers wish to include or emphasize higher-level objectives in their instruction, they may be forced to break this pattern and introduce additional objectives that round out pupil learning. Table 4.1 summarizes the advantages and disadvantages of textbook objectives and lesson plans. Key Assessment Tools 4.1 gives factors to consider when examining textbook objectives and lesson plans.

TABLE 4.1   ADVANTAGES AND DISADVANTAGES OF TEXTBOOK OBJECTIVES AND LESSON PLANS

Advantages	Disadvantages
Convenient, readily available objectives and plans	Designed for teachers and pupils in general, not necessarily for a given teacher or class
Can save valuable time in planning	
Provide an integrated set of objectives, plans, activities, and assessments	Heavy emphasis on lower-level objectives and activities
	Lesson activities tend to be didactic and teacher-led
Contain many ancillary materials for planning, instructing, and assessing	If accepted uncritically, can lead to inappropriate instruction for pupils

Key Assessment Tools 4.1

BASIC FACTORS TO CONSIDER WHEN EXAMINING TEXTBOOK OBJECTIVES AND LESSON PLANS

Textbook Objectives

1. **Clarity:** Are objectives clearly stated, especially the process and knowledge?

2. **Comprehensiveness:** Do the objectives include most learner outcomes for this topic?

3. **Level:** Do the objectives include both higher- and lower-level thinking behaviors?

4. **Prerequisites:** Do pupils have the prerequisite skills needed to master the objectives?

5. **Time:** Can pupils reasonably be expected to master the objectives in the time available for instruction?

Lesson Plans

1. **Pertinence:** Do plans help foster the stated objectives?

2. **Level:** Do plans include activities for fostering both higher- and lower-level objectives?

3. **Realism:** Are plans realistic given pupil ability, learning style, reading level, attention span, and so on?

4. **Resources:** Are the resources and materials needed to implement plans and activities available?

5. **Follow-up:** Are follow-up materials (e.g., worksheets, enrichment exercises, and reviews) related to the objectives and do they reinforce lesson plans and activities?

> **Key Assessment Tools 4.2**
>
> ### KEY POINTS TO CONSIDER IN JUDGING TEXTBOOK TESTS
>
> 1. The decision to use a textbook test must come *after* a teacher identifies the objectives that he or she has taught and now wants to assess.
> 2. Textbook tests are designed for the typical classroom, but since few classrooms are typical, most teachers deviate somewhat from the text to accommodate their pupils' needs.
> 3. The more classroom instruction deviates from the textbook objectives and lesson plans, the less valid the textbook tests are likely to be.
> 4. The main consideration in judging the adequacy of a textbook test is the match between its test questions and what pupils were taught in their classes:
>   a. Are questions similar to the teacher's objectives and instructional emphases?
>   b. Do questions require pupils to perform the behaviors they were taught?
>   c. Do questions cover all or most of the important objectives taught?
>   d. Is the language level and terminology appropriate for pupils?
>   e. Does the number of items for each objective provide a sufficient sample of pupil performance?

Evaluating Textbooks Tests

Textbook tests furnish a ready-made instrument for assessing the objectives stressed in the textbook and can save classroom teachers much time. Test formats vary across textbook publishers in terms of length, layout, and question type. Look through the teacher's edition of some textbooks to see the range of tests available.

Before using these tests, teachers should consider the criteria that permit a teacher to use a textbook or teacher-made test with confidence. The basic concern is whether the items on the test match the instruction provided pupils. Key Assessment Tools 4.2 identifies important points to consider when deciding about whether or not to use a textbook test.

Regardless of whether a teacher is constructing his or her own test or judging the adequacy of a textbook test, the same basic validity issue must be considered: do the items on the test match the instruction provided pupils? The more a teacher alters and reshapes the textbook curriculum, the less valid its accompanying tests become. As one teacher put it, "The textbook tests look good and can be time-savers, but they often don't test exactly what I've been doing in the classroom. Every time I change what I do from what the text suggests I do, and every time I leave out a lesson or section of the text from my instruction, I have to look at the text test carefully to make sure it's fair for my pupils."

TABLE 4.2   COMMON PROBLEMS IN DEVELOPING OR SELECTING TESTS TO ASSESS PUPIL ACHIEVEMENT

1. Failure to consider objectives and instructional emphases when planning a test
2. Failure to assess all of the important objectives and instructional topics
3. Failure to select item types that permit pupils to demonstrate the desired behavior
4. Adopting a test without reviewing it for its relevance to the instruction provided
5. Including topics or objectives not taught to pupils
6. Including too few items to assess the consistency of pupil performance
7. Using tests to punish pupils for inattentiveness or acting out

---

To summarize, both textbook and teacher-made tests should (1) assess the objectives and instruction provided and (2) include sufficient questions to measure all or most of those objectives. That way, the test provides a valid sample of pupil learning. Table 4.2 summarizes the problems teachers encounter in addressing these two important aspects.

STATEWIDE ASSESSMENTS

Statewide standards for instruction have been around for many years, but in the past decade, the focus and emphasis of statewide assessment has greatly changed.

The Rising Stakes

Every state except Iowa has now adopted state curriculum frameworks or content standards. In addition, all of these states with the exception of Nebraska have implemented an assessment program designed to measure student achievement of these curricular standards (Quality Counts, 2002). By 2008, almost half of the states (24) will require students to pass a state test in order to graduate; this requirement will affect 70% of students nationwide (Center on Education Policy, 2002). These standards are at the heart of statewide educational reform. They are used to guide activities such as teachers' instructional emphases, textbook selection, and assessment methods. Instruction and assessment are coordinated to reflect the state standards. Teachers are strongly encouraged to incorporate these

State-mandated standards are used to assess pupils, teachers, and schools in a particular state. The standards are intended to guide statewide learning and assessments.

TABLE 4.3 SOME HIGH-STAKES TERMINOLOGY*

Standard: A generic statement of what a student should know and be able to do in a subject area.

Benchmark: A specific statement of what a student should know at a specific time.

Indicator: A specific statement of knowledge or skills that a student demonstrates in order to meet the benchmark.

Framework: The governing document for a subject area, to be used for developing curriculum in that area.

Curriculum framework: A state's contents, standards, and benchmarks for a subject area.

*These terms and definitions are now widely accepted and used, though not universally.

standards into their curricula, and in many states achievement tests that reflect the standards are administered statewide to pupils.

In many states, the state assessments have important consequences for teachers, schools, and pupils. In some states, ratings of teachers and schools are based on their pupils' performance on state standards and assessments. Schools that have a history of poor pupil performance on the assessments can be put on probation or closed. In a few states, teachers and schools whose pupils perform very well on the state assessments are rewarded with merit pay. In many states, pupils can be placed in remedial programs, held back from promotion, or denied a high school diploma if they perform poorly on statewide assessments.

Clearly the stakes are high, since statewide standards and testing are being used now to drive major changes at state and local levels in the shaping of educational policy and determining what funding or other support schools will receive. Table 4.3 defines some terms that are useful in understanding the issues.

The Variety of Statewide Standards

Table 4.4 shows information about standards and accountability for the fifty states and the District of Columbia. (The abbreviations ES, MS, and HS mean Elementary School, Middle School, and High School.) All except one have standards in the core subjects (English, math, and science), but some are judged clearer, more specific, and better grounded than others.

Different states produce different standards, but most states do have achievement standards.

Statewide standards can be expressed in a wide variety of forms. Figure 4.2 shows excerpts of a Tennessee standard on developing knowledge, skills, and attitude to enhance personal growth. Note the levels of focus and detail associated with the standard: (1) the statement of the standard, (2) the learning

TABLE 4.4   STANDARDS AND ACCOUNTABILITY, STATE BY STATE

	Overall Grade		State Has Adopted Standards in Core Subjects (2003–04)	Standards—40% of Grade State has standards that are clear, specific, and grounded in content (2003)		
				English/ Language Arts	Mathematics	Science
Louisiana	A	98	✓	ES MS HS	ES MS HS	ES MS HS
New York	A	97	✓	ES MS HS	ES MS HS	ES MS HS
Ohio	A	95	✓	ES MS HS	ES MS HS	ES MS HS
West Virginia	A	95	✓	ES MS HS	ES MS HS	ES MS HS
Florida	A	94	✓	ES MS HS	ES MS HS	ES MS HS
Kentucky	A	94	✓	ES	ES MS HS	ES MS HS
Maryland	A	93	✓	ES MS HS	ES MS HS	ES MS HS
South Carolina	A	93	✓	ES MS HS	ES MS HS	ES MS HS
Indiana	A–	92	✓	ES MS HS	ES MS HS	ES MS HS
Illinois	A–	91	✓	ES MS HS	ES MS HS	ES MS HS
Georgia	B+	89	✓	ES MS HS	ES MS HS	ES MS HS
Oklahoma	B+	89	✓	ES MS HS	ES MS HS	ES MS HS
Massachusetts	B+	89	✓	ES MS HS	ES MS HS	ES MS HS
Delaware	B+	87	✓	ES MS	ES MS HS	ES MS HS
Missouri	B+	87	✓		ES MS HS	ES MS HS
California	B	86	✓	ES MS HS	ES MS HS	ES MS HS
Tennessee	B	86	✓	ES MS	ES MS HS	ES MS
Arizona	B	85	✓	ES MS HS	ES MS HS	ES MS HS
Virginia	B	85	✓	ES MS HS	ES MS HS	ES MS
Michigan	B	85	✓		ES MS HS	ES MS HS
North Carolina	B	84	✓	ES MS HS	ES MS HS	ES MS HS
Pennsylvania	8	84	✓	ES MS HS	ES MS HS	ES MS HS
New Mexico	B	83	✓	ES MS HS	ES MS HS	ES MS HS
Oregon	B–	82	✓	ES MS HS	ES MS HS	ES MS HS
Mississippi	B–	82	✓	ES MS	ES MS HS	ES MS
Alabama	B–	82	✓	ES	ES MS HS	ES MS
Connecticut	B–	82	✓	ES HS	ES MS HS	ES MS HS

(continued)

SOURCE: Adapted from *Education Week* 22, no. 17 (January 9, 2003), p. 84.

TABLE 4.4   STANDARDS AND ACCOUNTABILITY, STATE BY STATE (continued)

	Overall Grade		State Has Adopted Standards in Core Subjects (2003–04)	Standards—40% of Grade State has standards that are clear, specific, and grounded in content (2003)		
				English/ Language Arts	Mathematics	Science
New Jersey	B–	81	✓	ES MS HS	ES MS HS	ES MS HS
Colorado	B–	81	✓	ES MS HS	ES MS HS	ES MS HS
Nevada	B–	80	✓	ES MS HS	ES MS HS	MS HS
Kansas	B–	80	✓	ES MS HS	ES MS HS	ES MS HS
Arkansas	C+	79	✓	ES MS	ES MS	ES MS HS
South Dakota	C+	79	✓	MS HS	ES MS HS	ES MS HS
Texas	C+	79	✓	ES HS	ES MS HS	ES MS
Wisconsin	C+	77	✓	ES MS HS	ES MS HS	
Hawaii	C+	77	✓		ES MS HS	ES MS HS
Utah	C+	77	✓	ES MS HS	ES MS HS	ES MS HS
Idaho	C+	77	✓	ES MS HS	ES MS HS	ES MS HS
Washington	C+	77	✓	ES	ES MS	ES MS HS
Maine	C	75	✓	MS HS	ES	ES MS HS
Vermont	C	75	✓			ES MS HS
Minnesota	C	73	✓	ES MS HS	ES MS HS	ES MS HS
Alaska	C–	71	✓		ES MS HS	ES MS HS
New Hampshire	C–	70	✓	MS	ES MS HS	ES MS HS
North Dakota	C–	70	✓	ES MS HS	ES MS HS	ES MS HS
Nebraska	D	66	✓	HS	ES MS HS	ES MS HS
Rhode Island	D	66	3 subjects			ES MS HS
Wyoming	D	65	✓		ES MS HS	
District of Columbia	D–	61	✓	ES MS HS	ES MS HS	ES MS HS
Montana	D–	60	✓			MS HS
Iowa	F	33				
U.S.	—	—	49	—	—	—

Standard

1.0 The student will develop knowledge, skills and attitudes to enhance personal growth.

Learning Expectations

The student will:

1. Demonstrate a sense of purpose and direction and make decisions based on positive goals and values (believes self can make a significant difference; nothing is left to chance or luck).

2. Demonstrate positive attitudes toward self and others (self-respect, self-confidence and self-esteem; feels worthwhile, confident, and competent).

3. Develop capacity for resiliency in relationships. . . .

4. Demonstrate self-management. . . .

5. Choose ethical courses of action (integrity and honesty).

6. Develop openness to new experiences and roles.

Performance Indicators: Evidence Standard Is Met

The student is able to:

1. Select, research, and organize a project after identifying and exploring a variety of options.

2. Demonstrate growth through reflection (e.g., journals, attitudinal surveys, . . .).

3. Use problem-solving techniques to interact with others.

4. Set a personal goal and create benchmarks to reach that goal.

5. . . . (and so forth)

Sample Performance Task

The student will:

1. Identify a problem within the school or community and implement an action plan. . . . .

2. Create a "This is Your Life" video for a student from a different cultural background.

3. Create a reflection portfolio including an end-of-semester self-assessment.

4. Write about times when he or she has experienced conflict and role-play to resolve the conflict.

5. . . . . (and so forth)

FIGURE 4.2
A Tennessee Standard for Personal Growth.

TABLE 4.5   COLORADO MODEL CONTENT STANDARDS FOR READING AND WRITING

1. Students read and understand a variety of materials.

2. Students write and speak for a variety of purposes and audiences.

3. Students write and speak using conventional grammar, usage, sentence structure, punctuation, capitalization, and spelling.

4. Students apply thinking skills to their reading, writing, speaking, listening, and viewing.

5. Students read to locate, select, and make use of relevant information from a variety of media, reference, and technological sources.

6. Students read and recognize literature as a record of human experience.

SOURCE: *http://www.cde.state.co.us/download/pdf/reading.pdf* (Colorado Content Standards adopted 7-13-95)

expectations—what students will learn, (3) the performance indicators—evidence of meeting the standard, and (4) sample performance tasks. The tasks help pupils and teachers to know how to focus on the standard.

Table 4.5 lists the six Colorado standards for reading and writing, and Figure 4.3 shows excerpts that elaborate on two of them in terms of expectations, broad rationale, and how each standard applies at three different levels of schooling.

Figure 4.4 from West Virginia shows a glimpse of a different statewide approach to standards. It gives an overview and objectives for a specific course.

The point of these examples is to show the variety of ways that states define standards. For your own edification, try to find and examine the standards that are in effect in the state in which you plan to teach.

Construction of Statewide Assessments

Most statewide assessments are based on criterion-referenced scoring and are constructed in the following way. First, the standards for the different subject areas are determined by statewide curriculum committees made up of teachers, administrators, parents, businesspeople, and other concerned citizens. The identified standards are often not confined to those presently taught in schools. Usually the standards include new curriculum areas not previously emphasized by all teachers.

Once the standards are identified, items are written to assess them. Of the states that assess their students statewide, most include items requiring writing in some form, such as a poem, and performance-type assessments, such as an oral presentation, or science project. Thus, a large portion of the items produced for statewide assessments are performance assessments of various kinds. The constructed items are then reviewed to determine

FIGURE 4.3
*Elaborations of
Colorado Standards
1 and 3.*

STANDARD 1

Students read and understand a variety of materials.

To meet this standard, students will:

◆ Use comprehension skills such as previewing, predicting, inferring, comparing and contrasting, rereading and self-monitoring, summarizing, etc.

◆ Make connections between their reading and what they already know, and identify what they need to know about a topic before reading about it.

◆ Adjust reading strategies for different purposes such as reading carefully idea by idea; skimming and scanning, etc.

◆ Use word recognition skills and resources such as phonics, context clues, picture clues, etc.

◆ Use information from their reading to increase vocabulary and enhance language usage.

Rationale: The goal for students at all levels is that they know and can use strategies—various ways of unlocking the meaning of words and larger blocks of text—to become successful readers. The strategies are applied in increasingly difficult reading material at each grade level. At all levels, students should be challenged to read literature and other materials that stimulate their interests and intellectual abilities. Reading from a wide variety of texts, both assigned and student selected, provides experience in gaining information and pleasure from diverse forms and perspectives.

Grades K–4. In grades K–4, what the students know and are able to do includes using a full range of strategies to comprehend materials such as directions, nonfiction material, rhymes and poems, and stories.

Grades 5–8. As students in grades 5–8 extend their knowledge, what they know and are able to do includes using a full range of strategies to comprehend technical writing, newspapers, magazines, poetry, short stories. Students extend their thinking and understanding.

Grades 9–12. As students in grades 9–12 extend their knowledge, what they know and are able to do includes using a full range of strategies to comprehend essays, speeches, autobiographies.

For students extending their English/language arts education beyond the standards, what they know and are able to do may include using a full range of strategies to comprehend literary criticism and literary analysis, professional and technical journals.

STANDARD 3

Students write and speak using conventional grammar, usage, sentence structure, punctuation, capitalization, and spelling.

To meet this standard, students will:

◆ Know and use correct grammar in speaking and writing.

◆ Apply correct usage in speaking and writing.

(continued)

FIGURE 4.3
Elaborations of Two Colorado Standards (continued).

◆ Use correct sentence structure in writing.

◆ Demonstrate correct punctuation, capitalization, and spelling.

Rationale: Students need to know and be able to use standard English. Proficiency in this standard plays an important role in how the writer or speaker is understood and perceived. All skills in this standard are reinforced and practiced at all grade levels and should be monitored by both the teacher and student to develop lifelong learning skills.

Grades K–4. In grades K–4, what the students know and are able to do includes knowing and using subject/verb agreement; knowing and using correct modifiers; knowing and using correct capitalization.

Grades 5–8. As students in grades 5–8 extend their knowledge, what they know and are able to do includes:

◆ Identifying the parts of speech such as nouns, pronouns, verbs, adverbs.

◆ Using correct pronoun case, regular and irregular noun and verb forms, and subject-verb agreement involving comparisons in writing and speaking.

◆ Using modifiers, homonyms, and homophones.

◆ Using simple, compound, complex, and compound/complex sentences.

Grades 9–12. As students in grades 9–12 extend their knowledge, what they know and are able to do includes:

◆ Using pronoun references correctly in writing and speaking.

◆ Using phrases and clauses for purposes of modification and parallel structure in writing and speaking.

◆ Using internal capitalization and punctuation of secondary quotations in writing.

◆ Using manuscript forms specified in various style manuals for writing.

SOURCE: *http://www.cde.state.co.us/download/pdf/reading.pdf* (Colorado Content Standards adopted 7-13-95)

Most statewide assessment programs use performance-based items and tasks, although some states also include multiple-choice items.

whether they actually do assess the intended standard or objective, are culturally unbiased, and are at an appropriate language level for pupils in that grade. Items are then assembled into tests. Often the items are tried out on some pupils to determine how well they will work, though not on pupils in the grades to be assessed.

When the purpose of statewide assessments is to provide information about achievement at the school or school district level, it is not necessary for every pupil in a school or district to answer every test question. For school or district reporting purposes, the amount of information gathered can be maximized and the amount of assessment time minimized by having each pupil answer only some of all the items developed. Suppose a curriculum committee identified 12 science standards that it felt seventh

FIGURE 4.4
West Virginia
Standard for
Algebra I.

Algebra I Objectives

Algebra I is a course that provides the gateway to all higher mathematics courses. This course uses a conceptual approach to mathematics and does not focus on algorithmic methods. Algebraic representations will be used to generalize, and the algebraic method will be viewed as a problem-solving tool. In planning for instruction, consideration should be given to the student's readiness for abstract concepts. Manipulatives, such as algeblocks, should be used to bridge the gap from the concrete to the abstract. Available technology such as calculators, computers, and graphing utilities are to be used as tools to enhance learning.

Students will:

♦ demonstrate understanding of patterns, relations, and functions;

♦ represent and analyze mathematical situations and structures using algebraic symbols;

♦ use mathematical models. . . .

Algebra I Objectives

Students will:

A1.2.1   simplify and evaluate algebraic expressions using grouping symbols, order of operations and properties of real numbers with justification of steps.

A1.2.2   solve multi-step linear equations in one variable and apply skills toward solving practical problems. . . .

A1.2.3   . . . .

Performance Descriptors

♦ **Distinguished** The student demonstrates exceptional and exemplary performance. . . .

♦ **Above Mastery** The student demonstrates competent and proficient performance. . . .

♦ **Mastery** The student demonstrates fundamental course or grade level knowledge . . .

♦ **Partial Mastery** The student demonstrates basic but inconsistent performance. . . .

♦ **Novice** The student demonstrates substantial need for the development of fundamental knowledge. . . .

SOURCE: West Virginia Department of Education **Policy 2520.2. Effective Jul 1, 2003.**
http://wvde.state.wv.us/csos/

graders statewide ought to learn. Suppose also that 10 items were written to assess each of the 12 standards, thus producing a total of 120 seventh grade science items. Rather than giving each seventh grade pupil a 120-item test, the items could be divided into four tests of 30 items each. All four tests would then be administered at random to seventh graders in each school or district in the state, but each pupil would be required to take only

Statewide assessments can include all pupils or schools if scoring is based on individual schools and pupils, or samples of schools and pupils if overall statewide information is desired.

one of the tests. Summing the results of all four tests across pupils would yield a very good estimate of school or district performance on all 12 of the seventh grade science standards. It is important to recognize, however, that if the purpose of a statewide test is to make a decision about an individual pupil's performance, promotion, graduation, or placement, it is necessary to give all pupils the same assessment. That is the only fair way to make pupil-by-pupil decisions. Different states use different types of assessments in high-stakes testing. Figure 4.5 showing three different types is just a glimpse of the wide variety of approaches.

Scoring Statewide Assessments

Assigning grades to pupils based on a comparison with other pupils is called norm-referencing.

Scoring statewide assessments is usually carried out using a criterion-referenced approach. In general, criterion-referenced scoring is used to make decisions about individual pupil performance and grouped norm-referenced results are used to compare state performance to those of other states. Since each state has its own, unique statewide assessment, the only way comparisons across states can be obtained is with commercial standardized tests that are used nationally.

For criterion-referenced scoring, predetermined performance levels are established and pupil performance is compared to the levels. Two types of criterion-referenced standards are used in statewide scoring: percentage and performance scoring. In percentage scoring, passing the assessment is based on obtaining a given percentage of the items correct. The percentage selected is often called a **cut score** or a cutoff score. For example, if a state defines mastery as a cut score of 70 percent or above on a statewide assessment, pupils who correctly answer 70 percent or more of the items pass. Pupils answering fewer than 70 percent of the items correctly do not pass the assessment. Percentage scoring is not limited to pass-fail decisions. The statewide assessment in Massachusetts, for example, uses the cut score approach to place pupils into one of four scoring categories: fail, needs improvement, proficient, and advanced.

Performance scoring is used to score assessments that require pupils to write essays, perform a process, or present a portfolio. Percentage scoring is often difficult and cumbersome to implement for complex performances such as writing an essay, oral reading, performing a science experiment, or judging a portfolio. Instead, performances and portfolios are typically scored using rubrics. Figure 4.6 shows a rubric that could be used to score the quality of third graders' writing for personal expression in a state-based assessment program. There are four criteria associated with writing for personal expression: development, organization, focus on audience, and language. The rubric contains four levels of performance, labeled 3 to 0. Scorers read a third grader's essay and assign it to one of the categories, depending on which category best describes the quality of the pupil's writing. A class, school, or district with many 1's and 0's would be alerted to

FIGURE 4.5   *High-Stakes Test Items from Three States.*

Kansas

Sample question for the sixth grade social studies test:

Which of the following is the *best* example of an American export?

A. The United States produces steel.   C. The United States is selling wheat to Russia.

B. Japan produces excellent cars.   D. The United States is buying salmon from Canada.

Answer: C

Michigan

Prompt for the 1999 fifth grade writing test:

Topic:

Memories

Pretest directions:

Talk about these questions with your group, making sure everyone gets to speak.

Thinking about the topic:

Can you think of funny or happy memories? Do you remember celebrating a holiday or going to a wedding, a festival, or a birthday party?

Can you think of any sad, frightening, or embarrassing memories? Do you remember saying goodbye to a friend, being involved in an emergency, or getting a bad haircut?

Do you remember any exciting moments? Do you have memories of cooking dinner by yourself? Riding on an airplane? Waiting for an announcement about making a team? Getting a part in a play?

Test directions: writing about the topic:

Writers often write about past experiences. They often recall a favorite memory, an event like a celebration, or a time when they were happy, embarrassed, proud, or frightened. *Write about a memory.*

You might, for example, do one of the following:

◆ Write about an exciting or funny time you remember very well.

◆ Explain why some memories become important and others do not.

◆ Write about a family memory you've heard over and over.

◆ Write about a memory that includes a person who is important to you.

◆ Write about the topic in your own way.

You may use examples from real life, from what you read or watch, or from your imagination. Your writing will be read by interested adults.

Massachusetts

Question from the 2001 tenth grade mathematics test:

At the first stop, 3/4 of the passengers on the bus got off and 8 people got on. A total of 16 passengers were left on the bus. Write an equation that can be solved to show how many passengers were on the bus before the first stop. Let x represent the number of passengers on the bus before the first stop. (You do *not* have to solve the equation.)

FIGURE 4.6 *Scoring Rubric for Expressing Personal Ideas.*

Scoring rubric: writing to express personal ideas.

3 points
- ◆ *Development:* consistently develops ideas into a complete, well-developed whole.
- ◆ *Organization:* sequences in a logical and effective manner.
- ◆ *Focus on audience:* anticipates and answers the audience's needs and questions.
- ◆ *Language:* consistently uses language that enhances the writing.

2 points
- ◆ *Development:* partially develops the ideas and does not provide a complete, well-developed whole.
- ◆ *Organization:* purposely orders ideas for reader to follow.
- ◆ *Focus on audience:* usually anticipates and answers the audience's needs and questions.
- ◆ *Language:* frequently uses language to enhance the writing.

1 point
- ◆ *Development:* rarely develops ideas or produces poorly developed and incomplete ideas.
- ◆ *Organization:* usually orders ideas but with some interruptions in the flow.
- ◆ *Focus on audience:* occasionally anticipates and answers the audience's needs and questions.
- ◆ *Language:* sometimes uses language that enhances the writing.

0 points
- ◆ *Development:* no development of ideas into a complete whole.
- ◆ *Organization:* rarely evidences logical ordering of ideas.
- ◆ *Focus on audience:* does not anticipate and answer the audience's needs and questions.
- ◆ *Language:* fails to use language that enhances the writing.

Blank—no written response

Focus—did not answer the stated question

Unreadable—writing is illegible, writing not comprehensible

Statewide assessments are scored by criterion-referencing using a cut score or a rubric.

the need to reexamine its curriculum to determine why many pupils did poorly. Note that the state-based results do not *dictate* changes in curriculum, but they do provide information that can help in deciding whether or not instruction in an area needs to be revised.

Examples of Comprehensive Statewide Assessment

One of the most highly developed and pervasive statewide assessment programs is one developed in North Carolina in the early 1990s. (North Carolina Department of Public Instruction, 1992). It provides an example of how states are trying to use assessment to focus and improve teaching and learning. The North Carolina assessment program is linked to the North Carolina statewide standard course of study, which is the state-adopted curriculum that defines what pupils are to know and do in school subjects at all grade levels. All statewide assessments are constructed to match closely the standard course of study. Note that in addition to the assessments mandated by the state, local school districts may also administer additional commercial achievement test batteries of their choice to pupils.

The features of the North Carolina statewide assessment program are outlined below.

Grades 1 through 8

Assessment in grades 1 and 2 are done by portfolios of pupils' work. The samples of pupils' work can be reviewed by parents and teachers to determine pupil progress towards the designated goals.

In grades 3 through 8, three different mandated assessments are administered:

1. The North Carolina End-of-Grade (EOG) Tests will be administered at the end of each school year to assess mastery of grade-level knowledge and skills. Pupils will be assessed annually in five subject areas: reading, writing, mathematics, science, and social studies.

2. The Minimum Skills Diagnostic Tests (MSDT) will be given at the end of the year in grades 3, 6, and 8 to pupils who score below the state-designated passing score on the End of Grade Tests and who show other forms of difficulty with schoolwork. The primary purpose of the Minimum Skills Diagnostic Tests is to identify a pupil's strengths and weaknesses so proper instruction and remediation can be planned. The MSDT is administered in reading, mathematics, and language.

3. North Carolina Competency Tests (NCCT) are administered to pupils in grade 8 in the subjects of reading, mathematics, and writing. Pupils in grade 8 who score below the cut score on these tests will be retested every year until they reach the minimum passing score in all three subjects. Obtaining a passing score on all three tests is necessary to receive a high school diploma.

Grades 9 through 12

Two types of mandated assessment are carried out in these grades:

1. The North Carolina Competency Tests (NCCT) are administered yearly to those pupils who failed to attain the minimum passing score in reading, mathematics, and writing in grade 8.

2. The North Carolina End-of-Course (EOC) Tests are administered at the end of each course in the following subject areas: algebra I and II, geometry, biology, physical science, physics, chemistry, U.S. history, economic/legal/political systems, English I and II, and others.

The North Carolina state assessment program is more extensive than most other statewide assessments, mainly because very few other states have specific end-of-course or end-of-grade tests to determine pupil and schoolwide progress. North Carolina is, however, one of a growing number of states that link statewide standards in subject areas to the state-based assessment program. In other respects, the North Carolina assessments are different from those in other states.

Features of statewide assessment programs that are common to most programs include the following:

♦ A sizable amount of assessment is required.

♦ Part of the assessment includes performance-portfolio-based information.

♦ Decisions about performance are made by comparing a pupil's score to a predetermined, statewide passing score.

♦ The assessments have important implications for pupils and schools.

♦ Because poor performance on the assessment can affect pupils' opportunities, teachers must decide how much time they will devote to preparing pupils for the assessments.

♦ Combining performance across pupils provides information that can be used for district, school, or teacher accountability.

IMPLICATIONS OF HIGH-STAKES TESTING

It is not clear yet that high-stakes testing is an effective way to increase student motivation to learn and actual learning, but it is affecting teachers' classroom work, including what they focus on and how they allocate time.

Although teachers have little influence over statewide standards and assessment programs, the programs can and do influence teachers considerably. Statewide assessments, especially those with important consequences for schools, teachers, or pupils, increase the pressure on school districts and teachers to revise their curricula to better match the state standards and assessments. Teachers tend to increase the amount of instructional time devoted to the standards because the better their pupils learn them, the more the district and its teachers and pupils are rewarded. Indeed, one of the main reasons for statewide standards and aligned statewide assessments is to define and standardize the instructional emphases across a state.

There is a very large domain of information related to high-stakes assessment issues. More than 75 analyses have been conducted to determine the impact of high-stakes testing on pupils, teachers, parents, and administrators. One recent study in states that make extensive use of high-stakes testing looked at four independent achievement measures (SAT, ACT, and AP test scores, plus the National Assessment of Educational Progress) to see whether the high-stakes approach measurably increased student motivation to learn and increased actual student learning (Amrein & Berliner,

2003). The report concluded that it did not. In the rest of this section we will focus on the impact of high-stakes testing and some problems that it raises for teachers and their classroom work.

The Impact on Teachers and Teaching

Teachers' sense of the impact of high-stakes assessment was explored recently in a national survey (Pedulla, Abrams, Madaus, and others, 2003). It consisted of 80 items in the form of questions or statements related to statewide testing. Responses were gathered from throughout the country, some coming from teachers in states where assessments are clearly "high-stakes," others from teachers where the stakes are currently regarded as lower.

Many of the items were geared toward capturing the beliefs of teachers about the influence of their state's test on classroom instruction and student learning. The survey was based, in part, on other surveys used in Arizona (Smith, Nobel, Heinecke, et al., 1997), Maryland (Koretz, Mitchell, Barron, & Keith, 1996), Michigan (Urdan & Paris, 1994) and Texas (Haney, 2000), as well as on the National Science Foundation (NSF) study of the Influence of Testing on Teaching Math and Science in Grades 4–12 (Madaus, West, Harmon, Lomax, & Viator, 1992) and a study of the Effects of Standardized Testing (Kellaghan, Madaus, & Airasian, 1980).

The survey addressed the following topics:

◆ Information about state and district testing programs
◆ School climate
◆ Relationship of the mandated test to the state curriculum frameworks and standards
◆ Beliefs about teaching, learning, and assessment
◆ Classroom activities relating to instructional and testing practices
◆ Test preparation and administration
◆ Use and reporting of test results
◆ Professional development related to the state-mandated test
◆ Perceived effects of the state-mandated test

The Extent to Which Teachers Are Affected

Survey results were broken down according to whether responses came from elementary, middle, or high school teachers. One broad conclusion of the study was that state-mandated test results influence elementary teachers' instruction with much greater frequency than was the case for high school teachers. More elementary teachers reported using the results of the state-mandated test to aid in decisions about instruction, assess their own teaching effectiveness, provide feedback to parents, evaluate students, and group students in their class than did high school teachers. This may occur because the tests now focus elementary instruction on the standards tested, giving elementary teachers who must teach a variety of subjects much greater direction on what should be taught. These findings may also indicate that the state-mandated tests narrow or shape elementary curriculum to a greater degree than is the case at the high school level. Conversely, high school teachers' instruction may be least influenced by the state tests, because these teachers have always taught a specific subject area (e.g., math or history), and the test is measuring, for the most part, content they were already teaching. In general, high school teachers are least likely to use state-mandated test results. Middle school teachers fall somewhere between elementary and high school teachers in terms of subject matter specialization, and therefore the influence of the state test results on their instruction is somewhere between that for the other two groups, although generally closer to the elementary teachers.

A second broad conclusion was that, clearly, the stakes attached to the results of the state-mandated tests affect the extent to which teachers use them for various instructional and feedback activities. When the stakes are high for students and teachers, teachers use the results to the greatest extent; when they are low, they tend to use them less often.

More teachers in states with high stakes for students than in states with lesser stakes indicated that they spent more time on instruction in tested areas and less on instruction in noncore subject areas (e.g., fine arts, physical education, foreign languages, industrial/ vocational education) and on other activities (e.g., field trips, enrichment activities). In general, the influence of state testing programs on teachers' instructional practices is more closely related to the stakes for students than those for schools.

More elementary and middle school teachers than high school teachers reported that they increased the amount of time spent on tested areas and decreased the time spent on noncore subject areas and other activities. The impact of testing programs is generally stronger in elementary and middle schools than in high schools.

Across all types of testing programs, teachers reported increased time spent on subject areas that are tested and less time on areas not tested. They also reported that testing has influenced the time spent using a variety of instructional methods such as whole-group instruction, individual seatwork, cooperative learning, and using problems similar to those on the test.

The Problem of Pressure

Table 4.6 summarizes responses to a number of items about the pressure that teachers feel as a result of high-stakes testing. While teachers at all levels reported pressure, the numbers show that elementary and middle school teachers reported more pressure and stress than their high school colleagues.

TABLE 4.6   TEACHER PERCEPTIONS OF PRESSURE FROM HIGH-STAKES TESTING

Pressure-Related Items	Percentage Responding "Yes" School Type		
	Elementary	Middle	High
Teachers feel pressure from the district superintendent to raise scores on the test.	93	92	85
Teachers feel pressure from the building principal to raise scores on the test.	84	85	76
Teachers feel pressure from parents to raise scores on the state test.	56	56	51
Administrators in my school believe students' state-mandated test scores reflect the quality of teachers' instruction.	63	63	56
The state-mandated testing program leads some teachers in my school to teach in ways that contradict their own ideas of good educational practice.	78	73	67
There is so much pressure for high scores on the state-mandated test that teachers have little time to teach anything not on the test.	79	77	61
Teacher morale is high in my school.	47	44	43
Teachers in my school want to transfer out of the grade where the state-mandated test is administered.	43	29	24

SOURCE: J. Pedulla, L. M. Abrams, G. F. Madaus, et al. (2003), *Perceived Effects of State Mandated Testing Programs on Teaching and Learning: Findings from a National Survey of Teachers.* (Boston: National Board on Educational Testing and Public Policy)

A larger majority of teachers felt that there is so much pressure for high scores on state-mandated tests that they have little time to teach anything not covered on the tests. This response was most pronounced in states where high levels of accountability are demanded of districts, schools, teachers, and students. The finding supports the contention that state testing programs have the effect of narrowing the curriculum. Also, teachers in states with high-stakes were more likely than those in states with low-stakes to report feeling pressure from district superintendents and, to a lesser degree, principals to raise test scores.

Additional pressure is put on teachers because performance on statewide assessments is usually reported in newspapers. Parents and school administrators follow state-based assessment scores with the same intensity that they follow baseball pennant races and the Dow Jones averages. This interest produces pressure on schools and districts to "look good" relative to other schools and districts in the state. In Massachusetts for example, state-based assessment results have been reported not only on a district-by-district basis, but also in smaller groupings composed of districts

TECHNOLOGY AND ASSESSMENT

COMPUTER-BASED PRACTICE FOR STATE TESTING

Several states are using technology to help their students prepare for state tests by offering computer-based practice exams. These practice exams range from tutorials that mainly serve to guide students through an online testing format to those that test students' knowledge of content related to state standards.

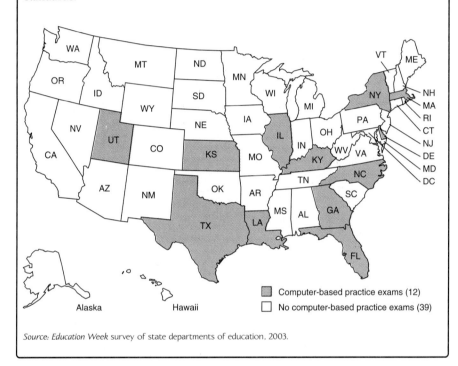

Source: *Education Week* survey of state departments of education. 2003.

of similar size, location, and socioeconomic status. A district's results are reported along with the results of similar districts in its group.

The consequences associated with most statewide standards and assessments put pressure on teachers, students, and administrators to obtain high scores.

The publication of these results creates pressure on the low-scoring districts to improve their performance. This message is echoed in districts across the nation when statewide assessment results are made public. Parents pressure administrators, who then pressure teachers to respond to the low performance, usually by rearranging the curriculum to spend more time on assessed topics. This pressure is magnified when comparisons are also made among the individual schools within a given school district. A general rule describing the impact of statewide assessment on instruction is that whenever the results of an assessment have important consequences for pupils, teachers, or school districts, the assessment will be taken seriously and there will be pressure to incorporate the assessed objectives into the school curriculum.

TABLE 4.7   TEACHER PERCEPTIONS OF FAIRNESS IN HIGH-STAKES TESTING

Student Achievement Items	Percentage Responding "Yes" School Type		
	Elementary	Middle	High
Scores on the state-mandated test results accurately reflect the quality of education students have received.	18	17	18
The state-mandated test is as accurate a measure of student achievement as a teacher's judgment.	17	18	17
The state-mandated test is *not* an accurate measure of what students who are acquiring English as a second language know and can do.	95	94	90
The state-mandated test is *not* an accurate measure of what minority students know and can do.	78	72	71
Score differences from year to year on the state-mandated test reflect changes in the characteristics of students rather than changes in school effectiveness.	83	85	77
Differences among schools on the state-mandated test are more a reflection of students' background characteristics than of school effectiveness.	85	88	83
Performance differences between minority and non-minority students are smaller on the state-mandated test than on commercially available standardized achievement tests (e.g., Stanford 9, ITBS, CAT).	21	22	20

SOURCE: J. Pedulla, L. M. Abrams, G. F. Madaus, et al. (2003), *Perceived Effects of State Mandated Testing Programs on Teaching and Learning: Findings from a National Survey of Teachers.* (Boston: National Board on Educational Testing and Public Policy)

The Problem of Fairness

In Table 4.7 we see that mainly elementary school teachers are most concerned about the fairness of high-stakes testing. The middle items in the table are key in this regard. Elementary teachers strongly agree that high-stakes testing does not measure accurately pupils who speak English as a second language or are members of a minority. They also view mandated tests as more reflective of student background characteristics than of school effectiveness.

While results suggest that high school teachers placed less value on state tests than teachers in lower grades, elementary teachers showed a greater concern for the accuracy of the test as an indicator of school effectiveness. Greater percentages of elementary (83 percent) and middle (85 percent) than high school teachers (77 percent) reported that school testing differences from year to year reflect changes in the characteristics of students rather than in school effectiveness.

In addition, while a substantial majority of teachers at all three levels agreed with the statements that state-mandated tests are not an accurate measure of what Limited English Proficiency and minority students know, once again the elementary teachers showed the highest concern.

Reconsidering High-Stakes Testing

olc

CHAPTER CASE STUDY

Visit the text OLC to read the case study for this chapter: A school district decides to use standardized achievement test results as a graduation requirement. Teachers spend a significant effort preparing students for the test. Some students inevitably don't pass, failing high school in spite of doing fairly well in their courses. How should the school district handle this situation?

www.mhhe.com/
airasian5e

One critic of high-stakes testing urges policymakers to recognize that federal, state, and local stakeholders (such as parents, students, and teachers) have differing needs, and performance measurements must take those differing needs into account (White & Medrich, 2002). A system of statewide testing that consumes weeks of teachers' and students' time every year to gather data on every student is not likely to be the best way to do this. The unfortunate fact is that data from most states' accountability tests have almost no value for improving teaching and learning (Popham, 2003). For state or federal policy-making purposes, there are more efficient ways to collect needed data than by employing every teacher to exhaustively test every student.

Another critic (Goldberg, 2004) summarizes many of the problems by asking the following questions:

1. Are the tests and testing movement as currently conceived worthwhile in the first place?
2. Are we really going to fail students who do everything right—except pass a single test?
3. How do we avoid nonrandom human error and other test problems to create an accurate assessment system?
4. What is the probable effect of a tough retention policy that requires students to pass a high-stakes test or repeat a grade? Higher drop-out rates seem likely.

Another critic from Nebraska, a state which has resisted the regimentation of initiatives like No Child Left Behind (which we will discuss shortly), sees a great danger when top-down accountability programs cause teachers to feel disempowered. Calling teachers the key to genuine change, he urges them to "turn the tables" by publicly asking crucial questions and letting voters and policymakers know what is educationally best for their students. He offers 10 questions for teachers to raise about any system of accountability (Gallagher, 2004):

1. Any accountability system should regard classroom teachers as *leaders.* Does this one?
2. Does the system focus on building capacity, or merely on control?

3. Does the system foster commitment, or merely compliance?

4. Does the system promote an integration of accountability with actual school improvement?

5. Does it risk the complexity that is an inherent part of education, rather than demand simplicity?

6. Does it include all students or merely those on the margins?

7. Does it engage all teachers?

8. Does it engage all other relevant stakeholders?

9. Does it keep pedagogy at its center?

10. Does it encourage *high-impact* assessment that truly benefits students and teachers, or simply *high-stakes* assessment that merely punishes them?

Motivating Pupils and Teachers for Statewide Testing

In addition to becoming aware of state standards and building them into their classroom teaching in a balanced way, how can teachers motivate pupils to do their best on these tests? Table 4.8 lists strategies used in various states (some more widely than others). That such strategies are being used is testimony to the impact of high-stakes testing on American education.

TABLE 4.8   STRATEGIES TO MOTIVATE PUPILS TO STUDY FOR STATEWIDE ASSESSMENTS

Discuss importance of good performance	Require/recommend summer school
Hold assemblies to motivate students	Retain students in grade
Publicly recognize students for good performance	Use scores for assigning grades
	Place students in classes
Schedule special activities (e.g., pizza party, field trips)	Exempt students who do well from required course work
Link performance to eligibility in extracurricular activities	Examine your state to determine the impact of high stakes in your state.
Give prizes to reward students	

SOURCE: J. Pedulla, L. M. Abrams, G. F. Madaus, et al. (2003), *Perceived Effects of State Mandated Testing Programs on Teaching and Learning: Findings from a National Survey of Teachers* (Boston: National Board on Educational Testing and Public Policy).

FIGURE 4.7
Recommendations for Preparing Pupils and Teachers for High-stakes and No Child Left Behind Testing.

1. Recognize and inform teachers about the nature of the assessment.
2. If possible, practice items similar to those in the tests.
3. Provide quality classroom materials as well as guidelines for aligning instruction and assessment.
4. Recognize and inform teachers and pupils about the cognitive assessments linked to assessment.
5. Avoid comparisons of teachers and schools—this approach limits useful and important teacher and school interactions.

The survey summary report also included a set of recommendations to states, shown in Figure 4.7.

Staying Focused on Quality in the Classroom

Coping with the pressures of high-stakes testing and other mandates from above may be easiest for the teacher who has clear personal and professional standards for the proper role of assessment in the classroom. Reiterating earlier themes from this book, here are five basic questions with which to judge the soundness of one's own approach to assessment (Popham, 2003):

♦ Do my classroom assessments measure genuinely worthwhile skills and knowledge?
♦ Will I be able to promote my students' mastery of what is measured in my classroom assessments?
♦ Can I describe what skills and knowledge my classroom tests measure in language that is clear enough for my own instructional planning?
♦ Do my classroom assessments yield results that allow me to tell which parts of my instruction were effective or ineffective?
♦ Do my classroom tests take too much time away from my instruction?

NO CHILD LEFT BEHIND

The most recent major effort to improve education in the United States has taken the form of federal legislation called No Child Left Behind (NCLB). NCLB was passed in January 2002, beginning a multiyear project to improve the educational performance of American educational administrators, schools, and teachers. NCLB is a high-stakes accountability program very similar to those described earlier for the states.

Expectations and Outcomes of NCLB

As might be expected, NCLB encompasses a broad range of expectations and outcomes, a key aspect of which is accountability. Annual "report cards" will provide comparative information on the quality of schools. It is hoped this will also empower parents to make more informed choices about their children's education. Other accountability features include the following:

The No Child Left Behind legislation is extremely ambitious in terms of what schools and states are going to be expected to do.

1. All states must submit plans and evidence of content and achievement standards and aligned assessments, school report cards, procedures, and statewide systems for holding schools and districts accountable for the achievement of their students. States must develop a single statewide accountability system to determine the progress of all public schools, districts, and the state overall.

2. Results of assessments in reading or language arts and mathematics will be used as the primary measure of school, district, and state progress. As a target, all students will be at or above proficiency in these subject areas by the end of the 2013–2014 school year. While the results of the annual science assessments will not be included in the determinations, the results must be included in the annual state and district reports consistent with the statute and regulations. States and districts were required to issue their first reports at the beginning of the 2002–2003 school year.

3. Data will be disaggregated for students by poverty levels, race, ethnicities, disabilities, and limited English speakers.

4. States also must report on school safety on a school-by-school basis.

5. Districts and schools that do not make sufficient yearly progress toward state proficiency goals for their students will be targeted for assistance.

It is important to keep in mind the link between state high-stakes testing and NCLB. They are not separate entities; rather, they will work together as supporting activities, with each state continuing to have its own assessment methods, types of teaching, and so on. However, NCLB is providing money to carry on research related to high-stakes standards, and will make judgments about the quality of the standards. For example, by the 2005–2006 school year, states must develop and implement assessments annually in reading and mathematics for grades 3 through 8, and at least once in grades 10 through 12. By 2008–2009, states also must administer science assessments at least once in grades 3 through 5, grades 6 through 9, and grades 10 through 12. These assessments must be aligned (brought into agreement) with state academic content and achievement standards. Deciding how to measure whether there is an effective alignment is a challenge in itself (Bhola, Impara, & Buckendahl, 2003). Also, the assessments must involve multiple measures, including measures of higher-order thinking and understanding.

Current Status of NCLB

It remains to be seen what NCLB will accomplish and how much public support it will have.

According to a poll taken in May and June of 2003, the American public felt generally ignorant of what NCLB was actually about. Even among parents of public school children, 78 percent said they knew "very little" or "nothing at all" about it (Rose & Gallup, 2003). The results of the poll also suggested that knowing more about NCLB was not likely to lead to greater public support for it.

NCLB is in a formative period. While high-stakes testing has existed for a number of years, the melding of it with NCLB is in its infancy. As time passes, we will have a better perspective on the linking of state programs and NCLB. It is likely that, over time, practice and experience will alter some aspects of both.

Though little discussed, a critical need continues for highly accurate, consistent measurements of school, teacher, and administrator performance.

Federal Accommodations for Disabilities

The NCLB legislation did not address the issue of how the assessment of pupils requiring accommodations for disabilities might be standardized or regulated across the states. This becomes an issue because educators and advocates want schools to be accountable for high standards in teaching these pupils, but they do not want schools or school districts to be penalized because certain pupils with disabilities cannot succeed at grade-level, standards-based assessments.

However, federal regulations issued in December 2003 give states and districts permission to administer alternate assessments that do not use grade-level standards to students with special needs who cannot take the grade-level tests even with accommodations (Goldstein, 2003). To prevent this allowance from becoming a "loophole" for states in the assessment process, the regulation says that only 1 percent of students can be tested in this way and have their scores counted by the state toward showing adequate yearly progress.

Controversial Issues for NCLB

The partnership concept of NCLB raises many questions and possible problems. Here are a few of them in brief:

1. The NCLB legislation is extremely ambiguous in terms of what schools and states are expected to do.

2. Can NCLB be equitable? Standards are likely to be harder in one state than another, and performance may vary for social and economic reasons over which the state has little control. Will NCLB turn out to reward some states for lowering their standards or other states for performing well on less demanding standards? State-to-state comparability has been an elusive goal since the early 1960s. It seems unlikely that NCLB can be applied equitably across all states.

3. Can accountability work in education? Accountabilty has worked in for-profit sectors of our economy like agriculture and industry. But education is not about making profits. If accountability is mainly a financial concept, how can it work in education?

4. Annual test results are not a good measure of school quality, especially for relatively small schools. Anyone who has taught knows that there are year-to-year differences in how students respond. Will small schools especially be penalized because of statistical fluctuations in performance? Will schools fall into the same trap as industries that constantly seek short-term profits or other signs of success at the expense of long-term gains?

5. What is the government's expectation? How realistic is it to expect school performance to improve quickly and dramatically as a result of federal legislation? Is federal regulation—with its costs in time and money—really the way to improve classroom teaching?

NCLB takes a concept of accountability that has worked in agriculture and industry and applies it to education, but to expect school performance to improve dramatically because of federal accountability legislation is probably wishful thinking.

One problem with rigid accountability systems is obvious to anyone who has taught in a classroom: there are year-to-year differences in how students respond.

CHAPTER SUMMARY

◆ Textbooks are available in many forms and levels. Assessments from textbooks are useful, but must be considered in terms of the intended desired outcome.

◆ The use of a textbook needs to be tailored to the objectives of the individual classroom teacher and the needs of his or her pupils.

◆ Planning instruction is greatly influenced by textbooks and their accompanying aids and resources. Although it is appealing to uncritically accept textbook objectives, plans, activities, and assessments, teachers must remember that every class is different. They must assess the textbook and its resources in light of their own class's unique needs, readiness, and learning styles.

◆ Statewide standards describe outcomes that pupils in a state are expected to learn. One important aim of statewide standards is to homogenize desired outcomes statewide. Almost every state has developed statewide standards.

◆ Standards are usually accompanied by statewide assessments that provide information about how pupils, teachers, or schools are doing to meet the state standards.

olc

CHAPTER REVIEW

Visit Chapter 4 of the Online Learning Center at **www.mhhe.com/ airasian5e** to take chapter quizzes, link to related websites, read PowerWeb articles and news feed updates, and access study tools, including the case study referenced in the chapter.

♦ Different states vary greatly in the types of statewide testing they use.

♦ High-stakes testing does have a considerable impact on teaching. Elementary school teachers experience more pressure from state-mandated assessment than teachers in higher grades, possibly because state expectations currently constrain the curriculum most closely in the lower grades.

♦ The challenge of high-stakes testing is to prepare pupils to reach grade-level expectations for their state without narrowing the curriculum to constantly "teaching to the test."

♦ Another criticism of statewide testing is that it may not fairly assess pupils who come from minority groups or whose first language is not English.

♦ No Child Left Behind is a federal program that aims at building a national system of accountability into statewide standards and assessment. The program is in its infancy, but parts of it are already in place.

QUESTIONS FOR DISCUSSION

1. Have you ever noticed one of your teachers pursuing a teaching objective that wasn't mirrored in the textbook you were using? What challenges or opportunities did that create?

2. What role should textbook materials play in instructional planning and assessment?

3. What system of statewide standards is in place in the state where you went to school or where you intend to teach? What evidence have you seen of this system at the classroom level? Is your state typical?

4. What kinds of concerns, efforts, and influences are shaping state-mandated testing? Is it good that these efforts are often viewed as "high stakes"?

5. How do you think the No Child Left Behind legislation is likely to play out in coming years? Is the net effect likely to be positive? How so?

5. Is any pupil more likely to be left behind because of No Child Left Behind?

ACTIVITIES

1. Visit your curriculum library or a local school to examine a set of textbook materials. Select a chapter from the teacher's edition and list all the materials and activities in or related to the chapter. Evaluate what you find as objectives and assessment tools.

2. Research three different state-mandated assessment programs (including the state in which you plan to teach) by finding sample test statewide assessments items from each. Select a grade and compare the items for that grade across the three states.

3. Find out what "campus-wide standards" exist for student performance and assessment at your college or university. Write a brief plan for improving existing standards or for creating new ones.

REVIEW QUESTIONS

1. What three criteria should teachers use to screen textbook objectives? Why?

2. What will make a textbook assessment valid or invalid as a classroom assessment tool? How should teachers evaluate and make use of textbook tests?

3. How widespread are statewide standards? What do they generally contain?

4. How are statewide standards and assessments created?

5. What are some good and bad effects of high-stakes testing on teachers and pupils at different levels of education?

6. What is No Child Left Behind? How is it related to state standards and state assessments?

7. What is the promise of No Child Left Behind? What are some possible problems?

REFERENCES

Amrein, A. L., Berliner, D. C. (2003). The effects of high-stakes testing on student motivation and learning. *Educational Leadership, 60*(5), 32–38.

Bhola, D. S., Impara, J. C., Buckendahl, C. W. (2003). Aligning tests with states' content standards: Methods and issues. *Educational Measurements: Issues and Practices, 22* (3), 21–27.

Center on Education Policy (2002). *State high school exit exams: A baseline report.* Washington, DC: Center on Education Policy.

Daniels, H., Zemelman S. (2004). Out with textbooks, in with learning. *Educational Leadership, 61*(4), 36–40.

Gallagher, C. W. (2004). Training the accountability tables: Ten progressive lessons from one 'backward' state. *Phi Delta Kappan,* January 352–360.

Goldberg, M. F. (2004). The test mess. *Phi Delta Kappan, (85)* 5,361–366.

Goldstein, L., "Final Rules Allow Alternate Assessments," *Education Week on the Web,* December 10, 2003.

Haney, W. (2000). The myth of the Texas miracle in education. *Education Policy Analysis Archives,* 8(41). Retrieved April 13, 2001 from http://epaa.asu.edu/epaa/v8n41.

Kellaghan, T., Madaus, G., & Airasian, P. (1980). *The effects of standardized testing.* Educational Research Centre: St. Patrick's College, Dublin, Ireland and Boston College: Chestnut Hill, MA.

Koretz, D., Mitchell, K., Barron, S., & Keith, S. (1996). *Final report: Perceived effects of the Maryland school performance assessment program.* (CSE Technical Report 409). Los Angeles: National Center for Research on Evaluation, Standards, and Student Testing.

Madaus, G., West, M., Harmon, M., Lomax, R., & Viator, K. (1992). *The influence of testing on teaching math and science in grades 4–12.* Boston: Center for the Study of Testing, Evaluation, and Educational Policy, Boston College.

North Carolina Department of Public Instruction (1992). Quick reference for parents and teachers: Testing at various grade levels. *Parent Involvement,* September–October.

Pedulla J., Abrams, L. M., Madaus, G. F., and others. (2003). *Perceived Effects of State Mandated Testing Programs on Teaching and Learning: Findings from a National Survey of Teachers.* Boston: National Board on Educational Testing and Public Policy.

Popham, W. J. (2003). The seductive allure of data. *Educational Leadership, (60)* 5, 48–51.

Quality Counts 2004. Count me in, special education in an era of standards. *Education Week on the Web, 23 (17),* 104.

Rose, L. C, Gallup, A. M. (2003). The 35th annual Phi Delta Kappa/Gallup poll of the public's attitudes toward the public schools. *Phi Delta Kappan, (85)* 1, 41–52.

Smith, M., Nobel, A., Heinecke, W., Seck, M., Parish, C., Cabay, M. et al. (1997). *Reforming schools by reforming assessment: Consequences of the Arizona student assessment program (ASAP): Equity and teacher capacity building.* (CSE Technical Report 425). Los Angeles: University of California. National Center for Research on Evaluation, Standards, and Student Testing.

Urdan, T. & Paris, S. (1994). Teachers' perceptions of standardized achievement tests. *Educational Policy, 8*(2), 137–156.

White, R., Medrich, E. (2002). Performance measurement for accountability: Lessons from the school-to-work experience. *Phi Delta Kappan, (84)* 4, 289–294.

ASSESSMENT DURING INSTRUCTION

KEY TOPICS

- *Assessment Tasks during Instruction*

- *Validity and Reliability in Instructional Assessment*

- *Improving Assessment during Instruction*

- *Questioning: Purposes and Strategies*

- *Accommodations during Instruction*

CHAPTER OBJECTIVES

After reading this chapter, you will be able to:

♦ Distinguish between planning and instructional assessment
♦ Describe what teachers do in the course of instructional assessment
♦ Explain the use of level of tolerance and practical knowledge
♦ Identify problems that influence validity and reliability in instructional assessment
♦ Write or ask higher-level and lower-level questions and convergent and divergent questions
♦ Cite strategies for effective questioning
♦ Accommodate students with disabilities during instruction and instructional assessment

THINKING ABOUT TEACHING

What are the most important activities a teacher should prepare for while planning for instruction?

Instructional assessment refers to those assessments made during instruction that indicate how well the lesson is going.

The assessment activities that teachers carry out when planning instruction are very different from those carried out when delivering instruction as Table 5.1 shows. Planning assessments are developed during quiet time, when the teacher can reflect and try to identify appropriate objectives, content topics, and assessment activities for pupils. Instructional assessments take place on the firing line, during teaching, and are focused upon making instantaneous and very specific decisions about what to do, say, or ask next in order to keep instruction flowing smoothly. Planning instruction allows the teacher to consider, weigh, and synthesize many kinds of information in making decisions. Conversely, assessments during instruction require the teacher to rely heavily on informal pupil cues such as attention, facial expressions, posture, and questions.

TABLE 5.1 CHARACTERISTICS OF PLANNING AND INSTRUCTIONAL ASSESSMENTS	
Planning Assessment	**Instructional Assessment**
1. Occurs before or after instruction	1. Occurs during instruction
2. Carried out away from class	2. Carried out in front of class
3. Allows for reflective decisions	3. Requires instantaneous decisions
4. Focuses on identifying objectives, content, and activities	4. Focuses on pupil reactions to content and activities presented
5. Based on many kinds of formal and informal evidence	5. Based mainly on informal pupil cues and responses

But of course planning and delivering instruction are integrally related. The instructional process constantly cycles from planning instruction to delivering instruction to revised planning to delivering, and so on. There is a logical, ongoing, and natural link between the two processes and both are necessary for successful teaching.

Although good planning reduces uncertainty during instruction, it rarely eliminates it. The teaching process must, to some extent, be free-flowing and adaptable, allowing for interruptions, digressions, and unexpected happenings. What the teacher does influences what the pupils do, which in turn influences what the teacher does, and so on throughout the instructional process. To understand the process of assessment during instruction, it is necessary to look beyond the teacher's written lesson plans to examine the classroom as a learning society.

Good planning reduces uncertainty. Rather than preventing a teacher from taking advantage of unexpected teaching opportunities, it frees the teacher to watch for such moments and adapt instruction.

This chapter discusses how teachers think of instructional assessment, how they carry it out, and how they can ensure the quality of their ongoing assessment. It goes into depth about the use of questioning and also describes accommodations appropriate for students with disabilities during instruction and in-class assessments.

ASSESSMENT TASKS DURING INSTRUCTION

Once instruction begins, teachers carry on two tasks: they deliver the instruction that they have planned and they constantly assess the progress and success of their instruction in order to modify it if necessary. For many reasons, things do not always go as planned. Interruptions, misjudgments about pupil readiness and attention, shifts in pupil interest, and various events (e.g., fire drills, assemblies, squawk box interruptions) can alter planned instruction. As a result, the teacher must constantly sense the mood and learning of the class to make decisions about what to do next. Thus, once the teacher initiates instruction, he or she engages in an ongoing process of assessing its progress and deciding about pupils' reactions to it.

Note that when planning instruction, the focus is on pupil characteristics, readiness, subject matter objectives, and learning activities. Once instruction actually begins, the focus shifts to more action-oriented concerns, especially on how pupils are reacting to the instructional process. This shift is logical, of course, the result of being caught up in the here and now of a complex teaching process. During instruction, teachers collect assessment data to help monitor factors such as:

◆ Interest level of individual pupils and the class as a whole
◆ Apparent or potential behavior problems
◆ Appropriateness of the instructional technique or activity being used
◆ Most appropriate pupil to call on next

- ♦ Adequacy of a pupil's answer
- ♦ Pace of instruction
- ♦ Usefulness and consequences of pupils' questions
- ♦ Smoothness of transitions from one concept to another and from one activity to another
- ♦ Suitability of examples used to explain concepts
- ♦ Degree of comprehension on the part of individual pupils and the class as a whole
- ♦ Desirability of starting or ending a particular activity

Such monitoring, of course, is a complicated task, since instruction, assessment, and decision making are taking place almost simultaneously. For example, during class discussion:

> . . . a teacher must listen to student answers, watch other students for signs of comprehension or confusion, formulate the next question, and scan the class for possible misbehavior. At the same time, the teacher must attend to the pace of the discussion, the sequence of selecting students to answer, the relevance and quality of the answers, and the logical development of the content. When the class is divided into small groups, the number of simultaneous events increases, and the teacher must monitor and regulate several different activities at once (Doyle, 1986).

Certainly, many decisions are required during instruction, and these decisions, in turn, are informed by assessments that teachers make as part of the instructional process.

Figure 5.1 illustrates this process of ongoing assessment. Once *teaching* begins, the teacher continually *assesses* its progress by observing pupil reactions and asking them questions. On the basis of these reactions and

FIGURE 5.1
Steps in Instructional Assessment.

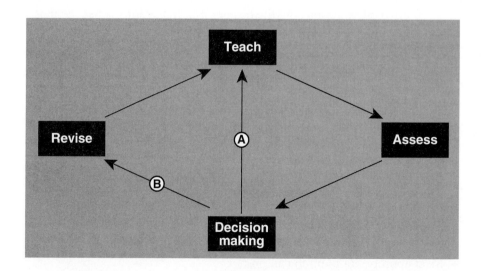

responses, the teacher makes a *decision* about how instruction is going. If the teacher decides that the lesson is progressing satisfactorily, he or she continues teaching as planned (path A). If the teacher senses a problem, such as lack of pupil understanding or interest, the planned instructional activity should be *revised* to alleviate the problem and another teaching activity or strategy initiated (path B). This cycle is repeated many times in the course of a single lesson.

Teachers' Thinking during Instruction

A large proportion of teachers' thinking during instruction concerns the adequacy of their instruction. Teachers described much of their thinking in terms such as these:

I was thinking about the need for another example of this concept.

I was trying to get him to see the relationship between the Treaty of Versailles and Hitler's rise to power without actually telling him.

I was thinking about a worksheet that would reinforce the idea.

I decided that it was necessary to review yesterday's lesson.

Teachers' thoughts are particularly concerned with the *effect* of instruction on pupils; that is, how much they are attending to and profiting from instruction. This form of teacher thinking is closest to the concept of reading the audience and is expressed through thoughts such as:

Teachers tend to look more for signs of student engagement than of student learning.

I realized that they didn't understand the concept of borrowing at all.

I thought, at least everyone is concentrating on the topic.

I figured I'd better call on Larry, just to make sure he was with us.

I asked Mike to explain the material because I thought he would know it and could explain it in a way many pupils could understand.

Assessing Abnormal and Normal Behavior

Over time, through observations and experience, teachers establish **levels of tolerance** that indicate what is normal pupil or class behavior. These tolerance levels vary from class to class and teacher to teacher. In some classrooms, for example, "normal" tolerance of noise during seatwork is very low; pupils are not permitted to interact, converse, or speak out. In other classrooms, "normal" tolerance permits more noise, pupil movement around the room, and conversation. Tolerance levels are also established for individual pupils. When we hear a teacher say things like, "Tariq acted out much more than usual today. He must be upset about something"; "Anush is mad at her

Instructional assessment includes noticing abnormal behavior in order to maintain the right level of tolerance.

parents again because she had that sulky expression and didn't say a word in class"; or "Eugenio turned in a sloppy, unfinished homework assignment today. Something's wrong," we are witnessing teacher decision making based upon pupil behaviors that are "out of tolerance" based upon normal pupil behavior.

Part of the process of "reading" the class during instruction involves knowing when the class or some pupils are exhibiting out-of-tolerance behaviors that call for a response from the teacher. Thus, a large proportion of teachers' decisions during instruction result from monitoring signs that tell the teacher whether the pupils' behavior is in or out of tolerance.

But teachers' decisions during instruction are not based solely on perceptions of unusual pupil behavior. Many relate to normal classroom routines. For example, many teacher decisions are the result of a pupil's question ("If Pedro doesn't understand, I'd better review this topic for the whole class") or the teacher's need to choose a pupil to respond during instruction ("Lilli hasn't raised her hand to answer for three days; I'll call on her"). Likewise, when there is a transition point in the lesson from one activity to another, when the teacher anticipates a problem teaching a concept, when there is insufficient time to complete planned activities, or when there is a shortage of materials, the teacher must make a decision about the course and nature of subsequent instruction.

The Need for Practical Knowledge

Caught up in the special demands of instruction, teachers rarely can deal with broad issues, questions, or decisions. Instead, they deal with specific pupils and situations. A teacher must focus on disciplining Xavier when he misbehaves, not on trying to apply general theories of classroom behavior and management. A teacher must have at his or her fingertips insights and strategies that will suggest how to explain a difficult concept to Joyce, not a list of general techniques for teaching complex principles. Furthermore, disciplining Xavier or explaining something to Joyce probably call for different techniques than disciplining Anastasia or explaining something to Tabatha. Teachers must know who can be pushed for a correct answer, who responds to reinforcement, who needs encouragement, and who can be relied on to help Martha with her accommodation.

While general theories of behavior or instruction provide some direction for a teacher, they cannot alone identify the reason why Clarise can't understand or Derrick won't listen. The teachers of Clarise and Derrick must pull together their own personal knowledge about these pupils to decide the best course of action to take. They must have a store of practical knowledge that fits pupils and the class as a whole to enable them to carry out instruction and manage the classroom.

Most of the observations, interpretations, and decisions that occur during instruction are made on the basis of the teacher's practical knowledge of the pupils. **Practical knowledge** comprises those beliefs, insights, perceptions, and habits that enable teachers to do their work in school and in the classroom. Practical knowledge, in contrast to theoretical knowledge, is time-bound and situation-specific. It is relevant to a particular class and to particular individuals in the class. It changes from year to year as the characteristics of pupils and the class change. Each class has its own personality, strengths, weaknesses, and challenges, and every year the teacher must rely on early assessments to help build up a new store of practical knowledge about the new class. Consider how the following teacher comments underscore the importance of practical knowledge.

> . . . the teacher's job is to recognize each student's particular needs, even very minor needs. The amount of attention the teacher gives a student or the tone of voice used to speak to or reprimand a student must be considered in terms of the student's individual needs and makeup. Moreover, the teacher must recognize when a student is troubled, simply by the look on his or her face. The teacher must recognize potential behavior problems before they occur and know how to prevent them.

> The room was alive with enthusiasm and curiosity; 20 of the 21 students were watching me demonstrate exchanging air from one underwater cup to another to displace the water. Letty's attention was everywhere but on the experiment, so I asked Letty to come up to the front and try to displace the water with air. Knowing Letty, I knew that this would gain her interest, but not make her uncomfortable. Letty got up and smiled as she hurried to the front of the room to demonstrate to the class. If I had tried that with Peter or James, they would have fallen apart.

> Of course every child is different. Some children will do anything to impress a class. Those kids I ask to speak to later, alone. Another child I may scold in front of his or her peers. There is one child who all I have to do is give a look and that's enough. Teaching and discipline are heavily based on personality. What works for one pupil or class may not be the solution for another.

Assessment Indicators during Instruction

Given the pace and complexity of instructional activities and the need to keep instruction flowing smoothly, it is no surprise that teachers rely much more heavily on informal than formal indications to monitor their instruction. They rely on behavioral cues from the students, such as attention or facial expressions, rather than more formal paper-and-pencil assessments. The latter could break the flow of the lesson and pupil involvement.

To determine what types of indicators teachers use to monitor and judge the success of their instruction, they were asked how they knew when their instruction was successful. Their responses included the following:

> It is easy to tell when things are not running as planned. Children get impatient; facial expressions become contorted; their body language, voice level, and eyes tell the story of their reaction to instruction.

Teachers should supplement their informal assessments of instruction with formal feedback such as homework, worksheets, and lesson reviews.

Oral questioning is the most common form of instructional assessment.

Good teachers can sense the success or failure of their instruction just as a skillful actor can sense the reaction of an audience.

The assessment information that teachers gather during instruction comes mostly from informal observation of their pupils.

olc
CHAPTER CASE STUDY

Visit the text OLC to read the case of Karen Lee, a first-year Spanish teacher. Karen takes over a high school Spanish III class midyear and faces an unruly group of students. One student in particular seems determined to make her miserable.

www.mhhe.com/ airasian5e

If my class is daydreaming—looking blankly out the window and unresponsive— that tells me something. At times like these I have to decide what to do, since I don't want the pupils to think that by acting disinterested they always can make me change my plans.

Some examples of a good lesson are when the pupils are eager to be called on, raise their hands, give enthusiastic answers, look straight at me, scream out answers, show excitement in their eyes. During a bad lesson, the kids have their heads on the desk, look around the room, play with little objects at their desks, talk to their neighbor, or go to the bathroom in droves.

Responding to a variety of immediate classroom needs allows teachers little time to reflect on what they are doing or the motives for their actions. Nonetheless, most teachers feel that they have a good sense of their instructional success, which implies that they do assess many environmental cues.

To summarize this section, the direction, flow, and pace of instruction are dictated by the chemistry of the classroom at any given time. The teacher's assessment task during instruction is to monitor the progress and success of the instruction. In most classrooms, monitoring boils down to assessing the appropriateness of the instructional procedures and the pupils' reaction to them. Decisions that teachers make during instruction are prompted by (1) unusual pupil behavior that requires a response or reaction from the teacher and (2) typical issues that arise during instruction, such as responding to a pupil's question, deciding whom to call on next, and deciding whether to move on to the next topic. The assessment information that teachers gather when they monitor their instruction comes mostly from informal observations of the pupils. These cues, plus the teacher's knowledge of the class, support the quick assessments and decisions that teachers make during classroom instruction. Assessments of abnormal behavior help to maintain whatever level of tolerance the teacher intends to allow. Above all, ongoing assessment is rooted in a teacher's practical knowledge of the class.

VALIDITY AND RELIABILITY IN INSTRUCTIONAL ASSESSMENT

Because there is little time for teachers to reflect on what is observed or to collect additional information during instruction, they must make decisions and act on the basis of incomplete and uncertain evidence. Even so, good teachers are quite successful in overcoming these difficulties and do carry out informative instructional assessments. In spite of the success of some teachers, however, it would be naive and inappropriate to overlook problems of quality associated with instructional assessment.

Problems That Affect Instructional Validity

Validity relates to collecting evidence that will help teachers correctly interpret observed pupil performance and make appropriate decisions about pupils' attention, comprehension, and learning as well as the pace and suitability of the instructional activities. As mentioned previously, during instruction, teachers assess these areas mainly by observing pupil attentiveness and by the verbal reactions and responses of their pupils. An important validity question is, do these pupil indicators provide the information teachers need to make appropriate decisions about instructional success? Two potential threats to validity are (1) the lack of objectivity by teachers when judging their own instruction and (2) the incompleteness of the evidence used to make decisions about instruction and pupil learning.

Objectivity of the Teacher as an Observer

Being a participant in the instructional process can make it difficult for the teacher to be a dispassionate, detached observer who can make unbiased judgments about his or her own instruction. Teachers have a stake in the success of instruction and derive their primary rewards from it; they have a strong personal and professional investment in the instructional process. Every time teachers make a favorable judgment about instruction or pupil learning, they are also rewarding themselves. Because teachers rely heavily on their observations to assess instruction, it can be asked whether teachers see only what they want to see—that is, only those things that will give them reinforcement. If so, the evidence they use to assess their instruction is potentially invalid.

Because teachers want to feel good about their instruction, there is the danger that they will look only for positive student reactions.

Evidence of invalid assessments of instruction is not hard to find. For example, the types of questions teachers ask can influence their sense of personal effectiveness. Simple, factual questions are likely to produce more correct pupil responses than open-ended, complex ones. Concentration on lower-level rote skills and information, rather than on higher-level skills and processes, can ensure more pupil participation and mastery. Teacher comments, such as "This topic is too hard for my pupils, so I'll skip over it," may be a realistic appraisal of pupil readiness or they may simply be a way for teachers to avoid instructional disappointments. In short, the desire to achieve teaching satisfaction may bias teachers' observations and produce invalid conclusions about the success of instruction, with harmful consequences for pupils.

Teachers sometimes ask easy, low-level questions in order to get correct answers that make them feel good about their instruction.

Bias also occurs when a factor such as race, native language, gender, or disability influences scoring so that a pupil so labeled receives a higher or lower score than he or she otherwise would *(Joint Committee on Standards for Educational Evaluation, 2003).*

Incompleteness of Instructional Indicators

The primary indicators that teachers use to monitor instruction are those that are most readily available, most quickly surveyed, and least intrusive: reactions from students such as facial expressions, posture, participation, questions, and attending. Using such indicators, teachers "read" a pupil or the class and judge the success of their teaching. But the real criterion of teachers' instructional success is *pupil achievement.* Although the *process* of instruction—its flow, pace, and student reactions—is important and should be assessed, it does not provide direct evidence of pupil learning. It deals only with intermediate events that may or may not lead to a more important outcome, namely, learning.

Instructional assessment should focus on student learning as well as student involvement.

Being attentive and involved in instruction is desirable, but does not necessarily mean that learning is taking place. Thus, valid assessment of instruction should include appropriate information about both pupil involvement and pupil learning. If it does not or if it focuses only on pupil interest and facial expressions, judgments about the ultimate goal—how well pupils are learning—may be invalid.

Problems That Affect Instructional Reliability

Reliability is concerned with the stability or consistency of the assessment data that are collected. However, one of the features of teaching is the fast-changing nature of instruction. If the message a teacher gets from his or her observations changes each time new evidence is gathered, the teacher cannot rely upon that evidence to help in decision making. Since teachers obtain most of their information about the success of instruction by observing their pupils, the broader the group of pupils observed, the more reliable the information.

Instructional assessment that involves feedback from a broad range of students is more reliable than assessments based on the reactions of one or two students.

Often because of seating arrangements or an unconscious preference for certain pupils, teachers tend to use an overly narrow sample of pupils when assessing the success of instruction. This inadequate sampling, of course, reduces the reliability of their assessment. It must be understood, however, that problems of narrow sampling during instruction result as much from the rapidity of classroom events as from the teacher's inattention to particular class members.

Key Assessment Tools 5.1 summarizes validity and reliability problems in instructional assessment.

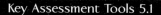

Key Assessment Tools 5.1

VALIDITY AND RELIABILITY PROBLEMS
OF INSTRUCTIONAL ASSESSMENT

Validity Problems

1. Lack of objectivity by the classroom teacher

2. Concentrating instruction on objectives and assessments that will provide the teacher maximum reinforcement but which narrow instruction for pupils

3. Focusing on instructional process indicators (e.g., facial expressions, posture, or participation) without also considering instructional outcome indicators (e.g., pupil learning)

Reliability Problems

1. Fast pace of classroom activities and decision making inhibit the collection of corroborative evidence

2. Focusing on a limited number of pupils to obtain information about the process of instruction and pupil learning

---

IMPROVING ASSESSMENT DURING INSTRUCTION

In basketball we often talk about a player who has a shooting "touch." Beyond the mechanics of knowing how to shoot a basketball, the player has an intangible ability to put the ball into the basket with unusual success. Likewise, an actor's ability to "read" the audience and react to it goes beyond the technical aspects of acting; it involves a special sensitivity to the audience. Just as the basketball player needs "touch" and the actor must be able to "read" an audience, successful instructional assessment depends upon a teacher's "feel" for the instructional process. This "feel" is dependent in large measure upon the teacher's early assessments and practical knowledge of the pupils' typical behavior. It permits the teacher to anticipate instructional problems, select the correct instructional procedure from the many options available, and utilize a few valid indicators to determine how instruction is going.

Assessments during instruction depend in some measure on an intangible, unarticulated process. To try to describe the instructional assessment process by spelling out a detailed list of rules and procedures would be to corrupt the natural flow of classroom events and likely destroy the process altogether. Teachers will always have to rely in part upon their "feel" for the classroom situation when gathering assessment information and making decisions during instruction. However, this does not mean that the process cannot be made more valid and reliable, so that decision making is improved and pupil learning enhanced.

To improve assessment during instruction does not mean to make the teacher an automaton blindly following a set of prescribed rules. It is, after all, the feel of teachers for their pupils and classroom situations that makes it impossible for machines to replace teachers. However, keeping the following recommendations in mind during instruction should improve the validity and reliability of the assessment process.

Great teachers will always be those who develop a feel for how things are going, moment by moment in the classroom.

1. *Include a broad sample of pupils when assessing instruction.* As discussed earlier, teachers evaluate themselves largely in terms of pupil involvement and attention during instruction. Consequently, they may observe or call on only those higher-achieving pupils whose behaviors or answers are likely to reinforce their perception of instructional success. Likewise they may be tempted to focus on lower-level instructional activities that are more easily attained by their pupils. To avoid these pitfalls, teachers must make an effort to sample a wide range of pupils in the class.

    Do not wait for hands to be raised to determine if pupils are following what is going on. Scan the room when a question is posed, surveying the eyes of the pupils. If they know the answer, they will look you in the eye and raise their hands. If they look away, they probably don't understand the question or don't know the answer. Directing attention only at the few pupils who always know the answer might cause the teacher to lose touch with the class as a whole. Unless the teacher attends to a wide range of pupils, evidence about the progress and success of instruction may be unreliable.

2. *Supplement informal assessment information with more formal information about pupil learning.* To get a more complete and reliable picture of instructional success, teachers should supplement their informal observations with more formal types of evidence taken from sources such as homework papers, chapter and lesson review exercises, and worksheets. Each of these are valuable sources of information that can tell the teacher something about how well pupils have mastered the lesson objectives. They should be examined closely to help identify misunderstandings and problem areas. If most pupils' homework fails to demonstrate mastery of the concept of regrouping when subtracting, the next instructional segment could begin by reviewing this concept and talking through the solutions to the homework problems. If the workbook exercise shows that pupils cannot differentiate between a fact and an opinion, succeeding instruction that will clarify the difference should be planned.

3. *Use appropriate questioning techniques and strategies to assess pupil learning.* During instruction, teachers have a limited number of ways

to determine if pupils are learning the desired objectives. It is impractical to stop instruction to give a quiz or test every time instructional effectiveness is in doubt. Similarly, most paper-and-pencil procedures like worksheets and homework take time to complete and, consequently, cannot provide the immediate feedback that teachers need. Therefore, to gather information about pupil learning during instruction, teachers rely heavily on oral questions. Oral questions are the major instructional assessment technique for most classroom teachers, with some teachers asking as many as 300 to 400 questions a day (Morgan and Saxton, 1991; Christensen, 1991). Questions facilitate learning by stimulating thinking and inquiry and provide assessment information to teachers.

Except for lecturing, questioning is the most dominant teaching strategy at all levels of education and, together with discussion, comprises the most common form of pupil-teacher interaction. Since questioning is so important, let's now look at it more closely.

QUESTIONING: PURPOSES AND STRATEGIES

Teachers need to be effective questioners in the classroom. Skillfully asked questions keep pupils involved in the lesson. At the same time, asking questions enables the teacher to pace a lesson and monitor pupil behaviors and learning. Questioning also lets members of the class hear ideas and explanations from their peers that they themselves might not have considered.

Purposes and Types of Questioning

During instruction, teachers ask questions for many reasons:

1. *To promote attention.* Questioning is a way to keep pupils' attention during a lesson, a way to engage them actively in the process of learning.
2. *To promote deeper processing.* Questioning lets pupils verbalize their thoughts and ideas, thereby promoting the thinking and reasoning that lead to deeper processing of information.
3. *To promote learning from peers.* Questioning allows pupils to hear their peers' interpretations and explanations of ideas, processes, and issues. Often, other pupils explain things in ways that are more in tune with the minds of their peers.
4. *To provide reinforcement.* Questioning is used by teachers to reinforce important points and ideas. The questions teachers ask cue pupils regarding what and how they should be learning.

Teachers ask questions in order to reinforce important points, to diagnose problems, to keep students' attention, and to promote deeper processing of information.

5. *To provide pace and control.* Questions that require brief, correct responses keep pupils engaged in learning and require them to pay continuous attention. Questions that are more general and open-ended slow the pace of instruction so pupils can reflect upon and frame their answers and explanations.

6. *To provide diagnostic information.* Questions provide the teacher with information about pupils and class learning. Teachers' questions can supplement their informal observations of pupil learning in the least disruptive way. Also, for group or cooperative learning activities, questioning of group members after completion of their task is a useful way to assess the success of the group.

Convergent questions are those that have a single correct answer, whereas divergent questions may have several appropriate answers.

Questions differ also in other respects. There are higher- and lower-level questions and convergent and divergent questions. **Convergent questions** have a single correct answer: What is the capital of Brazil? Who is credited with the discovery of radium? How many corners does a cube have? **Divergent questions** may have many appropriate answers: What are the benefits of a good education? Describe some differences between the American and French systems of government. What kinds of jobs do people in your neighborhood have? Divergent questions tend to demand more thought than convergent questions, although it should be recognized that both types are important to use during instruction (Wiggins and McTighe, 1998).

Christensen (1991) has developed a typology of questions that shows the breadth of information that can be obtained from varying types of questions.

♦ Open-ended questions	What is your reaction to this poem?
♦ Diagnostic questions	What is the nature of the problem in this short story?
♦ Information questions	What was the last state to be admitted to the United States?
♦ Challenge questions	What evidence is there to support your conclusion?
♦ Action questions	How can we go about solving the problem of high school dropouts?
♦ Sequence questions	Given limited resources, what are the two most important steps to take?
♦ Prediction questions	What do you think would happen if the government shut down for three months?
♦ Extension questions	What are the implications of your conclusion that grades should be abolished in schools?
♦ Generalization questions	Based on your study of classroom assessment, how would you sum up the general concept of validity?

Questions also can be categorized by whether they require higher or lower levels of pupil thinking. Lower-level thinking, requiring recall or memorization, resides in the lowest category of Bloom's Taxonomy. All succeeding levels of the taxonomy are considered higher level, because they require pupils to perform processes more complicated than pure memorization, such as understanding conceptual knowledge and applying procedural knowledge.

Lower-level questions generally begin with words such as "who," "when," "what," and "how many": "When did the American Civil War take place?" "What is the definition of *taxonomy?*" "Where is the city of Beijing located?" "How much is 9 times 8?" Such questions focus on factual information that the pupil is expected to remember and produce when questioned. Higher-level thinking often depends upon factual knowledge.

Most teachers want their pupils to apply, analyze, and synthesize the factual knowledge they have attained in order to help them solve new problems. Higher-level questions typically start with words such as "explain," "predict," "relate," "distinguish," "solve," "contrast," "judge," and "produce": "Explain in your own words what the main idea of the story was." "Predict what will happen to the price of oil if the supply increases but the demand remains the same." "Distinguish between statements of fact and statements of opinion in the passage we have just read." "Give three examples of how the self-fulfilling prophecy might work in a school." Questions such as these pose tasks that require pupils to think and to go beyond factual recall. Note that if the answers to these questions had been specifically taught to pupils during instruction, they would not be higher-level questions because pupils could answer them from memory, rather than having to construct an answer for themselves.

Lower-level, factual questions generally begin with words such as who, what, and when, whereas higher-level questions begin with action words such as explain, predict, distinguish, and solve.

Table 5.2 provides examples of questions at different levels of Bloom's Taxonomy. While the taxonomy provides a useful model, it is less important to ask questions at specific taxonomic levels than it is to focus generally on a range of questions that stimulate both memory and reflection.

The questions teachers ask should match the learning objectives. Although most teachers want their pupils to attain both lower- and higher-level outcomes from instruction, they tend to focus instruction and classroom questions on lower-level questions. Only about 10 to 20 percent of teachers' classroom questions are higher level. Pupils are not frequently asked to explain ideas in their own words, apply knowledge in unfamiliar situations, analyze components of an idea or story, synthesize different pieces of information into a general statement or conclusion, or judge the pros and cons of particular courses of action. This emphasis on lower-level questions also can be found in some teacher's edition textbooks and assessments of statewide standards.

Four factors explain this emphasis on lower-level questions. First, memory-focused questions are utilized heavily in the lesson plans. Second, lower-level questions are the easiest for pupils to answer, because they usually have already been taught. Focusing questions at lower levels

TABLE 5.2   EXAMPLES OF QUESTIONS FOR THE LEVELS OF BLOOM'S
                       COGNITIVE TAXONOMY

Knowledge (remembering)	What is the definition of a noun?
	How many planets are in our solar system?
	In what year did the Boston Tea Party occur?
Comprehension (understanding)	Summarize the story in your own words.
	Explain what $E = MC^2$ means.
	Paraphrase the author's intent.
Application (using information to solve new problems)	What is a real-world example of that principle?
	Predict what would happen if the steps in the process were reversed.
	How could the Pythagorean theorem be used to measure the height of a tree?
Analysis (reasoning, breaking apart)	Which of these statements are facts and which are opinions?
	How did the main character change after her scary nightmare?
	Explain the unstated assumption that underlies this argument.
Synthesis (constructing, integrating)	What do all these pictures have in common?
	Describe a generalization that follows from these data.
	State a conclusion supported by these facts.
Evaluation (judging)	What was the most important moment in the story and why?
	What is your opinion of the school policy for grades and extracurricular participation?

gives pupils the best chance to reply correctly, and thus promotes a feeling of instructional success among teachers. Third, teachers themselves are most likely to know the answers to lower-level questions, so they feel more confident in asking such questions. Finally, lower-level questions are much easier to create than higher-level questions. Figure 5.2 provide examples of each level of questioning in Bloom's Taxonomy for a unit on the solar system. While Bloom's Taxonomy provides a useful model, it is less important to ask questions at specific taxonomic levels than it is to focus generally on asking a range of questions that stimulate both memory and reflection.

UNIT: Solar System

Knowledge: What are the names of the nine planets in the solar system?

Comprehension: Explain in your own words the important characteristics of the moon.

Application: How would you determine the distance between the earth and Mars?

Analysis: What are three differences between the sun and the moon?

Synthesis: What is one characteristic that all the planets in the solar system have?

Evaluation: Which planet is most like the earth? Explain why.

FIGURE 5.2
Sample Questions for Each Level of Bloom's Taxonomy.

Training Students to Self-Assess

Beyond using questions to extract assessment information and keep pupils engaged in the class, teachers can train students to take more responsibility for their own learning by becoming effective questioners themselves (Chappuis, Stiggins, 2002). Teachers can both model and encourage pupils to ask effective self-assessment questions by which they can identify high-quality work, evaluate their own work, become aware of their own learning strategies, and set goals to improve them. To do this, teachers should model questions that focus on student process and work ("Have I proofread my paper?" "Does my story have a title?"), rather than on approval or disapproval ("Did I do a good job?"). Key Assessment Tools 5.2 suggests some ways to encourage pupils in this direction.

Key Assessment Tools 5.2

ENCOURAGING PUPIL QUESTIONING SKILLS AND SELF-ASSESSMENT OF LEARNING

1. Model and encourage the use of three basic self-assessment questions:
   Where am I going?
   Where am I now?
   How do I close the gap?

2. Show students samples of anonymous work and teach them how to ask and answer questions about the attributes of good performance.

3. Involve students in constructing lists of questions or criteria to serve as a scoring guide for a specific assignment. Start with just one question and gradually increase the number.

4. Have pupils create their own sets of questions for practice tests; discuss the merits of the questions.

5. Have pupils communicate with others about their progress toward a goal.

6. Display learning objectives in the classroom. Ask pupils to rephrase them.

Source: Adapted from Chappuis, S., Stiggins, R. J. (2002). *Classroom assessment for learning. Educational Leadership.* (60) 1, 40–43.

Questioning Strategies

The following strategies can be used to increase the effectiveness of oral questioning.

1. *Ask questions that are related to the objectives of instruction.* Teachers' questions communicate what topics are important and the ways these topics should be learned, so there should be consistency among objectives, instruction, and questioning. This consistency is especially important when higher-level objectives are stressed. It is useful to prepare a few higher-level questions before instruction begins and then incorporate them into the lesson plan.

2. *Avoid global, overly general questions.* Do not ask, "Does everyone understand this?" because many pupils will be too embarrassed to admit they do not and others will think they understand what has been taught when in reality they do not. Ask questions that probe pupils' comprehension of what is being taught. Similarly, avoid questions that can be answered with a simple yes or no unless the pupils are also expected to explain their answers.

3. *Involve the entire class in the questioning process.* Do not call on the same pupils time after time. Occasionally call on nonvolunteers in order to keep everyone attentive. Arranging pupils into a circle or a U and asking questions in a variety of ways in order to adapt them to pupils' varying ability levels increases pupil participation. Finally, support the response efforts of weak pupils and encourage everyone who tries.

4. *Be aware of patterns in the way questions are distributed among pupils.* Some teachers call on high-achieving pupils more frequently than low achievers, on girls more than boys, or on those in the front rows more than those in the back. Other teachers do the opposite. Be sensitive to such questioning patterns and strive to give all pupils an equal opportunity to respond.

5. *Allow sufficient "wait time" after asking a question.* This permits pupils to think about and frame a response. Pupils need time to process their thoughts, especially to a higher-level question. Remember, silence after a question is good because it means the pupils are thinking. Three to five seconds is a suitable "wait time" that permits most pupils, even the slower ones, to think about an answer to the question. Giving pupils time to think also leads to improved answers.

6. *State questions clearly and directly to avoid confusion.* Avoid vague questions or prompts like "What about the story?" or "Talk to me about this experiment." If pupils are to think in desired ways, the

teacher must be able to state questions in ways that focus and produce that type of thinking. Clarity focuses thinking and improves the
quality of answers. Again, preparing key questions before teaching a
lesson is a useful practice.

7. *Probe pupil responses with follow-up questions.* Probes such as
"Why?" "Explain how you arrived at that conclusion," and "Can you
give me another example?" indicate to pupils that the "whys" or logic
behind a response are as important as the response itself and will
encourage them to articulate their reasoning.

8. *Remember that instructional questioning is a social process that
occurs in a public setting.* Consequently, all pupils should be treated
with encouragement and respect. Incorrect, incomplete, or even
unreasonable answers should not evoke demeaning, sarcastic, or
angry teacher responses. Be honest with pupils; do not try to bluff
them when they pose a question that you cannot answer. Find the
answer and report it to pupils the next day.

9. *Allow private questioning time for pupils who are shy or have difficulty engaging in the questioning process.* If possible, allow private
questioning time for these pupils, perhaps during seatwork or study
time. Then, as they become more confident in their private
responses, gradually work them into public discussions, first with
small groups and then with the whole class.

10. *Recognize that good questioning also involves good listening and
responding.* In addition to framing good questions, it is important to
be both a good listener and responder to pupils' answers to questions.
Good listening means hearing the meaning and implications of
pupils' responses. Good responding means following up a pupil's
answers with comments that will benefit the pupil.

11. Avoid questions that require only a yes or no response.

12. Avoid always asking pupils the same types of questions. Ask for facts,
judgments, and so forth.

ACCOMMODATIONS DURING INSTRUCTION

As we stressed in Chapter 3, an important aspect of planning and delivering instruction is accommodating pupil needs and disabilities. Clearly,
pupil needs and disabilities span a broad range, from pupils with severe
cognitive, affective, or psychomotor disabilities to pupils with mild attention problems (Cegelka and Berdine, 1995; Cartwright, Cartwright, and Ward,
1995). While it is not possible here to address all available accommodation

strategies for instruction, we will review a sample of useful strategies to illustrate the breadth of options. For an excellent in-depth survey of strategies to accommodate varied pupil needs and disabilities, see Price and Nelson (2003, chapter 6).

Common Disabilities and Accommodations

For a hearing impaired pupil the teacher can:

♦ Use written rather than oral directions
♦ Speak slowly and distinctly
♦ Use sign language

For a vision impaired pupil the teacher can:

♦ Use large print
♦ Listen to recorded materials
♦ Let other pupils read out loud
♦ Seat the pupil near the blackboard

For a pupil with poor comprehension the teacher can:

♦ State directions orally and in writing
♦ Increase available time
♦ Sequence directions
♦ Shorten directions

For a pupil with a lack of attention the teacher can:

♦ Repeat major points
♦ Change the tone of voice
♦ Call pupil's name before questioning
♦ Ask frequent questions
♦ Have the pupil write down directions

Dealing with cleaning up classroom work sites:

♦ Establish and reinforce cleanup rules
♦ Practice cleaning up
♦ Praise pupils who are neat and begin to clean up first
♦ Make a checklist of cleanup tasks

TECHNOLOGY AND ASSESSMENT

Computer Adaptive Testing (CAT)

CAT is an advance in computer administration that enables interaction between the test and the test taker. By interaction with test takers, adaptive tests provide an optimal number of test items for each test taker. For example, when a test taker correctly answers an item, the test responds by providing a more difficult item. If the test taker answers incorrectly, the test produces an easier item. Adaptive tests use fewer items and are more accurate.

Dealing with pupil disrespect:

◆ Inform the pupil that such behavior is unacceptable.
◆ Make the consequences of future disrespect clear.
◆ Try to determine the basis for the pupil's disrespect.
◆ Have an individual conference or a conference with a mediator such as the pupil's advisor.
◆ Model respect to students.

Figure 5.3 provides more suggestions. Many other strategies apply to pupils with specific disabilities. For example, for pupils who have difficulty maintaining attention, provide a seat near an adult or quiet peers; seat them away from high traffic areas of the classroom; seat them at a single desk, not a table; provide more breaks or task changes; and use more active participation activities. For pupils having difficulty beginning a task, provide a cue card of steps on the desk that the pupil can check off as steps are completed; go to the pupil quickly at the start of the task and help him or her get started (indicate that you will return to check progress); and provide a peer helper. For pupils having difficulty organizing, list assignments and materials needed on the board or a transparency; have students use notebooks with pocket dividers; color code materials needed for various subjects; and provide time to gather books and materials at the start and end of school (Nissman, 2000; Price and Nelson, 1999).

These accommodations represent only a few of the ways lessons can be planned to help pupils get the most out of instruction. Based on the knowledge gained from early assessment and the teaching of initial lessons, teachers should begin to identify needs and appropriate accommodations for pupils. With this knowledge, teachers can plan and implement accommodations for students who need them to learn most effectively, thus improving the validity of their instruction and assessments.

FIGURE 5.3 *Interventions.*

Problem	Solution
Listening	Provide visual displays (e.g., flowcharts, pictorials, wheels); prereading questions/terms at end of chapter; assigned reading; keyword note-taking system to expand memory jogs during daily review; advance note-taking organizers from subtitles in textbook.
Distractibility	Minimize visual distractors in the environment; don't have interesting activities going on in one corner of the room while expecting the student to do his or her seatwork; provide a "quiet corner" for anyone who wishes a distraction-free place to work.
Attention Span	Have student work in short units of time with controlled activity breaks (i.e., reading break or magazine break); activities need to be interspersed throughout instruction.
Short-Term Memory	Offer review systems in a flashcard style so frequent practice can be done independently; material may need to be reviewed frequently.
Task Completion	Present work in short units (i.e., five problems on paper cut into quarters rather than on one sheet); time frames should be short, with clear deadlines and checkpoints to measure progress; have a model available so product can be examined if directions can't be retained.
Impulsivity	Have as few distractions as possible;
Inattention to Detail Test Taking	Show the student how to do the work; have a checklist for what he needs to do, and have a reward system tied to the completion of all the steps.
	Emphasize detail through color coding or isolation.
	Have the student review critical details and main ideas in a flashcard system to support attention and practice specific retrieval.

SOURCE: Rooney, (1995). Teaching students with attention disorders. *Intervention in School and Clinic, 30*(4), 221–225. Copyright 1995 by PRO-ED, Inc. Reprinted by permission.

Common Disabilities and Accommodations When Planning

Accommodations when planning content:

♦ If students have fallen behind in the curriculum, teach what is most generalizable.

♦ Teach learning strategies along with teaching content subject area.

♦ Select content based on student interests; for example, allow pupils to read the sports page to practice reading skills.

Accommodations when planning objectives:

◆ Pretest before teaching to make sure the objective is appropriate for the students.
◆ Determine whether the objective can be altered for some students; for example, can pupils who have poor writing skills demonstrate their knowledge orally?

Accommodations when deciding on instructional methods:

◆ Recognize that pupils with some learning and behavior disabilities often need very explicit directions.
◆ Evaluate the level of structure pupils need to be successful; do not assume that all students learn best with unstructured approaches.
◆ If pupils have fallen behind in the curriculum, use time-efficient methods.
◆ Be sure pupils have the necessary skills to be successful in the instructional method being used.

Accommodations when planning the lesson:

◆ Provide directions, procedures, and rules; describe them orally and in writing.
◆ Follow up by asking questions or by having pupils repeat or paraphrase what they are to do.
◆ Repeat key words often, using the same wording.
◆ Ask for frequent active responses.
◆ Break up information: teach a couple of steps, practice, teach a few more steps, practice. Keep reminding pupils of the whole task. Stop often to summarize.
◆ Point to steps on a written list as they are demonstrated.

Common Nondisability Teacher-Pupil Issue

Dealing with an argumentative pupil:

◆ Do not confront the pupil in a group situation.
◆ Evaluate the situation that led to the confrontation.
◆ Allow the pupil to have his or her say.
◆ Do not make threats that cannot be backed up.

CHAPTER SUMMARY

olc

CHAPTER REVIEW

Visit Chapter 5 of the Online Learning Center at **www.mhhe.com/ airasian5e** to take chapter quizzes, link to related websites, read PowerWeb articles and news feed updates, and access study tools, including the case study referenced in the chapter.

♦ During instruction, teachers must accomplish two tasks simultaneously. They must deliver instruction to pupils and they must constantly assess the progress and success of that instruction.

♦ Instructional assessments are more spontaneous and informal than planning assessments and focus on indicators such as body language, facial expressions, inattentiveness, and pupil questions.

♦ Studies of teachers' thoughts during instruction indicate that most attention is given to how learners are attending to and profiting from instruction, followed by teachers' own thoughts about their instructional actions. Teachers also assess to maintain class order at their level of tolerance.

♦ Among the factors teachers monitor and assess during instruction are pupil interest and behavior, instructional pace, usefulness of examples, most appropriate pupil to call on, and need to begin or end an activity.

♦ Because of its informal, spontaneous nature, assessment during instruction must overcome some validity problems, including a lack of objectivity by the classroom teacher regarding the success of instruction and the tendency to judge instructional success by facial expressions and participation, not by actual pupil achievement.

♦ Reliability problems during instructional assessment center on the teachers' difficulty of observing pupils given the fast pace of instruction and their tendency to observe or call on only certain pupils in the class, thus limiting their perception of the interest and understanding of the class as a whole.

♦ Instructional assessments can be improved by observing a broader sample of pupils, supplementing informal assessment information with more formal information, and using appropriate questioning techniques during instruction.

♦ Questioning is the most useful strategy a teacher can employ to assess the progress of instruction. It gives the teacher information about pupil learning, lets pupils articulate their own thoughts, reinforces important concepts and behaviors, and influences the pace of instruction.

♦ Good questioning techniques include asking both higher- and lower-level questions, keeping questions related to the objectives of instruction, involving the whole class in the process, allowing sufficient "wait time" for pupils to think about their responses, probing responses with followup questions, and never demeaning or embarrassing a pupil for a wrong or unreasonable answer.

♦ Numerous types of accommodation can be made during instruction and ongoing assessment for pupils with disabilities.

QUESTIONS FOR DISCUSSION

1. What challenges do you see during instruction in the need to both monitor your pupils' learning and maintain the right level of tolerance? What is likely to be difficult for you about doing both more or less at the same time?

2. In what situations should a teacher change instruction in response to pupil interest and attentiveness, and in what situations should a teacher not change instruction?

3. Under what circumstances would you call on a shy pupil who never raises a hand for oral questions?

ACTIVITIES

1. Throughout the next 24 hours, try to notice what questions you tend to ask or not ask of those around you. In writing, summarize how well your current question-asking skills are likely to serve in the classroom. What might you do to improve them?

2. Interview a teacher about how he or she knows when a lesson is going well or poorly. Ask the teacher to recall a recent lesson and ask what his or her main thoughts were during the lesson.

REVIEW QUESTIONS

1. How is assessment different for planning instruction and delivering instruction?

2. What are a teacher's main assessment tasks during instruction?

3. What is the relevance of the concept of "level of tolerance" to instructional assessment?

4. What are the main kinds of evidence teachers collect to assess instruction and what are the problems with this kind of evidence?

5. What are three main points of advice for improving assessment during instruction?

6. What are the validity and reliability issues in delivering instruction?

7. What are the purposes of oral questioning?

8. What strategies of oral questioning can a teacher use to make assessment during instruction more valid and reliable?

9. What accommodations can be made for pupils with disabilities during instruction?

REFERENCES

Bloom, B. S., et al. (1956). *Taxonomy of educational objectives: Handbook 1: Cognitive Domain.* New York: McKay.

Cartwright, P. G., Cartwright, C. A., & Ward, M. (1995). *Educating special learners,* 4th edition. Belmont, CA: Wadsworth Publishing.

Cegelka, P. T., & Berdine, W. H. (1995). *Effective instruction for students with learning difficulties.* Needham Heights, MA: Allyn and Bacon.

Christensen, C. R. (1991). The discussion teacher in action: Questioning, listening, and response. In C. R. Christensen, D. A. Garvin, and A. Sweet, *Education for Judgment.* Boston: Harvard Business School Press.

Doyle, W. (1986). Classroom organization and management. In M. C. Wittrock, *Handbook of research on teaching* (pp. 392–431). New York: Macmillan.

Joint Committee on Standards for Educational Evaluation (2003). *The student evaluations standards: How to improve evaluations of students.* Thousand Oaks, CA: Corwin Press.

Morgan, N., & Saxton, J. (1991). *Teaching, questioning, and learning.* New York: Routledge.

Nissman, B. (2000). *Teacher-tested classroom management strategies.* Upper Saddle River, NJ: Merrill.

Price, K. M. & Nelson, K. L. (2003). *Daily planning for today's classroom: A guide to writing lesson and activity plans.* 2nd edition. Belmont, CA: Wadsworth Publishing.

Wiggins, G., & McTighe, J. (1998). *Understanding by design.* Alexandria, VA: Association for Supervision and Curriculum Development.

OFFICIAL ASSESSMENTS

KEY TOPICS

- *Formative and Summative Assessments*

- *The Logic of Formal Assessment*

- *Planning an Official Assessment*

- *Preparing Pupils for Official Assessments*

CHAPTER OBJECTIVES

After reading this chapter, you will be able to:

- Contrast official assessment with initial and instructional assessment
- Differentiate formative and summative assessment
- Explain the difference between good teaching and effective teaching
- Describe the decisions needed to develop and plan an official assessment
- State activities that help prepare pupils for official assessments

THINKING ABOUT TEACHING

In what ways can teachers use the results of assessments to improve pupil learning? Cite three or more ways.

 hus far we have seen that assessment plays an important role in classrooms and that teachers use assessment to help them

- Get to know pupils early in the school year
- Establish the classroom as a learning community with rules and order
- Select appropriate educational objectives for pupils
- Develop lesson plans
- Select and critique instructional materials and activities
- Monitor the instructional process and pupil learning during instruction

The chapter explores the logic of the summative phase of assessment—assessment that takes place after learning has occurred. All teachers assess their pupils' achievements with more than one approach, and the official tests that they give also vary. For example, one test might mainly attempt to measure how much you remember while another goes after higher-level thinking. But all good tests have much in common. The chapter lays a basis for preparing yourself and your pupils for effective summative assessment.

FORMATIVE AND SUMMATIVE ASSESSMENTS

Much of the evidence that supports teachers' decisions comes from informal observations and perceptions. Rarely written down or saved in formal records, they are used to guide teachers' interactions with pupils during both instructional and noninstructional classroom encounters. These observations and perceptions help teachers make moment-to-moment decisions about specific pupil problems, control of the class, what to do next in a lesson, and how pupils are reacting to instruction. Such informal assessments are used primarily to "form" or alter ongoing classroom processes or activities, and are called *formative assessments*. They provide information when it is still possible to influence or "form" the everyday processes that are at the heart of teaching.

Formative assessments are used to alter or improve instruction while it is still going on.

Although critical to teachers' decision making, informal assessments should be supplemented by more formal kinds of evidence. Such formal assessments usually come at the end of a classroom process or activity, when it is difficult to alter or rectify what has already occurred. Called *summative assessments*, these later procedures are used mainly to assess the outcomes of instruction and are exemplified by end-of-chapter tests, projects, term papers, and final examinations. Table 6.1 contrasts formative and summative assessments.

Summative assessments are used to evaluate the outcomes of instruction and take the form of tests, projects, term papers, and final exams.

Early assessment and assessment during instruction are the categories of assessment that were covered in chapters 2 and 5. Summative assessments represent a third type of classroom assessment called *official assessment*. Official assessment is more formal and systematic than either teachers' early observations or instructional assessment. It helps teachers to make decisions that the school bureaucracy requires of them: testing, grading, and grouping pupils; recommending whether pupils should be promoted or placed in an honors section; and referring pupils to special education services if they have special needs. The most common form of official assessments are unit and chapter achievement tests and report card grades.

Official assessments are needed by the school bureaucracy for purposes such as pupil testing, grading, and placement.

Unlike other assessments based largely on informal assessments, official assessments are usually formal, appearing in report cards, school record

TABLE 6.1 COMPARISON OF FORMATIVE AND SUMMATIVE ASSESSMENTS		
	Formative	**Summative**
Purpose	To monitor and guide a process while it is still in progress	To judge the success of a process at its completion
Time of assessment	During the process	At the end of the process
Type of assessment technique	Informal observation, quizzes, homework, pupil questions, and worksheets	Formal tests, projects, and term papers
Use of assessment information	Improve and change a process while it is still going on	Judge the overall success of a process; grade, place, promote

folders, and standardized test reports, as well as in reading group or ability level designations. Further, most official assessment decisions are about individual pupils rather than groups or classes. Usually we grade, promote, honor, and place individuals, not groups. Because they have important public consequences for pupils and must often be defended by teachers, official assessments are generally based upon systematically gathered evidence. In the classroom, official assessments almost always focus on pupils' cognitive performance, usually how well pupils have learned what has been taught.

Official, summative assessments and their resulting decisions are usually administered at the end of a unit of instruction or the end of a grading period. As a consequence, they occur much less frequently than formative assessments.

Teachers have mixed emotions about official assessments, and especially about tests, as the following comments show.

> I hate giving them. I find the testing situation to be one where tests become public expressions of what I already knew about the kid and what the kid already knew about the subject matter. In other words, I knew who would get A's and who would get F's because I taught the class. I knew who knew it and who didn't, so when kids take a test it is a public transmission to say "yes, you know it" or "no, you don't know it."

> I need to use tests in algebra for grading my students and having objective information I can show parents when they complain about their child's grade. With so much emphasis on grades, I'm sure my students work mostly for a test grade and not for their enjoyment or understanding of the subject matter.

> The pressure to perform is too great for anyone, let alone a seven-year-old who's still trying to figure out what in the world he needs education for. Because the school system requires it, I test my students once a week in math and vocabulary and about once every two weeks in science, social studies, and religion. The only advantage I see in testing is that it gives the teacher a number on which to base the student's academic progress.

> Each test gives me some feedback on what I'm doing right and what I'm not, as well as what the class is learning best. I like to give a large number of tests to get this feedback and because I feel that the larger the number of test grades, the better indication I have of a pupil's learning.

Official assessments can have important consequences for students and should be taken quite seriously by teachers.

> My tests are helpful in that they offer concrete evidence to show parents if the student is deficient in an area. I'll tell a parent that Johnny can't add and they'll sometimes respond "I know he can add when he wants to." Then I show them a classroom test which shows Johnny's deficiency. One drawback to the tests, especially in the early grades, is that a child sometimes will become upset during testing, either because the child is having difficulty with the test or because the child wants to be doing something more enjoyable.

The statewide standards are supposed to focus and guide my instruction and assessment. In some respects they are useful because they specify specifically what pupils are to learn, but it is also true that many of my students are not well prepared enough to begin instruction where the standards decree they should. This causes problems with planning my instruction.

Clearly, teachers differ in their views of official assessments, but no matter how they feel about them, teachers must use them at least some of the time in their classrooms.

Despite their sometimes lukewarm endorsement by teachers, it is a grave mistake to underestimate the importance of official assessments. Official assessments have important consequences for pupils and should be taken quite seriously by teachers, especially so-called high-stakes assessments, such as statewide tests of basic skills that may be required for graduation. They provide the teacher with additional information about pupil learning. Moreover, pupils, their parents, and the public at large consider them to be very important and take them very seriously. The grading, placement, promotion, and other decisions that result from official assessments can influence pupils' lives both in and out of school. They are the public record of a pupil's school accomplishments and are often the sole evidence a parent has of how his or her child is doing in school. The following teacher comments illustrate the degree of importance parents and students attach to official assessments.

> Every year at open house I can count on at least one parent asking how much test scores count in the final grade and another asking me if I allow children to make up a poor test grade in some way. Test scores are like the currency of the classroom for many of them.

> The kids are forever asking "Do we have to know this?" "Is this going to be on the test," and "Will this be a big part of the test?" They define what's valuable and important in terms of what's going to be on the test.

For pupils, teachers, and administrators, official assessments are, in some respects, the "coin of the realm" for assessments.

THE LOGIC OF FORMAL ASSESSMENT

There is an important difference between teaching and effective teaching. Teaching refers to a *process* of instruction while *effective* teaching refers to the *outcomes* of instruction (Did pupils learn?). A teacher is one who, among other things, provides a review at the start of a new lesson, states appropriate objectives, maintains an appropriate level of lesson difficulty,

Good teaching refers to what teachers do during instruction, while effective teaching refers to the outcomes of instruction.

engages pupils in the learning process, emphasizes important points during instruction, gives pupils practice doing what they are expected to learn, and maintains an orderly classroom.

But effective teaching goes one step beyond to focus upon whether pupils actually learn from instruction. An effective teacher is one whose pupils learn what they have been taught. Official assessments seek to obtain evidence about teaching effectiveness, so they should be linked to the objectives, activities, and instruction provided pupils. It is impossible to evaluate pupils' achievement if the things assessed do not match the things pupils were taught.

The primary aim of assessing achievement is to provide pupils an opportunity to demonstrate what they have learned from the instruction provided.

Always remember that the primary aim in assessing pupil achievement is to *provide pupils a fair opportunity to demonstrate what they have learned from the instruction provided.* The primary aim is not to trick pupils into doing poorly, entertain them, or ensure that most of them get A's. It is not to determine the total knowledge pupils have accumulated as a result of their learning experiences, both in and out of school. It is simply to let pupils show what they have learned from the things they have been taught in their classroom.

PLANNING AN OFFICIAL ASSESSMENT

At the time for formal achievement testing, usually at the completion of instruction on a unit or chapter, the teacher must decide the following:

olc

CHAPTER CASE STUDY

Visit the text OLC website to read the case of Diane News, an elementary school teacher who must choose only four students for the school district's gifted & talented program. How does she make the choice?

www.mhhe.com/ airasian5e

1. What should be tested?
2. What type of assessment items should be used?
3. How long should the assessment take?
4. Should a teacher-made or textbook assessment be used?

Mr. Wysocki is a seventh grade English teacher who is teaching his class about descriptive paragraphs. Based upon earlier assessments, the pupils' previous English curriculum, the textbook, and other instructional resources available to him, Mr. Wysocki decides that the unit will focus on the following objectives, to which we have added labels from Bloom's Taxonomy.

1. The pupil can name the three stages of the writing process (i.e., prewriting, writing, and editing). (knowledge)
2. The pupil can explain in his or her own words the purposes of the three stages of the writing process. (comprehension)
3. The pupil can select the topic sentences in given descriptive paragraphs. (application)

4. The pupil can write a topic sentence for a given descriptive writing topic. (analysis)

5. The pupil can write a descriptive paragraph with a topic sentence, descriptive detail, and a concluding statement. (synthesis)

Using a Table of Specifications

To organize his objectives, Mr. Wysocki develops a table of specifications that identifies the cognitive processes pupils are to demonstrate, the content on which they are to demonstrate these processes, and the amount of emphasis each objective receives in instruction (low, middle, or high). Table 6.2 shows Mr. Wysocki's specifications.

The table of specifications has two dimensions, content and process. The content dimension includes the main topics of instruction and assessment. The process dimension, which you will recognize as the six categories of Bloom's Taxonomy, lists the cognitive processes related to each content topic. In Mr. Wysocki's table, for example, the intersection of knowledge (process dimension) and stages of writing (content dimension), represented by the X, refers to the objective: *the pupil can name the three stages of the writing process* (i.e., prewriting, writing, and editing); that is, the pupil will remember the names of the three writing stages. The L after the X refers to the amount of time allotted to this objective. Since it is a simple memorization task, a low (L) amount of time is spent teaching it. The intersection of comprehension (process dimension) and stages of writing (content dimension) refers to the objective: *the pupil can explain in his or her own words the purposes of the three stages of the writing process.* Notice that stages of writing relate to two different objectives, because Mr. Wysocki is concerned with two processes, remembering and explaining. Notice also that Mr. Wysocki places more emphasis on the pupils' own explanation of

TABLE 6.2	TABLE OF SPECIFICATIONS					
Content Dimension	**Process Dimension**					
	Knowledge	**Comprehension**	**Application**	**Analysis**	**Synthesis**	**Evaluation**
Stages of writing	X (L)	X (M)				
Topic sentences			X (M)	X (L)		
Writing essay					X (H)	
L = Low	M = Middle	H = High				

the three stages (M) than on remembering the stages (L). He also could have stated the planned number of test items to be used with each intersection of content and process instead of using L, M, and H.

Mr. Wysocki's third and fourth objectives indicate that he wants his pupils to both select and write their own topic sentences. Selecting calls for an analysis that differentiates topic sentences from other types of sentences. Writing a topic sentence calls for application of a procedure. Writing an essay, the final objective, calls for a correct synthesis of the three stages of descriptive writing. The writing objective is the most important and complex outcome, so more time is allotted to it than to the other four objectives.

Once his objectives are identified and organized, Mr. Wysocki develops lesson plans for them. In selecting activities, he considers the ability levels of his pupils, their attention spans, the suggestions made in the textbook, and the additional resources available to supplement and reinforce the textbook. He also plans activities that will give pupils practice in each objective. One of the benefits of a table of specifications is that it emphasizes the different processes that intersect with the content. Thus, the table reminds Mr. Wysocki that he needs both remembering and explaining activities to attain his first two objectives.

With the objectives and the planned activities identified, Mr. Wysocki commences instruction. First, he introduces pupils to the three steps in the writing process: (1) prewriting (identifying the intended audience, purpose, and initial ideas); (2) writing; and (3) editing what has been written. He tells pupils they are expected to memorize the names of the three stages. Next, he assigns pupils topics and has them describe how they will go through the three steps. He has them give reasons why each step is necessary for good writing. He then introduces them to the concept of a paragraph, and they read descriptive paragraphs to find a common structure. He notes that a paragraph is made up of a topic sentence, detail sentences, and a concluding sentence. Then he has the pupils select the topic sentences in several paragraphs. Later, he has them write their own topic sentences. The instruction should be linked to the objectives. Different instructional techniques are linked to different types of objectives. Objectives focus on memorizing factual information and other objectives that are higher level, such as application and synthesis.

Instruction seems to go along fairly well except that pupils have a hard time finding the common structure in paragraphs. Mr. Wysocki has to give additional explanation to the class. Even after instruction, his end-of-lesson assessments indicate that many pupils have the mistaken idea that the topic sentence always comes first in a paragraph, so he devises a worksheet in which many of the topic sentences are not at the beginning of the paragraph.

Finally, Mr. Wysocki has pupils write descriptive paragraphs. First, he has them write on the same topics so they can compare topic sentences and the amount of detail in each other's paragraphs. He thinks this strategy is useful because pupils can learn from one another's efforts. Homework assignments are returned to pupils with suggestions for improvement, and pupils are required to edit and rewrite their paragraphs. Later, pupils are allowed to construct descriptive paragraphs on topics of their choice.

Not all teachers would have instructed their pupils in this fashion; different teachers have different pupils, resources, and styles. But Mr. Wysocki did what he judged was best for his particular class. He instituted instructional procedures that gave pupils practice on the behaviors they were expected to learn, provided feedback on pupil performance during instruction, and revised his plans based upon his observations during instruction. He demonstrated the characteristics of a good teacher.

Mr. Wysocki felt that he had a fair sense of how well the class had mastered the objectives. Although he knew something about the achievement of each pupil, he was not sure about each one's achievement of all five objectives. He felt a formal, end-of-unit assessment would provide information about each pupil's mastery of all he had taught. Then he would not have to rely upon incomplete, informal perceptions when grading his pupils. To develop the assessment, however, he had to make some decisions about the nature of the test he would administer, including those in the following section.

The most useful strategy to assess the progress of instruction is oral questioning, which serves a number of purposes from both instructional and assessment prospects. Unfortunately, most classroom questions tend to be lower level and convergent.

Decisions in Planning a Test

As a running example, we continue to analyze systematically what Mr. Wysocki did.

1. *What should I test?* The first important decision when preparing to assess pupil achievement is to identify the information, processes, and skills that will be tested. A valid achievement test is one that provides pupils a fair opportunity to show what they have learned from instruction. Therefore, in deciding what to test, it was necessary for Mr. Wysocki to focus attention upon both his objectives and the actual instruction that took place. Usually the two are very similar, but sometimes it is necessary to add or omit an objective once teaching begins. In the final analysis, the things that are actually presented during instruction are the most important to assess.

A fair and valid test covers information and skills similar to those covered during instruction.

Mr. Wysocki knew, then, that he had to gather information about how well pupils could memorize and explain in their own words the three stages of the writing process, select topic sentences in a paragraph, write suitable topic sentences, and compose a descriptive paragraph with a topic sentence, descriptive detail, and summarizing statement. But what about other important skills such as taking notes on a topic or knowing the difference between a descriptive and an expository paragraph? These are also useful, so should they be on Mr. Wysocki's test?

The answer to this question is no! There will always be more objectives to teach than there is time to teach them. There will always be useful topics and skills that have to be omitted from tests because of lack of time. This is why thoughtfully planning instruction in terms of pupils' needs and resources is so important. Including untaught skills on an achievement test diminishes its validity, making it less than a true and fair assessment of what pupils have learned from classroom instruction.

By confining his test questions to what he actually taught, Mr. Wysocki could say to himself, I decided what the important objectives were for pupils, I provided instruction on those objectives, I gave pupils practice performing the objectives, and I gave a test that asked pupils to do things similar to those I taught. The results of the test should fairly reflect how much the pupils have achieved in this unit and permit me to grade fairly.

The type of assessment procedure chosen depends on the nature of the objective being assessed.

2. *What type of assessment should be given?* This question is answered by reference back to the learning objectives. Each objective contains a target process or behavior that students have been taught. For example, three of Mr. Wysocki's objectives referred respectively to comprehending (explain in one's own words), applying (write a topic sentence), and synthesizing (integrate and write an essay). These three processes are best assessed by *supply questions,* questions that require the pupil to produce (supply) an answer or product. Another one of his objectives referred to analyzing (selecting a topic sentence). This type of behavior is best assessed by *selection questions,* questions that present the pupil with a set of choices of which the pupil selects one or more. Yet another of Mr. Wysocki's objectives referred to remembering (name the three stages of the writing process). This behavior can be assessed by either a supply question (list or orally state the three stages) or a selection question (pick out the three stages from a set of choices). Thus, the format used to assess learning is largely predetermined by the statement of the objective.

Many teachers feel that only essay tests are good. Others use multiple-choice items as much as possible, and still others believe that tests should contain a variety of question types. Here is how several teachers responded when asked about the kinds of questions they use in their tests:

I always give the kids essay tests because that's the only way I can see how well they think.

Multiple-choice items are easy and fast to score, so I use them most of the time to test pupils' achievement.

I make sure that every test I make up has some multiple-choice questions, some fill-in questions, and at least one essay question. I believe that variety in the kinds of questions keeps students interested and gives all students a chance to show what they know in the way that's best for them.

Each of these teachers states a reason for following a particular classroom testing strategy. The reasons are neither wrong nor inappropriate, but they are secondary to the main purpose of official achievement testing, which is *to permit pupils to show how well they have learned the behaviors or processes they were taught.* Thus, no single type of assessment item is applicable all the time. What makes a particular procedure useful is whether it matches the objectives and instruction provided.

3. *How long should the test take?* Since time for testing is limited, choices must be made in deciding the length of a test. Usually, practical matters such as the age of the pupils or the length of a class period are most influential. Since the stamina and attention span of young pupils is less than that of older ones, a useful strategy to follow with elementary school pupils is to test them fairly often using short tests that assess only a few objectives. Because of their typical attention spans, 15- to 30-minute tests, depending on the grade and group, are suggested for elementary pupils.

The age of the students, the subject being tested, and the length of the class period all impact the length of a test.

Curricula for some school subjects such as history, social studies, and English are composed of relatively discrete, self-contained units. In other subjects such as mathematics, foreign language, and science, knowledge must be built up in a hierarchical sequence. Whereas topics in history may stand on their own, topics in mathematics or Spanish usually cannot be understood unless prior math and Spanish lessons have been mastered. Consequently, when teaching in a hierarchical subject area, it is useful to give more frequent tests to keep pupils on task in their studying and to make sure they grasp the early ideas that provide the foundation for subsequent, more complex ideas. Testing in middle, junior, and high schools is usually restricted by the length of the class period. Most teachers at these levels plan their tests to last almost one complete class period.

Mr. Wysocki's class periods are 50 minutes long. He wanted a test that would take about 40 minutes for most pupils to complete. A 40-minute test would allow time for distribution and collection of the tests, as well as a few minutes for those pupils who always want "one more minute" before handing in their test.

In deciding how many questions to ask for each objective, Mr. Wysocki tried to balance two factors: (1) the instructional time spent on each objective and (2) its importance. Some objectives are usually more important than others. These objectives tend to be the more general ones that call for the integration of several narrower objectives. Even though a great deal of instructional time was spent on writing and identifying topic sentences, Mr. Wysocki values this skill less for its own sake than for its contribution to the more general objective of constructing a descriptive paragraph. Thus, the number of test questions dealing with writing and identifying topic sentences was not proportional to the instructional time he spent on it. It is not necessary to include an equal number of questions for each objective, but all objectives should be assessed by some items. On the basis of these factors and the instruction he had provided, Mr. Wysocki felt that a test with the following format would be fair to pupils and would provide a valid and reliable assessment of their learning.

The number of test questions per objective depends on the instructional time spent on each objective and its importance.

♦ The pupil can *name* the three stages of writing. Use one supply question: list the three names.

♦ The pupils can *explain* in their own words the three stages of the writing process (i.e., prewriting, writing, and editing). Use a short essay question.

♦ The pupils can *select* the topic sentence in a given descriptive paragraph. Use three multiple-choice questions, each consisting of a paragraph and a list of possible topic sentences from which the pupil has to select the correct one.

♦ The pupils can *write* a topic sentence for a given descriptive topic. Use three short-answer questions that give the pupils a topic area and require them to write a topic sentence for each area.

♦ The pupils can write a descriptive paragraph using a topic sentence, descriptive detail, and a concluding statement. Use an essay question in which each pupil writes a descriptive paragraph on a topic of his or her choice. The paragraph cannot be on a topic the pupil used previously during instruction or practice.

Mr. Wysocki thought that writing topic sentences was an important enough skill to state it as a separate objective. Because he spent considerable time teaching the objective, he should test it separately. When teachers focus their tests solely upon their general, integrative objectives, pupils may answer questions incorrectly because they cannot successfully integrate the separate skills they have learned. Pupils often get no credit on such questions, even though they may have learned all the more specific skills they were taught.

4. *Should a teacher-made or a textbook test be used?* Teachers are inevitably confronted with the question of whether to use the textbook test or to construct their own. The very availability of textbook tests is seductive and causes many teachers to think: after all, the test comes with the textbook, seems to measure what is in the chapter I'm teaching, looks attractive, and is readily available, so why shouldn't I use it? Mr. Wysocki asked himself the same question.

Notice that the decision about using a textbook test or constructing one cannot be answered until *after* the teacher has reflected on what was taught and has identified the topics and behaviors to be tested. The usefulness of any achievement test (high stakes or low stakes) cannot be judged without reference to the planned objectives and actual instruction.

Textbook tests furnish a ready-made instrument for assessing the objectives stressed in the textbook and can save classroom teachers much time. Test formats vary across textbook publishers in terms of length, layout, and question type. Look through the teacher's edition of some textbooks to see the range of tests available.

Before using these tests, teachers should consider the criteria that permit a teacher to use a textbook or teacher-made test with confidence. The basic concern is whether the items on the test match the instruction provided pupils.

Regardless of whether a teacher is constructing his or her own test or judging the adequacy of a textbook test, he or she must consider the same basic validity issue: Do the items on the test match the instruction provided pupils? The more a teacher alters and reshapes the textbook curriculum, the less valid its accompanying tests become. As one teacher put it, "The textbook tests look good and can be time-savers, but they often don't test exactly what I've been doing in the classroom. Every time I change what I do from what the text suggests I do, and every time I leave out a lesson or section of the text from my instruction, I have to look at the text test carefully to make sure it's fair for my pupils." This concern also pertains to statewide testing.

Remember that it is possible to combine textbook items and teacher-constructed items into an assessment. Often the textbook test has some appropriate assessment items that can be used in conjunction with the items the teacher has constructed. This approach is commonly used by many teachers. The key issue, however, is the relevance of the assessment items to the instruction provided the pupils. Key Assessment Tools 6.1 relates to judging a textbook.

To summarize, both textbook and teacher-made tests should (1) clearly relate to the objectives of instruction, (2) include enough questions to assess all or most of the objectives, and (3) use assessment methods suited to the backgrounds and prior experiences of the pupils (Joint Advisory

The main consideration in judging the adequacy of a textbook test is the match between its questions and what pupils were actually taught in class.

Key Assessment Tools 6.1

KEY POINTS TO CONSIDER IN JUDGING TEXTBOOK TESTS

1. The decision to use a textbook test or pre-made standard achievement test must come *after* a teacher identifies the objectives that he or she has taught and now wants to assess.

2. Textbook and standard tests are designed for the typical classroom, but since few classrooms are typical, most teachers deviate somewhat from the text in order to accommodate their pupils' needs.

3. The more classroom instruction deviates from the textbook, the less valid the textbook tests are likely to be.

4. The main consideration in judging the adequacy of a textbook or standard achievement test is the match between its test questions and what pupils were taught in their classes:

   a. Are questions similar to the teacher's objectives and instructional emphases?

   b. Do questions require pupils to perform the behaviors they were taught?

   c. Do questions cover all or most of the important objectives taught?

   d. Is the language level and terminology appropriate for pupils?

   e. Does the number of items for each objective provide a sufficient sample of pupil performance?

Key Assessment Tools 6.2

COMMON PROBLEMS IN DEVELOPING OR SELECTING TESTS TO ASSESS PUPIL ACHIEVEMENT

1. Failing to consider objectives and instructional emphases when planning a test.
2. Failing to assess all of the important objectives and instructional topics.
3. Failing to select item types that permit pupils to demonstrate the desired behavior.
4. Adopting a test without reviewing it for relevance to the instruction provided.
5. Including topics or objectives not taught to pupils.
6. Including too few items to assess the consistency of pupil performance.
7. Using tests to punish pupils for inattentiveness or acting out.

Committee, 2002). Tests that meet these criteria will provide a valid indication of pupil learning. Key Assessment Tools 6.2 provides a summary of common problems teachers encounter in judging achievement tests.

PREPARING PUPILS FOR OFFICIAL ASSESSMENTS

The rest of this chapter discusses how to prepare pupils for testing. Many of these practices may appear to be commonsensical things that all teachers would normally do. However, such is not the case. It is remarkable how often these commonsense practices are ignored or overlooked. Failure to carry out these activities can jeopardize the validity of tests.

Issues of Test Preparation

Fair and valid assessment involves preparing appropriate objectives, providing good instruction on these objectives, and determining how these objectives are best assessed.

We use tests and other assessments to help make decisions about pupils' learning in some content area. A pupil's performance on a test or assessment is meant to represent the pupil's mastery of a broader body of knowledge and skills than just the specific examples included on the test or assessment. Remember from Chapter 1 that when Ms. Lopez described Manuela's and Chad's scores of 100 on her long division with remainder test, she said, "Manuela and Chad can do long division with remainder items very well." She did not say, "Manuela and Chad can do the 10 specific long division with remainder items that were on my test." Thus, tests and other assessments gather a sample of a pupil's behavior and use that sample to generalize how the pupil is likely to perform if confronted with similar tasks or items. For example, the performance of a pupil who scores 90 percent on a test of poetry analysis, chemical equation balancing, or capitalization rules is interpreted as indicating that the pupil has mastered about 90 percent of the general content domain he was taught and tested on. The specific tasks or test items are selected to represent the larger group of similar tasks and items.

Objectives, instruction, and the test *should* all be related to each other. After all, the purpose of an achievement test is to determine how well pupils have learned what they were taught. By definition, an achievement test must be related to instruction, and instruction is, in a real sense, preparation for the test. The important question, however, is: when does the relationship between objectives, instruction, and the test become so close that it is inappropriate or unethical?

Achievement tests should give information about how well a student can answer questions similar but not identical to those taught in class.

There is an important ethical difference between teaching to the test and teaching the test itself. Teaching to the test involves teaching pupils the general skills, knowledge, and processes that they need to answer the questions on a test. This is an appropriate and valid practice. It is what good teaching and testing are all about. But teaching the test itself—that is, teaching pupils the answers to specific questions that will appear on the test—is neither appropriate nor ethical. It produces a distorted, invalid picture of pupil achievement. Such a test will give information about how well pupils can remember the specific items they were taught, but it will not tell how well they can do on questions that are similar, but not identical, to the ones they have been taught. Teachers have an educational and ethical responsibility not to corrupt the validity of pupils' achievement test performance by literally teaching them the exact items that will be on the test.

There is an important difference between teaching to the test and teaching the test itself.

Another problematic practice difficult to classify is teachers' limiting instruction to overly narrow objectives that sometimes accompany a text. When working with a predetermined curriculum, it is appropriate for teachers to confine their instruction to the objectives that will be tested, so long as they do not prepare the pupils for the specific test items that will be used to measure these objectives. However, it is improper for teachers to consciously exclude important objectives from their instruction solely because those objectives are not on the test provided by a text or other outside source. Instead of linking assessment to the curriculum objectives, such teachers have let the test objectives define their curriculum.

Mel Levine, MD, professor of pediatrics at the University of North Carolina Medical School in Chapel Hill, suggests a "do no harm" approach to testing practices that states some important and useful strategies. See Key Assessment Tools 6.3.

> **Key Assessment Tools 6.3**
>
> ## "DO NO HARM" TESTING PRACTICES
>
> 1. Testing can help elevate education standards, but not if it creates larger numbers of students who are written off as unsuccessful. When a student does poorly, determine which link in the learning chain is uncoupled. Always have constructive, nonpunitive contingency plans for students who perform poorly on a test. Testing should not be an end in itself, but rather a call to action.
>
> 2. Not all students can demonstrate their strengths in the same manner. Allow different students to demonstrate their learning differently, using the means of their choice (portfolios, expert papers, oral presentations, and projects, as well as multiple-choice tests).
>
> 3. Never use testing as justification for retaining a student in a grade. Retention is ineffective and seriously damaging to students. How can you retain a child while claiming you are not leaving anyone behind?
>
> 4. Some students who excel on tests might develop a false sense of security and confidence, failing to realize that adult careers tap many abilities that no test can elicit. Take care to nurture vital capacities that are not testable.
>
> 5. Avoid the hazard of teachers' teaching to the tests because your work or school is being judged solely on the basis of examination scores. Teachers should never have their students rehearse or explicitly prepare for tests. Testing should be unannounced. Good results on such tests should be the product of the regular, undisturbed curriculum.
>
> *Source:* Levine, 2003.

The following sections describe other actions that teachers should carry out to prepare their pupils for achievement tests. As you read these sections, bear in mind the preceding list of inappropriate practices. Also bear in mind that concern about test preparation is not confined to paper-and-pencil tests, but also includes other assessment strategies and tasks.

Provide Good Instruction

Good instruction is the most important preparation for formal achievement testing.

The single most important thing a teacher can do to prepare pupils for formal classroom achievement tests is to provide them with good instruction. Earlier it was noted that good teaching includes activities such as providing a review at the start of a new lesson, setting an appropriate difficulty level for instruction, emphasizing important points during instruction, giving pupils practice on the objectives they are expected to learn, and maintaining an orderly classroom learning environment. These practices will prepare pupils for testing better than anything else a teacher might do. A primary ethical responsibility of teaching, therefore, is to provide the best

---

TECHNOLOGY AND ASSESSMENT

INTERACTIVE MULTI-MEDIA EXERCISES (IMMEX)

IMMEX is a computer-based system that allows students to work on complex problems in a number of disciplines. As a student works on a given problem, IMMEX records every step and decision made by that student. This progression of decisions and the student's final solution are examined together to classify the student's current state of knowledge and to identify the problem-solving strategies applied by the student. By tracking the problem-solving strategies a student applies across several problems, IMMEX is also able to help teachers assess the extent to which the student's problem-solving skills change over time. IMMEX is a rare example of an assessment instrument that examines both the process and the ultimate solution when providing information about a student's current skills and examining changes in those skills over time.

For more information on IMMEX, see http://www.immex.ucla.edu

---

instruction possible, without corrupting the achievement test in the ways described above. In the absence of good instruction, all aspects of assessment are greatly diminished.

Review before Testing

While teaching a unit or chapter, many objectives are introduced, some early and others at the end of instruction. Because the topics pupils most remember are the ones most recently taught, it is good practice to provide pupils a review prior to formal testing. The review can take many forms: a question and answer session, a written or oral summary of main ideas, or administration of a review test. The review serves many purposes: to refresh pupils on objectives taught early in the unit, to provide one last chance to practice important behaviors and skills, and to afford an opportunity to ask questions about things that are unclear. Often, the review exercise itself provokes questions that help pupils grasp partially understood ideas.

The review should cover the main ideas and skills that were taught. Many teachers fail to conduct a review because they feel the review might "tip off" pupils to the kinds of things that will be on the test. This is faulty reasoning. A review is the final instructional act in the chapter or unit. It provides pupils an opportunity to practice skills and clarify misunderstandings about the content. If the review focuses mainly on peripheral topics and behaviors in an attempt to "protect" the areas to be tested, pupils will not be afforded a final practice on the important outcomes. They will not have their questions answered, and, after experiencing a few irrelevant review sessions, will cease taking them seriously.

Test reviews often provoke questions that help students grasp partially understood ideas.

The purpose of a review, especially a review for a test or assessment, is to prepare pupils for the test. In essence, the review is the teacher's way of saying, "These are examples of the ideas, topics, and skills that I expect you to have learned. Go over this review and see how well you have learned them. Practice one last time before I ask you to demonstrate your learning on the test that counts toward your grade. If you have questions or difficulties, we'll go over them before the test. After that, you're on your own." A classroom achievement test should not trick pupils, make them answer topics they haven't been taught, or create a high-anxiety test situation. It should give pupils a fair chance to show what they have learned. A pertinent review prior to the test will help them do this.

The review exercises or questions should be similar, but not identical, to the exercises or questions that will make up the final test. If they are the actual test questions, then a valid assessment of pupil learning cannot be obtained, because the test will have been reduced to a short-term memory exercise rather than a measure of long-term mastery of general learning objectives. Most textbooks contain chapters or unit reviews to use prior to testing. Go to your curriculum center or library or to a local school and examine the chapter tests and reviews in a variety of textbooks.

Ensure Familiarity with Question Formats

If students are not familiar with the types of questions used on a test, the test does not produce a valid assessment of what they have learned.

If a classroom test contains questions that use an unfamiliar format, pupils should be given practice with that format prior to testing. The need for such practice is especially important in the elementary and middle grades where pupils first encounter matching, multiple-choice, true-false, short-answer, and essay questions. Pupils must learn what is expected of them for each type of question, and how to record their answer. One opportune time to familiarize pupils with question formats is during the review exercises prior to the chapter or unit test. Pretest practice with new types of question and response formats can reduce anxiety and permit a more valid assessment of pupil learning. In addition to familiarizing pupils with new types of questions and response formats, there is a general set of test-taking guidelines that can help pupils do their best on tests. These guidelines will not enable pupils to overcome the handicaps of poor teaching and lack of study, but they can help focus pupils during testing. Table 6.3 lists some advice that you may want to give pupils before a test (Ebel & Frisbie, 1991).

Another set of skills, called **testwise skills,** help pupils identify errors on the part of the question writer that provide clues to the correct answer. For example, when responding to multiple-choice questions, the testwise pupil applies the following probabilities:

♦ If the words "some," "often," or similar vague words are used in one of the options, it is likely to be the correct option.

TABLE 6.3   COMMON TEST-TAKING STRATEGY ADVICE FOR PUPILS

- ◆ Read test directions carefully.
- ◆ Find out how questions will be scored. Will all questions count equally? Will points be taken off for spelling, grammar, neatness?
- ◆ Pace yourself to ensure that you can complete the test.
- ◆ Plan and organize essay questions before writing.
- ◆ Attempt to answer all questions. Guessing is not penalized, so guess when you don't know the answer.
- ◆ When using a separate answer sheet, check often to make certain that you are marking your responses in the correct space.
- ◆ Be in good physical and mental condition at the time of testing by avoiding late-night cram sessions.

- ◆ The option that is longest or most precisely stated is likely to be the correct one.
- ◆ Any choice that has grammatical or spelling errors is not likely to be the correct one.
- ◆ Choices that do not attach smoothly to the stem of the question are not likely to be correct.

To be testwise is to be able to identify unintended clues to the correct answers.

Teachers should be aware of common test errors so they can guard against them when they construct or select test items. Ensure that pupils who answer test questions correctly do so because they have mastered the content or skill taught so the validity of the test will be strong.

There are many other testwise strategies that pupils use to overcome a lack of content knowledge. More detailed descriptions of these can be found in Chapter 7. With regard to one's own classroom tests, it is best to make pupils aware of such general test-taking skills and then concentrate on writing fair, appropriate test questions that do not contain errors that can be "psyched out." Chapter 7 describes how to write or select test questions that have few of the faults that testwise pupils thrive on.

Scheduling the Test

It has already been recommended that teachers not administer an achievement test immediately after completing instruction on a chapter or unit in order to provide pupils the opportunity to review, study, and reflect on the instruction before being tested. However, there are other considerations about the times when pupils are most likely to show their best performance. For example, if a teacher were to test pupils the day of the school's championship football game, the period after an assembly or lunch, or on the first day after a long school vacation, it is likely that pupils would give a subpar test performance. Likewise, a teacher should not schedule a test on a day that he or she will be away just so the substitute teacher will have something to keep the pupils busy. The substitute may not be able to answer pupils' questions about either the test or the meaning of particular questions. Furthermore, if it is an elementary classroom, the presence of a stranger in the classroom may make the pupils uncomfortable and unable to do their best.

In the elementary school there is more flexibility in scheduling tests than in the middle school or high school, where 50-minute periods and departmentalized instruction mean that pupils must be in certain places at certain times. The algebra teacher who has a class immediately after lunch has no choice but to test pupils then. While no teacher has complete control over scheduling tests, it is useful to bear in mind that there are some times when pupils are able to perform better on tests than others.

Giving Pupils Information about the Test

Usually the beginning of a chapter or unit review alerts pupils to anticipate a formal assessment for grading purposes. It is a good idea, however, to let them know when the test will be given, what areas will be covered, what types of questions it will contain, how much it counts, and how long it will take. These factors undoubtedly influence your own test preparation. By providing this information, the teacher can help reduce some of the anxiety that inevitably accompanies the announcement of a test. When information is provided, the test becomes an incentive to make pupils study.

The hardest achievement test for pupils to prepare for is the first one they take in a class. Even if a teacher provides detailed information about topics to be covered, types of items, number of questions, and the like, pupils always have some uncertainty about the test. It is not until they take a teacher's first test that they get a sense of how that teacher tests and whether the review given by the teacher can be trusted as a basis for test preparation. Once pupils know the teacher's style, they have a sense of what to expect on subsequent tests and whether the teacher's pretest information is useful.

Hastily planned tests too often focus on memory items and fail to cover a representative sample of the instruction provided.

Of course, unless a teacher has thought about the nature of the test to be given, it is impossible to provide the pretest information pupils need to prepare for the test. The specifics of test content, types of questions, and test length need to be considered well before the test is given. Hastily planned tests too often focus mainly on memorization skills and fail to cover a representative sample of the instruction provided to pupils. Thus, to inform pupils about test characteristics, a teacher cannot put off planning the test until the last minute.

CHAPTER SUMMARY

◆ Official assessments help teachers make decisions that the school bureaucracy requires of them, such as assigning grades, recommending pupils for promotion, placing pupils in groups, and referring pupils to special education services.

◆ Unlike early and instructional assessments, official assessments are summative—that is, based on formal, systematically gathered, end-of-instruction evidence.

◆ The main types of official assessment instruments are teacher-made tests, textbook tests, and standardized high-stakes tests.

◆ Official assessments are taken very seriously by pupils, parents, school administrators, and the public at large because they result in tangible consequences for pupils.

◆ Good official assessments have three features: (1) pupils are expected to perform what the teacher has stated in the objectives and instruction; (2) the questions provide a representative sample of the things pupils were taught; and (3) the questions, directions, and scoring procedures are clear and appropriate. Incorporating these three features in official assessments will provide valid and reliable information for decision making.

◆ Because the aim of official assessments is to provide pupils a fair opportunity to show what they have learned from instruction, it is very important that assessments reflect what pupils have been taught. This is the most basic requirement for official assessments.

◆ The methods used to gather information about pupil learning are dependent on the objectives and instruction provided. Methods that permit the pupils to show the behaviors taught are essential for valid assessment. Use multiple-choice, matching, or true-false questions when pupils are taught to "choose" or "select" answers; short-answer or essay questions when pupils are taught to "explain," "construct," or "defend" answers; and actual performances when pupils are taught to "demonstrate" or "show."

◆ A table of specifications can be used to see that test items relate to specific objectives.

◆ Test length is determined by the age and attention span of the pupils and the type of test questions used.

◆ The decision whether to construct one's own test or use a textbook test depends upon how closely instruction followed the lead of the textbook. The more a teacher supplements or omits material from the textbook, the less likely the textbook test will be a valid indication of pupils' learning.

◆ Preparing pupils for official assessments requires careful thought and planning on the part of the teacher. First and foremost, teachers should provide the best instruction possible prior to assessment. Good instruction

olc

CHAPTER REVIEW

Visit Chapter 6 of the Online Learning Center at **www.mhhe.com/ airasian5e** to take chapter quizzes, link to related websites, read PowerWeb articles and news feed updates, and access study tools, including the case study referenced in the chapter.

should be followed up by a review that gives pupils a chance to ask questions and practice important behaviors and skills that will be tested. Use of textbook review tests is one way to prepare pupils. Pupils, especially those in early elementary grades, should be given practice with unfamiliar item formats before testing. Pupils should be informed in advance of the time, nature, coverage, and format of the test.

♦ The test should be scheduled, when possible, at a time that will permit pupils to show their best work.

♦ In preparing pupils for testing, the teacher should *not* focus instruction only on item formats used on the test, use classroom examples taken directly from the test, or give pupils practice taking the actual test. These practices corrupt the validity of the test results. Instruction should be focused on the general skills and knowledge teachers want pupils to learn in a subject area, not on the specific questions that will be asked about those areas on the test.

QUESTIONS FOR DISCUSSION

1. What are some things that a teacher can do to help prepare students for classroom testing? What are some dangers of test preparation that should be avoided?

2. If higher-level thinking requires pupils to work with material and concepts they have not been taught specifically, what are some ways to prepare pupils to take tests that include higher-level items?

3. What are the hallmarks of *effective* teaching?

4. How do official assessments differ from early assessments and instructional assessments?

5. What are the criteria for judging how good a classroom achievement test is? Aside from what is on the test, what other information would you need to judge a test's validity and reliability?

ACTIVITY

Select a chapter from a teacher's edition of a textbook. Read the chapter and examine the aids and resources provided for planning, delivering, and assessing instruction. Compare the objectives of the chapter to the suggestions for instruction provided by the textbook author. Will the suggested instructional experiences help pupils attain the objectives? Is there a match between objectives and instructional experiences? Examine the end-of-chapter test. Is it a good test in terms of the chapter's objectives and the instructional suggestions? Do the types of test items used match the objectives? What is the proportion of higher- and lower-level items in the test?

REVIEW QUESTIONS

1. What is the fundamental purpose of assessing pupils' achievement? What decisions must a teacher make when preparing to assess pupil achievement?

2. How should the validity of an achievement test be determined?

3. List some ethical and unethical ways to prepare pupils for achievement testing. Why are the unethical ways you identified unethical?

4. What factors should be considered in determining whether to use a textbook test or construct your own?

5. In what way are the methods used to gather information about pupil learning dependent on the teacher's objectives and the instruction provided?

6. What are the characteristics of a good official assessment?

REFERENCES

Ebel, R. L., and Frisbie, D. A. (1991). *Essentials of educational measurement,* 5th edition. Englewood Cliffs, NJ: Prentice-Hall.

Joint Advisory Committee (1993). Principles for fair student assessment practices for eduction in Canada. Edmonton, Alberta: University of Alberta.

Joint Advisory Committee, Centre for Research in Applied Measurement and Evaluation (2002). *Principles for fair student assessment practices for education in Canada.* Edmonton, Alberta: University of Alberta. *http//www.2Learn.ca/ Projects/Together/fair.html.*

Levine, M. (2003). Celebrating diverse minds. *Educational Leadership,* (61) 2, 12–18.

CHAPTER 7

PAPER-AND-PENCIL TESTING

KEY TOPICS

- *Selection and Supply Test Items*

- *Higher-Level Questions*

- *Guidelines for Writing and Critiquing Test Items*

- *Accommodations: Substitutions for Paper-and-Pencil*

After reading this chapter, you will be able to:

- ◆ Define basic item-writing terms such as selection items, supply items, item stem, and specific determiner
- ◆ Distinguish between higher-level and lower-level test items
- ◆ Write correctly stated supply and selection items
- ◆ Identify and correct flaws in supply and selection items

THINKING ABOUT TEACHING

Write a multiple-choice, true-false, short answer, and essay question appropriate to the grade you wish to teach.

At most grade levels, paper-and-pencil tests are the most commonly used procedure for gathering formal evidence about pupil learning. These tests may be constructed by teachers, textbook publishers, statewide test constructors, or standardized test publishers. We have seen that a good assessment plan takes many things into consideration: identifying important instructional objectives, selecting question formats that match these objectives, deciding whether to construct one's own test or use one from the textbook, providing good instruction, and providing a review and information about the test. The success of these important preparatory steps can be undone, however, if the actual test questions are poorly constructed, unclear, or subjectively scored. Such problems do not give pupils a fair chance to show what they have learned and, consequently, do not provide a valid basis for decision making. No matter whether one is concerned with teacher-made, textbook, statewide, or standardized tests, it is important that teachers be able to differentiate between well-constructed and poorly constructed test questions.

Tests are composed of short communications called questions or **items.** Each question must be brief and must set a clear problem for the pupil to think about. Each question must also be complete in itself and independent of other questions. Further, because pupils will mentally debate the nuances of each word to be sure they are not misinterpreting the intent of the item, it is crucial that questions be stated in clear, precise language. This chapter examines and contrasts different types of paper-and-pencil test questions and provides general guidelines for writing or judging the adequacy of each kind of item. It also illustrates the link between educational objectives and student assessments.

SELECTION AND SUPPLY TEST ITEMS

Multiple-choice, true-false, and matching questions are examples of selection items. Supply items are those in which the student constructs his or her own answer.

There are two basic types of paper-and-pencil test questions: **selection items** and **supply items.** As their names suggest, selection items require the pupil to select the correct answer from among a number of choices, while supply items require the pupil to supply or construct his or her own answer.

Selection Items

Within the general category of selection items are multiple-choice, true-false, and matching questions.

Multiple-Choice Item

Multiple-choice items consist of a stem, which presents the problem or question, and a set of options from which the pupil selects an answer.

Multiple-choice items consist of a **stem,** which presents the problem or question to the pupil, and a set **options,** or choices, from which the pupil selects an answer. The multiple-choice format is widely used in achievement tests of all types, primarily to assess learning outcomes at the factual knowledge and comprehension levels. However, with suitable introductory material, this format can also be used to assess higher-level thinking involving application, analysis, and synthesis. (Item 3 from the following examples is a multiple-choice item that assesses higher-level thinking.) The main limitations of the multiple-choice format are that it does not allow pupils to construct, organize, and present their own answers, and it is susceptible to guessing.

Here are examples of multiple-choice items.

1. You use me to cover rips and tears. I am made of cloth. What am I?
   A. perch   B. scratch   C. patch   D. knot

2. What is the smallest state in the United States?
   A. Massachusetts
   B. South Carolina
   C. Rhode Island
   D. Illinois

3. Read the following passage.
   (1) For what men say is that, if I am really just and am not also thought just, profit there is none, but the pain and the loss on the
   (3) other hand is unmistakable. But if, though unjust, I acquire the reputation of justice, a heavenly life is promised to me. Since then
   (5) appearance tyrannizes over truth and is lord of happiness, to appearance I must devote myself. I will describe around me a

(7) picture and shadow of virtue to be the vestibule and exterior of my house; behind I will trail the subtle and crafty fox.

Which one of the following states the major premise of the passage?

A. For what men say (line 1)

B. if I am really just (line 1)

C. profit there is none, but the pain and the loss (line 2)

D. appearance tyrannizes over truth and is the lord of happiness (lines 5–6)

E. a picture and shadow of virtue to be the vestibule and exterior of my house (lines 7–8)

True-False Items

The true-false format requires pupils to classify a statement into one of two categories: true or false; yes or no; correct or incorrect; fact or opinion. True-false items are used mainly to assess factual knowledge and comprehension behaviors, although they also can be used to assess higher level ones (Frisbie, 1992). The main limitation of true-false questions is their susceptibility to guessing.

The main limitation of true-false questions is their susceptibility to guessing.

The following are typical true-false items.

1. $5 + 4 = 8$ T F

2. In the equation $E = mc^2$, when m increases E also increases.   T F

3. Read the statement. Circle T if true and F if false. If the statement is false, rewrite it to make it true by <u>changing only the underlined part of the statement</u>.

   The level of the cognitive taxonomy that describes recall and memory behaviors is called the <u>synthesis</u> level.   T F

Although primarily used to assess knowledge and comprehension, both multiple-choice and true-false items can be used to assess higher-level thinking.

Matching Items

Matching items consist of a column of **premises,** a column of **responses,** and directions for matching the two. The matching exercise is similar to a set of multiple-choice items, except that in a matching question, the same set of options or responses is used for all the premises. Its chief disadvantage is that it is limited mainly to assessing lower-level behaviors. The following is an example of a matching exercise.

Matching items consist of a column of premises, a column of responses, and directions for matching the two. They assess mainly lower-level thinking.

On the line to the left of each invention in column A, write the *letter* of the person in column B who invented it. Each name in column B may be used only once or not at all.

Column A

_____ (1) telephone

_____ (2) cotton gin

_____ (3) assembly line

_____ (4) polio vaccine

Column B

A. Eli Whitney

B. Henry Ford

C. Jonas Salk

D. Henry McCormick

E. Alexander Graham Bell

Most often, multiple-choice questions do not effectively test higher-level thinking, but multiple-choice interpretive questions can do so. We will discuss them later in the section "Higher-Level Questions."

Supply Items

Supply items consist of short-answer and completion (also called fill-in-the-blank) items, essay questions, or questions requiring the pupil to create things such as diagrams or concept maps.

Short-Answer and Completion Items

Short-answer items use a direct question to present a problem; completion items use an incomplete sentence. Both tend to assess mainly factual knowledge and comprehension.

Short-answer and completion items are very similar. Each presents the pupil with a question to answer. The short-answer format presents the problem with a direct question (e.g., What is the name of the first president of the United States?), while the completion format may present the problem as an incomplete sentence (e.g., The name of the first president of the United States is _____) or a picture, map, or diagram that requires labeling. In each case, the pupil must supply his or her own answer. Typically, the pupil is asked to reply with a word, phrase, number, or sentence, rather than with a more extended response. Short-answer questions are fairly easy to construct and diminish the likelihood that pupils will guess answers. However, they tend to assess mainly factual knowledge or comprehension.

The following are examples of completion and short-answer items.

1. Scientists who specialize in the study of plants are called _____.

Next to each state write the name of its capital city.
2. Michigan   _____
3. Massachusetts   _____
4. South Carolina _____

5. In a single sentence, state one way that inflation lowers consumers' purchasing power.

Essay Items

Essay questions are most useful for assessing higher-level thinking skills but are time-consuming to answer and score and favor the student with writing ability.

Essay questions give pupils the greatest opportunity to supply and construct their own responses, making them the most useful for assessing higher-level thinking processes like analyzing, synthesizing, and evaluating (more about this is discussed below). The essay question is also the primary way teachers assess pupils' ability to organize, express, and defend ideas. The main limitations of essays are that they are time-consuming to answer and score, permit testing only of a limited amount of pupils' learning, and place a premium on writing ability.

Here are some examples of essay questions.

1. What is the value of studying science? Give your answer in complete, correct sentences. Write at least five sentences.

2. "In order for revolutionary governments to build and maintain their power, they must control the educational system." Discuss this statement using your knowledge of the American, French, and Russian revolutions. Do you agree with the statement as it applies to the revolutionary governments in the three countries? Include specific examples to support your conclusion. Your answer will be judged on the basis of the similarities and differences you identify in the three revolutions and the extent to which your conclusion is supported by specific examples. You will have 40 minutes to complete your essay.

Comparing Selection and Supply

Supply questions are much more useful than selection questions in assessing pupils' ability to organize thoughts, present logical arguments, defend positions, and integrate ideas. Selection questions, on the other hand, are more useful when assessing application and problem-solving skills. Given these differences, it is not surprising that knowing the kind of item that will be on a test can influence the way pupils prepare for the test. In general, supply items encourage global, integrative study, while selection items encourage a more detailed, specific focus.

Supply questions are most useful for assessing students' ability to organize and present their thoughts, defend positions, and integrate ideas.

While supply and selection items consume approximately the same amount of time to construct and score, each format allocates its time differently. Selection items are time-consuming to construct, but can be scored quickly. Supply items are less time-consuming to construct, but are more time-consuming to score. Table 7.1 summarizes the differences.

Selection items are most useful when application and problem-solving skills are assessed.

HIGHER-LEVEL QUESTIONS

There is a growing emphasis on teaching and assessing pupils' higher-level thinking. As the following quotes show, teachers recognize the importance of pupils' learning how to understand and apply their knowledge. They know that knowledge takes on added meaning when it can be used in real-life situations.

Facts are important for pupils to learn in all subjects, but if pupils do not learn how to understand and use the facts to help them solve new problems, they haven't really learned the most important part of instruction.

The kids need to go beyond facts and rote learning. You can't survive in society unless you can understand, think, reason, and apply what you know.

TABLE 7.1	COMPARISON OF SELECTION AND SUPPLY TEST ITEMS	
	Selection Items	**Supply Items**
Types of Items	Multiple-choice, true-false, matching, interpretive exercise	Short-answer, essay, completion
Behaviors Assessed	Factual knowledge and comprehension; thinking and reasoning behaviors like application and analysis when using interpretive exercises	Factual knowledge and comprehension; thinking and reasoning behaviors like organizing ideas, defending positions, and integrating points
Major Advantages	1. Items can be answered quickly so a broad sample of instructional topics can be surveyed on a test. 2. Items are easy and objective to score. 3. Test constructor has complete control over the stem and options so the effect of writing ability is controlled.	1. Preparation of items is relatively easy; only a few questions are needed. 2. Affords pupils a chance to construct their own answers; only way to test behaviors such as organizing and expressing information. 3. Lessens chance the pupils can guess the correct answer to items.
Major Disadvantages	1. Time-consuming to construct. 2. Many items must be constructed. 3. Guessing is a problem.	1. Time-consuming to score. 2. Covers small sample of instructional topics. 3. Bluffing is a problem.

It would be so boring to only teach facts. Some recall or memorization is needed, of course, but day after day of memorization instruction would be demeaning to my pupils and me. I have to make room in my curriculum for more complex thinking and reasoning skills such as understanding and applying new knowledge.

What is more exciting for a pupil and her teacher than that moment when pupil's eyes light up with recognition that he or she can solve a new problem? Something that was confusing all of a sudden became clear and a whole new skill is born. That kind of excitement doesn't come very often when instruction is focused on rote, memorization-oriented behaviors.

Many people believe that the only way to test higher-level thinking skills is with essay items. That is not the case! Any test question that demands more from a pupil than memory is a higher-level item. Thus, any item that requires the pupil to solve a problem, interpret a chart, explain something in his or her own words, or identify the relationship between two phenomena qualifies as an item of higher-level thinking. Similarly, any assessment that requires pupils to demonstrate their ability to carry out an activity (e.g., give an oral talk, construct a mobile, or read an unfamiliar foreign language passage aloud) also qualifies as being higher level.

Essay Questions

Essay questions provide an important tool to assess higher-level thinking. Good essay questions require pupils to organize, understand, apply, integrate, and defend ideas. Questions that can be answered using only factual knowledge are better tested by more structured item types such as multiple-choice, true-false, or completion. The following are examples of essay questions that can elicit higher-level thinking from pupils. In all cases it is assumed that the pupils have been taught material similar, though not identical, to that in the items.

1. Explain whether the reasoning in the following statements is correct or incorrect.
   All dogs have tails.
   This animal has a tail.
   Therefore, this animal is a dog. (seventh grade English)
2. In what ways were the events leading up to the start of World War I the same as the events leading up to the start of World War II? In what ways were they different? Focus your answer on military, social, and economic factors. (high school history)
3. Describe in your own words how an eclipse of the sun happens. (third grade science)
4. Why are some parts of the world covered by forests, some parts by water, some parts by grasses, and some parts by sand? Tell about some of the things that make a place a forest, an ocean, a grassland, or a desert. (fourth grade social studies)

Interpretive Exercises

The interpretive exercise is a common form of multiple-choice item that can assess higher-level thinking. An interpretive exercise gives pupils some information or data and then asks a series of selection-type questions based on that information. Item 3 on page 174–175 is an example of an interpretive exercise. Figure 7.1 contains two more examples. Generally, multiple-choice items that ask for interpretations of graphs, charts, reading passages, pictures, or tables (e.g., What is the best title for this story? According to the

Interpretive exercises assess higher-level skills because the pupils must interpret or apply given information.

FIGURE 7.1   *Examples of Interpretive Exercises.*

Example 1

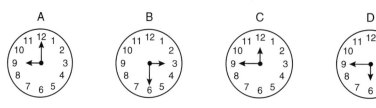

A   B   C   D

Use Oral Questions

What clock shows the time that school starts?   Ⓐ B C D

What clock shows the time closest to lunch time?   A B Ⓒ D

What clock shows half past the hour?   A Ⓑ C D

Example 2

1. The cartoon illustrates which of the following characteristics of the political party system in the United States?

   Ⓐ Strong party discipline is often lacking.

   B   The parties are responsive to the will of the voters.

   C   The parties are often more concerned with politics than welfare.

   D   Bipartisanship often exists in name only.

2. The situation shown in the cartoon is *least* likely to occur at which of the following times?

   A   During the first session of a new Congress

   B   During a political party convention

   C   During a primary election campaign

   Ⓓ During a presidential election campaign

SOURCE: Educational Testing Srvice, *Making the Classroom Test: A Guide for Teachers,* p. 6. Copyright © 1973 by Educational Testing Service (Princeton, NJ). Used by permission of the publisher.

chart, which year had the largest decline?) are classified as interpretive exercises. Such exercises can assess higher-level behaviors like recognizing the relevance of information, identifying warranted and unwarranted generalizations, recognizing assumptions, interpreting experimental findings, and explaining pictorial materials.

To answer the questions posed, pupils have to interpret, comprehend, analyze, apply, or synthesize the information presented. Interpretive exercises assess higher-level skills because they contain all the information needed to answer the questions posed. Thus, if a pupil answers incorrectly, it is because he or she cannot do the thinking or reasoning required by the question, not because the pupil failed to memorize background information.

The principle of testing pupils' higher-level skills by providing them with necessary information and then asking questions that require them to use that information can be applied beyond the realm of interpretive exercises. Compare what might be tested in these two versions of the same question.

Version 1

In one or two sentences, describe what Henry Wadsworth Longfellow is telling the reader in the first two verses of his poem "A Psalm of Life," which we read in class but did not discuss.

Version 2

In one or two sentences describe what Henry Wadsworth Longfellow is telling the reader in these lines of his poem "A Psalm of Life."

> Tell me not, in mournful numbers,
>   Life is but an empty dream!—
> For the soul is dead that slumbers,
>   And things are not what they seem.
> Life is real! Life is earnest!
>   And the grave is not its goal;
> Dust thou art, to dust returnest,
>   Was not spoken of the soul.

If a pupil does poorly on the first version, the teacher does not know whether the pupil failed to remember the poem or, remembering the poem, could not interpret what Longfellow was trying to say. In the second version, memory is made irrelevant by providing the needed lines of the poem.

Like the essay question, the interpretive exercise is a useful way to assess higher-level thinking. However, unlike the essay question, interpretive exercises cannot show how pupils organize their ideas when solving a problem or how well they can produce their own answers to questions.

Other disadvantages of interpretive exercises are the difficulty of constructing them and the heavy reliance they often place on reading ability. Pupils who read quickly and with good comprehension have an obvious

olc

CHAPTER CASE STUDY

Visit the text OLC to read the case of Elizabeth Rhodes, a high school math teacher. Elizabeth is frustrated by her advanced-placement (AP) calculus students who want to work only for solutions to problems and do not want to apply higher-order reasoning skills.

advantage over pupils who do not. This advantage is particularly evident when the test involves reading and interpreting many passages in a limited amount of time.

Most teachers do not construct their own interpretive exercises, preferring to use exercises supplied by textbook publishers or other sources. Regardless of whether one is constructing or selecting an interpretive exercise, the exercise should meet five general guidelines before it is used to assess pupil achievement.

1. *Relevance.* The exercise should be related to the instruction provided pupils. If it is not, it should not be used.
2. *Similarity.* The material presented in the exercise should be new to the pupils, but similar to material presented during instruction.
3. *Brevity.* There should be sufficient information for pupils to answer the questions, but the exercises should not become tests of reading speed and accuracy.
4. *Answers not provided.* The correct answers should not be found directly in the material presented. Interpretation, application, analysis, and comprehension should be needed to determine correct answers.
5. *Multiple questions.* Each interpretive exercise should include more than one question to make most efficient use of time.

Table 7.2 summarizes the pros and cons of the different types of paper-and-pencil test items.

GUIDELINES FOR WRITING AND CRITIQUING TEST ITEMS

Whether writing test items or selecting those prepared by others, there are three general guidelines that help insure good tests: (1) cover important objectives; (2) write clearly and simply; and (3) review items before testing. This section discusses and illustrates these guidelines.

Cover Important Objectives

Test items should reflect important topics and skills emphasized during instruction, should be stated briefly and clearly, and should be self-contained.

Note that the following discussion pertains to teacher-prepared tests and to textbook tests. Simply because a ready-made test is available with a textbook is no reason for a teacher to assume that the test adequately assesses his or her instruction on the chapter or unit. Each classroom teacher has a responsibility to decide about the suitability of a textbook test for assessing his or her instructional emphases.

| TABLE 7.2 ADVANTAGES AND DISADVANTAGES OF TYPES OF TEST ITEMS |||

Test Type	Advantages	Disadvantages
Multiple-choice items	1. Large number of items can be given in a short period 2. Higher- and lower-level objectives can be assessed 3. Scoring is usually quick and objective 4. Less influenced by guessing	1. Takes substantial time to construct items 2. Not useful when "show your work" is required 3. Often hard to find suitable options 4. Reading ability can influence pupil performance
True-false items	1. A large number of items can be given in a short time 2. Scoring is usually quick and objective	1. Guessing correct answer is a problem 2. Difficult to find statements that are clearly true or false 3. Items tend to stress recall
Matching items	1. An efficient way to obtain a great deal of information 2. Easy to construct 3. Scoring is usually quick and objective	1. Focus is mainly on lower-level outcomes 2. Homogeneous topics are required
Short-answer items	1. Guessing is reduced; pupil must construct an answer 2. Easy-to-write items 3. Broad range of knowledge can be assessed	1. Scoring can be time-consuming 2. Not useful for complex or extended outcomes
Essay items	1. Directly assess complex higher-level outcomes 2. Take less time to construct than other item types 3. Assess integrative, holistic outcomes	1. Difficult and time-consuming to score 2. Provide a deep but small sample of pupils' performance 3. Bluffing and the quality of writing can influence scores
Interpretive exercise items	1. Assess integrative and interpretive outcomes 2. Assess higher-level outcomes 3. Scoring is usually quick and objective	1. Heavily dependent on pupils' reading ability 2. Difficult to construct items

One important guideline to keep in mind when preparing tests is not to focus exclusively on trivial knowledge and skills. Studies that examined the nature of the test items written by classroom teachers have found that the vast majority assessed memory-level behaviors (Marso & Pigge, 1989, 1991). From elementary school to the university, items that stress recall and memory are used much more extensively than items that assess higher-level thinking and reasoning, mainly because it is much easier to write short-answer or multiple-choice questions. In far too many instances the richness of instruction is undermined by the use of test items that trivialize the breadth and depth of the concepts and skills taught.

Each example that follows states the objective taught, the test item used to assess it, and an alternative item that would have provided a more suitable assessment of the objective. Note that the poor items trivialized higher-level objectives by assessing them with a memory item.

1. **Objective:** Given a description of a literary form, the pupils can classify the form as fable, mystery, folktale, or fantasy.
   Poor item: What kind of stories did Aesop tell? _____.
   A. fables   B. mysteries   C. folktales   D. fantasies
   Better item: A story tells about the year A.D. 2020 and the adventures of a young Martian named Zik, who traveled to other worlds to capture strange creatures for the zoo at Martian City. This story is best classified as a

   _____.
   A. fable   B. mystery   C. folktale   D. fantasy

2. **Objective:** The pupils describe similarities and differences in chemical compounds and elements.
   Poor item: Chlorine and bromine are both members of a chemical group called the _____.
   Better item: Chlorine and bromine are both halogens. What similarities do they possess that make them halogens? What are two differences in their chemical properties?

3. **Objective:** The pupils can explain how life was changed for the Sioux Indians when they moved from the forests to the grasslands.
   Poor item: What animal did the Sioux hunt on the grasslands?
   Better Item: What are three changes in the life of the Sioux that happened when they moved from the forests to the grasslands?

Test items that do not reflect the important topics of instruction are not valid indicators of student achievement.

There are two main reasons for ensuring that the questions in an achievement test align with the important topics and skills that were emphasized during instruction. First, if there is not a good alignment between instruction and the test questions, performance on the test will be a poor indication of actual learning. Pupils may have learned what was taught but were stymied by an invalid test. Low grades usually accompany such invalid tests and can diminish pupils' effort and confidence.

Second, tests that do not align with instruction have little positive influence on motivating and focusing pupil study. If pupils find little relationship between instruction and test content, they will undervalue instruction. You can remember instances when you prepared well for a test based on the teacher's instruction and review only to find that the test contained many questions that focused either on picky, isolated details or on types of problems that were not discussed in class. Recall how you felt when you tried to prepare for the next test given by that teacher.

The problem of mismatch between tests and instruction can be overcome to a large degree by thinking about testing earlier than the day before the test is to be given. With relatively little advance planning, tests that assess the important aspects of instruction can be prepared.

Write Clearly and Simply: Seven Rules

If test questions use ambiguous words or sentence structure, include inappropriate vocabulary, or contain clues to the correct answers, the test will not be a valid indicator of pupil achievement. The most important skill in writing or selecting good test items is the ability to express oneself clearly and succinctly. Test items should be (1) briefly stated so pupils do not spend a disproportionate amount of time reading, (2) clearly expressed so pupils understand their task, and (3) capable of standing alone since each item provides a separate measurement.

Following are seven rules for writing sound test items. Each is illustrated by some confusing test items prepared by teachers who knew the content they wanted to test but who were unable to clearly state their intent. A better version of the same items is also shown for comparison.

Rule 1: Avoid ambiguous and confusing wording and sentence structure. Pupils must understand test questions. If the wording or sentence structure is confusing and prevents pupils from figuring out what they are being asked, pupils cannot demonstrate their learning. Consider the following test items.

1. All but one of the following is not an element. Which one is not?
   A. carbon   B. salt   C. sugar   D. plastic

2. Maine is not the only state that does not have a border with a neighboring state.   T F

In these examples, the wording and sentence construction are awkward and confusing. The pupil has to sort through multiple negatives to figure out what is being asked. It is better, therefore, to phrase questions briefly, directly, and in the positive voice, as shown in these edited versions.

1. Which one of these is an element?
   A. carbon   B. salt   C. sugar   D. plastic

2. Maine borders another state.   T F

Other items, such as examples 3 and 4, are more than just confusing, they are virtually incomprehensible.

3. What is the relative length of the shortest distance between Chicago and Detroit and Sacramento? _____

4. The _____ produced by the _____ is used by the green _____ to change _____ and _____ into _____. This process is known as _____.

Test items should be brief, clearly written, and free of ambiguous words so that comprehension is not an issue.

What is a reasonable answer to each? Taken individually, the words in example 3 are not overly difficult, but their sequencing makes their intent altogether unclear. Example 4 is so mutilated with blank spaces that a pupil has to be a mind reader to figure out what is being asked. No pupil should be confronted by such a question. Pupils will answer items like examples 3 and 4 incorrectly regardless of how well they have mastered the information and skills taught them. The following changes overcome the problems in these two examples.

3. Which is closer to Sacramento, Chicago or Detroit? _____

4. The process in which green plants use the sun's energy to turn water and carbon dioxide into food is called _____.

If a pupil answers the revised items incorrectly, it is because he or she does not know the desired answer. That is acceptable. Remember, the purpose of a test item is not to guarantee correct answers, but to give pupils a *fair* chance to show how much they know about the things they were taught. To do this, test items must be readily comprehended.

Another factor that prevents pupils from being able to focus quickly and clearly on the question being posed is the use of ambiguous words or phrases. Read examples 5, 6, and 7 and try to identify a problem in each that could cause pupils difficulty in deciding how to answer.

5. Shakespeare was the world's greatest playwright.   T F

6. The most important city in the Southeast is _____.
   A. Atlanta   B. Miami   C. New Orleans   D. Tuscaloosa

7. Write an essay in which you consider the future of atomic energy.

Each example contains an ambiguous term that could be puzzling to pupils and make their choice of an answer difficult. The true-false example contains the undefined word *greatest*. Did the teacher mean that Shakespeare wrote more plays than any other playwright? that more of his plays are still being performed than those of any other playwright? that his plays are required reading in more American classrooms than those of any other playwright? Until pupils know what the teacher means by *greatest*, they will have difficulty responding. Example 6 has the same fault. What does the phrase *most important* mean? Each of these cities is important in many ways. Words like *greatest, most important, best,* and similar ambiguous words should he replaced by more specific language, regardless of the type of test item used.

Note the rewritten versions of examples 5 and 6.

5. More of William Shakespeare's plays are required reading in American classrooms than those of any other playwright.　　　　　T　F

6. The main transportation center for train and airplane traffic in the Southeast is _____.

   A. Atlanta　　B. Miami　　C. New Orleans　　D. Tuscaloosa

In example 7 the teacher wants the pupils to consider the future of atomic energy. Does the teacher mean compare and contrast atomic energy to fossil fuel; discuss the relative merits of fission versus fusion as a means of generating energy; or explain the positive and negative consequences of increased use of atomic energy? It is not clear. The item needs to be more specific for the pupils to respond in the way the teacher desires as shown in this revised version.

7. Describe the advantages and disadvantages of increased use of atomic energy in the automobile manufacturing process.

In most cases, the teachers who wrote the preceding examples knew what they wanted to ask pupils but were unable to write items that clearly conveyed their intent. Teachers must say precisely what they mean, not assume or hope that their pupils will interpret their test items in the ways intended.

Rule 2: Use appropriate vocabulary. The difficulty level of test questions can be influenced dramatically by vocabulary. If pupils cannot understand the vocabulary used in test questions, their test scores will reflect their vocabulary deficiencies rather than how much they have learned from instruction. Based on early assessments every teacher should take into account the vocabulary level of his or her pupils when writing or selecting the items for achievement tests. Note the difference in the following two ways of writing a true-false question to assess pupils' understanding of capillary action, a principle that explains how liquids rise in narrow passages.

> The postulation of capillary effectuation promotes elucidation of how pliant substances ascend in incommodious veins.　　　　　T　F
>
> The principle of capillary action helps explain how liquids rise in small passages.　　　　　T　F

Clearly, vocabulary level can affect the ability of pupils to understand what is being asked in a test question.

Rule 3: Keep questions short and to the point. Items should quickly focus pupils on the question being asked. Examine these questions.

Questions should be short, specific, and written at pupils' vocabulary level.

8. Switzerland
   A. is located in Asia.
   B. produces large quantities of gold.
   C. has no direct access to the ocean.
   D. is a flat, arid plain.

9. Billy's mother wanted to bake an apple pie for his aunt and uncle, who were coming for a visit. Billy had not seen them for many months. When Billy's mother saw that she had no apples in the house, she sent Billy to the store to buy some. Her recipe called for 8 apples to make a pie. If apples at the store cost 30 cents for two, how much money will Billy need to buy eight apples?

A. $.30   B. $.90   C. $1.20   D. $2.40

In example 8, the stem does not clearly set a problem for the pupil, that is, after pupils read the item stem Switzerland, they still have no idea of the question being asked. Only after reading the stem *and* all the options does the point of the item begin to become clear. The item could be more directly stated as follows.

8. Which of the following statements about the geography of Switzerland is true?

A. It is located in Asia.
B. It is a flat, arid plain.
C. It has no direct access to the ocean.
D. It has a tropical climate.

Example 9 is intended to determine whether the pupil can correctly calculate the cost of some apples. The information about the aunt and uncle's visit, how long it had been since Billy last saw them, or the lack of apples in the house is not important, can be distracting, and takes time away from relevant items. A better way to state the item is shown here.

9. To make an apple pie Billy's mother needed 8 apples. If apples cost 30 cents for two, how much will 8 apples cost?

A. $.30   B. $.90   C. $1.20   D. $2.40

In short-answer or completion items, the blanks should come at the end of the sentence so pupils know what kind of a response is required. Compare these two items and notice how placing the blank at the end helps convey what the item is about.

_____ and _____ are the names of two rivers that meet in Pittsburgh.

The names of two rivers that meet in Pittsburgh are _____ and _____.

Matching items can also be written to help pupils focus more quickly on the questions being asked. Look over example 10 and suggest a change that would focus pupils more clearly on the questions they have to answer.

10. Draw a line to match the president in column A with his accomplishment in column B.

Column A	Column B
G. Washington	signed the Emancipation Proclamation
T. Jefferson	president during the New Deal
U. Grant	first president of the United States
F. Roosevelt	head of Northern troops in Civil War
	main author of the Declaration of Independence

Most matching items can be improved by placing the column with the lengthier descriptions on the left and the column with the shorter descriptions on the right, as shown next.

10. Draw a line to match the president in column B with his accomplishment in column A. One accomplishment will not be used.

Column A	Column B
Signed the Emancipation Proclamation	G. Washington
President during the New Deal	T. Jefferson
First president of the United States	U. Grant
Head of Northern troops in Civil War	F. Roosevelt
Main author of the Declaration of Independence	

Rule 4: Write items that have one correct answer. With the exception of essay questions, most paper-and-pencil test items are designed to have pupils select or supply one best answer. With this goal in mind, read examples 11 and 12. See how many correct answers you can provide for each item.

With the exception of essays, most test items should have only one correct answer.

11. Who was George Washington? _____.

12. Ernest Hemingway wrote _____.

Each of these items has more than one correct answer. George Washington was the first president of the United States, but he also was a member of the Continental Congress, commander of the Continental Army, a Virginian, a surveyor, a slave owner, and a man with false teeth. Faced with such an item, pupils ask themselves, which of the many things I know about George Washington should I answer? Similarly, Ernest Hemingway wrote short stories and letters, in Spain, in pencil, as well as famous novels such as *The Old Man and the Sea.*

Examples 11 and 12 can be restated so that pupils know precisely what is being asked. Notice how each question asks for something specific—a name or a country—thus indicating to pupils the nature of the expected answer.

11. What is the name of the first president of the United States? _____.

12. The name of the author of *The Old Man and the Sea* is _____.

Items with more than one correct answer occur much more often in short-answer and completion items than in selection items. Unless short-answer or completion items are stated specifically and narrowly, the teacher can expect many different responses. The dilemma for the teacher then becomes whether to give credit for answers that are technically correct but not the desired one.

Rule 5: Give information about the nature of the desired answer. While the failure to properly focus pupils is common to all types of test items, it is most often seen in essay items. Despite pupils' freedom to structure their own responses, essay questions should still require pupils to demonstrate mastery of key ideas, principles, or concepts that were taught. An essay, like any other type of test item, should be constructed to find out how well pupils have learned the things they were taught.

Here are a few typical essay questions written by classroom teachers.

13. Compare and contrast the North and South in the Civil War. Support your views.

14. Describe what happened to art during the Renaissance.

15. Why should you study science?

In each of these questions, the pupils' task is not clearly defined. When pupils encounter global questions such as these they may have little idea of what the teacher is looking for and may end up with a poor grade because they incorrectly guessed the teacher's intent. This practice is unfair to pupils and produces test results that do not reflect their achievement.

Essay questions should focus students' answers on the major points covered by instruction.

To determine whether pupils have learned what was taught, essay questions should be narrowed to focus pupils on the areas of interest. Pupils should be informed about the nature and scope of the expected answer. While essay questions should provide the pupil freedom to select, organize, state, and defend positions, they should not give pupils total freedom to write whatever they want. Obviously, to develop a well-focused essay question the teacher must give considerable thought to the purpose and scope of the question before actually writing it.

Examples 13, 14, and 15 and have been rewritten to more precisely reflect the teacher's intent. Notice how the vague and ambiguous directions (support your views; describe) are made clearer to pupils in the revised questions.

13. What forces led to the outbreak of the Civil War? Indicate in your discussion economic conditions, foreign policies, and social conditions in the North and the South before the war. Which two factors were most influential in the start of the Civil War? Give two reasons to support your choice of each factor. Your answer will be graded on your discussion of the differences between the North and South at the start of the war and the strength of the arguments you advance to support your choice of the two factors most influential in the start of the war (30 minutes).

14. Compare art during the Renaissance to art prior to the movement in terms of the portrayal of the human figure, use of color, and emphasis on religious themes. Your essay will be judged in terms of the distinctions you identify between the two periods and the explanations you provide to account for the differences.

15. Give two reasons a third grade pupil should study science. What are some things that studying science teaches us? What are some jobs that use science? Write your answer in at least five complete sentences.

Certainly these are not the only ways that these essay items could have been rewritten, but these revisions point out the need for focus in essay questions. When pupils approach these revised items, they have a clear sense of what is expected of them; they no longer have to guess what the scope and direction of their answers should be. Note also that it is much more difficult for the pupil to bluff an answer to the revised items than it is to the initial, broadly stated items. The revised items call for answers specifically related to instruction, and therefore test what was taught and make scoring easier. To write such items, however, the teacher must have a clear sense of what he or she is trying to assess before administering the essay.

To summarize, regardless of the particular type of test item used, pupils should be given a clear idea of what their task is. In the case of multiple-choice items this may mean elaborating a stem in order to clarify the options. In matching items it may involve putting the longer options in the left column. In short-answer or completion items it may mean placing the blank at the end of the statement or specifying precisely the nature of the desired answer. In essay questions it may mean elaborating to include information about the scope, direction, and scoring criteria for a desired answer. In all cases, the intent is to allow the pupil to respond validly and efficiently to the items.

For all types of test items, pupils should have a clear sense of what is expected of them.

Rule 6: Do not provide clues to the correct answer. The item-writing rules discussed thus far have all been aimed at problems that inhibited pupils from doing their best. However, the opposite problem arises when test items contain clues that help pupils answer questions correctly even though they have not learned the content being tested. Many types of clues may appear in items: grammatical clues, implausible option clues, and specific determiner clues. Try to identify the clue in examples 16 and 17.

Test item writers should take care not to provide grammatical clues, implausible option clues, or specific determiner clues.

16. A figure that has eight sides is called an _____.
     A. pentagon   B. quadrilateral   C. octagon   D. ogive

17. Compared to autos of the 1960s, autos in the 1980s _____.
     A. more horsepower.
     B. to use more fuel.
     C. contain more safety features.
     D. was less often constructed in foreign countries.

These examples contain grammatical clues. In example 16, using the article *a* or *an* at the end of the question or stem indicates to pupils what letter will begin the next word. The *an* before the blank tells the pupil that the next word must begin with a vowel, so the options pentagon and quadrilateral cannot be correct. There are two ways to correct this problem: replace the single article with the combined *a(n)* or get rid of the article altogether by writing the question in the plural form.

16. Figures that have eight sides are called _____.
    A. pentagons   B. quadrilaterals   C. octagons   D. ogives

In example 17, only option C grammatically fits the stem. Regardless of pupils' knowledge, they can select the correct answer because of the grammatical clue. The corrected item might read:

17. Compared to autos of the 1960s autos in the 1980s _____.
    A. have more horsepower.
    B. use more fuel.
    C. contain more safety features.
    D. are always constructed in foreign countries.

Now try to find the clues in examples 18 and 19.

18. Which of the following best describes an electron?
    A. negative particle
    B. neutral particle
    C. positive particle
    D. a voting machine

19. Match the correct phrase in column A with the term in column B. Write the *letter* of the term in column B on the line in front of the correct phrase in column A.

    Column A   **Column B**
    _____ 1. type of flower   A. cobra
    _____ 2. poisonous snake   B. fission
    _____ 3. how amoebae reproduce   C. green
    _____ 4. color of chlorophyll   D. hydrogen
    _____ 5. chemical element   E. rose

Example 18 contains a clue that is less obvious than those in examples 16 and 18, but is quite common in multiple-choice items. One of the options is inappropriate or implausible and therefore is immediately dismissed by the pupils. Choice D, a voting machine, is dismissed as an unlikely answer by all but the most careless readers. As much as possible, options in test questions should be realistic and reasonable. A useful rule of thumb is to have at least three incorrect (but reasonable) options, or **distractors,** in each multiple-choice item.

A distractor is a reasonable but incorrect option in a multiple-choice item.

The more choices pupils have, the less likely it is that they can guess the correct answer. Understanding this, teachers sometimes write three or four good options for an item and then add a fourth or fifth, such as none of the above or all of the above. It is usually better to avoid such general options.

Example 19 is a very easy question; the topics are so different from one another that many of the options in column B are implausible matches to the statements in column A. The item does not test one homogeneous subject area.

Consider the following matching item, that tests pupils' knowledge of a single, homogeneous topic. Note the difficulty in answering this item compared to the previous version of example 19.

A matching item should test the students' knowledge of a single homogeneous topic.

19. Match the names of the animals in column A to their correct classification in column B. Write the *letter* of the correct classification on the line in front of each animal name. The choices in column B may be used more than once.

Column A
_____ 1. alligator
_____ 2. condor
_____ 3. frog
_____ 4. porpoise
_____ 5. snake
_____ 6. salamander

Column B
A. amphibian
B. bird
C. fish
D. mammal
E. reptile

The revised item is a better test of pupils' knowledge in two ways. First, it does not include the obvious matches and mismatches that occur when many unrelated topics are contained in the same matching item. The revised version focuses on a single topic, classification of animals into groups. Second, unlike example 19, the revised item has an unequal number of entries in columns A and B. Unequal entries in the two columns of a matching item prevent pupils from getting the last match correct by the process of elimination.

Look for the clues in examples 20 and 21.

20. Some people think the moon is made of green cheese.　　　T　F

21. One should never phrase a test item in the negative.　　　T　F

These items contain clues that are called **specific determiners.** In true-false questions, words such as *always, never, all,* and *none* tend to appear in statements that are false, and testwise pupils tend to answer accordingly. Conversely, words like *some, sometimes,* and *may* tend to appear in statements that are true. Thus, in example 20, it is reasonable to assume that *some* people think the moon is made of green cheese, so T should be marked. On the other hand, example 21 must be marked F if there is even a single situation in which a test item can reasonably be stated in the negative (e.g., Which one of these is *not* an example of democracy?).

Rule 7: Don't overcomplicate test items. Occasionally, teachers and textbooks overcomplicate test items. Consider the following item, which was given to sixth graders to test their mastery of applying the procedure to calculate simple interest.

> John borrowed $117.55 from Bob at an interest rate of 9.73 percent a year. How much simple interest must John pay Bob at the end of 15 months?

The numbers in this example are difficult and almost ensure that many sixth grade pupils will make computational errors. Unless the teacher was specifically testing computational accuracy, the following example would better assess the pupils' ability to apply the procedure.

> John borrowed $150.00 from Bob at an interest rate of 9.00 percent a year. How much simple interest must John pay Bob at the end of 1 year?

The latter item assesses pupils' mastery of simple interest without complicating the computation so much that errors are likely to occur.

Review Items before Testing

It is helpful to have a colleague or friend critique test items before the test is administered to students.

The best advice that can be given to improve most classroom tests is to review them before reproducing and administering them to pupils. Having written or selected the items for a chapter or unit test, it is recommended that a teacher wait one day and then reread them. The teacher should also ask a colleague, spouse, or friend to review the items critically.

Most of the links in the chain of achievement testing—the importance of providing pupils with good instruction, the decisions that must be made in planning achievement tests, the instructional review that should precede testing, and the construction or selection of test items that give pupils a fair chance to demonstrate their learning—have all been examined. Two additional links that influence the adequacy of achievement tests are (1) assembling and administering the test and (2) scoring the test. These will be covered in Chapter 8. Key Assessment Tools 7.1 summarizes advice regarding different types of items.

TECHNOLOGY AND ASSESSMENT

COMPUTER VERSUS PAPER TESTING

In a recent Oregon survey, third graders responded positively about their performance on a Web-based state reading exam, compared with a paper-and-pencil version of the Oregon state reading exam. While high school students were less positive, most still felt they either did better on the Web-based test or equally well on the Web and paper versions of the test.

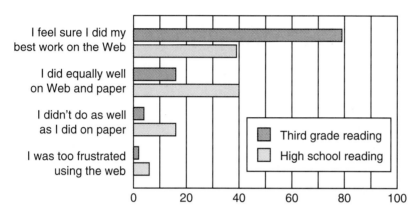

Note: Percentages do not add up to 100 because of rounding.

A majority of third graders found the online version of the Oregon state math test easier to use than the paper-and-pencil verson while 38 percent of high school students found the Web version easier to use and more enjoyable.

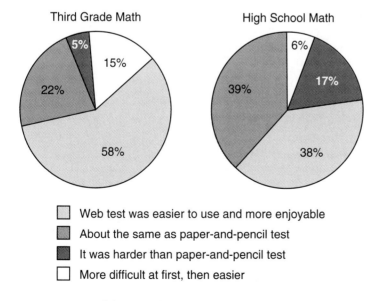

Source: Oregon Department of Education, Technology Enhanced Student Assessment (TESA), student survey, 2001.

Key Assessment Tools 7.1

WRITING TEST ITEMS

Multiple-choice items

1. Put each test item on a different line.
2. Place the pupil tasks in the item stem.
3. Put repeated terms in the item stem.
4. Construct at least three alternative choices.
5. Put options in logical order, if possible.
6. Avoid grammatical clues to the answer.
7. Be sure that items match pupils' reading level.
8. Do not include unneeded words.
9. If "no" is used, underline it.
10. Reread the item to identify spelling and other errors.
11. The item stem should clearly state the question to be answered.

True-false items

1. Make items clearly true or false.
2. Be sure that the item is important in the assessment.
3. Avoid specific determiners.
4. Make the true and false items about the same length.
5. Do not use items in a repetitive pattern.
6. Do not use textbook sentences.

Short-answer items

1. Make sure the item relates to the assessment being taught.
2. Provide a clear focus for the intended answer.
3. Make answers possible in short responses; construct item so that pupil answers are short.
4. Ask pupils to reply in only one or two responses.
5. Be sure item assesses the intended responses.
6. Put space for the item at the end of the item.
7. Avoid giving grammatical clues.

Matching answer items

1. Be sure the exercise relates to the assessment.
2. Compare homogeneous topics.
3. Make sure the directions are clear.
4. Put the longer options in the left-hand column.
5. Number one set of items; mark the other set with letters.
6. Do not ask for more than 10 responses in the assessment. If more responses are desired, begin a new matching test.

(continued)

> ## Key Assessment Tools 7.1 (*Continued*)
> ### WRITING TEST ITEMS
>
> 7. Provide one on two additional options on one column to avoid the final option being the correct answer by default.
>
> **Essay questions**
>
> 1. Use several short essays rather than one long one.
> 2. Be sure that the reading level is appropriate for pupils.
> 3. Be sure the essay relates to your objectives.
> 4. Base the essay on a fresh example, if examples are used.
> 5. Provide a clear focus of the desired outcome of the essay.
> 6. Do not use essays that require a great deal of memory.
> 7. Aid pupils by focusing them with terms such as "state and defend the topic," "apply the principle to," "develop a valid conclusion," and so on. These kinds of instructions focus pupils and also help to focus the grading.
> 8. Provide pupils with clear directions about the expected length of essay and the amount of time for completion.
> 9. Provide pupils with clear scoring criteria—for example, will spelling count?

ACCOMMODATIONS: SUBSTITUTIONS FOR PAPER-AND-PENCIL

The next chapter will include a discussion of various accommodations that can be arranged for students with disabilities in a testing situation. Here we will consider a few alternatives to conventional written or oral expression.

The simplest way to accommodate a pupil who is physically unable to respond in writing to a test of subject knowledge and ideas is to make the test oral, though obviously this does not test writing or written organizational skills. In some cases it may be appropriate for a student with a physical disability to use a computer in place of paper and pencil. In other cases, special equipment may be needed to make the computer itself accessible to such a pupil. There may be a special resources person or classroom in your school that can help with this type of problem, which is likely to require some forethought. Figure 7.2 is a suggestive rather than definitive list of products and website resources that can be useful. For pupils with extreme physical limitations there may be workable accommodations, such as speech-to-text software for pupils unable to type.

FIGURE 7.2   *Resources for Universal Design.*

Software

Built-in Accessibility of Operating Systems

Apple Special Needs
www.apple.com
(search for special needs)

Microsoft Enable
www.microsoft.com/enable

Text-to-Speech Software Programs

CAST eReader www.cast.org

Kurzwell 3000
www.kurzweiledu.com

ReadPlease 2003
www.readplease.com

TextHELP! www.texthelp.com

Write: OutLoud
www.donjohnston.com

WYNN
www.freedomscientific.com

Speech-to-Text Software Programs

Dragon Naturally Speaking
www.scansoft.com

IBM ViaVoice www.3.ibm.com

Accessible Multimedia

HiSoftware
www.hisoftware.com

Hardware

Portable Word Processors

AlphaSmart
www.alphasmart.com

CalcuScribe
www.calcuscribe.com

DreamWriter
www.brainium.com

LaserPC6
www.perfectsolutions.com

QuickPad www.quickpad.com

Handwriting Recognition Technologies

InkLink
www.siibusinessproducts.com

InkWell
www.apple.com/macrosx/
jaguar/inkwell.html

Logitech io Personal Digital Pen
www.logitech.com

PenReader
www.smarttech.com

Electronic Whiteboards

Mimio
www.mimio.com

SMARTBoard
www.smarttech.com

Online Resources

Digital Text

American Library Association
Great Sites for Children
www.ala.org/parentspage/
greatsites/lit.html

Berkeley Digital Library SunSite
http://sunsite.berkeley.edu

The Children's Literature Web Guide
www.ucalgary.ca/%7Edkbrown

Internet Public Library
www.ipl.org

Project Gutenberg
www.promo.net.pg

University of Virginia Library Electronic Text Center
http://etext.lib.virginia.edu/
ebooks

Organizations

Technology in Education

Association for the Advancement of Computing in Education (AACE)
www.aace.org

Association for Educational Communications and Technology (AECT)
www.aect.org

International Society for Technology in Education (STE)
www.iste.org

Network of Regional Technology in Education Consortia
www.rtec.org

U.S. Department of Education Office of Educational Technology
www.ed.gov/Technology

Accessibility

CPB/WGBH National Center for Accessible Media
http://ncam.wgbh.org

SOURCE: Curry, C. (2003). Universal design accessibility for all learners. *Educational Leadership,* (61) 2, 55–60.

FIGURE 7.3   *The Braille Alphabet, Numbers, and Punctuation.*

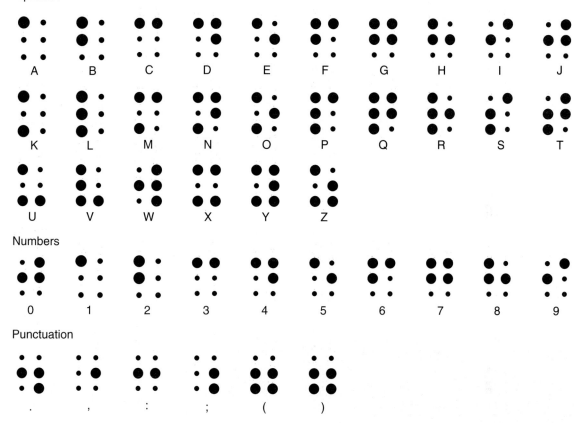

Two common disabilities, deafness and blindness, can require different interventions. While it is unlikely in the early grades to have a child with extreme hearing or vision limitations in a normally sighted and hearing classroom, the chances increase at the secondary school level, and many blind (and some deaf) students do college work among mainly sighted and hearing people.

Many teachers and students intending to teach become at least somewhat familiar with sign language or Braille in order to better aid those with hearing or vision disabilities that they teach. Figures 7.3 and 7.4 show the alphabets of these two systems.

FIGURE 7.4   *American Finger-Spelling Alphabet.*

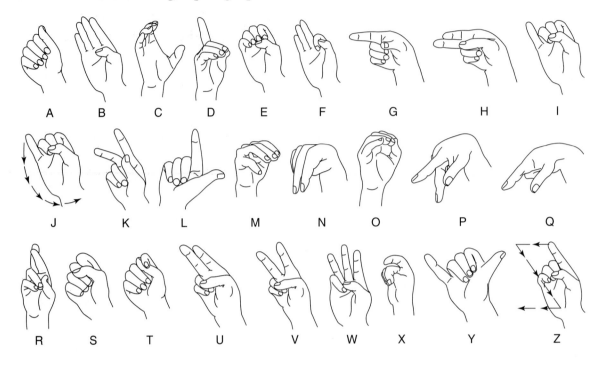

CHAPTER SUMMARY

♦ The central focus of achievement testing is to obtain a fair and representative indication of what pupils have learned from teachers' instruction.

♦ Paper-and-pencil tests are composed of two types of test questions: selection (multiple-choice, true-false, and matching) and supply (short-
answer, completion, and essay). Each general type can test both higher-
and lower-level thinking.

♦ Selection items can be answered quickly, can cover a broad sample of
instructional topics, and can be scored objectively. However, they are
time-consuming to construct and guessing answers is a problem.

♦ Supply items can be prepared easily, afford pupils the opportunity to
construct their own answers, and are rarely subject to guessing. However, they are difficult and time-consuming to score and tend to cover a
limited amount of instructional topics.

♦ Teachers should try to include higher-level questions in their instruction
and assessments. The interpretive exercise is a useful way to incorporate
higher-level skills into paper-and-pencil assessments.

◆ When writing or selecting paper-and-pencil test questions, three general guidelines should be followed: cover important topics and behaviors, write clearly and simply, and review items before testing.

◆ Most of the items in teacher-prepared and textbook tests are at the recall or memory level because such items are easier to write than higher-level questions. However, if tests are to be valid, they should reflect all the content and processes taught at both lower and higher levels. Tests that do not represent instruction can be invalid, provide a poor indication of pupil learning, and provide little influence in motivating pupils to study.

◆ Seven rules guide item writing: (1) avoid wording and sentence structure that is ambiguous and confusing; (2) use vocabulary appropriate for the pupils tested; (3) keep test items short and to the point; (4) write items that have one correct answer; (5) give pupils information about the characteristics of the desired answer; (6) avoid providing clues to test answers; and (7) don't overcomplicate test items.

◆ Paper-and-pencil test items should be aligned to the teacher's objectives and to the instruction provided.

◆ For pupils who can't take paper-and-pencil tests because of physical disabilities, accommodations are possible.

olc

CHAPTER REVIEW

Visit Chapter 7 of the Online Learning Center at **www.mhhe.com/ airasian5e** to take chapter quizzes, link to related websites, read PowerWeb articles and news feed updates, and access study tools, including the case study referenced in the chapter.

QUESTIONS FOR DISCUSSION

1. What are some objectives that are best assessed by supply items? What are some objectives that are best assessed by selection items?

2. How are early assessment, lesson plans, and instruction related to paper-and-pencil tests of pupil learning?

3. What are the pros and cons of giving pupils choices in answering essay items?

4. What harm could result if a teacher's tests produced invalid information about pupil learning?

5. Are higher-level objectives harder to teach and assess than lower-level ones? Why or why not?

ACTIVITIES

1. Each of the following eight test items has at least one fault. Read each item, identify the fault(s) in it and rewrite the item to correct the fault(s). When you have finished rewriting the items, organize them into a test to be given to students. Include directions for items and group items of a similar type together.

1. Robert Fulton, who was born in Scotland and came to the U.S. in 1843, is best known for his invention of the steamboat that he called the Tom Thumb.   T F

2. Minor differences among organisms of the same kind are known as
   A. heredity
   B. variations
   C. adaptation
   D. natural selection

3. The recall of factual information can best be assessed with a _____ item.
   A. matching
   B. objective
   C. essay
   D. short-answer

4. Although the experimental research completed, particularly that by Hansmocker, must be considered too equivocal and the assumptions viewed as too restrictive, most testing experts would recommend that the easiest method of significantly improving paper-and-pencil achievement test reliability would be to
   A. increase the size of the group
   B. increase the weighting of items
   C. increase the number of items
   D. increase the amount of testing time

5. F. Scott Fitzgerald wrote _____.

6. Boston is the most important city in the Northeast.   T F

7. An electric transformer can be used
   A. for storing up electricity
   B. to increase the voltage of alternating current (correct answer)
   C. it converts electrical energy into direct current
   D. alternating current is changed to direct current

8. The Confederate states were admitted back into the Union shortly after the Civil War.   T F

2. Below are five objectives. For each objective write one test item of the type specified in parentheses to assess the objective.

1. The student can match the symbols of chemical elements to their names.   (matching)

2. The student can identify the nouns in a sentence that contains more than one noun.   (multiple choice)

3. The student can indicate whether a statement about the U.S. Constitution is true or false.   (true-false)

4. The student can state the name of the Speaker of the House of Representatives.   (short answer)

5. The student can write the correct definition of an adverb. (short answer)

For objectives 4 and 5, describe the minimum answer that would receive full credit.

REVIEW QUESTIONS

1. What are the differences between selection and supply items? What are the advantages and disadvantages of each? What are common faults in each type?

2. What are the differences between higher- and lower-level test items?

3. Three guidelines for constructing paper-and-pencil test questions are: (1) cover important topics; (2) write clearly and simply; and (3) review items before testing. How does each of these guidelines lead to improved test questions?

4. What are examples of clues to be avoided in multiple-choice, true-false, completion, and matching items?

5. What is an interpretive exercise and why is it a useful method for assessing higher-level thinking?

6. How do tests of factual knowledge differ from tests of conceptual knowledge?

REFERENCES

Curry, C. (2003). Universal design accessibility for all learners. *Educational Leadership, 61* (2), 55–60.

Frisbie, D. A. (1992). The multiple true-false item format: A status review. *Educational Measurement: Issues and Practice, 11* (4), 21–26.

Marso, R. N., & Pigge, F. L. (1989). Elementary classroom teachers' testing needs and proficiencies: Multiple assessments and inservice training priorities. *Educational Review, 13*, 1–17.

Marso, R. N., & Pigge, F. L. (1991). The analysis of teacher-made tests: Testing practices, cognitive demands and item construction errors. *Contemporary Educational Psychology, 16*, 179–286.

CHAPTER 8

IMPROVING PAPER-AND-PENCIL ASSESSMENTS

KEY TOPICS

- *Assembling Tests*
- *Administering Tests*
- *Issues of Cheating*
- *Scoring Paper-and-Pencil Tests*
- *Analyzing Item Validity*
- *Discussing Test Results with Pupils*
- *Testing Students with Disabilities*

After reading this chapter, you will be able to:

- ♦ Define basic terms such as holistic scoring, analytic scoring, and objectivity
- ♦ State basic principles for assembling and administering tests
- ♦ Recognize the unacceptability of cheating on tests and identify strategies to reduce cheating
- ♦ Distinguish between objective and subjective scoring and holistic and analytic scoring
- ♦ Apply methods to improve the objectivity of essay scoring
- ♦ Recognize strategies to identify faulty test items
- ♦ Identify strategies for testing pupils with disabilities

THINKING ABOUT TEACHING

Apart from the validity and reliability of the test items themselves, what can a teacher do to make test results valid and reliable?

We have now examined most of the links in the chain of paper-and-pencil achievement testing. We have discussed the importance of providing pupils with good instruction, the decisions teachers must make in planning tests, the instructional review that should precede testing, and the construction or selection of test items that give pupils a fair chance to demonstrate their learning. Four final steps influence the adequacy of achievement tests: (1) assembling and administering the test, (2) understanding and dealing with cheating, (3) scoring the test, and (4) giving feedback to pupils about the results. This chapter addresses these topics along with pupil physical disabilities that interfere with paper-and-pencil work.

ASSEMBLING TESTS

Once test items have been written or selected and reviewed, they must be arranged into a test. If a teacher uses a textbook test or statewide assessment, the items will already be arranged and ready for copying. Often teachers cut and paste items from various sources into a single test. In assembling a test, similar types of items should be grouped together and kept separate from other item types. All of the short-answer questions should be together and separate from the multiple-choice, matching, completion, and essay questions. Grouping test items by type avoids the necessity of pupils shifting from one response mode to another as they move

When a test is assembled, test items of the same type should be grouped together. Supply items should be placed last.

from item to item. It also means that a single set of directions can be used for all of the items in that test section, helping pupils cover more items in a given time. Finally, grouping test items makes scoring easier.

Another important consideration in assembling the test is the order in which the item types are presented to pupils. In most tests, selection items come first and supply items come last. Within the supply section, short-answer or completion questions should be placed before essay questions. Supply items are placed at the end of the test so that pupils will not devote a disproportionate amount of time to this part of the test.

When arranging items on a test, remember these commonsense practices.

1. Designate a space for pupils to write their name and/or ID number.
2. Do not split a multiple-choice or matching item across two pages of the test. This can cause unintended errors when pupils flip from one page to the next to read the second half of a matching question or the last two options of a multiple-choice question.
3. Separate multiple-choice options from the stem by beginning the options on a new line.
4. Number test items, especially if pupils must record answers on a separate answer sheet or in a special place on the test.
5. Space items for easy reading and provide enough space for pupils to complete supply items. Remember that young pupils write big. Do not cram items closely together.
6. Proofread the test yourself or have someone else do so before photocopying.
7. Check the clarity of photocopied tests. Make a few extra copies.

Each section of the test should have directions telling students what to do, how to respond, and where to place their answers.

Each section of a test should have directions that focus pupils on what to do, how to respond, and where to place their answers. Lack of clear directions is one of the most common faults in teacher-prepared tests and often influences test validity. Here are some sample directions.

♦ Items 1–15 are multiple-choice items. Read each item carefully and write the *letter* of your answer on the line in front of the question number.
♦ Use words from the boxes to complete the sentences. Use each word only once.
♦ Answer each question by writing the correct answer in the space below the question. No answer should be longer than one sentence.
♦ For items 10 to 15, circle T or F (true or false).
♦ Use the chart to help you answer questions 27–33. Write your answers in the space provided after each question.

Directions such as these at the start of a test section focus pupils by telling them where and how to respond to the questions. To emphasize a point made earlier, it is especially important that each essay question spell out clearly for pupils the scope and characteristics of the desired answer. For older pupils, it is also helpful to indicate the number of points that will be given to each test section so they can make decisions about how to allocate their time.

The test should be reproduced so that each pupil has his or her own copy. Writing the test questions on the blackboard can be time-consuming, create problems for pupils with poor vision, and encourage pupils to look around the room during test taking. Orally reading questions can be used to pace pupils, but this approach places a premium on listening ability and prevents pupils from working at their own pace. This practice should be avoided unless one is assessing listening skills. In most circumstances, giving each pupil his or her own copy is the best way to present the test.

Tests that promote valid decisions also need to be reliable—that is, produce consistent scores. Without reliability a test can hardly provide the kind of information on which one would want to base decisions about a pupil's learning. The main factors in attaining reliable achievement tests are (1) the number and representativeness of the items included on the test and (2) the objectivity of scoring. In general, longer tests allow a teacher to look at a larger sample of pupil performance. For example, which test do you think would produce the more stable and consistent information about a pupil's spelling achievement; a test that consists of a single word selected from a 100-word list, or a test that contains a sample of 15 words selected from the same 100-word list? Key Assessment Tools 8.1 summarizes guidelines for assembling tests.

The more items on a test the higher its reliability, because the teacher can look at a larger sample of pupil performance.

Key Assessment Tools 8.1
GUIDELINES FOR ASSEMBLING A TEST

This list combines some suggestions from the discussion with several other good ideas.

◆ Organize the test by item type: selection before supply, essay last.

◆ Allow sufficient space for written responses, especially for young children's essay items.

◆ Do not split multiple-choice or matching items across two pages.

◆ Separate stem from options in multiple-choice questions.

◆ Number test items.

◆ Provide clear directions for each section of the test; for older pupils, indicate the value of each section or question.

◆ Provide enough questions to ensure reliability.

◆ Proofread the test before copying and make extra copies.

ADMINISTERING TESTS

The aim of test administration is to establish both a physical and psychological setting that permits pupils to show their best performance. The setting should also make it easy for pupils to keep track of the time.

Physical Setting

One way to minimize interruptions is to post a sign on the door indicating testing is occurring.

Pupils should have a quiet, comfortable environment in which to take the test. Interruptions should be minimized; some teachers post a sign on the door indicating that testing is in progress. During testing there is little one can do about interruptions like fire drills or announcements from the classroom squawk box. When such interruptions occur, the teacher must make a judgment about whether it is fair for pupils to continue with testing. Obviously a 1-minute interruption from the squawk box is less disruptive than a 20-minute fire drill, during which pupils may talk to one another about the test. If an interruption is judged sufficiently disruptive to diminish pupils' ability to provide a fair and representative indication of their achievement, testing should be terminated and repeated at another time.

Often interruptions occur when pupils ask questions during testing. A good way to minimize many of these questions is to proofread items and directions prior to administering the test. Occasionally, typographical errors or unclear items are not detected until testing has begun. Usually, a pupil raises his or her hand or approaches the teacher to ask a question or point out a problem. When such situations arise, an announcement should be made to the whole class informing them of the problem (e.g., "Please correct item 17 in the following way," or "Option B in item 29 should be changed to . . ."). In the end, the decision of whether and how to answer pupil questions rests with the individual teacher. Answering questions during testing is appropriate as long as the teacher is consistent in responding to all pupils who ask questions.

Psychological Setting

Test anxiety is diminished by giving students advance notice of the test, an opportunity to prepare for it, and by a pre-test review.

Establishing a productive psychological setting that reduces pupil anxiety and sets a proper atmosphere for testing is as important as providing a comfortable physical environment. Giving pupils good instruction, advance notice of the test, a day or two to prepare for it, and a good chapter or unit review will help diminish pupils' test anxiety. Even so, it is probably impossible to completely allay all test anxiety.

No teacher should precede test administration with a comment like, "This is the most important test you will take this term. Your grade and your future in this course will be determined primarily by how you do on

> **Key Assessment Tools 8.2**
>
> ## GUIDELINES FOR ADMINISTERING A TEST
>
> ♦ Provide a quiet, comfortable setting.
>
> ♦ Try to anticipate and avoid questions during the test by using good directions.
>
> ♦ Provide a good psychological setting; provide advance notice, review, and encouragement for pupils to do their best.
>
> ♦ Discourage cheating through seating arrangements, your own circulation about the room, and enforcement of rules and penalties.
>
> ♦ Help pupils keep track of time.

this test." A speech like this will raise pupils' anxiety levels appreciably and hamper their ability to show what they have learned. Conversely, test administration should not be prefaced with remarks such as, "Everybody knows that tests don't mean much; I just give tests because I have to" or "Don't worry about it—it counts very little in your final grade." Describing and treating a test as if it were a trivial interruption in the school day will diminish its ability to motivate pupil study and will interfere with pupils' test performances.

The line between overemphasizing and underemphasizing the importance of a test is hard to draw. Pupils should take tests seriously and they should be encouraged to do their best. The appropriate middle ground between over- and underemphasizing the importance of tests will vary with the age and characteristics of pupils. The more pupils know about the test, the more likely their anxiety will be lowered. Good instruction, a thorough review, and prior knowledge of which types of items will be on the test helps pupils relax at test time. Of course, fair, valid test items and no "surprises" such as unannounced tests, unfamiliar item types, and untaught topics will help allay test anxiety. Each teacher must find the middle ground for his or her class, knowing that whatever is done, there will be some pupils who will be very anxious about their performance and some who will not care.

Key Assessment Tools 8.2 summarizes important concerns in test administration.

Keeping Track of Time

During testing it often helps students if the teacher keeps track of the remaining time with announcements such as "There are 20 minutes left until the test is over." Such reminders can initially be made at 15-minute intervals, then changed to 5-minute intervals near the end of the test. Such reminders are most useful at the middle and high school levels during final exams, which usually take longer than a single class period to administer. In self-contained elementary school classrooms, where testing and instruction are ruled less by the bell schedule, the teacher has discretion regarding when and how to start and end testing.

ISSUES OF CHEATING

Teachers can discourage cheating with seating arrangements, careful proctoring, and swift punishment of those who do cheat.

Teachers should be alert to the possibility of cheating on tests, projects, quizzes, and assignments. Unfortunately, cheating is a common occurrence, both in school and in life. Students cheat for many reasons: external pressure from teachers or parents; failure to prepare and study for tests; internal pressure from being in an intensively competitive major or course that gives a limited number of high grades; danger of losing a scholarship; and, unfortunately, because "everybody else does it." Some even blame their cheating on the practices of others. For example, some try to justify cheating with excuses like, "No one near me was attempting to cover up their exam paper," "The course material is too difficult," "There's just too much material to learn," or "The instructor gives tests that are unfair."

However, no matter how and why it is done, cheating is an unacceptable, dishonest, and immoral classroom behavior. The argument that says, "So what, everybody does it. It's no big deal," is wrong. It *is* a big deal. Cheating is analogous to lying. When students cheat and turn in work or a test under the pretense that they did the work themselves, that is lying and should be recognized and called lying (Summergrad, 1999).

Types of Cheating on Tests

How do pupils cheat on tests? Cizek (1999) has written a useful and comprehensive book that explores cheating in depth and with understanding. He identifies and gives examples of a very large number of the ways that pupils cheat. The following examples adapted from Cizek's work represent a small sample of common ways pupils cheat. He provides many additional and esoteric ways.

1. Looking at another pupil's test paper during a test.
2. Dropping one's paper so that other pupils can cheat off it.
3. Dropping one's paper and having another pupil pick it up, cheat from it, and dropping it again so the original dropper can reclaim his or her paper.
4. Passing an eraser between two pupils who write test information on the eraser.
5. Developing codes such as tapping the floor three times to indicate that a multiple-choice item should be answered "C."

6. Looking at pupils' papers while walking up to the teacher to ask a question about the test.

7. Using crib notes or small pieces of paper to cheat. Crib notes can be hidden in many ingenious places.

8. Wearing a T-shirt with useful test information written on it.

9. Changing answers when teachers allow pupils to grade each other's papers.

Plagiarizing

Plagiarism is defined as presenting someone else's work as one's own, without attribution. There are four types:

1. Presenting someone else's whole paper as one's own.

2. Deliberately copying from someone else without indicating quotations and without acknowledging the source.

3. Copying in essence, disguised by changing words around or using synonyms.

4. Assuming the copied information is "common knowledge."

Why do pupils plagiarize?

◆ Out of ignorance that it's wrong.
◆ Because passing is important to graduation.
◆ Because they think they won't be caught.
◆ Because teachers don't bother to check for plagiarism.
◆ Because of parent pressure for good grades.
◆ Out of last-minute panic.
◆ Because "everybody does it."

Clearly, several of these causes are at least partially under a teacher's control.

Deterring Cheating

Teachers should monitor test taking in order to deter cheating and to enhance test validity. There are a number of methods that can be used to deter cheating, some relatively easy to apply and others more complicated. Three general approaches that help eliminate or lessen cheating are (1) providing pupils good instruction and information about the test, (2) knowing the common methods of pupil cheating, and (3) observing pupils during testing. Prior to testing, pupils' books and other materials should be out of sight under their desks or elsewhere. Pupils' seats should

olc
CHAPTER CASE STUDY

Visit the text OLC to read the case of Scott Donovan, a high school English teacher who discovers that four of his students plagiarized parts of an assignment.

be spread out in the classroom as much as possible. The author does not permit wearing baseball caps during testing because when the visors are tilted below the eyes, the author cannot see where the pupils' eyes are looking. During testing, the teacher should quietly move about the classroom and observe pupils as they take the test. While observation rarely "catches" a pupil cheating, the presence of the teacher moving about the classroom is a deterrent to cheating.

Table 8.1 shows a variety of strategies to deter plagiarism and other forms of cheating and the degree to which university students report that the strategies are successful. The Chapter 8 website contains more ideas. The fact that scrambled test forms are viewed as the best deterrent to cheating suggests that the main form of cheating is looking at other pupils' test answers. Scrambled forms are most useful in avoiding cheating from other pupils' tests. Note that the list of strategies includes different approaches. Some of the strategies are aimed at stopping cheating by putting up barriers (e.g., scrambled test forms, unique makeup exams, and assigning pupil seats for testing), while others are aimed at providing pupils with good instruction so they will not have to cheat (e.g., providing study guides and making old exams available to pupils).

Many schools and school systems develop honor codes or cheating rules that all pupils are to respect. Such codes or rules spell out in detail what is

TABLE 8.1   STUDENTS' PERCEIVED EFFECTIVENESS OF CHEATING-PREVENTION STRATEGIES

Rank	Strategy	% Rating Strategy as "Effective" or "Very Effective"
1.	Scrambled test forms	81.6%
2.	Small classes	69.8
3.	Using several proctors during examinations	68.4
4.	Using two or more test forms	66.6
5.	Providing study guides	54.8
6.	Making old examinations available for review	52.4
7.	Assigning seats for examinations	26.9
8.	Checking footnotes in student papers	26.4
9.	Giving more in-class tests, fewer take-home tests	23.7

SOURCE: From R. C. Hollinger and L. Lanza-Kaduce, 1996, "Academic Dishonesty and the Perceived Effectiveness of Countermeasures: An Empirical Survey of Cheating at a Major Public University," *NASPA Journal,* 33(4), p. 301. Copyright © 1996. Reprinted with permission of NASPA, Student Affairs Administrators in Higher Learning.

and is not cheating. Table 8.2 excerpts a cheating policy from a middle school in California.

It is the teacher's responsibility to discourage cheating with seating arrangements, careful proctoring, and other activities. If some pupils do cheat, those who do not can be unfairly penalized for their appropriate and ethical behavior, by receiving lower grades and the honors that come from grades. Teachers should discourage cheating and penalize pupils caught doing it, because it is an immoral activity and because it provides an invalid picture of a pupil's achievement. It is, however, important to have strong evidence to support charges of cheating, because pupils have due process rights if accused. Table 8.3 lists some clues for identifying plagiarized work.

TABLE 8.2   EXCERPTS FROM THE CHEATING POLICY OF HUNTINGTON MIDDLE SCHOOL

You are cheating if you:

♦ Copy, fax, or duplicate assignments that will each be turned in as an "original."

♦ Exchange assignments by printout, disk transfer, or modem, then submit as "original."

♦ Write formulas, codes, key words on your person or objects for use in a test.

♦ Use hidden reference sheets during a test.

♦ Use programmed material in watches or calculators, when prohibited.

♦ Exchange answers with others (either give or receive answers).

♦ Take someone else's assignment and submit it as your own.

♦ Submit material (written or designed by someone else) without giving the author/artist name and/or source (e.g., plagiarizing, or submitting work created by family, friends, or tutors).

♦ Take credit for group work, when little contribution was made.

♦ Do not follow additional specific guidelines on cheating as established by department, class, or a certain teacher.

Students caught cheating on any assignment (homework, tests, projects) will be referred to our Assistant Principal. The schoolwide citizenship grade will be lowered at least one grade and the parents will be called. Subsequent offenses may result in a "D" or "F" in citizenship, suspension, removal from elected positions and honorary organizations, the inability to participate in school activities, and similar consequences.

SOURCE: From Huntington Middle School Cheating Policy, by Huntington Middle School, San Marino (CA) Public Schools. Available: http://www.san-marino.k12.ca.us/~heh/BinderReminder/discipline.html. Reprinted with permission of Gary McGuigan, Principal, Huntington Middle School.

> **TABLE 8.3   CLUES FOR IDENTIFYING PLAGIARIZED WORK**
>
> 1. Writing style, language, vocabulary, tone, grammar, and so forth are above or below what the student usually produces. It doesn't sound like the student.
> 2. Spelling or idioms used are not found in the student's native language, using British spellings or phrasing in an American paper and vice versa.
> 3. Pronouns do not agree with the gender of the writer.
> 4. Essay is printed out from the student's Web browser.
> 5. A web address or other anomalous text appears at the top or bottom of the page.
> 6. There are references to graphs, charts, or accompanying material that isn't there.
> 7. Quotes in the paper do not have citations.
> 8. Citations in the bibliography or works cited cannot be verified.
> 9. All citations are to materials that are older than five years.
> 10. References are made to historical persons or events in the current sense.
> 11. Student cannot summarize the main points of the paper or answer questions about specific sections of the paper.
>
> SOURCES: Adapted from Peggy Bates and Margaret Fain, *Cheating 101: Paper Mills and You—Internet subject specific paper mills.* http://www.coastal.edu/library/mills5.htm. Revised September 17, 2003.

SCORING PAPER-AND-PENCIL TESTS

The product of test administration is a stack of tests that contain information about each pupil's achievement. However, to use this information, the teacher must summarize and score it. Scores provide a summary of each pupil's performance on the test. The process of scoring a test involves **measurement**—that is, assigning a number to represent a pupil's performance. In the case of achievement tests, performance on the test items is translated into a score that is used to make decisions about the pupil.

Of course, when pupil achievement is being scored, the same rules should be applied to all tested pupils. For example, if we score Jessica's performance on an achievement test by applying the rule "5 points for every correct answer," then we should score every pupil's performance using the same rule.

The complexity of scoring tests varies with their type. Selection-type items are easiest to score, short-answer and completion items are next easiest, and essays are the most difficult. The reason for this is obvious if one thinks about what a teacher has to do to score each item type. How much time and judgment is involved in scoring each? What precisely does the teacher have to look at to determine whether an item is correct or incorrect? Which type of item requires the most concentration to score? The answers to these questions illustrate the range of ease and difficulty encountered when scoring various item types.

Scoring Selection Items

Pupils respond to selection items by writing, circling, or marking the letter of their response. Scoring selection items is essentially a clerical task in which the teacher compares an answer **key** containing the correct answers to the answers the pupil has given. The number of matches indicates the pupil's score on the test. Before using an answer key, it is a good idea to check to make sure that the key is correct. Similarly, if the test is machine scored, it is good practice for the teacher to hand score a few answer sheets to determine if the machine scoring is accurate.

Subjective test scores are those for which independent scorers have difficulty arriving at the same or similar scores.

Scoring selection test items is relatively **objective**—that is, independent scorers will usually arrive at the same or very similar scores for a given pupil's test. Conversely, **subjective** scoring means that independent scorers would not arrive at the same or similar scores for a given pupil's test. In a subjective test, a pupil's performance depends as much on *who* scores the test as on the pupil's answers. Selection items produce objective scores because there usually is one clearly correct answer to each item, and that answer is identified by a single letter. However, as pupils' responses become more lengthy and complex—as they do with short-answer, completion, and essay items—the judgment of what is a correct or incorrect answer often blurs and scoring becomes more subjective. It has long been known that even when the same person scores the same essay test twice, there is no guarantee that the scores will be the same or similar (Starch and Elliott, 1912, 1913). This is a problem because, if we are to have confidence in a test score, it is important that the scores be objective. Fortunately, there are at least ways to make the scoring of essays less subjective, as we will see later.

Selection items can be scored objectively because they are usually brief and have only one correct answer.

To instill confidence in a test score, it is important that the score is as objective as possible.

Scoring Short-Answer and Completion Items

As long as short-answer and completion items are clearly written, focus pupils on their task, and call for a short response such as a word, phrase, date, or number, scoring is not difficult and can be quite objective. However, as items require lengthier responses from pupils, subjectivity of scoring will increase because more and more interpretations of what pupils know or meant to say will have to be made.

No matter how well a teacher has prepared and reviewed test items, he or she never knows how an item will work until *after* it is administered to pupils. Inevitably, there are times when pupil responses to an item reveal that most pupils misinterpreted it, and that the pupils' answers are correct given their interpretation, but incorrect given the teacher's intention. How should such responses be scored? Similarly, if a textbook test contains a few items that were not emphasized in instruction and pupils got them wrong, should adjustments be made in their scores?

In scoring unexpected responses, teachers must decide if wrong answers are the result of faulty test items or a lack of student learning.

How a teacher interprets pupils' unexpected responses or answers to untaught items can influence pupils' test scores and grades greatly. For example, suppose that one item in a 10-item test produces many unexpected responses from pupils. If the teacher simply marks these responses wrong because they do not match the answer key, he or she may be penalizing pupils for his or her own faulty test item. This 10 percent deduction could make a big difference in a pupil's test score or grade.

In reviewing unexpected responses and untaught items, the teacher must decide if wrong answers are the result of faulty items or a lack of pupil learning. Test scores should not automatically be raised simply because many pupils got an item wrong, but the teacher must make a judgment about the likely source of the problem and how it is best handled. At the very least, the problem items should be examined and analyzed.

Test scores that reflect ambiguous or untaught items are less valid indicators of student achievement.

In the end, scoring decisions rest with the teacher. Teachers must decide who is at fault when pupils misinterpret an item and whether pupils should lose credit for wrong answers on items that were not discussed in class. Two principles should be considered in making such decisions. First, since the test scores should reflect pupils' achievement on the chapter or unit, the scores should deal only with topics that were taught and items that are clearly written. If points are deducted for items not taught or for misinterpreting ambiguous questions, scores will not reflect pupils' true achievement. Second, whatever decision is made regarding the scoring of poor or untaught items, it should be applied uniformly to all pupils.

Three guidelines can help teachers overcome problems of scoring supply items.

1. Prepare an answer key before scoring. Know what you are looking for in pupil responses *before* scoring.
2. Determine how factors such as spelling, grammar, and punctuation, which are usually ancillary to the main focus of the response, will be handled in scoring. Should points be taken off for such factors? Decide before scoring and inform pupils before testing.
3. If pupil responses are technically correct but not initially considered in the scoring guideline, give credit to each unexpected but correct response.

Scoring Essay Items

Essay questions represent the ultimate in scoring complexity because they permit each pupil to construct a unique and lengthy response to the question posed. This means that there is no single definitive answer key that can be applied uniformly to all responses. Interpretation of the responses is necessary. Moreover, the answer to an essay question is presented in a form that contains many distracting factors that contribute to subjective scoring.

Think of an essay answer that you have written. Remember how it looked spread out over the page. Visualize your handwriting and the overall appearance of the written answer. Remember that the essay question was intended to determine how well you understood the ideas and information you had been taught. However, the teacher who scored your essay was probably influenced by one or more of the following factors:

♦ Handwriting

♦ Writing style, including sentence structure and flow

♦ Spelling and grammar

♦ Neatness

♦ Fatigue of the scorer

♦ Identity of the pupil

♦ Location of one's test paper in the pile of test papers

Many types of scorer subjectivity can influence how an essay item is scored.

Each of these factors can influence a teacher's reaction to an essay answer, although none of them has anything to do with the actual content of the pupil's response. For example, a pupil whose penmanship is so poor that it forces the teacher to decipher what each scribbled word means will frustrate the teacher and divert attention away from the content of the answer. The essay likely will get a lower score than that of another pupil who provides the same answer in more legible handwriting. A pupil who uses interesting words in a variety of sentence structures to produce an answer that flows smoothly from point to point likely will get a better score than a pupil who states the same points in a string of simple declarative sentences. Poor grammar and misspelled words create a negative impression in a teacher's mind. And neatness does count with teachers.

Scoring essays is a time-consuming and difficult task, so pupil scores may be influenced by how alert the teacher is when the essays are read. The first few essays that are read seem new and fresh, and pupils who wrote them tend to get good scores. However, after the teacher has read the same response 15 or more times, familiarity and fatigue set in, and responses similar to the initial ones often get lower scores. Thus, pupils who provide essentially the same answer to an essay question may get different scores depending upon when the scorer read their answer.

Knowledge of who wrote the essay can also influence the scoring process. In almost all essay questions there is at least one point when the teacher must interpret what a pupil was trying to say. Knowledge of who wrote the answer can influence the teacher's interpretation. For example, two pupils, Isobel and Keyshawn, have each written an essay that has some ambiguous statements. The teacher knows that Isobel is an interested, able pupil who always does well on tests and in class discussions. The teacher thinks, "Although Isobel didn't make this point clearly and it's not evident that she understands it, she probably knew the answer even though it didn't come out right. I'll give her the credit." The teacher also knows that Keyshawn generally does poorly in school and remembers his indifference to the topic during a recent class discussion. The teacher thinks, "Since Keyshawn doesn't care about this subject, rarely says anything in class except to disagree with me, and didn't make this point clearly, he probably had no idea of what was correct here. He will get no credit." One way to avoid such biased scoring is to identify papers by number or have pupils put their names on the last page of a test. Notice that knowing the pupil's identity is not a problem in scoring selection items, because there is little interpretation involved in scoring.

Consider the following situation. You are taking an essay examination. All the other pupils have finished and left the room. You are alone with the teacher. As you walk up to turn in your test paper, the teacher says to you, "You have worked hard on this test. I want to reward your effort. Here is the pile of test papers from all the other pupils in the class. When I score them, I shall start with the top paper and work down the pile in order. Because you have worked so hard, I will let you place your test paper anywhere in the pile you wish. Where would you like to place it?" Where would you place it? Could your choice within the stack make a difference in your score? If you think it could, you probably are correct. What does this say about the potential subjectivity of essay tests?

Holistic Versus Analytic Scoring

Holistic scoring provides a single, overall impression of the complete essay. Analytic scoring provides a separate score for each component of the essay.

Teachers typically use two approaches to scoring essay questions: holistic scoring and analytic scoring. **Holistic scoring** reflects a teacher's *overall impression* of the whole essay by providing a *single score or grade*. **Analytic scoring,** on the other hand, views the essay as being made up of many components and provides *separate scores* for each component. Thus, an essay that is scored analytically might result in separate scores for accuracy, organization, supporting arguments, and grammar and spelling. Analytic scoring provides detailed feedback that pupils can use to improve different aspects of their essays. In Chapter 6 Mr. Wysocki provided his pupils with detailed feedback from the practice paragraphs they wrote. Undoubtedly, he used analytic scoring to help his pupils improve. However, attempting to score more than three or four separate features often makes scoring confusing and time-consuming. In both holistic and analytic scoring, teachers should give helpful and encouraging suggestions on pupils' drafts and tests.

Steps to Ensure Objectivity

Regardless of whether a teacher uses holistic or analytic scoring, certain steps should be followed to ensure that pupils' essays are scored objectively. Although the following suggestions are time-consuming, they are necessary if scores are to be valid for decision making. In addition, scoring rubrics are very helpful (see Chapter 9).

1. *Define what constitutes a good answer before administering an essay question.* The less focused an essay question is, the broader the range of pupil responses will be and the more difficult it will be to apply uniform scoring criteria. Including information about the pupil's specific task, the scope of the essay, and the scoring criteria in the essay directions has numerous benefits. First, it helps pupils respond to a precise set of teacher expectations. This in turn will diminish scoring subjectivity. Second, by writing questions that clearly indicate the characteristics of a good answer, the teacher automatically has to confront the issue of scoring. The criteria that focus pupils' responses are also the basic criteria that will be used in scoring the pupils' answers.

2. *Decide and tell pupils how handwriting, punctuation, spelling, and organization will be scored.* Pupils should know in advance what factors will count in scoring the essay.

3. *If possible, score pupils anonymously.* This will help keep the scoring objective by eliminating knowledge and accompanying perceptions of the pupil's effort, ability, interest, and past performance. Each pupil should be scored on the basis of present performance, not in terms of teacher perceptions or past performance.

4. *In tests with multiple essay items, score all pupils' answers to the first question before moving to the second question.* If it is difficult to score a single essay question objectively, it is more difficult to score two or three different essay questions in succession. One must not only contend with the distractions present in each individual essay, but also must shift content orientation and criteria for each question. Scoring all the answers to a single essay question at one time ensures against the "carryover" effect, the tendency to let one's reaction to a pupil's initial essay influence one's perception of succeeding essays written by that same pupil.

5. *Read essay answers a second time after initial scoring.* The best way to check for objectivity in essay scoring is to have a second individual read and score pupils' papers using the same criteria the teacher

A well-focused essay item includes scoring criteria and specific information about the pupils' task.

Before scores of essay items are finalized, the teacher should check for objectivity by rereading and, if necessary, rescoring a sample of essays.

Key Assessment Tools 8.3

GUIDELINES FOR SCORING A TEST

This combines suggestions from the discussion with some other good ideas.

♦ Test scores should be based upon topics that were taught and items that are clearly written.

♦ Make sure the same rules are used to score all pupils.

♦ Be alert for the following distractors that may affect the objectivity of essay scores: writing style, grammar and spelling, neatness, scorer fatigue, prior performance, and carryover effects.

♦ Define what constitutes a good answer before administering an essay question.

♦ Score all answers to the first essay question before moving on to score the succeeding question.

♦ Read essay questions a second time after initial scoring.

♦ Carry out posttest review to locate faulty test items and, when necessary, to make scoring adjustments.

---

used to score them. Since this is usually impractical, except when making very important decisions (e.g., awarding a scholarship, selecting for an honor society), an acceptable procedure is for the teacher to reread and, if necessary, rescore a sample of the essays before finalizing the scores. Two scorings by the same person, even if done quickly and on only a sample of essays, are better than a single scoring and lead to more objective decision making.

Essay questions permit the assessment of many thought processes that can be assessed in no other way. When such thought processes are part of the instructional objectives and are actively taught to pupils, they should be assessed to obtain a representative picture of pupil learning. Nevertheless, when using essay questions, one must realize the difficulty inherent in scoring them and the dangers of scoring them improperly. A teacher should use essay questions if they are the best way to assess what has been taught, but time should be set aside to score them objectively so that their results can be used with confidence. Key Assessment Tools 8.3 summarizes guidelines to follow when scoring tests.

ANALYZING ITEM VALIDITY

Even though one has prepared pupils for testing and written or selected appropriate test items, poor test assembly, administration, and scoring can impair test validity. If there are distractions when pupils are taking the test, if the teacher knowingly or unknowingly heightens pupils' anxiety levels immediately before testing, if directions do not make clear to pupils what they are to do, or if scoring, particularly for essay questions, is haphazard and subjective, the validity of achievement tests is reduced. The steps described in the preceding section are intended to produce valid achievement test scores, which can be used with confidence in making decisions about pupil learning.

Although these steps will eliminate most of the common pitfalls found in classroom achievement tests, a teacher never really knows how well test items will work until after they have been administered to pupils. It is all but impossible to anticipate how pupils will react to a given item. Thus, a review of pupil performance after testing in order to identify faulty items is an important final step to ensure the validity of the test results. There are two reasons for performing such posttest reviews: (1) to identify and make scoring adjustments for any items that pupils' answers show were misunderstood or ambiguous and (2) to identify ways to improve items for use on future tests.

The Need for After-Test Reviewing: Two Examples

The following examples illustrate the need for posttest reviewing.

A social studies teacher who taught a unit on the Low Countries (e.g., Belgium, Luxembourg, and Holland) asked the following short answer question.

What are the Low Countries?

She expected that her pupils would respond with the names of the Low Countries even though the item did not ask explicitly for the names. While many students did supply the names, many others responded that the low countries were "a group of countries in Europe that are largely below sea level." How should the teacher treat the responses of this latter group of pupils?

A health teacher wrote the following multiple-choice question.

The main value of a daily exercise program is to:
  A. eat less
  B. develop musculature
  C. raise intelligence
  D. keep physically fit

Choice B was keyed as the correct answer, but many students selected D as their answer. What should the teacher do about the pupils who selected option D?

Notice that these problems did not become apparent until *after* the teacher looked over the pupil responses and found unexpected or odd response patterns in a few items: almost everyone missing a particular item; some pupils giving strange or unexpected answers to an item; all of the bright students doing poorly on an item; no consistency in the wrong answers to an item. As these scoring patterns emerge, teachers should inspect pupil responses to determine whether the problem was related to test construction or pupil learning. It is important to emphasize that test scores should not automatically be raised simply because many pupils got an item wrong. In each case, the teacher must make a judgment regarding the source of the problem and how it will be rectified, if at all. Recognize, however, that if problem items are not examined and analyzed, no reasonable decision can be made.

Problems in short-answer and completion items usually become evident when reading pupils' answers. The written responses give a good indication of how pupils understood and interpreted a test item. For example, in the preceding social studies item on the Low Countries, pupils' answers made it clear that the item did not focus students on the names of the Low Countries and, consequently, produced other responses that were correct but not what the teacher wanted.

Selective Reviewing of Multiple-Choice Items

Problems in selection items, especially multiple-choice ones, are harder to detect because pupils select rather than construct their own response, which provides little insight into their thinking. To identify problems with multiple-choice items, teachers must view response patterns on the various options provided. While it is desirable to review all items in a multiple-choice test, limitations in time make it more realistic to review those items that half or more of the pupils answered incorrectly. This is where most, if not all, of the faulty items are likely to be found.

There are many ways that patterns for multiple-choice items can be examined. A number of statistical indices can be calculated to describe each test item (Kubiszyn and Borich, 1999). For example, the **difficulty index** of an item describes the proportion of pupils who answered it correctly. Thus, an item of .70 difficulty (70 percent of the class answered correctly) is easier than one of .40 difficulty (40 percent of the class answered correctly). Items can be ranked in terms of their difficulty to identify pupils' strengths and weaknesses. The **discrimination index** describes how an individual item fares with pupils who scored high and low on the overall test. An item with positive discrimination is one that is more frequently answered correctly by pupils who score high on the test as a whole than by pupils who score low.

Because most classroom teachers lack the time and resources to perform the numerical analyses required to calculate difficulty and discrimination indices, they must rely upon simple methods to understand and improve those items that a large proportion of the class answered incorrectly. The following are examples of item response patterns teachers can use to answer the question "What's the problem, if any, with this item?" Each of these patterns indicates a different possible reason why large numbers of pupils might answer incorrectly. In each case, an asterisk indicates the keyed answer.

This first response pattern is typical of multiple-choice items that have two correct or defensible answers, similar to the health item shown previously. Two choices, A and C, were rarely selected. The majority of pupils split themselves almost evenly between options B and D. Only the pupils who marked B, the keyed response, received credit on the item when it was initially scored.

	Options	A	*B	C	D
Number of pupils choosing option		2	8	2	8

When the teacher saw that most pupils missed this item, he looked at option D, decided that it was also a correct choice, and decided to give full credit to those who selected D. Remember, the final decision about whether the item or the pupils are at fault rests with the teacher.

The next pattern is one where most pupils select an option other than the keyed one. In the example below, most pupils chose C rather than D, the keyed option. Many times this pattern is simply the result of miskeying on the part of the teacher. In this case the teacher wrote D next to this item when she meant to write C. While miskeying is not always the explanation for such a response pattern, it is a good starting point. If the item was not miskeyed, closer inspection of option C should provide a clue about why it was chosen so often. If not, pupils should be consulted to explain their answers.

	Options	A	B	C	*D
Number of pupils choosing option		2	1	15	2

Finally, consider the following pattern in which all options are selected by about the same number of pupils. Such a pattern may be an indication that pupils are guessing the correct answer. They probably have no idea which option is correct. Faulty wording or untaught material are likely explanations for such a response pattern.

	Options	*A	B	C	D
Number of pupils choosing option		5	6	4	5

After-test reviews using the above strategies can help teachers better understand how well their items are working and why pupils responded as they did. Asking pupils what they were thinking when they answered an item can also produce useful information. While the decision about how to score an item ultimately rests with the classroom teacher, information of the kind described in this section is helpful in making that decision. An after-test review will enhance the validity of the test scores and the decisions made from them.

DISCUSSING TEST RESULTS WITH PUPILS

Going over test results when pupils have the graded test in front of them is useful.

Pupils want information about their test performance. Teachers can provide this information through comments written on papers, tests, or projects that indicate to pupils what they did well and how they might improve. It also is helpful to go over the results of a test with pupils. This is especially useful when the pupils have their marked tests in front of them during the review. The teacher should pay special attention to items that a large proportion of the class got wrong in order to clear up misconceptions and to indicate the nature of the desired answer. For older pupils it also is helpful to explain how the tests were scored and graded. Finally, opportunity should be provided for shy pupils to discuss the test in private with the teacher.

TESTING STUDENTS WITH DISABILITIES

Accommodations can be made by modifying the format of presentation or response or the setting or timing of a test.

In Chapter 3 the history and key features of accommodating pupils with disabilities were described. In that chapter, the focus was on accommodating pupils with disabilities during instruction. In Chapter 7 we noted some alternatives to pencil-and-paper testing. In this chapter the focus is on other ways of accommodating pupils with disabilities during testing and assessment. There is some overlap between pupil accommodations for instruction and those for assessment, in large part because many disabilities call for the same or similar accommodations for both instruction and testing. In all cases, the purpose of accommodations is to minimize the effect of pupil attributes that are not related to the primary focus of the test. For example, if a pupil has a hearing disability that may interfere with performance on an oral test, the pupil may be provided with a written test. Or, a pupil who is new to the English language may be given the test in his or her own language, assuming the teacher or assistant knows the language; if the test must be taken in English the pupil may be given extra time to complete the test. In each of these cases, the idea is to provide an accommodation that will provide the pupil a fair chance to show what he or she knows, unencumbered by the handicap.

Pupil accommodations in testing can be divided into four general categories: modifying the presentation format of the test, modifying the response format of the test, modifying test timing, and modifying test setting. Following are common examples of accommodations in these four areas. The specific accommodations required for a given pupil will be guided by his or her Individual Education Plan (IEP).

Modifying the Presentation Format
- ◆ Read directions for each test section; read slowly.
- ◆ Provide verbal or oral directions as needed.
- ◆ Present directions as a sequence of steps for the pupil to follow.
- ◆ Have pupil repeat directions to ensure understanding.
- ◆ Read test questions aloud.
- ◆ Spread items over the page; put each sentence on a single line.
- ◆ Present test in Braille, large print, sign language, native language, or bilingually.
- ◆ Revise or simplify language level.

Modifying the Response Format
- ◆ Allow dictionaries, texts, or calculators.
- ◆ Allow responses in Braille, large print, sign language, native language, or tape recording.
- ◆ Provide verbal prompts to items.
- ◆ Provide a scribe to write pupil answers.
- ◆ Provide examples of expected test responses.
- ◆ Give pupil an outline for essay items.
- ◆ Include definitions or formulas for the pupil; allow the use of notes.
- ◆ Double-check pupil's understanding of the items and desired responses.
- ◆ Make test similar to what was taught during instruction.

Modifying Test Timing
- ◆ Provide extra time.
- ◆ Avoid timed tests.
- ◆ Test over a period of discrete testing sessions.
- ◆ Give extra breaks during testing.
- ◆ Allow unlimited time.

Modifying Test Setting
- ◆ Test in a separate and quiet location.
- ◆ Seat pupil away from distractions.
- ◆ Test one-on-one: one pupil, one test administrator.

TECHNOLOGY AND ASSESSMENT

ACCOMMODATING STUDENTS WITH DISABILITIES DURING TESTING

For more information about accommodating students with disabilities during testing, visit Chapter 8 of the text website to link to the following resources.

URLs for each organization can be found on www.mhhe.com/airasian5e.

♦ *The Council for Exceptional Children (CEC)*
  The Council for Exceptional Children gives teachers support for teaching students with special needs.

♦ *Special Education Resources on the Internet (SERI)*
  Search this site under categories including "Special Education Discussion Groups," "Learning Disabilities," "Classroom Accommodations," and "Inclusion Resources."

♦ *Attention Deficit Disorder Association*
  ADDA focuses especially on the needs of AD/HD adults and young adults with AD/HD. This site is packed with articles, personal stories, interviews with AD/HD professionals, book reviews, and links to other AD/HD-related sites.

♦ *Hard of Hearing and Deaf Students Resource Guide for Teachers*
  Often-asked questions, information and communication, and teaching strategies are included to help broaden your awareness and experience of the language and world of your student who is hard of hearing or deaf.

♦ *Learning Disabilities Association of America*
  LDA provides information, support, education and resources through its network of nearly 300 state and local affiliates in 50 states and Puerto Rico.

The above four areas include many of the most common accommodations used in classrooms. There are, of course, many other accommodations that can be applied to provide valid assessment of pupils with disabilities, but this list provides a useful beginning for our exploration into this area. The pupil's IEP will guide the teacher in preparing pupils for testing.

One additional issue requires attention. The above accommodations are generally those that all pupils in a classroom will notice during a test. While it is usually clear that pupils with disabilities are being treated differently from nondisabled pupils, teachers should try not to bring undue attention to pupils with disabilities during testing. For example, teachers could confer privately with pupils with disabilities when setting up needed accommodations. They can make the modified test similar in appearance to the regular test. They can try to be unobtrusive when helping pupils with disabilities during testing and try to monitor all pupils in the same way. The aim of such practices is to be sensitive to embarrassment to pupils with disabilities during testing and avoid it as much as possible.

Pupils with disabilities will increasingly be included in classrooms with their peers who do not have disabilities. This inclusion will have many benefits for all pupils, but teachers will be called upon to make accommodations for pupils with disabilities in the construction and administration of assessments.

CHAPTER SUMMARY

◆ In assembling items into a test, the various item types should be grouped together, with selection items placed at the start of the test and supply items at the end. Short-answer items should be placed before essay items.

◆ Each section of the test should have directions that tell pupils what to do, how to respond, and where to place their answers. Older pupils may also be helped by knowing how much each item is worth.

◆ Each pupil should have his or her own copy of the test.

◆ A proper physical climate for testing is one in which pupils are comfortable and interruptions are minimized.

◆ A proper psychological climate is more difficult to attain because some pupils are always more anxious about testing than others. Providing advanced warning of a test, reviewing important objectives, and encouraging pupils to do their best without exerting undo pressure will help set a suitable psychological climate in which pupils can perform their best. Make it easy for pupils to keep track of the time.

◆ Cheating is unacceptable and dishonest; it is also common. It is a teacher's responsibility to establish conditions that reduce cheating.

◆ Teachers can deter cheating by scrambling test forms, arranging pupil seating, circulating the classroom during testing, providing study guides, using more essay items, forbidding pupils to share materials, enforcing cheating rules and penalties, and other strategies.

◆ In higher grades, students should be informed about what constitutes plagiarism.

◆ Measurement is a form of scoring in which numbers are assigned to describe pupils' performance.

◆ An objective test item is one that independent scorers would score the same or similarly. A subjective item is one that independent scorers would not score the same. Factors that contribute to subjectivity include handwriting, style, grammar, and the teacher's perception of the pupil.

◆ Selection items are easy to score objectively. Supply items become increasingly subjective as pupils are given more freedom to construct their own answers. Essay items are the most subjective kind of item.

olc

CHAPTER REVIEW
Visit Chapter 8 of the Online Learning Center at **www.mhhe.com/ airasian5e** to take chapter quizzes, link to related websites, read PowerWeb articles and news feed updates, and access study tools, including the case study referenced in the chapter.

♦ Test scores should be based on the topics that were taught.

♦ The two principal methods of scoring essay tests are holistic scoring, which produces a single overall score, and analytic scoring, which produces a number of scores corresponding to particular features of the essay (e.g., organization, style, and so forth).

♦ To make essay scores objective, a teacher should decide what factors constitute a good answer before giving the test, provide those factors in the test item, read all responses to a single essay question before reading responses to other questions, and reread essays a second time to corroborate initial scores.

♦ After a test is scored, the teacher should review items that show unusual answers or response patterns to determine if the items are faulty. It faulty items are judged to be responsible, a scoring adjustment may be in order.

♦ It is good practice to conduct an after-test review with pupils in order to (1) help identify any misconceptions, (2) locate faulty test items and make necessary scoring adjustments, and (3) build up a permanent test item file.

♦ Testing accommodations can be provided for pupils with physical disabilities. Pupils whose physical disabilities rule out their use of paper and pencil can be accommodated by testing through other means.

QUESTIONS FOR DISCUSSION

1. What are some ways that scoring essay questions can be made more objective? What are some consequences of subjective essay scoring?

2. How can a teacher reduce pupils' test anxiety while maintaining their motivation to do well on a test?

3. How should a teacher respond to cheating? Should all forms of cheating be treated in the same way? What cautions should a teacher keep in mind before accusing a pupil of cheating?

ACTIVITIES

1. Rewrite the following essay question to make it more focused for pupils. Then state a set of criteria you would use to judge the quality of your pupils' answers.

   Compare the Democratic and Republican parties.

2. Talk to two teachers about how they deal with and prevent cheating on tests.

3. In a small group, talk with other students about types of cheating they have noticed and what can be done to reduce it.

REVIEW QUESTIONS

1. What is the fundamental purpose of assessing pupils' achievement? What decisions must a teacher make when preparing to assess pupil achievement?

2. How is the validity of an achievement test determined?

3. What are some differences between scoring selection and supply items?

4. What is the difference between objective and subjective scoring? What factors make it difficult to score essay questions objectively? What steps can a teacher take to make essay scoring more objective?

5. What guidelines should be followed in arranging the items in a test?

6. What are some strategies that can be used to limit cheating on tests?

7. How do holistic and analytic scoring differ? When should each be used?

8. What is the relationship among educational objectives, instruction, and achievement testing?

REFERENCES

Bates, P., Fain, M. (2003). *Cheating 101: Paper mills and you—Internet subject specific paper mills.* Conway, SC: Kimbel Library, Coastal Carolina University. http://www.coastal.edu/library/mills5.htm

Cizek, G. (1999). *Cheating on Tests: How to do it, detect it, and prevent it.* Mahwah, NJ: Lawrence Erlbaum Associates.

Kubiszyn, T., & Borich, G. (2003). *Educational testing and measurement,* 7th edition. Glenview, IL: Scott, Foresman.

Starch, D., & Elliott, E. (1912). Reliability of the grading of high-school work in English. *School Review, 20,* 442–457.

Starch, D., & Elliott, E. (1913). Reliability of grading work in mathematics. *School* Review, 21, 254–259.

Summergrad, D. (1999). Calling it what it is. *Education Week,* August 4, p. 46.

PERFORMANCE ASSESSMENTS

CHAPTER OBJECTIVES

After reading this chapter, you will be able to:

- Define checklist, rating scale, rubric, performance criteria, and other basic terms
- Contrast performance processes and performance products
- Contrast performance assessment with other assessment types
- Write well-stated performance criteria for a given process or performance
- Apply different scoring approaches for performance assessments
- Construct a scoring rubric
- Discuss portfolios and their use in assessment
- Identify strategies to improve the validity and reliability of classroom performance assessments

THINKING ABOUT TEACHING

In what ways can teachers use the results of assessments to improve pupil learning?

This chapter describes **performance assessment,** which is any form of assessment in which pupils carry out an activity or produce a product in order to demonstrate learning. This chapter tells how to develop such assessments and discusses their pros and cons, including questions of validity and reliability.

The following examples describe common classroom assessment practices. How could the validity of these practices be improved?

Ms. Landers taught her ninth grade science class a unit on microscopes. She taught her pupils how to set up, focus, and use a microscope. Each pupil used a microscope to identify and draw pictures of three or four objects on glass slides. At the end of the unit, she assessed the pupils' achievement by giving a paper-and-pencil test that asked them to label parts of a diagrammed microscope and answer multiple-choice questions about the history of the microscope.

In Mr. Cleaver's third grade class, oral reading skills are strongly emphasized, and he devotes a great deal of energy to helping pupils use proper phrasing, vocal expression, and clear pronunciation when they read aloud. All of the tests that Mr. Cleaver uses to grade his pupils' reading achievement are paper-and-pencil tests that assess pupils' paragraph comprehension and word recognition.

These examples illustrate an important limitation of many paper-and-pencil tests: they allow teachers to assess some, but not all, important school learning outcomes. In each of the two classrooms, the teacher relied solely on tests that measured *knowledge of performance* (remember factual knowledge), but not ability to actually *perform the skill* (apply procedural knowledge).

THE GENERAL ROLE
OF PERFORMANCE ASSESSMENTS

There are many classroom situations for which valid assessment requires that teachers gather formal information about pupils' performances or products. Teachers collect pupil products such as written stories, paintings, lab reports, and science fair projects, as well as performances such as giving a speech, holding a pencil, typing, and cooperating in groups. Generally, products produce tangible outcomes—things you can hold in your hand—while performances are things you observe or listen to. Table 9.1 contrasts the selection and supply items discussed in Chapter 7 with typical examples of performance and product assessments.

Performance assessments may also be called alternative or authentic assessments. They permit pupils to show what they can do in real situations (Wiggins, 1992). The difference between describing how a skill should be performed and actually knowing how to perform it is an important distinction in classroom assessment. Teachers recognize this distinction, as the following comments illustrate.

Performance assessments allow pupils to demonstrate what they know and can do in a real situation. Performance assessments are also called alternative and authentic assessments.

I want my pupils to learn to do math for its own intrinsic value, but also because math is so essential for everyday life. Making change, balancing checkbooks, doing a budget, and many other practical, real-world activities require that pupils know how to use their math knowledge.

The kids need to learn to get along in groups, be respectful of others' property, and wait their turns. I don't want kids to be able to recite classroom rules, I want them to practice them. These behaviors are just as important for kids to learn in school as reading, writing, and math.

Just because they can write a list of steps they would follow to ensure laboratory safety does not mean that in a given situation they could actually demonstrate that knowledge.

Some types of paper-and-pencil test items can be used to provide information about the thinking processes that underlie pupils' performance. For example, a math problem in which pupils have to show their work provides insight into the mental processes used to solve the problem. An essay question can show pupils' organizational skills, thought processes, and application of capitalization and punctuation rules. These two forms of paper-and-pencil test items can assess what pupils can do as opposed to the majority of paper-and-pencil test questions that reveal what pupils know. With most selection and supply questions, the teacher observes the *result* of the pupil's intellectual process, but not the thinking process that produced the result. If the pupil gets a multiple-choice, true-false, matching, or completion item correct, the teacher *assumes* that the pupil must have followed the correct process, but there is little direct evidence to sup-

TABLE 9.1   EXAMPLES OF FOUR ASSESSMENT APPROACHES

Selection	Supply	Product	Performance
Multiple choice	Completion	Essay, story, or poem	Musical, dance, or dramatic performance
True-false	Label a diagram	Research report	Science lab demonstration
Matching	Short answer	Writing portfolio	Typing test
	Concept map	Diary or journal	Athletic competition
		Science fair project	Debate
		Art exhibit or portfolio	Oral presentation
			Cooperation in groups

SOURCE: *If Minds Matter: A Forward to the Future,* vol. 2, edited by Arthur L. Costa, James Bellanca, and Robin Fogarty. © 1992 IRI/Skylight Publishing Inc. Reprinted by permission of Skylight Professional Development. www/skylightedu.com

port this assumption, since the only evidence of the pupil's thought process is a circled letter or a single written word. On the other hand, essays and other extended response items provide a product that shows how pupils think about and construct their responses. They permit the teacher to see the logic of arguments, the manner in which the response is organized, and the basis of conclusions drawn by the pupil (Bartz et al. 1994). Thus, paper-and-pencil assessments like stories, reports, or "show-your-work" problems are important forms of performance assessments. Table 9.2 shows some of the differences between objective test items, essay tests, oral questions, and performance assessments.

Chapters 2 and 5 discussed how teachers observe their pupils' performance in order to learn about them and also to obtain information about the moment-to-moment success of their instruction. Such observations are primarily informal and spontaneous. In this chapter, we are concerned with assessing more formal, structured performances and products, those that the teacher plans in advance, helps each pupil to perform, and formally assesses. These assessments can take place during normal classroom instruction (e.g., oral reading activities, setting up laboratory equipment) or in some special situation set up to elicit a performance (e.g., giving a speech in an auditorium). In either case, the activity is formally structured—the teacher arranges the conditions in which the performance or product is demonstrated and judged. Such assessments permit each pupil to show his or her mastery of the same process or task, something that is impossible with informal observation of spontaneous classroom performance and events.

TABLE 9.2   COMPARISON OF VARIOUS TYPES OF ASSESSMENTS

	Objective Test	Essay Test	Oral Question	Performance Assessment
Purpose	Sample knowledge with maximum efficiency and reliability	Assess thinking skills and/or mastery of how a body of knowledge is structured	Assess knowledge during instruction	Assess ability to translate knowledge and understanding into action
Pupil's Response	Read, evaluate, select	Organize, compose	Oral answer	Plan, construct, and deliver an original response
Major Advantage	Efficiency—can administer many items per unit of testing time	Can measure complex cognitive outcomes	Joins assessment and instruction	Provides rich evidence of performance skills
Influence on Learning	Overemphasis on recall encourages memorization; can encourage thinking skills if properly constructed	Encourages thinking and development of writing skills	Stimulates participation in instruction, provides teacher immediate feedback on effectiveness of teaching	Emphasizes use of available skill and knowledge in relevant problem contexts

SOURCE: Adapted from R. J. Stiggins, "Design and Development of Performance Assessments," *Educational Measurement: Issues and Practice,* 1987, *6*(3), p. 35. Copyright 1987 by the National Council on Measurement in Education Adapted by permission of the publisher.

PERFORMANCE ASSESSMENT IN SCHOOLS

Performance assessments reflect the recent emphasis on real-world problem solving.

The amount of attention that has recently been focused on performance assessment in states, schools, and classrooms might lead one to believe that performance assessment is new and untried, and that it can solve all the problems of classroom assessment. Neither of these beliefs is true (Madaus and O'Dwyer, 1999). Performance assessment has been used extensively in classrooms for as long as there have been classrooms. Table 9.3 provides examples of five common, long-standing areas of performance assessment in schools.

Many factors account for the growing popularity of performance assessment (Ryan and Miyasaka, 1995; Quality Counts, 1999). First, performance assessment is being proposed or mandated as part of formal statewide assessment programs. Second, increased classroom emphasis on problem solving, higher-level thinking, and real-world reasoning skills has created a

TABLE 9.3   FIVE COMMON DOMAINS OF PERFORMANCE ASSESSMENT

Communication Skills	Psychomotor Skills	Athletic Activities	Concept Acquisition	Affective Skills
Writing essays	Holding a pencil	Shooting free throws	Constructing open and closed circuits	Sharing toys
Giving a speech	Setting up lab equipment	Catching a ball	Selecting proper tools for shop tasks	Working in cooperative groups
Pronouncing a foreign language	Using scissors	Hopping	Identifying unknown chemical substances	Obeying school rules
Following spoken directions	Dissecting a frog	Swimming the crawl	Generalizing from experimental data	Maintaining self-control

reliance on performance and product assessments to demonstrate pupil learning. Third, performance assessments can provide some pupils who do poorly on selection-type tests an opportunity to show their achievement in alternative ways.

Performance-Oriented Subjects

All schools expect pupils to demonstrate communication skills, so reading, writing, and speaking are perhaps the most common areas of classroom performance assessment. Likewise, simple psychomotor skills such as being able to sit in a chair or hold a pencil, as well as more sophisticated skills such as setting up laboratory equipment or using tools to build a bird-house, are a fundamental part of school life. Closely related are the athletic performances taught in physical education classes.

There also is a growing emphasis on using performance assessment to determine pupils' understanding of the concepts they are taught and measure their ability to apply procedural knowledge. The argument is that if pupils really grasp a concept or process, they can explain and use it to solve real-life problems. For example, after teaching pupils about money and making change, the teacher may assess learning by having pupils count out the money needed to purchase objects from the classroom "store" or act as storekeeper and make change for other pupils' purchases. Or, rather than giving a multiple-choice test on the chemical reactions that help identify unknown substances, the teacher could give each pupil an unknown substance and have them go through the process of identifying it. These kinds of hands-on demonstrations of concept mastery are growing in popularity.

Teachers also constantly assess pupils' feelings, values, attitudes, and emotions. When a teacher checks the "satisfactory" rating under the category "works hard" or "obeys school rules" on a pupil's report card, the

Assessing students' understanding of concepts through hands-on demonstrations is becoming more common.

olc

CHAPTER CASE STUDY

Visit the text OLC to read the case of teacher Frank Oakley's science lesson. It will give you a feel for the challenges of performance assessment in a high school lab.

www.mhhe.com/ airasian5e

teacher bases this judgment on observations of the pupil's performance. Teachers rely upon observations of pupil performance to collect evidence about important behaviors such as getting along with peers, working independently, following rules, and self-control.

Most teachers recognize the importance of balancing supply and selection assessments with performance and product assessments, as the following comments indicate.

It is important for teachers to balance supply and selection assessments with performance and product assessments.

> It's not reasonable to grade reading without including the pupil's oral reading skills or their comprehension of what they read. I always spend some time when it's grading time listening to and rating my pupils' oral reading and comprehension quality.

> My kids know that a large part of their grade depends on how well they follow safety procedures and take proper care of the tools they use. They know I'm always on the lookout for times when they don't do these things and that it will count against them if I see them.

> I wouldn't want anyone to assess my teaching competence solely on the basis of my students' paper-and-pencil test scores. I would want to be seen interacting with the kids, teaching them, and attending to their needs. Why should I confine my assessments of my pupils solely to paper-and-pencil methods?

Early Childhood and Special Needs Pupils

While performance assessment cuts across subject areas and grade levels, it is heavily used in early childhood and special education settings. Because preschool, kindergarten, and primary school pupils are limited in their communication skills and are still in the process of being socialized into the school culture, much assessment information is obtained by observing their performances and products. Assessment at this age focuses on gross and fine motor development, verbal and auditory acuity, and visual development, as well as social behaviors. Key Assessment Tools 9.1 illustrates some of the important early childhood behaviors and skills that teachers assess by performance-based means. These examples provide a sense of how heavily the early childhood curriculum is weighted toward performance outcomes.

Early education teachers rely heavily on performance-based assessments became of their students' limited communication skills.

Many special needs pupils—especially those who exhibit multiple and severe disabilities in their cognitive, affective, and psychomotor development—are provided instruction focused on self-help skills such as getting dressed, brushing teeth, making a sandwich, and operating a vacuum cleaner. Pupils are taught to carry out these performances through many, many repetitions. Observation of pupils as they perform these activities is the main assessment technique special education teachers use to identify performance mastery or areas needing further work.

To summarize, performance assessment gathers evidence about pupils by observing and rating their performance or products. Although appropri-

---

Key Assessment Tools 9.1

EARLY CHILDHOOD BEHAVIOR AREAS

Gross motor development: Roll over, sit erect without toppling over, walk a straight line, throw a ball, jump on one or two feet, skip.

Fine motor development: Cut with scissors, trace an object, color inside the lines, draw geometric forms (e.g., circles, squares, triangles), penmanship, left-to-right progression in reading and writing, eye-hand coordination.

Verbal and auditory acuity: Identify sounds, listen to certain sounds and ignore others (e.g., tune out distractions), discriminate between sounds and words that sound alike (e.g., "fix" vs. "fish"), remember numbers in sequence, follow directions, remember the correct order of events, pronounce words and letters.

Visual development: Find a letter, number, or object similar to one shown by the teacher; copy a shape; identify shapes and embedded figures; reproduce a design given by the teacher; differentiate objects by size, color, and shape.

Social acclimation: Listen to the teacher, follow a time schedule, share, wait one's turn, respect the property of others.

---

ate at all grade levels, it is especially useful in subjects that place heavy emphasis on performances or products of some kind, such as art, music, public speaking, shop, foreign language, and physical education. It is also very useful with early childhood and special needs pupils whose lack of basic communication, psychomotor, and social skills forces the teacher to rely upon pupil performances to assess instructional success.

DEVELOPING PERFORMANCE ASSESSMENTS

A diving competition is an instructive example of a skill that is assessed by a performance assessment. Submitting a written essay describing how to perform various dives or answering a multiple-choice test about diving rules are hardly appropriate ways to demonstrate one's diving *performance.* Rather, a valid assessment of diving performance requires seeing the diver actually perform. And, to make the assessment reliable, the diver must perform a series of dives, not just one.

Diving judges rate dives using a scale that has 21 possible numerical scores that can be awarded (e.g., 0.0, 0.5, 1.0 . . . 5.5, 6.0, 6.5, . . . 9.0, 9.5, 10.0). They observe a very complicated performance made up of many body movements that together take about 2 seconds to complete. The judges do not have the benefit of slow motion or instant replay to review the performance and they cannot discuss the dive with one another. If their attention strays for even a second, they miss a large portion of the performance. Yet, when the scores are flashed on the scoreboard the judges inevitably are in very close agreement. Rarely do all judges give a dive the exact same score, but rarely is there more than a 1-point difference between any two judges' scores. This is amazing agreement among observers for such a short, complicated performance.

With this example in mind, let's consider the four essential features of all formal performance assessments, whether it be a diving competition, an oral speech, a book report, a typing exercise, a science fair project, or something else. This overview will then be followed by a more extensive discussion of each feature. Briefly, every performance assessment should:

1. Have a clear purpose that identifies the decision to be made from the performance assessment.
2. Identify observable aspects of the pupil's performance or product that can be judged.
3. Provide an appropriate setting for eliciting and judging the performance or product.
4. Provide a judgment or score to describe performance.

Define the Purpose of Assessment

Performances and products are normally broken down into specific, observable criteria, each of which can be judged independently.

In a diving competition, the purpose of the assessment is to rank each diver's performance in order to identify the best divers. Each dive receives a score and the highest total score wins the competition. Suppose, however, that dives were being performed during practice, prior to a competition. The diver's coach would observe the practice dives, but the coach's main concern would be not with the overall dive, but with examining the many specific features of each dive that the judges will score during a competition. Consequently, the coach would "score" the practice dive formatively, identifying the diver's strengths and weaknesses for all aspects of each dive. The specific areas in which the diver was weak would likely be emphasized in practice.

Performance assessments are particularly suited to diagnosis because they provide information about how pupils perform each specific criterion in a general performance.

Performance assessments are particularly suited to such diagnosis because they can provide information about how a pupil performs each of the specific criteria that make up a more general performance or product. This criterion-by-criterion assessment makes it easy to identify the strong and weak points of a pupil's performance. When the performance criteria are stated in terms of observable pupil behaviors or product characteristics, as they should be, remediation is made easy. Each suggestion for improvement can be described in specific terms—for example, "report to group project area on time," "wait your turn to speak," "do your share of the group work."

Teachers use performance assessment for many purposes: grading pupils, constructing portfolios of pupil work, diagnosing pupil learning, helping pupils recognize the important steps in a performance or product, providing concrete examples of pupil work for parent conferences. Whatever the purpose of performance assessment, it should be specified at the beginning of the assessment process so that proper performance criteria and scoring procedures can be established.

Teachers need to think ahead about whether a performance assessment's purposes will be formative or summative because their judgment task is very different depending on which is the case. When the goal of assessment is formative, the focus is on giving feedback to pupils about their strengths and weaknesses. When the goal is summative, the focus is on rating the ultimate level of achievement.

Identify Performance Criteria

Performance criteria are the specific behaviors a pupil should display in properly carrying out a performance or create a product. They are at the heart of successful performance assessment, yet they are the area in which most problems occur.

When teachers first think about assessing performance, they tend to think in terms of general performances such as oral reading, giving a speech, following safety rules in the laboratory, penmanship, writing a book report, organizing ideas, fingering a keyboard, or getting along with peers. In reality, such performances cannot be assessed until they are broken down into the more specific aspects or characteristics that comprise them. These more narrow aspects and characteristics are the performance criteria that teachers will observe and judge.

Studies show that many classroom teachers lack skill in assessing and are unprepared to assess their pupils, especially on performance assessments (Fager, Plake, and Impara, 1997). Relatively few teachers are required to pass a course in classroom assessment in their teacher preparation. Only about 20 states require that preservice teachers take an assessment course (Stiggins, 1999). Teachers tend to be better at providing interesting tasks and performances for their pupils than they are at identifying the criteria that describe what makes a good task or performance. Often, the first question a teacher asks is "What will we do?" A more appropriate question to ask first, especially with performance assessments, is "What do I want my pupils to learn?" (Arter, 1999.)

Key Assessment Tools 9.2 shows three sets of criteria for assessing pupils' performance when (1) working in groups, (2) playing the piano, and (3) writing a book report. Criteria such as these focus teachers' instruction and assessments in the same way that diving criteria enable judges to evaluate diving performance. Notice how the performance criteria clearly

Key Assessment Tools 9.2

EXAMPLES OF PERFORMANCE CRITERIA

Working in Groups	Playing the Piano	Writing a Book Report
Reports to group project area on time	Sits upright with feet on floor (or pedal, when necessary)	States the author and title
Starts work on own	Arches fingers on keys	Identifies the type of book (fiction, adventure, historical, etc.)
Shares information	Plays without pauses or interruptions	Describes what the book was about in four or more sentences
Contributes ideas		
Listens to others	Maintains even tempo	
Waits turn to speak	Plays correct notes	States an opinion of the book
Follows instructions	Holds all note values for indicated duration	Gives three reasons to support the opinion
Courteous to other group members	Follows score dynamics (forte, crescendo, decrescendo)	Uses correct spelling, punctuation, and capitalization
Helps to solve group problems	Melody can be heard above other harmonization	
Considers viewpoints of others		
Carries out share of group-determined activities	Phrases according to score (staccato and legato)	
Completes assigned tasks on time	Follows score pedal markings	

Performance criteria can focus on processes, products, or both.

identify the important aspects of the performance or product being assessed. Well-stated performance criteria are at the heart of successful efforts to instruct and assess performances and products.

To define performance criteria, a teacher must first decide if a process or a product will be observed. Will processes such as typing or oral reading be assessed, or will products such as a typed letter or book report be assessed? In the former case, criteria are needed to judge the pupil's actual performance of targeted criteria; in the latter, criteria are needed to judge the end product of those behaviors. In some cases, both process and product can be assessed. For example, a first grade teacher assessed both process and product when she (1) observed a pupil writing to determine how the pupil held the pencil, positioned the paper, and manipulated the pencil and (2) judged the finished, handwritten product to assess how well the pupil formed his letters. Notice that the teacher observed different things according to whether she was interested in the pupil's handwriting *process* or handwriting *product*. It is for this reason that teachers must know what they want to observe before performance criteria can be identified.

The key to identifying performance criteria is to break down an overall performance or product into its component parts. It is these parts that will be observed and judged. Consider, for example, a product assessment of eighth graders' written paragraphs. The purpose of the assessment is to judge pupils' ability to write a paragraph on a topic of their choice. In preparing to judge the completed paragraph, a teacher initially listed the following performance criteria:

♦ First sentence
♦ Appropriate topic sentence
♦ Good supporting ideas
♦ Good vocabulary
♦ Complete sentences
♦ Capitalization
♦ Spelling
♦ Conclusion
♦ Handwriting

These performance criteria do identify important areas of a written paragraph, but the areas are vague and poorly stated. What, for example, is meant by "first sentence"? What is an "appropriate" topic sentence or "good" vocabulary? What should be examined in judging capitalization, spelling, and handwriting? If a teacher cannot answer these questions, how can he or she provide suitable examples or instruction for pupils? Performance criteria need to be specific enough to focus the teacher on well-defined characteristics of the performance or product. They must also be specific enough to permit the teacher to convey to pupils, in terms they can understand, the specific features that define the desired performance or product. Once defined, the criteria permit consistent teacher assessments of performance and consistent communication with pupils about their learning.

Following is a revised version of the performance criteria for a well-organized paragraph. Note the difference in clarity and how the revised version focuses the teacher and students on very specific features of the paragraph—ones that are important and will be assessed. Before assigning the task, the teacher wisely decided to share and discuss the performance criteria with the pupils.

♦ Indents first sentence.
♦ Topic sentence sets main idea of paragraph.
♦ Following sentences support main idea.
♦ Sentences arranged in logical order.
♦ Uses age-appropriate vocabulary.
♦ Writes in complete sentences.
♦ Capitalizes proper nouns and first words in sentences.
♦ Makes no more than three spelling errors.
♦ Conclusion follows logically from prior sentences.
♦ Handwriting is legible.

Cautions in Developing Performance Criteria

Three points of caution are appropriate here. First, it is important to understand that the previous example of performance criteria is not the only one that describes the characteristics of a well-written paragraph. Different teachers might identify varying criteria that they feel are more important or more suitable for their pupils than some of the ones in our example. Thus, emphasis should not be upon identifying the best or only set of criteria for a performance or product, but rather upon stating criteria that are meaningful, important, and can be understood by the pupils.

Very long lists of performance criteria (over 15) become unmanageable and intrusive.

Second, it is possible to break down most school performances and products into many very narrow criteria. However, a lengthy list of performance criteria becomes ineffective because teachers rarely have the time to observe and assess a large number of very specific performance criteria for each pupil. Too many criteria make the observation process intrusive, with the teacher hovering over the pupil, rapidly checking off behaviors, and often interfering with a pupil's performance.

For classroom performance assessment to be manageable and meaningful, a balance must be established between specificity and practicality. The key to attaining this balance is to identify the *essential* criteria associated with a performance or product; 6 to 12 performance criteria are a manageable number for most classroom teachers to emphasize.

Third, the process of identifying performance criteria is an ongoing one that is rarely completed after the first attempt. Initial performance criteria will need to be revised and clarified, based on experience from their use, to provide the focus needed for valid and reliable assessment. To aid this process, teachers should think about the performance or product they wish to observe and reflect on its key aspects. They can also examine a few actual products or performances as bases for revising their initial list of criteria.

The following list shows the initial set of performance criteria a teacher wrote to assess pupils' oral reports.

◆ Speaks clearly and slowly.
◆ Pronounces correctly.
◆ Makes eye contact.
◆ Exhibits good posture when presenting.
◆ Exhibits good effort.
◆ Presents with feeling.
◆ Understands the topic.
◆ Exhibits enthusiastic attitude.
◆ Organizes.

Note the lack of specificity in many of the criteria: "slowly," "correctly," "good," "understands," and "enthusiastic attitude." These criteria hide more than they reveal. After reflecting on and observing a few oral presentations, the teacher revised and sharpened the performance criteria as shown in the following list. Note that the teacher first divided the general performance into three areas (physical expression, vocal expression, and verbal expression) and then identified a few important performance criteria within each of these areas. It is not essential to divide the performance criteria into separate sections, but sometimes it is useful in focusing the teacher and pupils.

Like other writing assignments, good performance criteria need to be revised and clarified over time.

1. Physical expression
   ♦ Stands straight and faces audience.
   ♦ Changes facial expression with changes in tone of the report.
   ♦ Maintains eye contact with audience.

2. Vocal expression
   ♦ Speaks in a steady, clear voice.
   ♦ Varies tone to emphasize points.
   ♦ Speaks loudly enough to be heard by audience.
   ♦ Paces words in an even flow.
   ♦ Enunciates each word.

3. Verbal expression
   ♦ Chooses precise words to convey meaning.
   ♦ Avoids unnecessary repetition.
   ♦ States sentences with complete thoughts or ideas.
   ♦ Organizes information logically.
   ♦ Summarizes main points at conclusion.

Developing Observable Performance Criteria

The value and richness of performance and product assessments depend heavily on identifying performance criteria that can be observed and judged. It is important that the criteria be clear in the teacher's mind and that the pupils be taught the criteria. The following guidelines should prove useful for this purpose.

The value of performance assessments depends on identifying performance criteria that can be observed and judged.

1. *Select the performance or product to be assessed and either perform it yourself or imagine yourself performing it.* Think to yourself, "What would I have to do in order to complete this task? What steps would I have to follow?" It isn't a bad idea to actually carry out the performance yourself, recording and studying your performance or product.

2. *List the important aspects of the performance or product.* What specific behaviors or attributes are most important to the successful completion of the task? What behaviors have been emphasized in instruction? Include important aspects and exclude the irrelevant ones.

3. *Try to limit the number of performance criteria, so they all can be observed during a pupil's performance.* This is less important when one is assessing a product, but even then it is better to assess a limited number of key criteria than a large number that vary widely. Remember, you will have to observe and judge performance on each of the criteria identified.

4. *If possible, have groups of teachers think through the important criteria included in a task.* Because all first grade teachers assess oral reading in their classrooms and because the criteria for successful oral reading do not differ much from one first grade classroom to another, a group effort to define performance criteria will likely save time and produce a more complete set of criteria than that produced by any single teacher. Similar group efforts are useful for other common performances or products such as book reports and science fair projects.

When teachers within a school develop similar performance criteria across grade revels, it is reinforcing to pupils.

5. *Express the performance criteria in terms of observable pupil behaviors or product characteristics.* Be specific when stating the performance criteria. For example, do not write "The child works." Instead, write "The child remains focused on the task for at least four minutes." Instead of "organization," write " Information is presented in a logical sequence."

6. *Do not use ambiguous words that cloud the meaning of the performance criteria.* The worst offenders in this regard are adverbs that end in *ly.* Other words to avoid are "good" and "appropriate." Thus, criteria such as "appropriate organization," "speaks correct*ly,*" "writes neat*ly,*" and "performs graceful*ly*" are ambiguous and leave interpretation of performance up to the observer. The observer's interpretation may vary from time to time and from pupil to pupil, diminishing the fairness and usefulness of the assessment.

7. *Arrange the performance criteria in the order in which they are likely to be observed.* This will save time when observing and will maintain primary focus on the performance.

8. *Check for existing performance criteria before defining your own.* The performance criteria associated with giving an oral speech, reading aloud, using a microscope, writing a persuasive paragraph, cutting with scissors, and the like have been listed by many people. No one who reads this book will be the first to try to assess these and most other common school performances. The moral here is that one need not reinvent the wheel every time a wheel is needed.

Key Assessment Tools 9.3 summarizes the foregoing guidelines. Regardless of the particular performance or product assessed, clearly stated performance criteria are critical to the success of both instruction and assessment. The criteria define the important aspects of a performance or

---

Key Assessment Tools 9.3

GUIDELINES FOR STATING PERFORMANCE CRITERIA

1. Identify the steps or features of the performance or task to be assessed by imagining yourself performing it, observing pupils performing it, or inspecting finished products.

2. List the important aspects of the performance or product.

3. Try to keep the number of performance criteria small so that they can be reasonably observed and judged; a good range to use is 6 to 12 criteria.

4. Have teachers think through the criteria as a group.

5. Express the criteria in terms of observable pupil behaviors or product characteristics.

6. Avoid vague and ambiguous words like "correctly," "appropriately," and "good."

7. Arrange the performance criteria in the order in which they are likely to be observed.

8. Check for existing performance assessment instruments to use or modify before constructing your own.

---

product, guide what pupils should be taught, and produce a focus for both the teacher and pupil when assessing performance. Clear performance criteria are needed, and the tasks used to teach and assess the desired performance should be aligned to the criteria (McTighe, 1996).

Provide a Setting to Elicit and Observe the Performance

Once the performance criteria are defined, a setting in which to observe the performance or product must be selected or established. Depending on the nature of the performance or product, the teacher may observe behaviors as they naturally occur in the classroom or set up a specific situation in which the pupils must perform. There are two considerations in deciding whether to observe naturally occurring behaviors or to set up a more controlled exercise: (1) the frequency with which the performance naturally occurs in the classroom and (2) the seriousness of the decision to be made.

If the performance occurs infrequently during normal classroom activity, it may be more efficient to structure a situation in which pupils must perform the desired behaviors. For example, in the normal flow of classroom activities, pupils rarely have the opportunity to give a planned 5-minute speech, so the teacher should set up an exercise in which each pupil must develop and give a 5-minute speech. Oral reading, on the other hand, occurs

Teachers may observe and assess naturally occurring classroom behaviors or set up situations in which they assess carefully structured performances.

Formally structured performance assessments are needed when teachers are dealing with low-frequency behaviors and making important decisions.

olc

CHAPTER CASE STUDY

Visit the text OLC to read the case of Leigh Scott, a high school social studies teacher. Leigh is confronted by an angry student to discuss how she arrived at his report card grade.

www.mhhe.com/ airasian5e

frequently enough in many elementary classrooms that performance can be observed as part of the normal flow of reading instruction.

The importance of the decision to be made from a performance assessment also influences the context in which observation takes place. In general the more important the decision, the more structured the assessment environment should be. A course grade, for example, represents an important decision about a pupil. If performance assessments contribute to grading, evidence should be gathered under structured, formal circumstances so that every pupil has a fair and equal chance to exhibit his or her achievement. The validity of the assessment is likely to be improved when the setting is similar and familiar to all pupils.

Regardless of the nature of the assessment, evidence obtained from a single assessment describes only one example of a pupil's performance. For a variety of reasons such as illness, home problems, or other distractions, pupil performance at a single time may not provide a reliable indication of the pupil's true achievement. To be certain that one has an accurate indication of what a pupil can and cannot do, multiple observations and products are useful. If the different observations produce similar performance, a teacher can have confidence in the evidence and use it in decision making. If different observations contradict one another, more information should be obtained.

Multiple observations of pupil performances provide more reliable and accurate information.

Develop a Score to Describe the Performance

Holistic scoring (a single overall score) is good for such things as group placement or grading; analytic scoring (scoring individual criteria) is useful in diagnosing student difficulties.

The final step in performance assessment is to score pupils' performance. As in previous steps, the nature of the decision to be made influences the judgmental system used. Scoring a performance assessment can be holistic or analytic, just like scoring an essay question. In situations such as group placement, selection, or grading, holistic scoring is most useful. To make such decisions, a teacher seeks to describe an individual's performance using a single, overall score. On the other hand, if the assessment purpose is to diagnose pupil difficulties or certify pupil mastery of each individual performance criterion, then analytic scoring, with a separate score or rating on each performance criterion, is appropriate. In either case, the performance criteria dictate the scoring or rating approach that is adopted. (See Chapter 8 for a discussion of holistic and analytic scoring.)

In most classrooms, the teacher is both the observer and the scorer. In situations where an important decision is to be made, additional observers/scorers may be added. Thus, it is common for performance assessments in athletic, music, debate, and art competitions to have more than a single judge in order to make scoring more fair.

A number of options exist for collecting, recording, and summarizing observations of pupil performance: anecdotal records, checklists, rating scales, and rubrics, and portfolios. The following sections explore these options in detail.

ANECDOTAL RECORDS, CHECKLISTS, AND RATING SCALES

Anecdotal Records

Written accounts of significant, individual pupil events and behaviors the teacher has observed are called **anecdotal records**. Only those observations that have special significance and that cannot be obtained from other classroom assessment methods should be included in an anecdotal record. Figure 9.1 shows an example of an anecdotal record of pupil Lynn Gregory. Notice that it provides information about the learner, the date of observation, the name of the teacher observing, and a factual description of the event.

Most teachers have difficulty identifying particular events or behaviors that merit inclusion in an anecdotal record. What is significant and important in the life of a pupil is not always apparent at the time an event or behavior occurs. From the hundreds of observations made each day, how is a teacher to select the one that might be important enough to write down? It may take many observations over many days to recognize which events really are significant. Moreover, anecdotal records are time-consuming to prepare and need to be written up soon after the event or behavior is observed, while it is fresh in the teacher's mind. This is not always possible. For these reasons, anecdotal records are not used extensively by teachers. This does not mean that teachers do not observe and judge classroom events—we know they do. It simply means that they seldom write down descriptions of these events.

Anecdotal records such as checklists, rating scales, and portfolios are options available to record and collect observations of pupils.

Anecdotal records are written accounts of significant events and behaviors the teacher has observed in a pupil.

Checklists

A **checklist** is a written list of performance criteria. As a pupil's performance is observed or product judged, the scorer determines whether the performance or the product meets each performance criterion. If it does, a

PUPIL *Lynn Gregory*	DATE *9/22/2004*
OBSERVER *J. Ricketts*	

All term Lynn has been quiet and passive, rarely interacting w/classmates in class or on the playground. Today Lynn suddenly "opened up" and wanted continual interaction w/classmates. She could not settle down, kept circulating around the room until she became bothersome to me and her classmates. I tried to settle her down, but was unsuccessful.

FIGURE 9.1
Anecdotal Record for Lynn Gregory.

FIGURE 9.2 *Checklist Results for an Oral Presentation.*

NAME: *Rick Gray*   DATE: *Oct. 12, 2004*

I. Physical Expression

    ✓ A. Stands straight and faces audience.

    _____ B. Changes facial expression with changes in tone of the presentation.

    ✓ C. Maintains eye contact with audience.

II. Vocal Expression

    ✓ A. Speaks in a steady, clear voice.

    ✓ B. Varies tone to emphasize points.

    _____ C. Speaks loudly enough to be heard by audience.

    ✓ D. Paces words in an even flow.

    _____ E. Enunciates each word.

III. Verbal Expression

    _____ A. Chooses precise words to convey meaning.

    ✓ B. Avoids unnecessary repetition.

    ✓ C. States sentences with complete thoughts or ideas.

    ✓ D. Organizes information logically.

    ✓ E. Summarizes main points at conclusion.

A checklist, which is a written list of performance criteria, can be used repeatedly over time to diagnose strengths, weaknesses, and changes in performances.

checkmark is placed next to that criterion, indicating that it was observed; if it does not, the checkmark is omitted. Figure 9.2 shows a completed checklist for Rick Gray's oral presentation. The performance criteria for this checklist were presented earlier in this chapter.

Checklists are diagnostic, reusable, and capable of charting pupil progress. They provide a detailed record of pupils' performances, one that can and should be shown to pupils to help them see where improvement is needed. Rick Gray's teacher could sit down with him after his presentation and point out both the criteria on which he performed well and the areas that need improvement. Because it focuses on specific performances, a checklist provides diagnostic information. The same checklist can be reused, with different pupils or with the same pupil over time. Using the same checklist more than once is an easy way to obtain information about a pupil's improvement over time.

There are, however, disadvantages associated with checklists. One important disadvantage is that checklists give a teacher only two choices for each criterion: performed or not performed. A checklist provides no middle ground for scoring. Suppose that Rick Gray stood straight and faced the audience most of the time during his oral presentation, or paced his words evenly except in one brief part of the speech when he spoke too quickly and ran his words together. How should his teacher score him on these performance criteria? Should Rick receive a check because he did them most of the time, or should he not receive a check because his performance was flawed? Sometimes this is not an easy choice. A checklist forces the teacher to make an absolute decision for each performance criterion, even though a pupil's performance is somewhere between these extremes.

A second disadvantage of checklists is the difficulty of summarizing a pupil's performance into a single score. We saw how useful checklists can be for diagnosing pupils' strengths and weaknesses. But what if a teacher wants to summarize performance across a number of criteria to arrive at a single score for grading purposes?

Checklists cannot record gradations in performances.

One way to summarize Rick's performance into a single score is to translate the number of performance criteria he successfully demonstrated into a percentage. For example, there were 13 performance criteria on the oral presentation checklist and Rick demonstrated 9 of them during his presentation. Assuming each criterion is equally important, Rick's performance translates into a score of 69 percent ($9/13 \times 100 = 69\%$). Thus, Rick demonstrated 69 percent of the desired performance criteria. (In Chapter 10 we will discuss the way scores like Rick's 69 percent are turned into grades.)

A second, and better, way to summarize performance would be for the teacher to set up standards for rating pupils' performance. Suppose Rick's teacher set up the following set of standards:

Excellent	12 or 13	performance criteria shown
Good	9 to 11	performance criteria shown
Fair	5 to 8	performance criteria shown
Poor	5 or less	performance criteria shown

These standards allow the teacher to summarize performance on a scale that goes from excellent to poor. The scale could also go from a grade of A to one of D, depending on the type of scoring the teacher uses. The same standard would be used to summarize each pupil's performance. Rick performed 9 of the 13 criteria, and the teacher's standard indicates that his performance should be classified as "good" or "B." Of course, there are many such standards that can be set up and the one shown is only an example. In establishing standards, it is advisable to keep the summarizing rules as simple as possible.

Summarizing performances from a checklist can be done by setting up rating standards or by calculating the percentage of criteria accomplished.

Rating Scales

The three most common types of rating scales are numerical, graphic, and descriptive (also called scoring rubrics).

Although they are similar to checklists, **rating scales** allow the observer to judge performance along a continuum rather than as a dichotomy. Both checklists and rating scales are based upon a set of performance criteria, and it is common for the same set of performance criteria to be used in both a rating scale and a checklist. However, a checklist gives the observer two categories for judging, while a rating scale gives more than two.

Three of the most common types or rating scales are the numerical, graphic, and descriptive scales. Figure 9.3 shows an example of each of these scales as applied to two specific performance criteria for giving an oral presentation. In numerical scales, a number stands for a point on the rating scale. Thus, in the example, "1" corresponds to the pupil *always* performing the behavior, "2" to the pupil *usually* performing the behavior, and so on. Graphic scales require the rater to mark a position on a line divided into sections based upon a scale. The rater marks an "X" at that point on the line that best describes the pupil's performance. Descriptive rating scales, also called **scoring rubrics,** require the rater to choose among different descriptions of actual performance. (We will say more about rubrics in the next section.) (Wiggins and McTighe, 1998; Goodrich, 1997.) In descriptive rating scales, different descriptions are used to represent different levels of pupil performance. To score, the teacher picks the description that comes closest to the pupil's actual performance. A judgment of the teacher determines the grade.

Descriptive rating scales, or scoring rubrics, require the rater to choose among different descriptions of actual performance.

Regardless of the type of rating scale one chooses, two general rules will improve their use. The first rule is to limit the number of rating categories. There is a tendency to think that the greater the number of rating categories to choose from, the better the rating scale. In practice, this is not the case. Few observers can make reliable discriminations in performance across more than five rating categories. Adding a larger number of categories on a rating scale is likely to make the ratings less, not more, reliable. Stick to three to five well-defined and distinct rating scale points, as shown in Figure 9.3.

Having too many scales tends to distract the rater from the performance, making the ratings unreliable.

The second rule is to use the same rating scale for each performance criterion. This is not usually possible in descriptive rating scales where the descriptions vary with each performance criterion. For numerical and graphic scales, however, it is best to select a single rating scale and use it for all performance criteria. Using many different rating categories requires the observer to change focus frequently and will decrease rating accuracy by distracting the rater's attention from the performance.

Whereas checklists measure only the presence or absence of some performance, a rating scale measures the degree to which the performance matches the criteria.

Figure 9.4 shows a complete set of numerical rating scales for Sarah Jackson for an oral presentation. Note that its performance criteria are identical to those on the checklist shown in Figure 9.2. The only difference between the checklist and the numerical rating scales is the way performance is scored.

FIGURE 9.3   *Three Types of Rating Scale for an Oral Presentation.*

Numerical Rating Scale

Directions: Indicate how often the pupil performs each of these behaviors while giving an oral presentation.
For each behavior circle **1** if the pupil **always** performs the behavior, **2** if the pupil **usually** performs the
behavior, **3** if the pupil **seldom** performs the behavior, and **4** if the pupil **never** performs the behavior.

Physical Expression

A. Stands straight and faces audience

    1   2   3   4

B. Changes facial expression with changes in tone of the presentation

    1   2   3   4

Graphic Rating Scale

Directions: Place an **X** on the line which shows how often the pupil did each of the behaviors listed while giving
an oral presentation.

Physical Expression

A. Stands straight and faces audience

    always   usually   seldom   never

B. Changes facial expression with changes in tone of the presentation

    always   usually   seldom   never

Descriptive Rating Scale

Directions: Place an **X** on the line at the place which best describes the pupil's performance on each behavior.

Physical Expression

A. Stands straight and faces audience

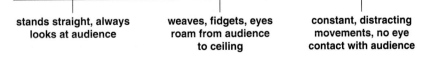

    **stands straight, always   weaves, fidgets, eyes   constant, distracting
    looks at audience   roam from audience   movements, no eye
                                   to ceiling   contact with audience**

B. Changes facial expression with changes in tone of the presentation

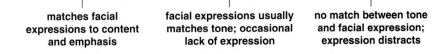

    **matches facial   facial expressions usually   no match between tone
    expressions to content   matches tone; occasional   and facial expression;
    and emphasis   lack of expression   expression distracts**

FIGURE 9.4 *Types of Rating Scales.*

NAME: *Sarah Jackson*   DATE: *Nov. 8, 2004*

Directions: Indicate how often the pupil performs each of these behaviors while giving an oral presentation.
For each behavior **circle 4** if the pupil **always** performs the behavior, **3** if the pupil **usually**
performs the behavior, **2** if the pupil **seldom** performs the behavior, and **1** if the pupil **never**
performs the behavior.

I. Physical Expression

④ 3 2 1   A. Stands straight and faces audience

4 3 ② 1   B. Changes facial expression with changes in tone of the presentation

4 ③ 2 1   C. Maintains eye contact with audience

II. Vocal Expression

④ 3 2 1   A. Speaks in a steady, clear voice

4 ③ 2 1   B. Varies tone to emphasize points

4 3 ② 1   C. Speaks loudly enough to be heard by audience

4 ③ 2 1   D. Paces words in an even flow

4 3 ② 1   E. Enunciates each word

III. Verbal Expression

4 3 ② 1   A. Chooses precise words to convey meaning

4 ③ 2 1   B. Avoids unnecessary repetition

④ 3 2 1   C. States sentences with complete thoughts or ideas

④ 3 2 1   D. Organizes information logically

4 ③ 2 1   E. Summarizes main points at conclusion

While rating scales provide more categories for assessing a pupil's performance, and thereby provide detailed diagnostic information, the multiple
rating categories complicate the process of summarizing performance across
criteria to arrive at a pupil's overall score. With a checklist, summarization is
reduced to giving credit for checked criteria and no credit for unchecked, criteria. This cannot be done with a rating scale because performance is judged
in terms of *degree,* not presence or absence. A teacher must treat ratings of
"always," "usually," "seldom, and "never" differently from each other, or there
is no point to having the different rating categories.

Numerical summarization is the most straightforward and commonly used approach to summarizing performance on rating scales. It assigns a point value to each category in the scale and sums the points across the performance criteria. For example, consider Sarah Jackson's ratings in Figure 9.4. To obtain a summary score for Sarah's performance, one can assign 4 points to a rating of "always," 3 points to a rating of "usually," 2 points to a rating of "seldom," and 1 point to a rating of "never." The numbers 4, 3, 2, and 1 match the four possible ratings for each performance criterion, with 4 representing the most desirable response and 1 the least desirable. Thus, high scores indicate good performance. Note that before summarizing Sarah's performance into a single score, it is important for the teacher to identify areas of weakness so that Sarah can be guided to improve her oral presentations.

Sarah's total score, 39, can be determined by adding the circled numbers. The highest possible score on the rating scale is 52; if a pupil was rated "always" on each performance criterion, the pupil's total score would be 52 (4 points × 13 performance criteria). Thus, Sarah scored 39 out of a possible 52 points. In this manner, a total score can be determined for each pupil rated. This score can be turned into a percentage by dividing it by 52, the total number of points available ($39/52 \times 100 = 75\%$).

RUBRICS

Besides numerical summaries, scoring rubrics or descriptive summarizations provide another way to summarize performance on checklists and rating scales. A rubric is a set of clear expectations or criteria used to help teachers and pupils focus on what is valued in a subject, topic, or activity. A rubric describes the level at which a pupil may be performing a process or completing a product. It focuses on academic work and is based on and linked to the teacher's curriculum. A rubric describes what is to be learned rather than on how to teach. It lays out criteria for different levels of performance, which are usually descriptive, rarely numerical. Figure 9.5 lists ways in which rubrics help both the teacher and the pupil.

As with all performance assessments, rubrics are based on clear and coherent performance criteria.

Rubrics summarize performance in a general way, whereas checklists and rating scales provide specific diagnostic information about pupil strengths and weaknesses.

Two Methods of Scoring

There are two basic methods of scoring rubrics, holistic and analytic, similar to essay scoring methods. Holistic scoring is used to assess the overall performance of a pupil across all the performance criteria. Previous examples in this chapter exemplify holistic scoring. The teacher selects the

FIGURE 9.5
Rubrics Aid Teachers and Pupils.

Rubrics help teachers by

♦ specifying criteria to focus instruction on what is important;

♦ specifying criteria to focus pupil assessments;

♦ increasing the consistency of assessments;

♦ limiting arguments over grading because of the clear criteria and scoring levels that reduce subjectivity; and

♦ providing descriptions of pupil performance that are informative to both parents and students.

Rubrics help pupils by

♦ clarifying the teacher's expectations about performance;

♦ pointing out what is important in a process or product;

♦ helping them to monitor and critique their own work;

♦ providing informative descriptions of performance; and

♦ providing clearer performance information than traditional letter grades provide.

description that most closely matches the pupil's overall performance on the process or product. Analytic scoring is used to assess individually each performance criterion stated in the rubric. Each criterion is rated separately using different levels of performance. Figure 9.6 illustrates holistic scoring for foreign language assessment. There are four scoring levels, each including multiple criteria. The assessor selects the scoring level that best describes the pupil's overall language proficiency.

Devising Rubrics

Consider the following set of performance criteria that were developed for a fifth grade book report by one of the author's students.

1. Tell why you chose the book.
2. Describe the main characters of the book.
3. Explain the plot of the book in three to five sentences.
4. Describe the main place or setting of the book.
5. Explain in three sentences how the main characters have changed through the book.
6. Write in complete sentences.
7. Check spelling, grammar, punctuation, and capitalization.
8. Describe whether or not you enjoyed the book and why.

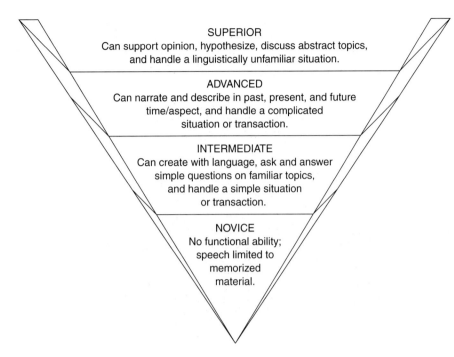

FIGURE 9.6
An Example of Holistic Scoring. **ACTFL Proficiency Levels.**
SOURCE: Adapted from *Oral Proficiency Interview: Tester Training Manual* (n.p.) by the American Council on the Teaching of Foreign Languages. Copyright 1989 by The American Council on the Teaching of Foreign Languages. Adapted by permission.

Of course, these criteria could be added to or subtracted from, based on the pupils in a class and what characteristics of a book report the teacher wishes to emphasize. Different teachers might select different performance criteria.

Scoring rubrics for processes and products are developed by stating levels of the performance criteria that indicate different qualities of pupil performance. For example, the scoring rubric constructed for the fifth grade book report contained three levels of performance labeled "excellent," "good," and "poor." Read each description and note how the authors describe different levels of performance for the criteria.

Excellent: Pupil gives two reasons why the book was chosen; all main characters described in great detail; describes the plot in a logical, step-by-step sequence; gives detailed description of the place in which the book takes place; describes how each main character changed during the book in five sentences; all sentences are complete; no more than a total of five spelling, grammar, punctuation, or capitalization errors; states opinion of the book based on book content.

Good: Pupil gives one reason why the book was chosen; all main characters described too briefly; plot described but one main aspect omitted; provides general description of the book setting; briefly describes how most of the main characters changed during the book; a few nonsentences; more than five spelling, grammar, punctuation, or capitalization errors; states opinion of the book but no reference to the book content.

> **Key Assessment Tools 9.4**
>
> ### GENERAL STEPS IN PREPARING AND USING RUBRICS
>
> 1. Select a process or product to be taught.
> 2. State performance criteria for the process or product.
> 3. Decide on the number of scoring levels for the rubric, usually three to five.
> 4. State description of performance criteria at the highest level of pupil performance (see "excellent" description of the book report rubric).
> 5. State descriptions of performance criteria at the remaining scoring levels (e.g., the "good" and "poor" levels of the book report rubric).
> 6. Compare each pupil's performance to each scoring level.
> 7. Select the scoring level closest to a pupil's actual performance or product.
> 8. Grade the pupil.

Poor: Pupil fails to state why book was chosen; not all main characters are described; superficial plot description with key aspects omitted; little information about where the book takes place; incorrectly describes changes in the main characters during the book; a few nonsentences; many spelling, grammar, punctuation, or capitalization errors; no opinion of the book provided.

To score the book report, the teacher would read a pupil's book report, compare it to the three levels, and determine which of the three levels best describes the quality of the pupil's book report. Is it most like the "excellent" description, the "good" description, or the "poor" description? The selected description determines the grade for the pupil's book report. Different rubrics can have different numbers of scoring levels and different descriptions for the levels. Key Assessment Tools 9.4 gives the steps in preparing and using rubrics.

Consider the rubric in Table 9.4 that is used to assess pupils' response journal questions. The rubric has four scoring levels ranging from "excellent" to "poor" performance. After reading the "excellent" scoring level, can you identity the teacher's intended performance criteria? If the criteria are clear you should be able to identify them from the "excellent" rubric.

We can apply the steps in Key Assessment Tools 9.4 to the response journal rubric in Table 9.4:

Step 1: Select a performance process or product: journal response questions.
Step 2: Identify performance criteria based on best pupil performance:

- ♦ Answers complete and accurate
- ♦ Answers supported with information from readings
- ♦ Answers include direct quotations
- ♦ Answers show varied and detailed sentences
- ♦ Appropriate spelling, capitals, and punctuation

> **TABLE 9.4 SCORING RUBRIC FOR FIFTH GRADE RESPONSE JOURNAL QUESTIONS**
>
> **3—Excellent.** Answers are very complete and accurate. Most answers are supported with specific information from the reading, including direct quotations. Sentence structure is varied and detailed. Mechanics are generally accurate, including spelling, use of capitals, and appropriate punctuation.
>
> **2—Good.** Answers are usually complete and accurate. These answers are supported with specific information from the reading. Sentence structure is varied. Mechanics are generally accurate, including spelling, use of capitals, and appropriate punctuations.
>
> **1—Needs improvement.** Answers are partially to fully accurate. These answers may need to be supported with more specific information from the reading. Sentence structure is varied, with some use of sentence fragments. Mechanics may need improvement, including spelling, use of capitals, and appropriate punctuation.
>
> **0—Poor.** Answers are inaccurate or not attempted at all. Sentence structure frequently incomplete. Mechanics need significant improvement.
>
> SOURCE: Used with permission of Gwen Airasian.

Step 3: Decide on the number of scoring levels: four.
Step 4: State the description of the performance criteria at the highest level: see the "excellent" category in Table 9.4.
Step 5: State descriptions of criteria at the remaining scoring levels: compare the quality of the "excellent" scoring level to the "good," "needs improvement," and "poor" levels.
Step 6: Compare each pupil's performance to the four scoring levels.
Step 7: Select the scoring level that best describes the level of the pupil's performance on the response journal.
Step 8: Assign grade to pupil.

One important aspect of developing and using rubrics is the construction of scoring levels. The bases for developing good scoring levels are the performance criteria and a set of terms that differentiate levels of pupil performance. For example, go to Table 9.4 and read the four scoring levels. Notice that in each scoring level except the "poor" one, we can see the same aspects of the performance criteria: answers complete and accurate, supported from readings, sentence structure, and mechanics. Even the "poor" level includes three of the four criteria. Note what makes the scoring levels different. It is not the criteria per se. It is the level of performance used to describe each criterion. For example, in the "excellent" level, answers are *very* complete and accurate; in the "good" level, answers are *usually* complete and accurate; in the "needs improvement" level, answers are *partially* accurate; and in the "poor" level, answers are *inaccurate or not attempted*. Try the same analysis with the remaining criteria in the table.

Many common sets of terms are used to describe scoring levels in rubrics. For instance, excellent, good, needs improvement, poor were used in the preceding examples. Other description levels are always, mostly, sometimes, seldom, never; exemplary, competent, inconsistent, lacking; advanced, proficient, basic, in progress; and all, some, few, incomplete. These and many other groups of differentiating labels are used to develop scoring levels.

There are also generic rubrics that can be used to assess a variety of processes and products. Usually, generic rubrics state only the description of the highest level of the scoring rubric. The user must provide his or her own scoring levels to differentiate pupil performance. One example of a description from a generic rubric is "goes beyond expectation, includes extra information, makes no mistakes, demonstrates exceptional grasp of the topic, understands abstract concepts, and finds links among parts." This generic rubric could be applied to many types of performance assessments.

TECHNOLOGY AND ASSESSMENT

PERFORMANCE ASSESSMENT RESOURCES

olc Visit Chapter 9 of the text website (www.mhhe.com/airasian5e) to link to the following web-based resources.

Scoring Rubrics: What, When, & How?

♦ This article also appears in *Practical Assessment, Research, & Evaluation*, authored by Barbara M. Moskal. The article discusses what rubrics are, and distinguishes between holistic and analytic types. Examples and additional resources are provided.

A Process for Designing Performance Assessment Tasks

♦ Staff in the Prince George's County Public Schools in Maryland have developed this page that provides a very informative description of the steps involved in the design of performance tasks. This page provides an overview of the steps and includes links provided to more detailed information and discussions, including a page of rubric samples.

Performance Assessments Index

♦ Faculty and staff in the Pattonville School District in Missouri have collected samples of performance tasks, including rubrics, and categorized them by grade level.

Portfolio Assessment

♦ Staff in the Prince George's County Public Schools (Maryland) have developed this page that describes what portfolios are and why teachers may want to consider using them. Included are links to additional pages discussing characteristics of effective portfolios, different types of portfolios, and how to get started and evaluate student portfolios.

What descriptions for an average and a poor scoring level might follow from the exemplary generic description? For example, if a particular exemplary description is "goes beyond expectation," what phrasing could be used to describe an average or poor level for "goes beyond expectation"? Two possible "average" examples might be "performs adequately" or "exhibits average expectation." A description of a third, poor level of performance might be stated as "performs inadequately" or "exhibits below average expectation." Now, given the generic exemplary description "makes no mistakes," what average and poor level examples can you identify for the generic example? Scoring rubrics may have only two levels or may use up to six, but rarely does the number of scoring levels exceed four or five. Too many scoring levels makes judging the pupil's appropriate level for grading more difficult and unreliable.

More Examples of Rubrics

Rubrics come in various forms to assess various processes and products. A few more examples here will provide a wider glimpse of their usefulness. Figure 9.7 shows a small portion of a first grade report card that is presented as a rubric. The entire report card has a number of such rubrics as well as a cover page sent home to explain the report form to parents. The outcomes reported to parents are the language arts and mathematics outcomes the

FIGURE 9.7 *Scoring Rubric Used in First Grade Report Card.*

NOT YET—1	2	DEVELOPING—3	4	ACHIEVING—5		EXTENDING

Such as: May demonstrate one or *more* of following:
 	
Identifies the topic but does not identify any details from the book.
Cites information incorrectly.
Draws only from personal experience rather than from evidence in the book.
Identifies details but not topic.
		Such as: May demonstrate one or *more* of following:
		
		Identifies topic and one (1) detail from the book.
		Identifies several details, but needs prompting to clearly state the main topic.
				Criteria: Demonstrates <u>all</u> of following:
				
				Identifies from an informational book:
				  topic of book,
				  two or more supporting
				  details.
				
				Such as:
				  "This book is about whales. The blue whale is the largest animal on earth. Whales have babies that are born alive—not hatched."
						EXTENDING →
						
						Identifies main ideas.
						Identifies background knowledge.
						Distinguishes between what she or he already knew and what was just learned.
						Identifies topic and details of an informational book <u>read by student.</u>

SOURCE: Reprinted by permission of the Ann Arbor Public Schools, Ann Arbor, Michigan.

district has identified as most crucial for teachers to monitor and for students to achieve. Notice that each desired outcome is defined by specific performances or products at each of the three rubric levels: not yet, developing learner, and achieving learner.

Table 9.5 shows a rubric to assess eleventh grade history pupils. There are five scoring levels for each of the two rubrics shown. Can you identify the performance criteria for the two rubrics?

Key Assessment Tools 9.5 shows a general four-level persuasive writing rubric that can be used at varied grade levels. Identify the terms in this rubric that are used to differentiate levels of pupil performance (e.g., "clearly," "consistently," "thoroughly maintained").

Analytic scoring breaks down the general description of a holistic process or product into separate scores for each criterion. For example, consider the persuasive writing rubric. Unlike a holistic score, analytic scoring would provide a score for each of the five performance criteria. Thus, the teacher might score the criteria in the following manner for the first two performance criteria.

Take a position and clearly state their point of view

Completely
Generally
Partially
Not at all

Consistently use facts and/or personal information to develop support for their position

Extensively
Partially
Rarely

Note that analytic scoring can use letters (A, B, C, etc.), numbers (4, 3, 2, 1), and descriptions as in the examples above.

Write analytic scoring forms for the remaining three performance criteria.

Involving Pupils in the Use of Rubrics

When using rubrics a teacher should inform the pupils about the criteria that will be used to judge their performance or product *before* assessment takes place. Obviously, the teacher should have identified the criteria before the beginning of instruction and assessment. The criteria—and, ideally, specific examples of good and poor performance—should be described and illustrated for the pupils. Pupils should know what makes a good lab report, oral speech, persuasive essay, "show-your-work" math problem, dissection of a frog, analysis of a poem, bar graph, journal response, or any of a thousand other classroom processes and products.

TABLE 9.5 CALIFORNIA ASSESSMENT PROGRAM 1990 HISTORY–SOCIAL SCIENCE GRADE 11 SCORING GUIDE: GROUP PERFORMANCE TASK

	Level I Minimal Achievement	Level II Rudimentary Achievement	Level III Commendable Achievement	Level IV Superior Achievement	Level V Exceptional Achievement
Communication of Ideas 20	(1–4) Position is vague. Presentation is brief and includes unrelated general statements. Overall view of the problem is not clear. Statements tend to wander or ramble.	(5–9) Presents general and indefinite position. Only minimal organization in presentation. Uses generalities to support position. Emphasizes only one issue. Considers only one aspect of problem.	(8–12) Takes a definite but general position. Presents a somewhat organized argument. Uses general terms with limited evidence that may not be totally accurate. Deals with a limited number of issues. Views problem within a somewhat limited range.	(13–16) Takes a clear position. Presents an organized argument with perhaps only minor errors in the supporting evidence. Deals with the major issues and shows some understanding of relationships. Gives consideration to examination of more than one idea or aspect of the problem.	(17–20) Takes a strong, well-defined position. Presents a well-organized, persuasive argument with accurate supporting evidence. Deals with all significant issues and demonstrates a depth of understanding of important relationships. Examines the problem from several positions.
Knowledge and Use of History 30	(1–6) Reiterates one or two facts without complete accuracy. Deals only briefly and vaguely with concepts or the issues. Barely indicates any previous historical knowledge. Relies heavily on the information provided.	(7–12) Provides only basic facts with only some degree of accuracy. Refers to information to explain at least one issue or concept in general terms. Limited use of previous historical knowledge without complete accuracy. Major reliance on the information provided.	(13–18) Relates only major facts to the basic issues with a fair degree of accuracy. Analyzes information to explain at least one issue or concept with substantive support. Uses general ideas from previous historical knowledge with fair degree of accuracy.	(19–24) Offers accurate analysis of the documents. Provides facts to relate to the major issues involved. Uses previous general historical knowledge to examine issues involved.	(25–30) Offers accurate analysis of the information and issues. Provides a variety of facts to explore major and minor issues and concepts involved. Extensively uses previous historical knowledge to provide an in-depth understanding of the problem and to relate it to past and possible future situations.

SOURCE: California Department of Education, 1990. Reprinted with permission.

Key Assessment Tools 9.5

GENERIC RUBRIC TO SCORE WRITING TO PERSUADE

When describing observables to incorporate in a rubric to assess student responses to a specific prompt, it is important to address all of the specific criteria that were included in the prompt itself. In addition, we need to consider how skillfully the response was crafted and how effectively it addressed the writer's ability to persuade. To assist you with identifying these factors, the following observables are provided at varying score points.

Students at Level 1:
◆ Take a position and clearly state their point of view.
◆ Consistently use facts and/or personal information to develop support for their position.
◆ Organize details in a logical plan that is thoroughly maintained.
◆ Consistently enhance what they write by using language purposefully to create sentence variety.
◆ Incorporate appropriate mechanics (spelling, capitalization, punctuation). Any errors that occur are due to risk taking.

Students at Level 2:
◆ Take a position and adequately attempt to clarify their point of view.
◆ Frequently use facts and/or personal information to develop support for their position.
◆ Organize details in a logical plan that is adequately maintained.
◆ Frequently support their position by providing sufficient information.
◆ Frequently enhance what they write by using language purposefully to create sentence variety.
◆ Incorporate appropriate mechanics (spelling, capitalization, punctuation). Most errors that occur are due to risk taking.

Students at Level 3:
◆ Take a position and make a limited attempt to clarify their point of view.
◆ Generally use facts and/or personal information which may or may not support their position.
◆ Organize details in a plan that may or may not be adequately maintained.
◆ May or may not support their position by providing sufficient information.
◆ May or may not attend to mechanics (spelling, capitalization, punctuation).

Student at Level 4:
◆ Usually provide a position and limited information to support the position.
◆ Minimally organize details that include some support for the position.
◆ Seldom take their audience into consideration.
◆ Occasionally choose vocabulary that sufficiently supports the position.
◆ Seldom enhance what they write by varying sentence structure and incorporating appropriate mechanics (spelling, capitalization, punctuation).

Knowing the criteria of quality performance before assessment leads to a number of benefits for both pupils and teacher. First, knowledge of performance criteria provides information to pupils about what is expected of their work—what characteristics make the work good work. Second, knowledge of the criteria lends focus and structure to pupils' performances and product. They know what is expected of them and thus can concentrate on learning and demonstrating the desired knowledge and behaviors. This, in turn, saves the teacher time in scoring pupils' products or processes because the criteria narrow the breadth of pupil responses.

Many teachers let pupils help identify the important performance criteria for a classroom process or product. Involving pupils in identifying performance criteria gives them a sense of ownership of the rubric as well as an early preview of the important characteristics of the process or product they will be working on. Some teachers provide pupils with good and poor examples of the process or product they are teaching and ask pupils to identify what makes a good example. In the process of determining what makes good examples, the pupils are also identifying relevant criteria for the process or product. Figure 9.5 summarized some of the main advantages of rubrics for pupils.

It is very important to understand that there is a learning curve for mastering the construction and use of rubrics. It takes time to learn to use rubrics well. Trial and error as well as practice for both pupils and teachers are needed to help each gain the most out of rubrics. Start with simple and limited performance criteria and scoring levels—perhaps three or four criteria and two or three scoring levels. Explain the rubric process to the pupils: what rubrics are, why we use them, how they can help improve learning and clarify grading. Practice with the pupils. One approach is to have pupils use a rubric to revise their work before passing it in. A teacher should expect to revise a rubric a few times before he or she and the pupils feel comfortable with it.

PORTFOLIOS

An important addition to the growing use of classroom performance assessments is portfolio assessment. This assessment method is gaining use in schools and classrooms (Ryan and Miyasaka, 1995). A **portfolio** is a collection of selected student work. The term *portfolio* derives from the collections that models, photographers, and artists assemble to demonstrate their work. In the classroom, portfolios have the same basic purpose: to collect pupil performances to show their work and accomplishments over time. Portfolios do not contain haphazard, unrelated collections of a pupil's work. They contain consciously selected examples of work that is intended to

Key Assessments Tools 9.6

WHAT CAN GO INTO A PORTFOLIO

Media: videos, audiotapes, pictures, artwork, computer programs

Reflections: plans, statements of goals, self-reflections, journal entries

Individual work: tests, journals, logs, lab reports, homework, essays, poems, maps, inventions, posters, math work

Group work: cooperative learning sessions, group performances, peer reviews

Work in progress: rough and final drafts, show-your-work problems, science fair projects

show pupil growth and development toward important curriculum goals. Portfolios support instruction and learning and should be related to teachers' objectives.

A portfolio can be made up of many different pupil performances or it can be made up of a single performance. For example, a multifocused writing portfolio might contain writing samples, lists of books read, journal entries about books read, and descriptions of favorite poems. Conversely, a single-focus portfolio might contain multiple pieces of the same process or product, such as a portfolio containing only book reports, only written poems, or only chemistry lab reports. Key Assessment Tools 9.6 samples the range of materials that can go into a portfolio.

In one first grade class, pupils developed a reading portfolio. Every third week the pupils read a paragraph or two into their audiotape "portfolio." The teacher monitored pupil improvement over time and pupils could play back their pieces to measure their reading improvement. Also, periodically the pupils' reading portfolios were sent home for the parents to listen to their child's reading improvement, an opportunity parents appreciated.

Portfolios can contribute to instruction and learning in many ways:

♦ Showing pupils' typical work.
♦ Monitoring pupil progress and improvement over time.
♦ Helping pupils self-evaluate their work.
♦ Providing ongoing assessment of pupil learning.
♦ Providing diagnostic information about pupil performance.
♦ Helping teachers judge the appropriateness of the curriculum.
♦ Facilitating teacher meetings and conferences with pupils, parents, and both pupils and parents.
♦ Grading pupils.
♦ Reinforcing the importance of processes and products in learning.
♦ Showing pupils the connections among their processes and products.
♦ Providing concrete examples of pupil work.
♦ Encouraging pupils to think about what is good performance in varied subject areas.

♦ Focusing on both the process and final product of learning.

♦ Informing subsequent teachers about pupils' prior work.

Whatever a portfolio's use and contents, it is important that it have a defined, specific purpose that will focus the nature of the information that will be collected in the portfolio. Too often, teachers defer the question of the portfolio's purpose until *after* pupils have collected large amounts of their work in their portfolios. At that time the teacher is likely to be confronted with the question of what to do with a vast, undifferentiated collection of pupil information.

Perhaps the greatest contribution that portfolios provide for learning is that they give pupils a chance to revisit and reflect on the products and processes they have produced. For many pupils, life in school is an ongoing sequence of papers, performances, assignments, and productions. Each day a new batch of paperwork is produced and the previous day's productions are tossed away or lost, both mentally and physically. Collecting pieces of pupils' work in a portfolio retains them for subsequent pupil review, reflection, demonstration, and grading. With suitable guidance, pupils can be encouraged to think about and compare their work over time, providing them an opportunity rarely available in the absence of portfolios. For example, pupils might be asked to reflect on the following questions. Which of these portfolio items shows the most improvement and why? Which did you enjoy most and why? From which did you learn the most and why? In what areas have you made the most progress over the year and what was the nature of that progress? Portfolios allow pupils to see their progress and judge their work from the perspectives of time and personal development.

As noted, there is a great deal more to successful portfolio assessment than simply collecting bunches of pupils' work. Portfolio assessment is a type of performance assessment and thus depends on the same four elements that all types of performance assessment require: (1) a clear purpose, (2) appropriate performance criteria, (3) a suitable setting, and (4) scoring performance. There are a number of questions that must be answered in developing and assessing portfolios. Key Assessment Tools 9.7 lists the main questions that guide classroom use of portfolios.

Key Assessment Tools 9.7

PORTFOLIO QUESTIONS

1. What is the purpose of the portfolio?
2. What will go into and be removed from the portfolio during its use?
3. Who will select the entries that go into the portfolio: teacher, pupils, or both?
4. How will the portfolio be organized and maintained?
5. How will the portfolio be assessed?

Purpose of Portfolios

It is important to determine the purpose and guidelines for a portfolio's content before compiling it. Is it to grade, group, instruct, or diagnose pupils?

The items that go into a portfolio, the criteria used to judge the items, and the frequency with which items are added to or deleted from the portfolio all depend on the portfolio's purpose. If the purpose is to illustrate a pupil's typical work in various school subjects for a parent's night at the school, the portfolio contents would likely be more wide ranging than if its purpose is to assess the pupil's improvement in math problem solving over a single marking period. In the latter case, math problems would have to be obtained periodically throughout the marking period and collected in the portfolio.

If a portfolio is intended to show a pupil's best work in a subject area, the contents of the portfolio would change as more samples of the pupil's performance became available and as less good ones were removed. If the purpose is to show improvement over time, earlier performances would have to be retained and new pieces added.

Given the many and varied uses of portfolios, purpose is a crucial issue to consider and define in carrying out portfolio assessment. It is important to determine the purpose and general guidelines for the pieces that will go into the portfolio *before* starting the portfolio assessment. It is also critical that all pieces going into a portfolio be dated, especially in portfolios that aim to assess pupil growth or development. Without recorded dates for each portfolio entry, it may be impossible to assess growth and improvement.

Allowing students to help determine what goes into their portfolios gives them a sense of ownership.

To promote pupils' ownership of their portfolios, it is useful to allow pupils to choose at least some of the pieces that will go into their portfolios. Some teachers develop portfolios that contain two types of pieces, those required by the teacher and those selected by the pupil. It is also important that all pupil portfolio selections are accompanied by a brief written explanation of why the pupil feels that a particular piece belongs in her or his portfolio. This will encourage the pupil to reflect on the characteristics of the piece and why it belongs in the portfolio.

Performance Criteria

Performance criteria are needed to evaluate each of the individual pieces within a portfolio.

Performance criteria are needed to assess the individual pieces that make up a portfolio. Without such criteria, assessment cannot be consistent within and across portfolios. The nature and process of identifying performance criteria for portfolios is the same as that for checklists, rating scales, and rubrics. Depending on the type of performance contained in a portfolio, many of the performance criteria discussed earlier in this chapter can be used to assess individual portfolio pieces.

If pupil portfolios are required for all teachers in a grade or if portfolios are to be passed on to the pupil's next teacher, it is advisable for all affected teachers to cooperate in formulating a common set of performance criteria.

Cooperative teacher practice is useful because it involves groups of teachers in the process of identifying important performance criteria. It also helps produce common instructional emphases within and between grades and fosters discussion and sharing of materials among teachers (Herbert, 1992).

It is valuable to allow pupils to help identify performance criteria used for assessing the contents of a portfolio because this can give pupils a sense of ownership over their performance and help them think through the nature of the portfolio pieces they will produce. Beginning a lesson with joint teacher and pupil discussion of what makes a good book report, oral reading, science lab, or sonnet is a useful way to initiate instruction and get the pupils thinking about the characteristics of the process or product they will have to develop.

There is another very important reason why performance criteria are needed for portfolio assessment. The processes or products that will make up a portfolio should, like all forms of assessment, be related to the instruction provided to pupils. Performance criteria are like the teacher's objectives, identifying the important outcomes pupils need to learn. Without explicit criteria, instruction may not provide all the experiences necessary to carry out the desired learning, thereby reducing the validity of the portfolio.

The performance criteria used in evaluating portfolios should align with a teacher's instructional objectives.

Setting

In addition to a clear purpose and well-developed performance criteria, portfolio assessments must take into account the setting in which pupils' performances will be gathered. While many portfolio pieces can be gathered by the teacher in the classroom, others pieces cannot. When portfolios include oral speaking, science experiments, artistic productions, and psychomotor activities, special equipment or arrangements may be needed to properly collect the desired pupil performance. Many teachers underestimate the time it takes to collect the processes and products that make up portfolios and the management and record keeping needed to maintain them. Checking, managing, maintaining, and assessing pupil portfolios is time-consuming but important.

An important dimension of using portfolios is the logistics of collecting and maintaining pupil portfolios. Portfolios require space. They have to be stored in a safe but accessible place. A system has to be established for pupils to add or subtract pieces of their portfolios. Can pupils go to their portfolio at any time or will the teacher set aside special times when all pupils deal with their portfolios? If the portfolio is intended to show growth, how will the order of the entries be kept in sequence? Maintaining portfolios requires time and organization. Materials such as envelopes, crates, tape recorders, and the like will be needed for assembling and storing pupil portfolios.

Scoring

Scoring portfolios is a time-consuming process that involves judging each individual piece and the portfolio as a whole.

Scoring portfolios can be a time-consuming task. Not only does each individual portfolio piece have to be assessed, but the summarized pieces must also be assessed to provide an overall portfolio performance. Depending on the complexity and variety of the contents of the portfolio, assessing may require considerable time and attention to detail, further increasing assessment time.

Summative Scoring

Consider the difference in managing and scoring portfolios that contain varied processes or products compared to portfolios that contain examples of a single process or product. The multifocused portfolio provides a wide range of pupil performance, but at a substantial logistical and scoring cost to the teacher. The single-focus portfolio does not provide the breadth of varied pupil performances of the multifocused portfolio, but can be managed and scored considerably more quickly.

Figure 9.8 is a narrative description of one pupil's writing portfolio. When the purpose of a portfolio is to provide descriptive information about pupil performance for a parent-teacher night or to pass pupil information on to the next year's teacher, no scoring or summarization of the portfolio contents will be necessary. The contents themselves provide the desired information. However, when the purpose of a portfolio is to diagnose, track improvement, assess the success of instruction, encourage pupils to reflect on their work, or grade pupils, some form of summarization or scoring of the portfolio pieces is required.

Performance criteria used to assess an entire portfolio are different from those used to assess individual portfolio items.

The purpose of assessing an entire portfolio, as opposed to the individual pieces, is usually summative—to assign a grade. Such holistic portfolio assessment requires the development of a set of summarizing criteria. For example, improvement in writing might be judged by comparing a pupil's early pieces to later pieces in terms of these performance criteria: (1) number of spelling, capitalization, and punctuation errors, (2) variety of sentence structures used, (3) use of supporting detail, (4) appropriateness of detail to purpose, (5) ability to emphasize and summarize main ideas, (6) link and flow between paragraphs, and (7) personal involvement in written pieces. An alternative approach might be for the teacher to rate earlier written pieces using a general scoring rubric and compare the level of early performances to later performances using the same rubric.

Different portfolios with different purposes require different summarizing criteria. For example, how would you summarize a portfolio containing a number of tape recordings of a pupil's Spanish pronunciation or a portfolio made up of poems a pupil wrote as part of a poetry unit? What criteria would you use to judge *overall* progress or performance?

FIGURE 9.8 *Narrative Description of a Pupil's Writing Portfolio.*

Date	Genre	Topic	Reason	Length	Drafts
9/??	Self-Reflection	Thinking About Your Writing	Requested	1 page	1 draft
10/17	Narrative/Dramatic	Personal Monologue	Important	1 page	2 drafts
1/16	Response to Literature	On *The Lord of the Flies*	Unsatisfying	1 page	4 drafts
2/??	Self-Reflection	Response to Parent Comments	Requested	1 page	1 draft
2/28	Narrative/Dramatic	"The Tell-Tale Heart"	Free Pick	3 pages	2 drafts
5/22	Response to Literature	On *Animal Farm*	Satisfying	5 pages	2 drafts
6/??	Self-Reflection	Final Reflection	Requested	2 pages	1 draft

As a writer, Barry shows substantial growth from the beginning of the year in his first personal monologue to his last piece, a response to *Animal Farm.* Initially, Barry seems to have little control over the flow and transition of his ideas. His points are not tied together, he jumps around in his thinking, and he lacks specificity in his ideas. By January, when Barry writes his response to *The Lord of the Flies,* he begins a coherent argument about the differences between Ralph's group and Jack's tribe, although he ends with the unsupported assertions that he would have preferred to be "marooned on a desert island" with Ralph. Barry includes three reasons for his comparison, hinges his reasons with transition words, but more impressively, connects his introductory paragraph with a transition sentence to the body of his essay. In the revisions of this essay, Barry makes primarily word and sentence level changes, adds paragraph formatting, and generally improves the local coherence of the piece.

By the end of February when he writes his narrative response to Poe's "The Tell-Tale Heart," Barry displays a concern for making his writing interesting. "I like the idea that there are so many twists in the story that I really think makes it interesting." He makes surface-level spelling changes, deletes a sentence, and replaces details, although not always successfully (e.g., "fine satin sheets and brass bed," is replaced with the summary description "extravagant furniture"). Overall, it is an effective piece of writing showing Barry's understanding of narrative form and his ability to manipulate twists of plot in order to create an engaging story.

Barry's last selection in his portfolio is an exceptional five-page, typed essay on Orwell's *Animal Farm.* The writing is highly organized around the theme of scapegoating. Using supporting details from the novel and contemporary examples from politics and sports, Barry creates a compelling and believable argument. The effective intertextuality and the multiple perspectives Barry brings to this essay result largely from an exceptional revision process. Not only does he attempt to correct his standard conventions and improve his word choices, he also revises successfully to the point of moving around whole clumps of text and adding sections that significantly reshape the piece. This pattern of revision shows the control Barry has gained over his writing.

In Barry's final reflection he describes his development, showing an awareness of such issues as organizing and connecting ideas, choosing appropriate words and details, and making his writing accessible to his readers. "I had many gaps in my writing. One problem was that I would skip from one idea to the next and it would not be clear what was going on in the piece. . . . Now, I have put in more details so you don't have to think as much as you would. I also perfect my transitions and my paragraph form. . . . My reading . . . has improved my vocabulary and it helped me organize my writing so it sounds its best and makes the most sense possible. . . . There are many mistakes I have made throughout the year, but I have at least learned from all of them." I agree with him.

Source: P. A. Moss, et al., "Portfolios, accountability, and an interpretive approach to validity," *Educational Measurement: Issues and Practice,* 1992, *11*(3), p. 18. Copyright 1992 by the National Council on Measurement in Education. Used by permission of AERA.

> **TABLE 9.6 ASSESSING INDIVIDUAL PORTFOLIO PIECES**
>
> **Checklist**
>
> | | | |
> |---|---|---|
> | Selects correct solution method | Yes | No |
> | Draws and labels diagrams | Yes | No |
> | Shows work leading to solution | Yes | No |
> | Gets correct answer | Yes | No |
>
> **Rating Scale**
>
> | | | | |
> |---|---|---|---|
> | Selects correct solution method | Quickly | Slowly | Not at all |
> | Draws and labels diagrams | Completely | Partially | Not at all |
> | Shows work leading to solution | Completely | Partially | Not at all |
> | Gets correct answer | Quickly | Slowly | Not at all |
>
> **Rubric**
>
> Selects correct solution method; draws complete, labeled diagrams; shows all work; gets correct answer
>
> Selects correct solution method; draws complete but poorly labeled diagrams; shows partial work; gets partially correct answer
>
> Selects incorrect solution method; neither draws nor labels diagrams; shows very little work; gets incorrect answer

Scoring the Pieces

Individual portfolio pieces are normally judged using performance criteria that have been assembled into some form of checklist, rating scale, or rubric.

Individual portfolio pieces are typically scored using methods we have discussed: checklists, rating scales, and rubrics. Table 9.6 gives examples. Thus, each story, tape recording, lab report, handwriting sample, persuasive essay, or cooperative group product can be judged by organizing the performance criteria into a checklist, rating scale, or rubric.

Of course, the teacher does not always have to be the one who assesses the pieces. It is desirable and instructive to allow pupils to self-assess some of their portfolio pieces in order to give them practice in critiquing their own work in terms of the performance criteria.

Allowing students to self-assess their portfolio encourages pupil reflection and learning.

Consider how much more pupil involvement in the writing process portfolios provide, compared to when an assignment is given, passed in to the teacher, graded, returned to the pupil, and soon forgotten. Note also how this kind of assessment encourages pupil reflection and learning.

From the teacher's point of view, clearly there are both advantages and disadvantages to performances, product, and portfolio assessments. Table 9.7 summarizes the major trade-offs.

> **TABLE 9.7   ADVANTAGES AND DISADVANTAGES OF PERFORMANCE, PRODUCT, AND PORTFOLIO ASSESSMENTS**
>
> **Advantages**
>
> ♦ Chart pupil performance over time.
> ♦ Conduct pupil self-assessment of products and performances.
> ♦ Conduct peer review of products and performances.
> ♦ Provide diagnostic information about performances and products.
> ♦ Integrate assessment and instruction.
> ♦ Promote learning through assessment activities.
> ♦ Give pupils ownership over their learning and productions.
> ♦ Clarify lesson, assignment, and test expectations.
> ♦ Report performance to parents in clear, descriptive terms.
> ♦ Permit pupil reflection and analysis of work.
> ♦ Provide concrete examples for parent conferences.
> ♦ Assemble cumulative evidence of performance.
> ♦ Reinforce importance of pupil performance.
>
> **Disadvantages**
>
> Most disadvantages associated with performance, product, and especially portfolio assessments involve the time they require:
>
> ♦ To prepare materials, performance criteria, and scoring formats.
> ♦ To manage, organize, and keep records.
> ♦ For teachers and pupils to become comfortable with the use of performance assessments and the change in teaching and learning roles they involve.
> ♦ To score and provide feedback to pupils.

VALIDITY AND RELIABILITY OF PERFORMANCE ASSESSMENTS

Since formal performance assessments are used to make decisions about pupils, it is important for them to be valid and reliable. This section describes steps that can be taken to obtain high-quality performance assessments.

Scoring performance assessments is a difficult and often time-consuming activity. The process is often complex and lengthy. Unlike when scoring

Scoring performance assessments is a difficult, time-consuming activity.

selection items, teachers' interpretation and judgment are necessary for scoring performances and products. Each student produces or constructs a performance or product that is different from that of other students. This makes scoring difficult; the more criteria to address and the more variation in the products or performances students produce, the more time-consuming, fatiguing, and potentially invalid.

Distractions and personal feelings can introduce error into either the observation or judging process, thereby reducing the validity and reliability of the assessment.

Further, like essays, performance assessments are subject to many ancillary factors that may not be relevant to scoring but may influence the teacher's judgment of the performance assessments. For example, teachers' scoring of products such as essays or reports are often influenced by the quality of a pupil's handwriting, neatness, sentence structure and flow, and knowledge of the pupil being scored. These and similar factors are not key aspects of the product, but they often weigh heavily in scoring. Teachers can rarely be completely unbiased observers of what their pupils do, because they know their pupils too well and have a set of built-in predispositions regarding each one. In each case, there are many irrelevant and distracting factors that can influence the teacher's judgments and the validity and reliability of performance assessments.

The key to improving rating or scoring skills is to try to eliminate the distracting factors so that the assessment more closely reflects the pupil's actual performance. In performance assessments, the main source of error is the observer, who judges both what is happening during a performance and the quality of the performance. Beyond the issue of distractions, teachers can prepare their pupils well and ensure validity and reliability in various other ways.

Preparing Pupils

There are many ways teachers prepare their pupils for performance assessment. First and foremost, they provide good instruction. Pupils learn to set up and focus microscopes, build bookcases, write book reports, give oral speeches, measure with a ruler, perform musical selections, and speak French the same way they learn to solve simultaneous equations, find countries on a map, write a topic sentence, or balance a chemical equation. They are given instruction and practice. Achievement depends upon their being taught the things on which they are being assessed. One of the advantages of performance assessments is their explicit criteria, which focus instruction and assessment.

Unless students are informed about the performance criteria upon which they will be judged, they may not perform up to their abilities.

In preparing pupils for performance assessment, the teacher should inform and explain the criteria on which they will be judged (Mehrens, Popham, & Ryan, 1998). In many classrooms, teachers and pupils jointly discuss and define criteria for a desired performance or product. This helps them to understand what is expected of them by identifying the important dimensions of the performance or product. Another, less interactive way to do this is for the teacher to give pupils a copy of the checklist or rating form that will be used during their assessment. If performance criteria are not made clear to pupils, they may perform poorly, not because they are incapable, but because they were not aware of the teacher's expectations and the criteria for a good performance. In such cases, the performance ratings do not reflect the pupils' true achievement, and the grades they receive could lead to invalid decisions about their learning.

Validity

Validity is concerned with whether the information obtained from an assessment permits the teacher to make a correct decision about a pupil's learning. As discussed previously, either failure to instruct pupils on desired performances or the inability to control personal expectations can produce invalid information. Another factor that can reduce the validity of formal performance assessment is **bias**. When some factor such as race, native language, prior experience, gender, or disability differentiates the scores of one group from those of another (e.g., English-speaking and Spanish-speaking pupils, prior experience and inexperience, hearing disability and no hearing disability) we say the scores are biased. That is, judgments regarding the performance of one group of pupils are influenced by the inclusion of irrelevant, subjective criteria.

When irrelevant, subjective factors differentiate the scores of one group of pupils from another, the scores are said to be biased.

Suppose that oral reading performance was being assessed in a second grade classroom. Suppose also that in the classroom there was a group of pupils whose first language is Spanish. The oral reading assessment involved reading aloud from a storybook written in English. When the teacher reviewed her notes on the pupils' performances, she noticed that the Spanish-speaking pupils as a group did very poorly. Would the teacher be correct in saying that the Spanish-speaking pupils have poor oral reading skills? Would this be a valid conclusion to draw from the assessment evidence? A more reasonable interpretation would be that the oral reading assessment was measuring the Spanish-speaking pupils' familiarity with the English language rather than their oral reading performance. In essence, the assessment provided different information about the two groups (oral reading proficiency versus knowledge of English language). It would be a misinterpretation of the evidence to conclude that the Spanish-speaking pupils had poorer oral reading skills without taking into account the fact that they were required to read and pronounce unfamiliar English words. The results of the assessment were not valid for the teacher's desired decision about oral reading for the Spanish-speaking pupils.

Teachers should select performance criteria and settings that do not give an unfair advantage to any group of students.

When an assessment instrument provides information that is irrelevant to the decisions it was intended to help make, it is invalid. Thus, in all forms of assessment, but especially performance assessment, a teacher must select and use procedures, performance criteria, and settings that do not give an unfair advantage to some pupils because of cultural background, language, disability, or gender. Other sources of error that commonly affect the

Teachers should write down performance assessments at the time they are observed in order to avoid memory error.

Assessing pupils on the basis of their personal characteristics rather than on their performance lowers the validity of the assessment.

validity of performance assessments are teachers' reliance on mental rather than written record keeping and their being influenced by prior perceptions of a pupil. The longer the interval between an observation and the written scoring, the more likely the teacher is to forget important features of pupils' performance.

Often, teachers' prior knowledge of their pupils influences the objectivity of their performance ratings. Personality, effort, work habits, cooperativeness, and the like are all part of a teacher's perception of the pupils in his or her class. Often, these prior perceptions influence the rating a pupil is given: the likable, cooperative pupil with the pleasant personality may receive a higher rating than the standoffish, belligerent pupil, even though they performed similarly. Assessing pupils on the basis of their personal characteristics rather than their performance lowers the validity of the assessment. Each of these concerns threatens the validity of teacher interpretations and scores. These concerns are particularly difficult to overcome because of the complexity of performance assessment.

Reliability

Observing a performance more than once increases the reliability of the assessment but is time-consuming.

An important concern in interpreting performance assessments is the often low generalizability of pupils' performances, products, or portfolios.

Reliability is concerned with the stability and consistency of assessments. Hence, the logical way to obtain information about the reliability of pupil performance is to observe and score two or more performances or products of the same kind. Doing this, however, is not reasonable in most school settings; once a formal assessment is made, instruction turns to a new topic. Few teachers can afford the class time necessary to obtain multiple assessments on a given topic. This reality raises an important problem with the reliability of performance assessments: they may lack generalization. Performances, products, and portfolios are more complex and fewer in number than selection or short-answer assessments. Because of such discrepancies in the quantity of information obtained from particular assessments, the teacher who employs performance assessments sees fewer examples of pupil mastery than when more narrow assessment approaches are used. The teacher's question then becomes how reliable is the limited information I have obtained from pupils? Does a single essay, a few show-your-work problems or a portfolio provide enough evidence that students will perform similarly on other essays, show-your-work problems, or portfolios?

Teachers are put on the horns of a dilemma. Because they want their pupils to learn more than facts and narrow topics, they employ performance assessments to ensure deeper, richer learning. However, by employing an in-depth and time-consuming approach, they often diminish the reliability of the assessment. This is a dilemma faced in classroom teachers' own assessments and in more general, statewide pupil assessments. There are few easy ways to overcome the dilemma. However, it is better to use evidence from imperfect performance assessments than to make uninformed decisions about important pupil achievement.

Reliability is also affected when performance criteria or rating categories are vague and unclear. This forces the teacher to interpret them, and because interpretations often vary with time and situation, this introduces inconsistency into the assessment. One way to eliminate much of this inconsistency is to be explicit about the purpose of a performance assessment and to state the performance criteria and rubrics in terms of observable pupil behaviors. The objectivity of an observation can be enhanced by having several individuals independently observe and rate a pupil's performance. In situations where a group of teachers cooperate in developing criteria for a pupil performance, product, or portfolio, it is not difficult to have more than one teacher observe or examine a few pupils' products or performances to see whether scores are similar across teachers. This is a practice followed in performance assessments such as the College Board English Achievement Essay and in most statewide writing assessments.

Unclear or vague performance criteria increase teacher interpretation, which introduces inconsistency into the assessment.

Key Assessment Tools 9.8 contains guidelines for improving the validity and reliability of performance, product, and portfolio assessments:

Having more than one person observe and rate a performance increases the objectivity of the assessment.

Performance criteria should be realistic in terms of the students' developmental level.

Key Assessment Tools 9.8
IMPROVING VALIDITY AND RELIABILITY OF PERFORMANCE ASSESSMENTS

◆ Know the purpose of the assessment from the beginning.

◆ Teach and give pupils practice in the performance criteria.

◆ State the performance criteria in terms of observable behaviors and avoid using adverbs such as *appropriately, correctly,* or *well* because their interpretation may shift from pupil to pupil. Use overt, well-described behaviors that can be seen by an observer and therefore are less subject to interpretation. Inform pupils of these criteria and focus instruction on them.

◆ Select performance criteria that are at an appropriate level of difficulty for the pupils. The criteria used to judge the oral speaking performance of third-year debate pupils should be more detailed than those to judge first-year debate pupils.

◆ Limit performance criteria to a manageable number. A large number of criteria makes observation difficult and causes errors that reduce the validity of the assessment information.

◆ Maintain a written record of pupil performance. Checklists, rating scales, and rubrics are the easiest methods of recording pupil performance on important criteria, although more descriptive narratives are often desirable and informative. Tape recordings or videotapes may be used to provide a record of performance, so long as their use does not upset or distract the pupils. If a formal instrument cannot be used to record judgments of pupil performance, then informal notes of its strong and weak points should be taken.

◆ Be sure the performance assessment is fair to all pupils.

CHAPTER SUMMARY

olc

CHAPTER REVIEW

Visit Chapter 9 of the Online Learning Center at **www.mhhe.com/ airasian5e** to take chapter quizzes, link to related websites, read PowerWeb articles and news feed updates, and access study tools, including the case study referenced in the chapter.

♦ Performance assessments require pupils to demonstrate their knowledge by creating an answer, carrying out a process, or producing a product, rather than by selecting an answer. Performance assessments complement paper-and-pencil tests in classroom assessments.

♦ Performance assessments are useful for determining pupil learning in performance-oriented areas such as communication skills; psychomotor skills; athletic activities; concept acquisition; and affective characteristics.

♦ Performance assessments have many uses. They can chart pupil performance over time, provide diagnostic information about pupil learning, give pupils ownership of their learning, integrate the instructional and assessment processes, foster pupils' self-assessment of their work, and assemble into portfolios both cumulative evidence of performance and concrete examples of pupils' work. Performance assessments can be used in assessing the work of pupils with special needs. The main disadvantage of performance assessments is the time it takes to prepare for, implement, and score them.

♦ Successful performance assessment requires a well-defined purpose for assessment; clear, observable performance criteria; an appropriate setting in which to elicit performance; and a scoring or rating method.

♦ The specific behaviors a pupil should display when carrying out a performance or the characteristics a pupil product should possess are called performance criteria. These criteria define the aspects of a good performance or product. They should be shared with pupils and used as the basis for instruction.

♦ The key to identifying performance criteria is to break down a performance or product into its component parts, since it is these parts that are observed and judged. It is often useful to involve pupils in identifying the criteria of products or performances. This provides them with a sense of involvement in learning and introduces them to important components of the desired performance.

♦ The number of performance criteria should be small, between 10 and 15, in order to focus on the most important aspects of performance and simplify the observation process. Teacher collaboration on common assessment areas or performances is advisable.

♦ Ambiguous words that cloud the meaning of performance criteria (e.g., *adequately, correctly, appropriate*) should be avoided; state specifically what is being looked for in the performance or product. Criteria should be stated so explicitly that another teacher could use them independently.

♦ Performance assessments may be scored and summarized either qualitatively or quantitatively. Anecdotal records and teacher narratives are qualitative descriptions of pupil characteristics and performances. Checklists, rating scales, and scoring rubrics are quantitative assessments of performance. A rubric describes the level at which a pupil may be performing a task. Portfolios may include either qualitative, quantitative, or both kinds of information about pupil performance.

◆ Checklists and rating scales are developed from the performance criteria for a performance or product. Checklists give the observer only two choices in judging each performance criterion: present or absent. Rating scales provide the observer with more than two choices in judging: for example, always, sometimes, never or excellent, good, fair, poor, failure. Rating scales may be numerical, graphic, or descriptive. Performance can be summarized across performance criteria numerically or with a scoring rubric.

◆ Portfolios are collections of pupils' work in an area that show change and progress over time. Portfolios may contain pupil products or pupil performances.

◆ Portfolios have many uses: focusing instruction on important performance activities; reinforcing the point that performances are important school outcomes; providing parents, pupils, and teachers with a perspective on pupil improvement; diagnosing weaknesses; allowing pupils to revisit, reflect on, and assess their work over time; grading pupils; and integrating instruction with assessment.

◆ Portfolio assessment is a form of performance assessment, and thus involves these four factors: definition of purpose, identification of clear performance criteria, establishment of a setting for performance, and construction of a scoring or rating scheme. In addition to performance criteria for each individual portfolio piece, it is often necessary to develop a set of performance criteria to assess or summarize the entire portfolio.

◆ To ensure valid performance assessment, pupils should be instructed on the desired performance criteria before being assessed.

◆ The validity of performance assessments can be improved by stating performance criteria in observable terms; setting performance criteria at an appropriate difficulty level for pupils; limiting the number of performance criteria; maintaining a written record of pupil performance; and checking to determine whether extraneous factors influenced a pupil's performance.

◆ Reliability can be improved by multiple observations of performance or by checking for agreement among observers viewing the same performance, product, or portfolio and using the same assessment criteria.

QUESTIONS FOR DISCUSSION

1. What types of objectives are most suitably assessed using performance assessment?

2. How do formal and informal performance assessments differ in terms of pupil characteristics, validity and reliability of information, and usefulness for teacher decision making?

3. What are the advantages and disadvantages of performance assessments for teachers? For pupils?

4. How should a teacher determine the validity of a performance assessment?

5. How might instruction differ when a teacher desires to assess pupils' performances and products rather than their responses to selection-type tests?

6. What are some examples of how performance assessment can be closely linked to instruction? For example, how can performance assessment be used to involve pupils in the instructional process?

ACTIVITIES

1. Select a subject area you might like to teach and identify one objective in that subject matter that cannot be assessed by selection or essay questions. Construct a performance or product assessment instrument for this objective. Provide the following information:

   (a) the objective and a brief description of the behavior or product you will assess and the grade level at which it will be taught.

   (b) a set of at least 10 observable performance criteria for judging the performance or product.

   (c) a method to score pupil performance.

   (d) a method to summarize performance into a single score.

   The assessment procedure used may be in the form of a checklist or a rating scale. A two- to three-page document should adequately provide the needed information. Be sure to focus on the clarity and specificity of the performance criteria and on the clarity and practicality of the scoring procedure.

2. Rewrite in clearer form the following performance criteria for assessing a pupil's poem. Remember, what you are trying to do is write performance criteria that most people will understand and interpret the same way.

   ♦ Poem is original
   ♦ Meaningfulness
   ♦ Contains rhymes
   ♦ Proper length
   ♦ Well-focused
   ♦ Good title
   ♦ Appropriate vocabulary level

REVIEW QUESTIONS

1. How do performance assessments differ from other types of assessment? What are the benefits of using performance assessment? The disadvantages?

2. What four steps must be attended to in carrying out performance assessment? What happens at each of these steps?

3. Why are performance criteria so important to performance assessment? How do they help the assessor not only with judging pupils' performance and products but also with planning and conducting instruction?

4. What are the differences between checklists, rating scales, and rubrics? How is each used to assess performance and products?

5. What are the main threats to the validity of performance assessments? How can validity be improved?

6. In what ways are scoring performance assessments similar to scoring essay questions?

7. What makes an effective scoring rubric?

8. What are some pros and cons of portfolios?

REFERENCES

Arter, J. (1999). Teaching about performance assessment. *Educational Measurement: Issues and Practice, 18*(2), 30–44.

Bartz, D., Anderson-Robinson, S., & Hillman, L. (1994). Performance assessment: Make them show what they know. *Principal, 73*, 11–14.

Brennan, R. L, & Johnson, E. G. (1995). Generalizability of performance assessments. *Educational Measurement: Issues and Practice, 14*(4), 25–27.

Fager, J. J., Plake, B. S., & Impara, J. C. (1997). *Examining teacher educators' knowledge of classroom assessment: A pilot study.* Paper presented at the National Council on Measurement in Education National Conference, Chicago.

Goodrich, H. (1997). Understanding rubrics. *Educational Leadership, 54*(4), 14–17.

Herbert, E. A. (1992). Portfolios invite reflection from both students and staff. *Educational Leadership, 49*(8), 58–61.

Madaus, G. F., & O'Dwyer, L. M. (1999). A short history of performance assessment: Lessons learned. *Phi Delta Kappan, 80*(9), 688–695.

McTighe, J. (1996). Performance-based assessment in the classroom: A planning framework. In R. Blum & J. Arter (eds.), *Student performance assessment in an era of restructuring.* Alexandria, VA: Association for Supervision and Curriculum Development.

Mehrens, W. A., Popham, W. J., & Ryan, J. M. (1998). How to prepare students for performance assessments. *Educational Measurement: Issues and Practice, 17*(1), 18–22.

Quality counts '99. Rewarding results, punishing failure. *Education Week* (January 11, 1999).

Ryan, J., & Miyasaka, J. (1995). Current practices in teaching and assessment: What is driving the change? *NAASP Bulletin, 79,* 1–10.

Stiggins, R. (1999). Evaluating classroom assessment training in teacher education programs. *Educational Measurement: Issues and Practice, 18*(1), 23–27.

Swanson, D., Norman, G., & Linn, R. L. (1995). Performance-based assessment: Lessons from the health professions. *Educational Researcher, 24*(5), 5–11, 35.

Wiggins, G. (1992). Creating tests worth taking. *Educational Leadership, 44*(8), 26–33.

Wiggins, G., & McTighe, J. (1998). *Understanding by design.* Alexandria, VA: Association for Supervision and Curriculum Development.

CHAPTER 10

GRADING

KEY TOPICS

- *Rationale and Difficulties of Grading*

- *Grading as Judgment*

- *Four Types of Comparison for Grading*

- *Grading for Cooperative Learning and Pupils with Disabilities*

- *Deciding What to Grade*

- *Summarizing Varied Types of Assessment*

- *Two Approaches to Assigning Grades*

- *Other Methods of Reporting Pupil Progress*

CHAPTER OBJECTIVES

After reading this chapter, you will be able to:

♦ Define basic terms such as norm-referenced, criterion-referenced, and grading curve

♦ Contrast the characteristics of norm- and criterion-referenced grading

♦ Identify principles of grading and explain their importance

♦ Describe approaches for grading cooperative learning and pupils with disabilities

♦ State strategies for conducting effective parent-teacher conferences

THINKING ABOUT TEACHING

How do you think you will feel about grading pupils? What will be your grading model?

Grading is the process of judging the quality of a pupil's performance by comparing it to some standard of good performance.

We have seen that teachers use a variety of techniques to gather information about their pupils' learning. But teachers must do more than just gather pupils' performances, they also must make judgments about their quality. The process of judging the quality of a pupil's performance is called **grading.** It is the process that translates test scores and descriptive assessment information into marks or letters that indicate the quality of each pupil's learning and performance. Assigning **grades** to pupils is an exceptionally important professional responsibility, one a teacher carries out many times during the school year and one that has important consequences for pupils. Grades are the most common and important forms of classroom assessments that most pupils and parents experience.

Teachers assign grades to single assessments and to groups of assessments. When a pupil says, "I got a B on my book report," or "I got an A on my chemistry test," the pupil is talking about a grade on a single assessment. Report card grades, on the other hand, represent a pupil's performance across a variety of assessments that were completed during a term or grading period. Some people refer to the former process as "assigning grades" and the latter as "assigning marks," but the basic processes are similar, so we shall use the term "grading." Hence, grading is the process of judging the quality of a single assessment or multiple assessments over time.

In order to judge the quality of a pupil's performance, it must be compared to something or someone. There is no grading without comparison. When a teacher grades, he or she is making a judgment about the quality of a pupil's performance by comparing it to some standard of good performance. Suppose that Jamal got a score of 95 on a test. His score *describes* his performance—95 points. But does 95 indicate excellent, average, or poor achievement? This is the grading question—what is Jamal's performance worth? To answer this question, we need more than Jamal's test score. For example, we might want to know how many items were on Jamal's test and how much each item counted. A score of 95 does not provide this information. It would probably make a difference in the way Jamal's performance was judged if he got 95 out of 200 items right as opposed to 95 out of 100 items right. Or, we might like to know how Jamal did in relation to other pupils in the class. A score of 95 does not tell us this. It would make a difference in grading to know whether Jamal's score was the highest or the lowest in the class. Finally, one might like to know whether Jamal's 95 represents an improvement or a decline compared to his previous test scores. A score of 95 does not tell us this. Some form of comparison is needed to assign a grade.

RATIONALE AND DIFFICULTIES OF GRADING

The purpose of this chapter is to raise the questions teachers face when grading and to help answer these questions. While the main focus is on the process of assigning report card grades in academic subjects, the principles discussed are also appropriate for grading single tests or assessments. A logical place to begin discussion is with the question "Why grade?"

Why Grade?

The simplest and perhaps most compelling reason that classroom teachers grade their pupils is that they have to. All teachers grade, and grading is one type of official assessment that school teachers are required to carry out. Virtually all school systems demand that classroom teachers make periodic judgments about their pupils' performance. In recent years, with the rise of high-stakes testing and No Child Left Behind, the importance of grading has steadily grown. Table 10.1 lists some recent trends related to grading.

Grading is an official assessment required of teachers.

TABLE 10.1   RECENT TRENDS RELATED TO GRADING

- ◆ Increased reliance on computers for detailed information about pupil and teacher performance.
- ◆ More testing of all types.
- ◆ Increased use of standards-based testing.
- ◆ Increased information among parents about their child's performance and the performance of their child's school.
- ◆ More attention to student performance on tests as an indicator of teacher competence.

The form of these written judgments varies from one school system to another and from one grade level to another. Some schools require teachers to record pupil performance in the form of letter grades (e.g., A, A–, B+, B, B–, C+); some in the form of standards-based achievement categories (e.g., excellent, good, fair, poor); some in the form of percentage or other numerical grades (e.g., 100–90, 89–80); some in the form of pass-fail; some in the form of a checklist of specific skills or objectives that are graded individually; and some in the form of teachers' written narratives describing pupils' accomplishments and weaknesses. The most widely used systems are letter grades, which are the main grading system in upper elementary, middle, and high schools; and skill-based or objective-based ratings, which are used mainly in kindergarten and the primary grades.

Regardless of the grading system or reporting form used, grades are always based on teacher judgments.

Some school systems also require teachers to write comments about each pupil's performance on the report card, while others require teachers to grade performance in both academic subjects and social adjustment areas. There are many different varieties of grading forms, and Figures 10.1, 10.2, and 10.3 show three examples. Often, there are heated debates over the form of the report cards used in a school district, with some parents wanting the product-oriented A, B, C, D, and F grades and others wanting the more process-oriented checklist. Regardless of the particular system or report form used, grades are always based on teacher judgments.

The purpose of all grades is to communicate information about a pupil's academic performance to pupils, parents, and others. Within this general purpose are four more specific grading purposes: administrative, informational, motivational, and guidance.

Administrative reasons for grading include determining a pupil's rank in class, credits for graduation, and readiness for promotion.

Administratively, grades help determine such things as a pupil's rank in class, credits for graduation, and suitability for promotion to the next level. They may also be used to judge different teaching approaches and the quality of both teachers and administrators.

Informationally, grades are used to inform parents, pupils, and others about a pupil's academic performance and effort or lack of effort. Grades represent the teacher's summary judgment about how well pupils have mastered the content and processes taught in a subject area during a particular term or grading period. Because report card grades are given only four or five times a year, the judgments that they contain are summary. Grades rarely provide diagnostic information about pupil accomplishments and shortcomings. Teachers recognize this limitation (Hubelbank, 1994), but it does not diminish the importance of grades for pupils and parents. Grades are important, but bear in mind that grades are only one means of communicating with pupils and parents. Other methods such as parent conferences can provide more detailed information about school progress, and will be described later in this chapter.

Grades are used to motivate pupils to study and to guide them toward appropriate courses, course levels, colleges, and special services.

Grades are also used to motivate pupils to study. A high grade is a reward for learning. This motivational aspect of grading is, however, a two-edged sword. Pupil motivation may be enhanced when grades are high, but may be diminished when grades are lower than expected or when the same

FIGURE 10.1   *Example of an Elementary School Report Card.*

ALLSTON PUBLIC SCHOOL
Grades 1–3
Robert Sommers, Superintendent

NAME_____   GRADE_____   SCHOOL YEAR_____

SCHOOL _____   HOMEROOM TEACHER_____

KEY	
C Commendable	✓ denotes an area of weakness
S Satisfactory	M denotes modified program
N Needs Improvement	+ or - may be used to modify **S**

ATTENDANCE RECORD

TERM	I	II	III	IV	TOTAL
ABSENT					
TARDY					
DISMISSED					

	1	2	3	4		1	2	3	4
READING GRADE					**SOCIAL STUDIES (grade 3 only)** GRADE				
Effort					Effort				
Connects literature with other experiences					Demonstrates geographic awareness				
Learns and applies vocabulary					Understands cultural similarities and differences				
Comprehends teacher read selections					Understands historical concepts and ideas				
Understands story structure					**COMPUTERS** GRADE				
Uses word attack skills					Effort				
Applies appropriate reading strategies and skills					Conduct				
Reads with fluency					Understands concepts and ideas				
Reads with understanding					**WORK HABITS** GRADE				
Makes good use of independent reading time					Listens attentively				
LANGUAGE GRADE					Works cooperatively in a group				
Effort					Participates in class				
Organizes and expresses ideas orally					Completes homework				
Expresses ideas through writing					Completes work independently				
Develops and organizes ideas in written work					Uses time efficiently				
Writes with correct usage and mechanics					Has a positive attitude toward learning				
Edits and revises as necessary					Follows directions				
SPELLING GRADE					Seeks help when needed				
Effort					Organizes work and materials				
Masters assigned spelling words					Uses study skills				
Spells correctly in written work					**CONDUCT** GRADE				
HANDWRITING GRADE					Follows classroom rules				
Effort					Follows school rules				
Forms letters correctly					Demonstrates self control				
Writes neatly and legibly					Respects rights, opinions and property of others				
MATHEMATICS GRADE									
Effort									
Understands concepts									
Masters basic facts									
Works with accuracy									
Interprets information to solve problems									

FIGURE 10.2 *Example of a High School Report Card.*

STUDENT NAME	YEAR OF GRAD 2005	STUDENT I.D.	TELEPHONE	HOME ROOM	SEMESTER 1 2004 – 2005 PREV. CREDITS 62.00

SEMESTER SCHOLARSHIP REPORT

NO.	COURSE		TEACHER	1ST GRADE	1ST MISSED	2ND GRADE	2ND MISSED	EXAM	FINAL GRADE	CREDITS EARNED
11	HEALTH	34	Mr. Fleagle	A	1	A–		B	A–	1.00
133	ENGLISH	30	Mr. Turcotte	B	2	B+		B	B+	2.50
221	AP EUR HIS	30	Mrs. Golden	B	1	B+		B	B	2.50
321	GEOMETRY	30	Ms. Franklin	B	2	C+	1	C+	B–	2.50
433	PHYSICS	31	Mr. Wind	B–		B	2	B–	B	3.00
737	INTRO LAW	34	Mr. Tarot	B+	1	A–		B+	A–	2.50
	MERITS			100		100		100		

ATTENDANCE	THIS GRADING PER.	TOTAL THIS YEAR
DAYS ABSENT	0	0
TIMES TARDY	0	0
TIMES DISMISSED	1	1

ATTENDANCE IS RECORDED AS OF 01–19–05

FELTON HIGH SCHOOL
47 WEST STREET
WILSON, MASS. 01760

CREDITS TO DATE 76.00

GUIDANCE COUNSELOR
TELEPHONE

PARENT / STUDENT
PLEASE SEE REVERSE SIDE FOR EXPLANATION OF GRADES

ATTENDANCE — School Year 19 ___ -19 ___

EVALUATION KEY
G - Good   S - Satisfactory
I - Needs Improvement
N - Not expected at this time

	D	M	J
Absent			
Tardy			

Student's Name: _____

Teacher's Name: _____

KINDERGARTEN PROGRESS REPORT
Our Lady of Lourdes School
54 Brookside Avenue
Jamaica Plain, MA 02130
542-6136

READING READINESS

	D	M	J
Recognizes own name			
Knows alphabet in sequence			
Recognizes uppercase letters			
Recognizes lowercase letters			
Associates sounds with letters			
Is able to blend sounds into words			
Works from left to right			
Shows interest in books/stories			

LANGUAGE DEVELOPMENT

ORAL

	D	M	J
Speaks clearly			
Expresses ideas and feelings well			
Shares ideas and feelings well			
Uses adequate vocabulary			
Speaks in complete sentences			
Tells story in sequence			

WRITTEN

	D	M	J
Can print full name			
Prints alphabet			

MATH READINESS

	D	M	J
Can count in order			
Recognizes numbers to 10			
Recognizes numbers above 10			
Writes numbers clearly			
Applies knowledge of numbers			
Identifies basic shapes			
Understands math items			
Visually discriminates among likenesses and differences			

PHYSICAL DEVELOPMENT

SMALL MUSCLE

	D	M	J
Dresses self			
Buttons			
Zips			
Laces			
Controls pencil well			
Can cut well			
Colors neatly			
Pastes neatly			

LARGE MUSCLE

	D	M	J
Runs and jumps well			
Can catch, bounce, and throw ball			
Shows partiality to left or right			

DEVELOPMENT IN ART AND MUSIC

	D	M	J
Is eager to explore art materials			
Is imaginative with art materials			
Identifies colors, shapes, and sizes			
Shows enthusiasm for music			
Enjoys singing			

RELIGIOUS DEVELOPMENT

	D	M	J
Is learning to pray and talk to God			
Is learning about God and His creation			

SOCIAL DEVELOPMENT

	D	M	J
Accepts responsibility			
Respects others' property			
Respects others' feelings			
Respects authority			
Works well with others			
Plays well with others			
Listens when others talk			

WORK HABITS

	D	M	J
Observes rules and regulations			
Listens carefully			
Follows directions			
Has good attention span			
Completes activities promptly			
Works well independently			
Uses materials correctly			
Takes care of materials			
Cleans up after work period			
Finishes what has been started			
Values own work			
Is observant			

PERSONAL

	D	M	J
Knows full name			
Knows address			
Knows phone number			
Knows age and birthday			

pupils continually get low grades. Moreover, it is not desirable to have students study solely to get a good grade, so teachers should try to balance grading rewards with other kinds of rewards.

Lastly, grades are used for guidance. They help pupils, parents, teachers, and counselors to group pupils and to choose appropriate courses and course levels for them. They help identify pupils who may be in need of special services and they provide information to colleges about the pupil's academic performance in high school. Table 10.2 summarizes these various purposes.

Grades are used in schools for many reasons, and while there are periodic calls to abolish grades, it is difficult to envision schools in which judgments about pupils' performance would not be made by teachers and communicated to various interested parties. The basis on which teacher judgments are made may change, the format in which the grades are reported may be altered, and the judgments may no longer be called "grades," but the basic process of teachers judging and communicating information about pupil performance—that is, "grading"—will still go on.

Grades in whatever form are potent symbols in our society, symbols that are taken very seriously by teachers, pupils, parents, and the public at large. Regardless of your personal feelings about the value and usefulness

TABLE 10.2 PURPOSES OF GRADING	
Administrative	Determine pupil's suitability for promotion or graduation.
	Determine pupil's rank in class.
	Determine quality of teachers and teaching approaches.
	Determine quality of administration.
Informational	Judge and inform parents, pupil, and others about pupil's academic performance.
Motivational	Judge level of pupil effort.
	Reward good motivation.
	Motivate parents and pupil to improve a pupil's effort.
Guidance	Help pupils, parents, and counselors to choose appropriate courses and levels.
	Help teachers to group pupils by level of performance or need.

of grades and grading, it is necessary to take the grading process seriously. That means you should devise a grading system for your pupils that (1) is fair to your pupils and (2) delivers the message about pupil performance you wish to convey. Teachers have a responsibility to be objective and fair in assigning grades and should never use grades to punish or reward pupils the teacher likes or dislikes.

Because grades can affect students' chances in life, teachers are ethically bound to be as fair and objective as possible when grading pupils.

The Difficulty of Grading

Grading can be a very difficult task for teachers for four reasons: (1) few teachers have had formal instruction in how to grade their pupils (Brookhart, 1999); (2) school districts and principals provide little guidance to teachers regarding specific grading policies and expectations (Hubelbank, 1994); (3) teachers know that grades are taken seriously by parents and pupils and that the grades a pupil gets will be scrutinized and often challenged; and (4) the knowledge of each pupil's needs and characteristics that teachers must have to provide good instruction is difficult to ignore when the teacher is called upon to be a dispassionate, objective dispenser of grades.

Teachers inevitably face the dilemma of what constitutes fairness in grading. Must a teacher always be steadfast to the institution that expects dispassionate grading, or can fairness include consideration of a pupil's unique needs, circumstances, and problems? Which is the greater misuse of power, to ignore or to take into account individual pupil circumstances when grading? The special helping relationship that teachers have with their pupils makes it difficult for teachers to judge them on a solely objective or dispassionate basis (Hubelbank, 1994). This is especially so for grading, because the judgments made about pupils are public, taken very seriously, have real consequences for pupils, and can influence the pupil's educational, occupational, or home status.

The helping relationship that teachers have with their pupils makes it difficult to judge them on a completely objective basis.

The following remarks indicate some of the ambivalence teachers feel about grading.

> Report card time is always difficult for me. My pupils take grades seriously and talk about them with each other, even though I warn them not to. They're young (fourth graders) and some let their grades define their self-images, so grades can have a negative effect on some. Still, I guess it doesn't do a kid much good to let him think everything's great in his schoolwork when it really isn't . . . but putting it down on a report card makes it final and permanent . . . I agonize over the grades I give.

> The first report card of the year is always the toughest because it sets up future expectations for the child and his or her parents.

> At the high school level where I teach, grades are given more "by the book" than I think they are in the elementary school. Here we don't get to know our students as well as elementary school teachers and so we can be more objective

> **TABLE 10.3   DIFFICULTIES OF GRADING**
>
> ♦ Teacher's dual role: judgmental, disciplinarian relationship versus helping relationship.
> ♦ Preventing pupil's personal circumstances, characteristics, and needs from distorting judgment regarding academic achievement.
> ♦ Judgmental, subjective nature of grading; evidence always inconclusive.
> ♦ Lack of formal training in grading.
> ♦ Lack of universally accepted strategies for grading.

when grading. I have to admit, though, that I do recognize differences in pupil interest, effort, and politeness that probably influence my grades a little bit.

Sitting in judgment of students is always difficult, but report card grades are especially so for me. Subject matter grades are supposed to reflect only academic performance, so some good and desirable qualities of students get left out. Yet parents and many kids take these incomplete indicators very, very seriously. I try to cover each student's good, nonacademic qualities in my written report card comments. Another reason report card grades are so difficult for me is because my grade is the first one in which students receive letter grades in subject areas. Every time I give a report card grade, I am aware that I'm setting expectations for the student, the student's parents, and future teachers.

There are no uniformly accepted strategies for assigning grades.

These comments indicate that grading is a difficult, time-consuming process that demands considerable mental and emotional energy from teachers because grades have important consequences for pupils and others. Grading is further complicated by the lack of uniformly accepted strategies for assigning grades. Grading systems are not comparable from school to school nor from teacher to teacher, so each teacher must find his or her own answer to the many questions associated with the grading process. Table 10.3 summarizes some of the more difficult considerations teachers face when assigning grades to their pupils.

GRADING AS JUDGMENT

The most important aspect of the grading process is its dependence on teacher judgments.

The single most important characteristic of the grading process is its dependence upon teacher judgments. Ultimately, all grades are based on judgment. Although there are general guidelines to help develop a classroom grading system, all such systems rely on teacher judgment because the teacher knows the pupils and their accomplishments better than anyone else. Consequently, in assigning grades, teachers are granted considerable discretion and autonomy; no one else can or should make grading judgments for a teacher's pupils.

Teacher judgments require two things: (1) information about the person being judged (e.g., test scores, book reports, performance assessments) and (2) a basis of comparison that can be used to translate that information into grading judgments (e.g., what level of performance is worth an A, B, C, D, or F). Information provides the basis for judgment, but note that judgment is different from mere guessing. Guessing is what one does when there is no information or evidence to help make a judgment: "I have no information, so I'll just have to guess." To *judge* implies that the teacher has some evidence to consider in making the judgment. Thus, a teacher gathers evidence of various kinds to help make judgments and decisions about pupil learning.

A judgment is neither a guess nor a certainty but is based upon evidence the teacher deems valid and reliable.

But judgment also implies uncertainty, especially in the classroom setting. When there is complete certainty, there is no need for a teacher to judge. For example, when teachers state "Gerhard is a boy," "Svetlana's parents are divorced," or "Sigmund got the highest score on the math test," they are stating facts, not making judgments. Judgment, then, falls between guessing and certainty. Because the evidence for assigning a grade is rarely conclusive or complete, teachers are required to make a judgment. Using greater amounts of information can reduce, but rarely eliminate, the need for them to do so. Because assessment evidence is always incomplete, teachers must be concerned about the validity and reliability of judgments made from it.

To summarize our discussion of purpose, the goal of grading is to obtain enough valid evidence about pupil accomplishments to make a grading judgment that is fair, communicates the level of a pupil's academic performance, and can be supported with evidence. Because grades are important public judgments, they should be based mainly on formal evidence such as tests, projects, and performance assessments. The concreteness of these evidence types not only helps the teacher to be objective in awarding grades, but also can help to explain or defend a grade that is challenged. Bearing this in mind, there are three main questions to answer when making a **grading system:**

olc

CHAPTER CASE STUDY

Visit the text OLC to read the case of Sarah Hanover, a high school math teacher who is confronted by angry parents about her grading practices.

◆ Against what standard shall I compare my pupils' performance?
◆ What aspects of pupil performance shall I include in my grades?
◆ How should different kinds of evidence be weighted in assigning grades?

Embedded in these three questions are other questions that all teachers must address when grading. Unfortunately, few school districts have explicit grading policies that tell a teacher how to answer these questions. Most districts have particular grading formats teachers must use (e.g., A, B, C; good, satisfactory, poor), but teachers must work out the specific details of their grading systems for themselves. They must answer questions such as "What level of performance is A work and what is D work?" "What is the difference between good and satisfactory performance?" "Should pupils be failed if they're trying?" Even if a teacher does not consciously ask such questions when grading, he or she must implicitly answer them, because otherwise grades cannot be assigned.

FOUR TYPES OF COMPARISON FOR GRADING

As noted earlier, a grade is a judgment about the quality of a pupil's performance. But it is impossible to judge performance in the abstract. Comparison must be involved. Recall the difficulty we had in judging how good Jamal's test score of 95 was when that was our only piece of information. We needed to seek additional information that would allow us to compare Jamal's performance to some standard of goodness or quality. Thus, without comparison, there can be no grading.

Many bases of comparison can be used to assign grades to pupils. Those most commonly used in classroom grading compare a pupil's performance to:

A pupil's performance is most commonly compared to the performance of other pupils or to predefined standards of good and poor performance.

1. The performance of other pupils.
2. Predefined standards of good and poor performance.
3. The pupil's own ability level.
4. The pupil's prior performance (improvement).
5. The standards of state assessments.
6. The bases of No Child Left Behind.

The vast majority of teachers use one of the first two comparisons in assigning grades to their pupils (Brookhart, 1999). This is just as well, since for technical and substantive reasons the comparisons based on ability or improvement are not recommended.

Norm-Referenced Grading (Comparison with Other Pupils)

Norm-referenced grading is based upon a pupil's comparison with other pupils.

Assigning grades to pupils based upon a comparison with other pupils in the class is referred to as **norm-referenced grading.** Other names for this type of grading are "relative grading" and "grading on the curve." A high grade means that a pupil scored higher than most of his or her classmates, while a low grade means the opposite. When a teacher says things like "Garth is smarter than Omar," "Rowanda works harder in social studies than Tiffany and Tamika," and "Maria completes her math worksheets faster than anyone else in the class," the teacher is making norm-referenced comparisons.

In norm-referenced grading, not all pupils can get the top grade, no matter how well they perform. The system is designed to ensure that there is a distribution of grades across the various grading categories. In norm-referenced grading, the grade a pupil gets provides no indication of how well or poorly the pupil performed. Pupils get A grades for having higher scores than their classmates. If a pupil answered only 40 out of 100 test questions correctly, but was the highest scorer in the class, he or she would receive an A grade in norm-referenced grading, in spite of answering only 40 items correctly. The opposite is true at the other end of the scoring range: a pupil may answer 97 out of 100 questions correctly but get a C because most other pupils in the class got 98's, 99's, and 100's. Compared to classmates, a score of 97 falls in the middle of the group, even though, in absolute terms, it is very high performance.

In norm-referenced grading, teachers establish a **grading curve** that defines what percentage of the pupils can get A's, B's, C's, etc. This curve, which varies from teacher to teacher and is established before an assessment is given, sets up quotas for each grade. Following are two examples of grading curves.

A grading curve sets up quotas for each grade.

A	Top 20 percent of pupils		A	Top 10 percent of pupils
B	Next 30 percent of pupils		B	Next 40 percent of pupils
C	Next 30 percent of pupils		C	Next 45 percent of pupils
D	Next 10 percent of pupils		D	Last 5 percent of pupils
F	Last 10 percent of pupils			

If the curve on the left were applied to grading a chapter or unit test, the teacher would administer the test, score it, and arrange the pupils in order of their scores from highest to lowest. The highest scoring 20 percent of the pupils (including ties) would get an A grade; the next 30 percent, a B grade; the next 30 percent, a C grade; and so on. If the same curve were to be applied when giving report card grades, the teacher would first have to summarize the varied information about pupil performance that was gathered over the entire term. The summary score for each pupil would be arranged in order from highest to lowest, and the percentages in the curve would be applied to allocate grades.

There is no single best grading curve that should be used in every norm-referenced grading situation. Some teachers give mostly A's and B's, while others give mainly C's. Some teachers do not believe in giving pupils F's, while others give many F's. Teacher discretion determines the nature of the grading curve. However, if a teacher's curve gives too many high grades to mediocre pupils, pupils will not respect it. If it is too difficult even for bright, hardworking pupils to get an A, they will give up. In the end, one seeks a grading curve that is fair to the pupils and that represents academic standards that the teacher feels are appropriate and realistic for the pupils.

A grading curve that represents appropriate and realistic academic standards is fair.

The type of comparison that is used to assign grades to pupils can influence their effort and attitude. For example, norm-referenced grading tends to undermine the learning and effort of pupils who repeatedly score near the bottom of the class, since they continually receive poor grades. Norm-referenced grading poses a lesser threat to the top pupils in the class,

Norm-referenced grading makes a pupil's grade dependent on the performance of classmates, which can reduce student cooperation.

although it can spur competition among pupils for the high grades. Competitive, norm-referenced approaches that make a pupil's success or failure dependent on the performance of classmates can also reduce pupil cooperation and interdependence, because success for one pupil reduces the chance of success for other pupils.

Criterion-Referenced Grading (Predefined Standards)

Instead of grading by comparing one pupil to others, a teacher can compare a pupil's performance to preestablished performance standards. **Performance standards** define the level or score that a pupil must attain to receive a particular grade. All pupils who reach a given level get the same grade, regardless of how many pupils reach that level. The test for a driver's license is a simple, pass–fail example of performance standards. In many states, the driver's test contains two parts, a written section covering knowledge of the rules of the road and a performance section in which the applicant must actually drive an automobile around local roads. (Notice how paper-and-pencil tests *and* performance assessments are combined in driver's tests to make certain the all-important knowledge and skills of safe driving are assessed. This is a good example to keep in mind for your own classroom assessments.)

The written portion of the driver's test usually contains 20 multiple-choice items that must be passed before the performance portion is attempted. The written test is administered to groups of applicants in much the same way paper-and-pencil tests are administered in schools. In most states, passing the test depends upon getting 70 percent of the items correct. In this case, 70 percent is the performance standard. Whether any single applicant passes or fails depends only on how he or she compares to the performance standard of 70 percent. Passing has nothing whatsoever to do with how other applicants taking the test perform because applicants' scores are not compared to one another. They are compared to the predetermined 70 percent performance standard. In this system it is possible for all or none of the applicants to pass.

Grading that compares a pupil's achievement to preestablished performance standards rather than to other pupils' achievement is called criterion-referenced grading.

Grading that compares a pupil's achievement to predefined performance standards is called **criterion-referenced grading** or absolute grading. As in the driver's test, each pupil is graded on the basis of his or her own performance. Since pupils are not compared to one another and do not compete for a limited percentage of high grades, it is possible for all students to get high or low grades on a test. Criterion-referenced grading is the most commonly used grading system in schools. The criteria used to determine performance standards can be either performance-based or percentage-based.

Performance-Based Criteria

Performance-based criteria spell out in detail the specific learning pupils must demonstrate to receive a particular grade. For example, in some classrooms teachers utilize contract grading in which the pupil and teacher negotiate the quality and amount of work the pupil must satisfactorily complete to receive a particular grade. If the pupil meets the negotiated performance standard by the end of the semester, he or she receives the promised grade. Alternatively, a more narrow performance standard could be set up to grade each pupil who must give an oral speech. The teacher would observe the speech, concentrating on the specific activities listed in the oral speech performance standards. At the end of the speech, the teacher would refer to the performance standards or rubric and assign a grade to each pupil. A sample rubric based on preset performance standards for an oral speech is presented below. Again, notice that each pupil's grade depends upon how he or she performs in comparison to the standard, not in comparison to other pupils.

Criterion-referenced grading is the most commonly used grading system in schools.

In criterion-referenced grading, there is no limit to the number of pupils who can receive a particular grade.

A Pupil consistently faces audience, stands straight, and maintains eye contact; projects voice well and clearly; pacing and tone variation appropriate; well-organized points logically and completely presented; brief summary at end.

B Pupil usually faces audience, stands straight, and makes eye contact; voice projection good, but pace and clarity vary during talk; well organized but repetitive; occasional poor choice of words; incomplete summary.

C Pupil fidgety; some eye contact and facial expression change; uneven voice projection, not heard by all in room, some words slurred; loosely organized, repetitive, contains many incomplete thoughts; poor summary.

D Pupil's body movements distracting, little eye contact or voice change; words slurred, speaks in monotone, does not project voice beyond first few rows, no consistent or logical pacing; rambling presentation, little organization with no differentiation between major and minor points; no summary.

Percentage-Based Criteria

This second, more common type of criterion-referenced standard uses cutoff scores based on the percentage of items answered correctly. In the case of report card grading, an overall percentage of mastery across many individual assessments is used. The following cutoff percentages comprise perhaps the most widely used standard of this type.

90 to 100 percent of items correct = A

80 to 89 percent of items correct = B

70 to 79 percent of items correct = C

60 to 69 percent of items correct = D

Less than 60 percent of items correct = F

Any pupil who scores within one of the above performance standards will receive the corresponding grade. There is no limit on the number of pupils who can receive a particular grade and the teacher does not know what the distribution of grades will be until after the tests are scored and graded. Note that this is not the case in the norm-referenced approach.

Many teachers use percentage-based cutoff scores other than those shown here; some use 85 percent and higher as the cutoff for an A grade and readjust the cutoffs for the remaining grades accordingly. Others refuse to flunk a pupil unless he or she gets less than half (50 percent) of the items incorrect. Like the curve in norm-referenced grading, the grading standards used in criterion-referenced grading are based upon a teacher's judgment about what is suitable and fair for his or her class. Standards should be reasonable given the ability of the class and the nature of the subject matter, and they should be academically honest and challenging for the pupils.

Interpreting and Adjusting Grades

A criterion-referenced grading system is intended to indicate how much a pupil has learned of the things that were taught. Grades based on poor instruction, invalid assessments, or assessments that fail to cover the full range of what pupils were taught will convey an incorrect message about pupil learning. Of course, good instruction and valid instruments that fully assess what pupils have been taught should always be used, regardless of the grading approach. However, the focus on content mastery in criterion-referenced grading makes it especially crucial that teachers provide good instruction and develop assessments that are fair and that cover the full range of objectives taught.

In recent years students are being graded not only by their teachers, but also by statewide assessments.

In criterion-referenced grading, getting an invalid or unclear test item wrong can have major implications for pupil grades. Suppose that 2 out of 10 items on a teacher's test were not taught to pupils and as a consequence many pupils answered these two items incorrectly. The highest score these students could get would be 80 percent. If they made no other mistakes and were being graded on performance standards in which 80 percent or higher is a B grade, the highest grade these pupils could receive would be a B, even though the two items that they got wrong were not their fault.

Thus, before using assessment information to grade pupils, the quality of that information should be considered. Grades are only as meaningful as the information on which they are based. If grades are assigned subjectively, if scoring criteria change at random from pupil to pupil, if there are no established grading criteria, or if the teacher's attention wanders during scoring, grades will not accurately reflect pupil achievement. If unit tests are unfair to pupils or do not test a representative sample of what was taught, the scores pupils attain will not be valid indicators of their achievement. It is important for teachers to examine assessment results that are unusual or unexpected. Typically, unexpectedly low results provoke teacher concern and attention. Teachers ask themselves: do these low scores indicate a problem with the test or instruction, or a problem with the effort pupils put into preparing for the test? How should this result be handled in grading?

Suppose a teacher's test produced lower than usual scores for most pupils. When he compared the test items to what he had taught, he found that the test contained items on a section of the unit he had not taught. Thus, the match between the unit test and classroom instruction was not good. Pupils were being penalized because the teacher's instruction failed to cover many concepts included in the test. Thus, to use these scores would provide a distorted picture of the pupils' actual achievement, and this in turn would reduce the validity of their grades.

To avoid this, the teacher decided to change the pupils' scores on the test to better reflect their achievement. He estimated that about 20 percent of the items on the test were from the section he had not taught. After determining that most pupils had done poorly on these items, the teacher decided to increase each pupil's test score by 20 percentage points to adjust for the invalid items. He correctly reasoned that the increased scores would provide a better indication than the original scores of what pupils had learned *from the instruction provided.*

It is important to reiterate the critical need to make such adjustments when criterion-referenced grading is used. It is also important to note that the teacher adjusted the low scores on the test only *after* reexamining both the test and his instruction. He did not raise the scores to make the pupils feel better about themselves or to have them like him more. In this instance the test scores were raised to provide a more valid indication of how well pupils learned from the instruction. The raised grades better reflected the pupils' mastery of the subject matter.

Regardless of whether one employs a norm- or a criterion-referenced grading system, the grading curve or performance standards should be determined before assessment is carried out. Doing this helps teachers to think about expected performance and allows them to inform pupils of what will be needed to get high grades. When properly defined, a grading system tells pupils what constitutes high and low achievement. However, judgments are sometimes incorrect and need to be adjusted. Consequently, once established, performance standards and grading curves need not be set in stone. If, for some reason, a standard or grading curve turns out to be inappropriate or unfair, it can and should be changed before grades are assigned. While changes in performance standards or grading curves should not be made frivolously, it is better to make changes than to award incorrect and invalid grades. Usually, increased experience with a class helps a teacher arrive at a set of standards or a grading curve that is appropriate and fair. The discretion lies with the classroom teacher to make changes in grading curves and standards when he or she judges them to be invalid for some reason. Teacher discretion is at the heart of good grading.

Having made this point, it must also be emphasized that fairness to pupils does not mean selecting standards or curves to ensure that everyone

If a grading standard or curve proves to be inappropriate or unfair, it should be changed before grades are assigned.

TABLE 10.4   COMPARISON OF NORM-REFERENCED AND CRITERION-REFERENCED GRADING

	Norm-Referenced	Criterion-Referenced
Comparison made	Pupil to other pupils.	Pupil to predefined criteria.
Method of comparison	Grading curve; percentage of pupils who can get each grade.	Standard of performance; scores pupils must achieve to get a given grade.
What grade describes	Pupil's performance compared to others in the class.	Pupil's percentage mastery of course objectives.
Availability of a particular grade	Limited by grading curve. Not all pupils can get an A.	No limit on grade availability. All pupils could get an A.

Fairness means assessing what pupils were taught, using appropriate assessment procedures, and establishing realistic performance standards or grading curves.

gets high grades. Lowering standards or grading curves to guarantee high grades discourages pupil effort and diminishes the validity of the grades. Fairness means fully assessing what pupils were taught, using assessment procedures appropriate to the grade level and type of instruction used, and establishing performance standards or grading curves that are realistic if pupils work hard. These are the teacher's responsibilities in integrating instruction, assessment, and grading. Table 10.4 compares the main features of norm- and criterion-referenced grading.

Comparison to a Pupil's Ability

Teachers frequently make remarks such as "Dwayne is not working up to his ability," "Maurice is not doing as well as he can," or "Jaklyn continues to achieve much higher grades than I expected she would." When teachers make such statements, they are comparing a pupil's actual performance to the performance they expect, based on their judgment of the pupil's ability. The terms "overachiever" and "underachiever" are used to describe pupils who do better or worse than teacher judgments of what they should be doing. Many teachers assign grades by comparing a pupil's actual performance to their perception of the pupil's ability level.

In this ability-based grading approach, pupils with high ability who do excellent work would receive high grades, as would pupils with low ability who the teacher believed were achieving "up to their potential." Even though the actual performance of the low-ability pupils may be well below that of the high-ability, high-achieving pupils, each group would receive the same grade if each were perceived to be achieving up to their ability. Conversely, pupils with high ability who were perceived by their teacher to be underachieving—that is, performing below what the teacher thinks they are capable of performing—would receive low grades. An argument advanced in defense of this grading approach is that it motivates pupils to do their best and get the most from their ability. It also punishes lazy pupils who do not work up to their perceived ability.

However, grading based on pupil ability is not recommended for a number of reasons (Kubiszyn and Borich, 2003). First, the approach depends on the teacher having an accurate perception of each pupil's ability. In reality, teachers rarely know enough about their pupils to permit valid and precise assessments of their abilities. Teachers do have a general sense of pupils' abilities from their early assessments and the pupils' classroom performance, but this information is too imprecise to use as a basis for grading. Formal tests designed to measure ability are rarely precise enough to accurately predict a pupil's capacity for learning. Even for experts, it is all but impossible to make valid predictions about what a pupil of a certain general ability level is capable of achieving in any specific subject area.

Second, teachers often have a difficult time differentiating a pupil's ability from other pupil characteristics such as self-assurance, motivation, or responsiveness. This is especially problematic in light of recent constructivist thinking that pupils have numerous types of abilities or intelligences, not just one (Sternberg, 1997). Given these multiple abilities or intelligences that help pupils learn and perform in different modalities (e.g., oral, visual, written), which ones should a teacher focus on to judge a pupil's ability?

Third, grades comparing performance against expectations are confusing to people outside the classroom, especially parents. For example, a high-ability pupil who attained 80 percent mastery of the instruction might receive a C grade if perceived to be underachieving, while a low-ability pupil who attained 60 percent mastery might receive an A grade for exceeding expectations. An outsider viewing these two grades would probably think that the low-ability pupil mastered more of the course, because that pupil got the higher grade. In short, there is little correlation between grades and student mastery of course content in ability-based grading systems.

Teachers should not assign grades by comparing a pupil's actual performance to their perception of the pupil's ability level.

These reasons argue strongly against the use of a grading system that compares actual to predicted achievement. Some report cards do allow separate judgments about pupil achievement and ability. The teacher can record a subject matter grade based on the pupil's actual achievement, and then, in a separate place on the report card, indicate if he or she thinks the pupil is working up to expectations. Usually, the teacher writes comments or checks boxes to show whether the pupil "needs improvement," "is improving," or "is doing his best" relative to his or her ability. Even in this approach, teachers must be cautious about putting too much faith in their estimates of pupil ability and potential.

Comparison to Pupil Improvement

Even formal tests designed to measure ability are rarely precise enough to accurately predict a pupil's capacity for learning.

Basing grades on pupil improvement over time creates problems similar to those of grading estimates of pupil ability. Pupil improvement is determined by comparing a pupil's early performance to his or her later performance. Pupils who show the most progress or growth get the high grades and those who show little progress or growth get the low grades. An obvious difficulty with this approach is that pupils who do well early in the grading period have little opportunity to improve, and thus have little chance to get good grades. Low scorers at the start of the term have the best chance to show improvement, and thus tend to get high grades. It is not surprising that students graded on improvement quickly realize that it is in their best interests to do poorly on the early tests. They "play dumb" so early performance will be low and improvement can be shown easily.

There is little correlation between grades and student mastery of course content in ability-based grading systems.

Like comparing actual to predicted performance, grading on the basis of improvement also causes problems with grade interpretation. A pupil who improves from very low achievement to moderate achievement may get an A, while a pupil who had high achievement at the start and therefore improved little may get a B or a C, when it was the latter pupil who mastered more of the subject matter than the pupil who got the A grade.

The same grading system must be applied to all pupils in the class in order to convey a consistent and understandable message about classroom standards.

Some teachers recognize this difficulty and propose the following solution: give the pupils who achieve highly throughout the term an A grade for their high performance, but also give A grades to pupils who improve their performance a great deal over time. While this suggestion overcomes the problem noted above, it creates a new problem. In essence, these teachers are proposing to use two very different grading systems, one based on high achievement and the other on high pupil improvement. This approach provides rewards for both groups of pupils, but confuses the meaning of their grades, since the grades can mean two different things, achievement or improvement. Thus, grading systems based on improvement and ability, and grading systems based on combinations of these two, are not recommended. Grades can convey a consistent, understandable message only if the same approach is applied to all pupils.

GRADING FOR COOPERATIVE LEARNING AND PUPILS WITH DISABILITIES

Grading in Cooperative Learning

Classrooms at all levels of education are increasingly emphasizing group-based or cooperative learning strategies. In cooperative learning, small groups of two to six pupils are presented with a task or problem situation that they must solve together. While the problem given in a cooperative group can be posed in virtually any subject area, the main purpose of cooperative learning is to have pupils learn to work together to arrive at a single, group-generated solution.

In grading cooperative learning, teachers are usually concerned with assessing three important outcomes: (1) the interactive, cooperative processes that go on within the group, (2) the quality of the group's solution, and (3) each member's contribution to and understanding of that solution. While the assessment of the group processes is important, assessment of subject matter learning is equally important. However, conducting assessment of each individual group member is difficult because the group turns in a single, cooperatively reached product. At issue is how a teacher should assign individual pupil grades on the basis of a single group production.

The most common grading practice in cooperative learning is to assign a single grade to a group's solution and to give that grade to each group member. The difficulty with such a strategy is that it assumes equal contributions and understanding on the part of each group member. Both the pupil who contributed and learned a great deal and the pupil who contributed and learned very little receive the same grade. On the other hand, to push too hard for individual pupil solutions and contributions can destroy many of the benefits of cooperative problem solving. Thus, for many teachers, grading in cooperative learning situations creates problems not encountered in grading individual pupil performance.

There is no single acceptable solution to these problems. Many teachers see no difficulty in assuming equal contributions and learning from each group member and give identical grades to all of them. Other teachers mingle assessment of the group process with assessment of the group product, relying on their observations and interactions with pupils to provide them with an indication of the contribution and comprehension of each group member. Teachers then adjust individual grades according to their observations of pupil participation, contribution, and understanding. Still other teachers let the pupils self-assess their own contribution and understanding by grading themselves. This approach is less than ideal because pupils' self-assessments will often be based as much on their self-perceptions and self-confidence as on their actual contribution and learning.

Teachers can use follow-up activities with individual students to determine how well they understand the processes used in a group-based solution.

Another strategy that has some advantages over the preceding ones combines group and individual grades. All members of the group get the same grade for their single, group-based solution or product. Subsequently, the teacher requires each pupil to individually answer or perform follow-up or application activities related to the group problem or task. The purpose of these follow-up activities is to determine how well each pupil understands and can apply the group solution in solving similar types of problems. This approach blends both participation and contribution with subject matter learning in a way that helps the teacher know what each pupil has learned.

Grading Pupils with Disabilities

In earlier chapters, we discussed issues of instructing and assessing pupils with disabilities. We saw that more and more pupils with disabling conditions are being integrated into or "included" in regular education classrooms. While disabling conditions often prevent pupils from performing at a level similar to their nondisabled classmates in some areas, the intellectual and social benefits of inclusion warrant placing pupils who have disabilities with their nondisabled peers. However, because of the disparities in academic performance that often occur between some disabled and nondisabled pupils, grading can present classroom teachers with a variety of concerns. Indeed, one of the questions asked most frequently by classroom teachers is "How should I assign grades to my included pupils with disabilities?"

The Nature of the Problem

Embedded in the question above is a host of other questions. For example, who should be responsible for grading an included pupil: the classroom teacher, a special education teacher, or these two in combination? Should the same standards be used to assess pupils with and without disabilities? How should an included pupil's Individual Education Plan (IEP) enter into the grading process? What is the best way to report the performance of pupils with disabilities? These and many other questions face the classroom teacher who must grade pupils with disabilities (Guskey and Bailey, 2001).

Here we will examine issues associated with grading pupils with disabilities placed in regular classrooms. We will consider a variety of ways in which such grading can be done and the limitations of these methods. We will also identify the primary problem that confronts teachers who must grade pupils with disabilities and suggest how that grading can be made more manageable and informative.

Consider the question of who should be responsible for grading pupils with disabilities. The answer to this question depends on the extent of a pupil's inclusion in regular classrooms. Different pupils with different disabilities often spend different amounts of time in regular classrooms—from full-time inclusion, to part-time inclusion for instruction in particular subject areas, to no inclusion at all. Generally, the teacher who delivers the instruction in a subject area should be responsible for grading a student in that subject area. Thus, fully included pupils with disabilities should be graded by the regular classroom teacher, as should partially included students who take particular courses from a classroom teacher. Subject areas taught by special education teachers in separate education classrooms should be graded by the special education teacher. Our focus here is on the issues related to grading pupils with disabilities who are included part- or full-time in a regular classroom.

The main problem teachers face in grading pupils with disabilities is the often large disparity in their achievement compared to the achievement of nondisabled pupils. While it is important to understand that not all disabilities hamper a pupil's ability to achieve at a level comparable to nondisabled peers, many disabilities do. Teachers often ask two questions: Should grading standards be the same for all pupils in my class? and how can I take into account a pupil's disability when I assign grades to my class?

If a teacher applies the same grading standard to all pupils, many of the pupils with disabilities will receive low grades. If the teacher uses different standards for pupils with and without disabilities, the same grade will mean different things depending on which grading standard was applied to a given pupil. Notice that this is a problem whether a norm-referenced or criterion-referenced grading system is used. However, it is especially a problem for pupils with disabilities in criterion-referenced grading where the performance standards are rigid and inflexible (Polloway et al., 1994). The problem is heightened because pupils who are moved from special education classrooms to regular classrooms previously were graded on standards different than those used in regular classrooms (Valdes, Williamson, and Wagner, 1990), thereby creating more confusion about the meaning of a grade.

Some Possible Strategies

Many alternative grading strategies have been adopted to grade pupils with disabilities (Salend, 1990). All of the approaches are based on the objectives in a pupil's IEP, since these represent the instruction given and the desired pupil outcomes. Most of the approaches are based on a set of standards unique to each pupil, so that a pupil is compared to her- or himself in some way. An individual pupil grading strategy can be created by a team, sometimes including the classroom teacher, the student, his or her parents, and special education experts (Munk and Bursuck, 2003). Following are explanations of some of these alternative strategies.

◆ **Contract grading:** The teacher and the pupil jointly determine the type and quality of work a pupil will complete in order to receive a particular grade. The contract spells out what amount of work at what level of quality is needed for a pupil to receive an A, B, C, and so on. Different pupils have different contracts with different terms.

◆ **IEP-based grading:** Pupils are graded on the percentage of objectives in their IEP that they complete in a term or marking period. The grading standards would be criterion-referenced with different percentages of completion resulting in different grades (i.e., 80 percent or more completion is an A, 70 to 79 percent completion is a B, and so on). This approach is similar to grading a pupil based on her or his improvement over time.

♦ **Multiple grading:** The pupil receives different grades for different performances rather than a single, overall grade. For example, a pupil could receive separate grades for effort, participation, achievement, and progress. Such an approach allows the teacher to make some distinctions in the pupil's overall performance and to show areas of strength and weakness. A similar approach is to adjust grading weights for different pupils by, for example, counting effort or projects more than test results. Report cards that are similar in form to checklists or rating scales also permit more detailed descriptions of pupil performances.

♦ **Level-based grading:** Pupils are given grades that indicate both their achievement level and curriculum level. For example, a pupil who shows B-level achievement in an accelerated curriculum can be graded B(1), while a pupil who shows B-level achievement in a below grade level curriculum can be graded B(3). The number in parentheses represents the level of the curriculum in which a pupil is performing. This is another way of representing a pupil's ability level in a grade.

♦ **Narrative grading:** The teacher does not assign a grade per se, but provides a substantial written or oral description of the pupil's performance, achievements, strengths, and weaknesses based upon the teacher's observations and assessments of the pupil. Note that this is an informative, but time-consuming, grading approach.

A survey of non–special education teachers (Bursuck et al., 1996) indicates that classroom teachers utilize many of these strategies in grading pupils *both* with and without disabilities. The survey also showed that teachers use some strategies more than others in grading pupils with disabilities. Among the commonly used strategies are grading on the basis of improvement in IEP objectives; awarding separate grades for process (effort, participation) and achievement (test results); weighting pupil process more than product in grading; and using contract grading. For pupils with disabilities, teachers were less likely to change their grading standards, pass pupils just for high effort, or pass them no matter what their performance. While all of the above strategies are used by teachers, none avoid the grading problems of measuring improvement, determining ability, and applying differing grading standards.

The Need for Different Messages

The main problem most teachers face in grading classes that contain pupils both with and without disabilities is the inability of any single type of grade to convey the many important messages to the many different audiences interested in grades.

The most common grading system used in schools is the A, B, C, D, and F letter grade system (Polloway et al., 1994; Friedman and Frisbie, 1983). This system limits the information that can be conveyed in a grade because all a teacher can record for a pupil's grade is a single letter, perhaps with a plus or minus added. A, B, C, D, F grading conveys little of the specifics of what the student can or cannot do and has or has not learned. Letter grades create particular problems for teachers who want to take a pupil's disability into account when awarding a grade. As noted previously, regardless of whether teachers use a norm- or criterion-referenced grading system, many pupils with disabilities are likely to receive low grades. On the one hand, if teachers raise a grade because of a pupil's disability, they are constrained to do it within the letter grading system. This means that although a pupil with a disability performed less well than another pupil, both pupils were given the same grade. People who see the two grades will assume that they represent the same achievement. However, if teachers do not take the disability into account, many pupils with disabilities will continually receive low grades. This is the teacher's grading dilemma.

Reporting systems that allow teachers to provide more information about a pupil's grade than a single letter or number can help teachers with this dilemma. Systems such as the level-based and narrative grading approaches allow the teacher to provide important information about the meaning of the pupil's performance. The ability to describe a pupil's specific learning outcomes, the grade level of pupil performance, the amount of improvement, the weight given to effort and achievement, the availability of an aide for a pupil, or other pertinent factors related to pupil performance helps teachers in grading a pupil with a disability. Employing such information takes a pupil's disability into account in the grades a pupil receives and also provides the desired perspective on the meaning of the grades.

DECIDING WHAT TO GRADE

Once the comparative basis for assigning grades is decided on, it is necessary to select the particular pupil performances and products that will be used to award grades. If a teacher is grading a single test or a project, there is obviously only one performance to be considered. If a teacher is assigning report card grades, many formal and informal performances could be considered.

The quantity and the nature of the assessment information available to a teacher varies depending on the grade level and subject area. For example, assigning a term grade in spelling simply involves combining the results of each pupil's performance on the Friday spelling tests. In American history or social studies, however, a teacher may have information from quizzes, tests, homework, projects, reports, portfolios, and worksheets. High school math teachers have homework papers, quizzes, portfolios, and test results to consider in assigning grades, while English teachers have tests, essays, oral reports, homework, quizzes, portfolios, projects, and

Each teacher must decide which of the many formal and informal information sources available to use in determining a report card grade.

class discussion to consider. In addition to these formal indicators of achievement, teachers have informal perceptions of pupils' effort, interest, motivation, helpfulness, and behavior. Each teacher must decide which of all the available information will be used in determining report card grades. This decision is critical, because the performances that are included define what the grade really means. Two questions teachers have to ask about grading are "What do I want my grades to convey about pupil performance?" and "Do the assessments I've included in the grade reflect what I want to convey?" Note that it is not necessary or even desirable for teachers to include all available pupil information when assigning grades.

Grading can cover both formal academic achievement and the less formal area of "affective performance"—motivation, behavior, interest, and so forth.

Academic Achievement

Subject matter grades should reflect a pupil's academic achievement rather than such things as motivation, cooperation, and attendance.

Grades are usually viewed as an indication of how much pupils have learned from instruction. Formal assessments of pupils' achievement of the course objectives should be the major component of subject matter grades. Note that the more valid the assessments used in grading, the more valid the resulting grades (Brookhart, 1999). Affective performances should *not* be a major determinant of subject matter grades because affective characteristics pertain to pupil processes, not pupil learning. To judge pupils' academic achievement we look at the *results* of affect (effort, motivation, interest), as demonstrated in formal assessments.

Formal subject matter assessments such as teacher-made tests and homework provide the hard evidence to explain or defend a grade.

Formal subject matter assessments such as teacher-made and text-book tests, papers, quizzes, homework, projects, worksheets, portfolios, and the like are the best types of evidence to use in assigning report card grades. They are suitable in two respects. First, they provide information about pupils' academic performance, which is what grades are intended to describe. Second, as tangible products of pupils' work, they can be used to explain or defend a grade if the need arises. It is defensible to say to a pupil, "I gave a C grade because when I compared your test scores, projects, and homework assignments in this marking period to my grading standards, you performed at a C level." It is indefensible to say, "I gave a C grade because I had a strong *sense* that you were not working as hard as you could and because I have a negative *general perception* of your daily class performance." This rationale would be difficult to defend or explain to pupils, parents, or principals.

Because formal assessments of pupil achievement should be accorded major weight in assigning grades, it is important to stress that grades will be only as good as the instruction and formal assessments on which they are based. Grading as a process cannot be separated from the quality of the instruction and assessment information teachers collect prior to grading. Just as good instruction can be undermined by invalid assessment, good grading can be undermined by poorly constructed, invalid, and unreliable assessments. Irrelevant, invalid evidence about pupil achievement will produce irrelevant, invalid grades. The guidelines for constructing valid assessments described in Chapters 6 through 9 should underlie the assessments teachers construct and use in their grades.

As the culminating step in the process of assessing pupils' academic achievement, grading should be based upon a varied assortment of valid and reliable evidence. A general rule of grading is to draw on several different types of information rather than a single type, because this gives pupils more opportunity to show what they can do. Also, since pupils are required to remember, understand, and apply most subject areas, varied procedures are needed to assess all-important outcomes of instruction.

If subject matter grades were assigned by computers, it would be easy to grade solely on formal assessments of pupil achievement. We could program the computer and it would provide the grades. But teachers are not computers and teachers know a great deal more about their pupils than any computer ever could. Teachers know their pupils as whole persons, not one-dimensional scores or achievers. Teachers understand pupils' home backgrounds and know the effects grades will have on pupils and their parents. Because of this, teachers rarely can be completely objective and dispassionate dispensers of report card grades, as the following excerpts illustrate.

Pupils are given greater opportunity to demonstrate achievement when grades are based on several types of assessment information.

> Peter works harder than any pupil in my class, but he cannot seem to overcome his lack of ability. No one tries harder, yet his tests and projects are all failures. But I just can't in good conscience give Peter a failing grade because he tries so hard and an F would destroy him.

> Brianne had a terrible term. Her test scores dropped off, her attention during instruction was poor, and she failed to complete many homework assignments. The reason for these behaviors is in her home situation. Her father left the home, her mother had to find a job, and Brianne had to assume most of the household and babysitting responsibilities because she is the oldest child. How can I not take this into account when I grade her this term?

> Jermaine is the ultimate itch: constant motion, inattention, socializing around the classroom at inappropriate times. He drives me crazy. However, his classwork is well done and on time. When I sit down to grade him, I have to refrain from saying "OK Jermaine, now I'm going to get you for being such a distraction." I have a hard time separating his academic performance from his classroom behavior.

Affective Performances

Affective characteristics should not be major factors in report card grades, but because teachers do have perceptions of their pupils' affective characteristics means that they often enter into grading decisions. A common situation in which pupil motivation, interest, and effort enter into grades is their use in giving borderline pupils the benefit of the doubt. When a teacher awards a B+ to a pupil whose academic performance places her between a B and a B+ grade, but who is motivated, participates in class, and works diligently, the teacher is taking into account more than just formal assessments of achievement.

Pupil effort and participation can be used to adjust a grade but should not be the main determiner of the grade.

Teachers often nudge upward the grades they give to conscientious, participating pupils in order to keep them motivated. Strictly speaking, such adjustments distort the intended meaning of a grade, but most teachers do make them based upon their knowledge of particular pupil characteristics and needs. Grading is a human judgmental process, and it is virtually inevitable that such teacher adjustments will be made. These borderline decisions usually operate for the benefit of the pupil and the psychic comfort of the teacher.

A teacher should guard against allowing effort, motivation, interest, or personality to become the dominant factors in grades. If that happens, grades are distorted, providing little useful information about the pupil's academic achievement.

For example, to give an A grade to a pupil who is academically marginal but very industrious and congenial, would be misleading to the pupil, parents, and others who would interpret the grade as indicating high achievement. Pupils who work hard, are cooperative, and show great motivation and interest are desirable to have in class and deserve to be rewarded, but subject matter grades are not the proper arena for such rewards. Nor should grades be used to punish pupils for behavioral problems or late work unless timeliness is part of the formal performance criteria. Although few teachers can ignore nonacademic evidence like pupils' ability, effort, and improvement when they grade, most correctly use such evidence as a basis for adjustments in pupils' grades, not as the central determiner of grades (Brookhart, 1992; Griswold and Griswold, 1992; Nava and Loyd, 1992).

In the last three main sections of the chapter, we have seen that teachers must decide what standards of comparison to use in assigning grades. This means deciding upon either a norm-referenced or a criterion-referenced standard. Once this decision has been made, the teacher must establish a grading curve in the norm-referenced approach or a set of performance standards in the criterion-referenced approach. Next, the teacher must determine what performances will be included in the grade. Because grades are mainly intended to convey information about pupils' mastery of subject matter, rather than their personal qualities, grades should be based primarily upon formal assessments of pupil achievement. Although, teachers' subjective perceptions and insights inevitably influence the grading process to some extent, they should not be allowed to greatly distort the subject matter grade.

SUMMARIZING VARIED TYPES OF ASSESSMENT

Report card grades require teachers to summarize each pupil's performance on the many individual assessments gathered during the marking period. In some subject areas, summarization across a term is easy and straightforward. Suppose Ms. Fogarty is getting ready to assign report card grades in spelling. To do this she would refer to her grade book of her pupils' scores on each of the weekly spelling tests given during the grading period. It is very important that teachers maintain such grade books and that they be carefully guarded to ensure confidentiality of pupil grades. It is recommended that teachers keep two copies of the grade book, one kept in the classroom and one kept at home. Losing your only copy of a grade book leaves you with the difficult task of reconstructing it in order to grade.

Figure 10.4 shows a page from a fifth grade teacher's actual grade book for the first 5 weeks of term two in geography. At the bottom of the figure

FIGURE 10.4 *Fifth Grade Teacher's Rank Book.*

Subject: Geography Section: 02

Students	#	1st week (M T W T F)	2nd week (M T W T F)	3rd week (M T W T F)	4th week (M T W T F)	5th week (M T W T F)
Abra, G.	1	70 92 79	99 ı 91	ı √+ 81	60 47 √	80 82 85
Avakian, P.	2	50 95 79	92 ı 90	ı √+ 100	60 86 √+	100 91 100
Bornstein, E.	3	40 82 47	○ ı 74	ı ○	80 40 ı	80 64 55
Brooks, P.	4	70 76 89	86 ı 82	ı √+ 93	80 79 √+	90 99 100
Chang, M.	5	54 84 47	89 88 ı 67	⁻10	89 39 62	55 99 80
Chou, C.	6	60 91 84	100 ı 85	ı √+ 91	70 87 √	100 100 95
Davis, L.	7	49 67 47	○ ı 55	ı √+ 59	40 58 √	99 80
Garcia, G.	8	70 94 89	100 ı 86	ı √+ 92	40 93 √+	97 100
Haley, N.	9	69 68 100	83 ı 88	ı √+ 89	80 87 √+	100 77 90
Katz, W.	10	80 73 74	100 ı 99	ı √+ 0	20 73	70 100 80
Morgan, J.	11	39 73 47	98 ı 62	ı √+ 90	70 46	80 99 100
Nguyen, T.	12	70 76 89	92 ı 78	ı √+ 88	70 67 √	80 99 100
Ortiz, J.	13					
Rodriguez, H.	14	68 62 79	81 ab 69	ı √+ 31	ab 59 √	70 94 80
Schmitt, O.	15	63 79 74	98 ı 79	ı √+ 77	80 60 √	95 99
Vance, N.	16	59 34 60 58	92 ı 75	⁻10 ⊕ 86	100 67 ı	82 80
Winston, D.	17	71 87 100	85 ı 95	⁻10 89	100 59 √+	100 100 75
Zang, E.	18	80 79 100	83 ı 74	⁻10 √+ 6	100 53 √+	95 80 95

Assignment labels (columns):

1 — Weekly Geo #8 (10)
Current Event—Oct
Pictonitions Quiz (19)
2 —
3 —
4 — Weekly Geo #9 (14)
Around World in 26 letters
Current Event—Nov (25)
5 —
Mystery Post Card
American Squares
6, 7 — Weekly Geo #10 (18)
8 — Sit Report / Sec 2 Quiz (10) PR 26-30
Weekly Geo #11 (15)
December Cities
9 — Around World in 20 cards
10 — Weekly Geo #12 (11)

Term 2

is a list of all the assessments the pupils were expected to complete. Each pupil is assigned a grade for each of the assessments. Grades that have an empty circle indicate that the pupil has not yet turned in that assessment. Assessment topics that have no grades listed for all pupils, such as "Around World in 26 Letters," indicate assessments that are in process but not completed.

At the end of term, teachers must synthesize each pupil's assessments. Calculating each pupil's overall performance has been made easier with the use of spreadsheets and varied computer grading programs. The convenience of computer grading depends on the teacher keeping accurate assessment data to synthesize. Table 10.5 shows the results of a computer grading program. The scores for each assessment are shown in the columns numbered 1 to 13. The average of each pupil's assessments is shown on the left of the table under "Average." Scores shown in bold in the "Average" column indicate pupils who have not completed all the term assessments. Note that synthesizing pupils' term performance as shown does not produce pupil grades. The teacher must still apply grading standards to the scores to determine pupil grades.

TABLE 10.5   COMPUTER GRADING PROGRAM 2004, GEOGRAPHY, TERM 1

Student Names	Average	13	12	11	10	9	8	7	6	5	4	3	2	1
Achebe, K.	85.40	95	95	100	100	83	49	35	91	91	96	88	88	88
Ansary, T.	92.20	95	95	88	100	87	100	80	90	91	100	88	95	94
Chapman, G.	**85.16**		95		80	58	88	85	94	82	89	50	85	94
Cunningham, P.	94.40	95	95	100	100	82	88	85	98	100	100	88	95	94
Garcia, W.	86.53	92	92	88	90	75	98	80	83	55	100	100	85	94
Gaspari, F.	95.40	95	95	100	100	92	98	85	100	87	96	94	95	94
Griffiths, C.	74.93	85	95	88	65	82	88	25	76	36	71	88	85	88
Hussein, K.	94.87	95	95	100	100	92	100	85	92	100	100	94	92	94
Jones, T.	91.33	95	95	100	100	88	88	85	83	87	100	94	95	94
Jones, W.	77.67	95	88	100	90	87	63	85	45	64	82	88	88	100
Kelley, W.	77.60	95	95	87	50	58	87	95	63	73	100	56	85	94
Lee, J.	89.13	95	95	100	90	83	75	80	89	73	96	88	95	100
Mulera, R.	80.13	95	92	74	90	81	67	70	75	60	71	88	95	94
Pitzer, S.	82.13	95	95	100	70	83	100	60	65	64	100	88	82	100
Schell, M.	**75.01**		85	100	70	49	56	40	72	73	100	63	85	94
Sickafoose, T.	**89.24**	95	95	99	100	81	99	85	72	91	100	88		100
Stockbridge, J.	90.40	95	100	100	80	91	100	75	80	96	100	100	88	91

Returning to Ms. Fogarty's task of assigning report card grades for spelling, suppose there were 11 spelling tests for each pupil, each scored on the basis of 100 points. Ms. Fogarty must summarize the scores for each pupil and use the resulting number to assign a report card grade. This is a relatively easy task for her, since each test was scored on the basis of 100 total points and each test was worth the same amount. She would sum each pupil's score on the 11 tests and calculate the mean or average score.

Let us assume that Ms. Fogarty decided to assign spelling grades using a criterion-referenced approach with the following performance standards: 100 to 90 = A, 89 to 80 = B, 79 to 70 = C, and below 70 = D. She also decided not to flunk any pupils in the first term and not to award pluses and minuses, but instead to use only A, B, C, and D as possible grades. It is important to recognize that not all teachers would have made the same decisions as Ms. Fogarty. Some might have used a norm-referenced grading system, selected different performance standards, or made adjustments based on effort and motivation. There is no best way to assign grades in all classrooms; we can only discuss the topic in terms of examples that allow us to look at basic issues that should be considered in all grading situations. In this example, Ms. Fogarty would compare each pupil's spelling average to the performance standards and then award the corresponding letter grade: all pupils whose average scores were between 90 and 100 would be given an A, all between 80 and 89 a B, and so on.

This example provides a basic frame of reference for understanding the grading process. It shows how standards come into play in allocating grades, how formal assessment evidence is recorded in a marking book, and how individual scores are summarized to provide a summary of pupil performance for report card purposes. However, most grading situations are not as simple as this example. Consider the more typical example of Ms. Fogarty's marking book for social studies, shown in Figure 10.5.

Notice two important differences between the information Ms. Fogarty has available to grade social studies and the information that was available in the spelling example. In spelling, the only formal assessments were the weekly spelling tests. In social studies, Ms. Fogarty has collected many different kinds of assessment information. Four homework assignments, two quiz results, four unit test results, and two projects make up the information Ms. Fogarty can use to assign grades in social studies. In spelling, all test results were expressed numerically, on a scale of 0 to 100. In social studies, different grading formats are used for different assessments: homework assignments are rated ✓+, ✓, ✓−, quizzes and tests are recorded on a scale of 0 to 100; and the two projects are recorded as letter grades. Grading social studies will be a more complicated process than grading spelling.

Despite their differences, both grading processes start out with the same concerns. First, what standard of comparison will be used to award grades? Second, what specific performances will be included in the grade? Let us assume that, in social studies, Ms. Fogarty wishes to use a criterion-referenced grading approach and that she wishes to use pluses and minuses.

FIGURE 10.5 *Marking Book for Social Studies Assessments.*

	HW #1	HW #2	HW #3	HW #4	quiz	quiz	test unit 1	test unit 2	test unit 3	test unit 4	proj. Explor.	proj. Colon. Amer.
Avadis, P.	✓	✓	✓	✓‑	85	90	80	85	50	80	B+	B
Babcock, W.	✓	✓	✓	✓‑	90	90	85	80	60	80	B	B
Cannata, T.	✓	✓‑	✓	✓	80	75	70	70	45	75	C‑	C
Farmer, P.	✓+	✓+	✓+	✓	100	95	90	85	70	95	A‑	A‑
Foster, C.	✓+	✓+	✓	✓	90	80	85	90	65	80	B	B+
Gonzales, E.	✓	✓‑	✓‑	✓‑	70	75	60	70	55	70	C	B‑
Grodsky, F.	✓‑	✓‑	✓‑	✓‑	65	65	65	60	35	60	C	C
Miarka, S.	✓	✓	✓	✓	80	90	70	85	65	85	C	B
Picardi, O.	✓	✓	✓	✓	75	80	85	75	65	80	B	B‑
Ross, O.	✓+	✓	✓	✓	85	80	90	90	75	95	A	A‑
Sachar, S.	✓‑	✓	✓	✓+	80	85	75	80	40	80	B+	B
Saja, J.	✓	✓	✓	✓	75	80	85	85	50	80	B	B+
Stamos, G.	✓	✓+	✓+	✓	70	60	75	85	50	70	B‑	B
Whalem, W.	✓	✓	✓	✓	70	70	50	60	60	70	B‑	B‑
Yeh, T.	✓+	✓+	✓+	✓+	95	100	95	95	75	95	A	A‑

With this decision made, she must next determine which of the four different kinds of assessment information available to her will be included in the grade. She must not only decide which of these to include, but how much each kind of information will count in determining the grades. For example, should a project count as much as a unit test? Should two quizzes count as much as one unit test or four homework assignments? These are questions all teachers face when they try to combine different kinds of assessment information into a single indicator. The following sections contain suggestions for answering such questions.

What Should Be Included in a Grade?

Figure 10.5 shows four different formal indicators of Ms. Fogarty's pupils' academic performance: homework, quizzes, unit tests, and projects. In addition to these formal indicators, Ms. Fogarty also has many informal, unrecorded perceptions about each pupil's effort, participation in class, interest, behavior, and home situation. Should all the formal and informal information be included in her pupils' grades?

Almost all teachers would include the unit tests and the project results in determining their pupils' grades. These are formal, summative indicators of pupil achievement that should be reflected in the grade a pupil receives. Most teachers rightly assign grades based mainly on formal assessments. Many teachers would also include quiz results and homework, although there would be less unanimity among teachers on this point. Some teachers regard quizzes and homework as practice activities that are more closely tied to instruction than to assessment. Other teachers view homework and quizzes as indicators of how well pupils have learned their daily lessons and thus include them as part of the pupil's grade. Others would not count homework because it is never clear who actually does the work. As with most grading issues, the final decision is the classroom teacher's.

Some teachers view quizzes and homework as more closely tied to the instructional process than to the grading process.

Let us assume that Ms. Fogarty has decided to include three types of formal assessment information in her pupils' social studies grades: tests, projects, and quizzes. Let us also assume that she has decided not to include a formal rating of each pupil's effort, participation, interest, and behavior. Having decided what pupil performances will be included, she now must determine whether each kind of information will count equally or whether some kinds should be weighted more heavily than others.

Selecting Weights for Assessment Information

An immediate concern in summarizing pupil performance on different kinds of evidence is how each should be weighted. In general, teachers should give the more important types of pupil performance (e.g., tests, projects, and portfolios) more weight than short quizzes or homework assignments, since the former provide a more complete, integrated and valid view of pupils' subject matter learning. Ms. Fogarty decided that unit tests and projects should count equally and that both should count more than quiz results. She was fairly certain that she had used valid tests that reflected the important aspects of her instruction and that the projects assigned required pupils to integrate their knowledge about the topic. Thus, she was confident in using tests and projects as the main components of her social studies grade. Finally, she decided that the two quizzes would count as much as one unit test.

Although many teachers do not count homework directly in determining grades, they often warn pupils that if more than three or four homework assignments are not turned in, their report card grade will be lowered. Used this way, homework becomes more an indicator of effort or cooperation than of subject matter mastery. This lowers the validity and clarity of the grade. Some teachers do not actually compute pupil homework averages, but rely instead on an informal "sense" or "intuition" of how a pupil has performed. Although timesaving, this practice allows subjective factors such as the pupil's behavior or interest in the subject matter to influence the teacher's judgment. Neither lowering pupil grades for missed homework assignments nor determining grades on the basis of an informal sense of pupil performance is recommended.

Regardless of how a teacher weights each kind of assessment information, it is strongly suggested that the weightings be simple. It is better to weight some things twice as much as others than to weight some five times as much and others seven times as much. In most instances, the final grades arrived at using a simple weighting scheme will not differ greatly from those arrived at using a more complex, cumbersome weighting scheme.

After deciding on her weightings for quizzes, unit tests, and projects, Ms. Fogarty identified seven pieces of information that she would combine to determine her pupils' report card grades in social studies:

- ♦ One overall assessment of quiz results.
- ♦ Four scores from the unit tests.
- ♦ Two project grades.

In the final weightings, quiz results count one-seventh of the grade, unit tests count four-sevenths of the grade, and projects count two-sevenths of the grade. Ms. Fogarty next had to combine the available information according to the selected weights.

Methods for weighting the various types of assessment information should be kept simple.

Combining Different Assessment Information

Figure 10.5 shows that pupil performance on different assessments often is represented in different ways. Somehow Ms. Fogarty must combine the selected scoring formats into a single summary score that includes performance on tests, projects, and quizzes. Some of the information shown in Figure 10.5 will have to be changed into another format, preferably a numerical one. This means that the project letter grades will have to be converted into numerical scores on a scale of 0 to 100 percent, so that they will correspond to the scores for the quizzes and unit tests.

It is important to stress that all performance indicators should be expressed in terms of the same scale, so that they can be combined meaningfully. As another example, suppose a teacher gave two tests, one with 50 items and one with 100 items, and that the teacher wanted each test to count equally in determining a pupil's grade. Now suppose that two pupils, Terence and Marcus, each got a perfect score on one of the tests and a zero score on the other: Marcus got his perfect score on the 50-item test and Terence got his on the 100-item test. Because the tests are to count equally, one would think that the pupils' grades should be the same regardless of the number of items on each test. However, if the teacher calculates the average performance for Marcus and Terence using the *number* of items they got right across both tests, the resulting averages will be quite different: Marcus's average would be 25 $(50 + 0)/2 = 25$) and Terence's average would be 50 $(0 + 100)/2 = 50$). Terence would get a higher grade than Marcus, even though they each attained a perfect score on one test and a zero score on another and the tests were to count equally. Clearly, combining raw scores or number of items correct and finding their average does not give equal weight to each test.

The problem in the preceding example is that the teacher did not take into account the difference in the number of items on the two tests; the teacher did not put the two tests on the same scale before computing an average. If the teacher had changed the scores from number of items correct to percentage of items correct *before* averaging, Marcus and Terence would have had the same overall performance [Marcus = $(100 + 0)/2 = 50$; Terence = $(0 + 100)/2 = 50$]. Or if the teacher had expressed performance on both tests in terms of the 100-point test, the averages would have been the same, since Marcus's perfect score on a 50-item test would be worth 100 points on a 100 point scale. Once again, if scores are not expressed in a common scale, pupil performance will be distorted and grades will not reflect actual achievement. See the Technology and Assessment box for additional information on grading systems.

Each type of assessment information should be expressed in terms of the same scale so that all can be combined into a composite score.

TECHNOLOGY AND ASSESSMENT

NORM-REFERENCED AND CRITERION-REFERENCED GRADING SYSTEMS

olc Visit Chapter 10 of the text website (www.mhhe.com/airasian5e) to link to the following excellent Web resources on grading.

◆ **Grading Systems**

The Center for Teaching and Learning Services at the University of Minnesota developed this page, which offers good summaries of norm-referenced and criterion-referenced grading systems. Advantages and disadvantages, as well as possible modifications and questions to ask yourself before deciding on each type of system are included. Alternative systems such as contract grading and peer grading are also discussed.

◆ **Grading Systems**

The Center for Teaching and Learning at the University of North Carolina at Chapel Hill has also developed a site that offers a comprehensive discussion about norm-referenced ("relative") and criterion-referenced ("absolute") grading systems.

◆ **Grading Systems by Country**

This site provides brief summaries of the predominant grading systems in countries—and in some cases, provinces *within* countries—around the world. It is interesting to see how students are graded around the world—from Afghanistan to Zimbabwe.

TABLE 10.6	SOCIAL STUDIES ASSESSMENT SCORES PLACED ON THE SAME SCALE, SOCIAL STUDIES, TERM 1							
	Quiz 1	Quiz 2	Test 1	Test 2	Test 3	Test 4	Proj. 1	Proj. 2
Avadis, P.	85	90	80	85	50	80	88	85
Babcock, W.	90	90	85	80	60	80	85	85
Cannata, T.	80	75	70	70	45	70	72	70
Miarka, S.	100	95	90	85	70	95	92	92
Foster, C.	90	80	85	90	65	80	85	88
Gonzales, E.	70	75	60	70	55	70	75	82
Grodsky, F.	65	65	65	60	35	60	75	75
Martin, J.	80	90	70	85	65	85	75	85
Picardi, O.	75	80	85	75	65	80	85	82
Ross, O.	85	80	90	90	75	95	95	92
Sachar, S.	80	85	75	80	40	80	88	85
Saja, J.	75	80	85	85	50	80	85	88
Stamos, G.	70	60	75	85	50	70	82	85
Whalem, W.	70	70	50	60	60	70	82	82
Yeh, T.	95	100	95	95	75	95	95	92

Returning to Ms. Fogarty's grading task, a way must be found to express project performance on a scale that corresponds to the 0 to 100 percent scale used for quizzes and unit tests. She decided that for project grades, the following scale would be used to assign numerical scores to the projects: 95 = A, 92 = A−, 88 = B+, 85 = B, 82 = B−, 78 = C+, 75 = C, 72 = C−, 68 = D+, 65 = D, 62 = D−, less than 60 = F. If, for example, a pupil got a B− on one of the projects, that pupil's numerical score on the project would be 82. When Ms. Fogarty applied these values to the projects, she ended up with the information shown in Table 10.6. It is important to note that Ms. Fogarty's is not the only way that the different scores could be put on the same scale, nor is it without limitations. It is, however, one way she could accomplish her task with a method she felt comfortable using. With this task completed, Ms. Fogarty has to confront one additional issue prior to computing grades.

Validity of the Information

Grades are only as meaningful (valid) as the information upon which they are based.

Before combining assessment information into a grade, the quality of that information must be considered. Grades will be only as meaningful as the information on which they are based. If the project grades were assigned subjectively, with no clear criteria in mind and with shifting teacher attention during scoring, they will not accurately reflect pupil achievement. If the unit tests were unfair to pupils or did not test a representative sample of what was taught, the scores pupils attained will not be valid indications of their achievement. In this regard, Ms. Fogarty should examine the results of the unit 3 test, since they were much lower than scores on the other unit tests (see Figure 10.5). Do these scores indicate a problem with the test or a problem with the effort pupils put into preparing for the test? How should this result be handled in grading? These questions have to be answered before information can be combined and used for grading.

Ms. Fogarty noticed the poor performance on the unit 3 test when she scored the test, and no doubt asked herself why the scores were so low. Normally, questions about the match between an assessment instrument and the things pupils were taught occur *before* an assessment instrument is used. Sometimes, however, mismatches are overlooked or do not become apparent until after the instrument is administered and scored. Unexpectedly low scores typically provoke teacher concern and attention; rarely do unexpectedly high scores provoke the same reaction. The reason for this discrepancy in teacher reaction is that most teachers probably assume that unexpectedly low scores are the result of a faulty assessment instrument, while unexpectedly high scores are the result of their superior teaching.

Most teachers assume that unexpectedly low test scores are the result of a faulty assessment instrument, while unexpectedly high scores are the result of superior teaching.

Ms. Fogarty looked over the items in the unit 3 test (a textbook test), and compared the items to the topics and skills she had taught in that unit. She found that a large number of the test items had come from a section of the textbook that she had decided not to teach; by oversight she had failed to remove the items. Thus, the match between the unit test and classroom instruction was not good, and her pupils had been penalized by being asked questions about material they had not been taught. Clearly, the unit 3 test scores did not reflect her pupils' actual achievement and, if used in grading, would reduce the validity of the grades.

If unexpectedly low scores on some part of a test indicate a mismatch with instruction, then grading adjustments should be made.

To avoid this, Ms. Fogarty decided to change the pupils' scores on the unit 3 test to better reflect their achievement. She estimated that about 20 to 25 percent of the items on the test were from the section she had not taught. She checked and saw that most pupils had done poorly on these items, so she decided to increase each pupil's unit 3 score by 20 percentage points. She correctly reasoned that the increased scores would provide a better indication than the original scores of what pupils had learned from the instruction provided. Adjusting each pupil's unit 3 score places all of the assessment information on a common scale that ranges from 0 to 100 and indicates the percentage of mastery by each pupil on each assessment.

It is important to point out that Ms. Fogarty adjusted the low scores on the unit 3 test only after reexamining both the test and her instruction. She did not raise the scores to make the pupils feel better about themselves, to have them like her more, or for other, similar reasons. The test scores were raised so that they would provide a more valid indication of how well pupils learned from their instruction. It made her grades better reflect her pupils' subject matter mastery. Low assessment scores should not be raised simply because they are low or because the teacher is disappointed with them.

Computing Overall Scores

Having decided on score equivalents for the project assessments and having adjusted scores on the unit 3 test to correct the partial mismatch between instruction and assessment, Ms. Fogarty is ready to compute her pupils' social studies grades. To do this, she must (1) give each kind of assessment information the weight she decided on; (2) sum the scores; and (3) divide by 7, which is the number of assessment items she is using to grade (one overall quiz score, four unit test scores, and two project scores). This computation will provide an average social studies score for each pupil's marking period. Table 10.7 shows the seven components to be included in each pupil's grade, their total, and their average. To make her task simpler, Ms. Fogarty decided that all fractions would be rounded off to the nearest whole number.

Strictly speaking, the actual weight that a particular assessment carries in determining a grade depends on the spread of scores on that assessment compared to the spread of scores on other assessments (Frisbie and Waltman, 1992). The greater the spread of scores on an assessment, the greater the influence that assessment will have on the final grade when averaged with other assessments. Fairly simple and straightforward techniques are available for equalizing the influence of assessments whose scores are widely spread. However, this is not a major problem with most classroom

TABLE 10.7   COMPUTATION OF PUPILS' SOCIAL STUDIES GRADES, SOCIAL STUDIES, TERM 1

	Quizzes	Test 1	Test 2	Test 3	Test 4	Proj. 1	Proj. 2	Total Score	Average
Avadis, P.	88	80	85	70	80	88	85	576	82
Babcock, W.	90	85	80	80	80	85	85	585	84
Cannata, T.	78	70	70	65	70	72	70	495	71
Miarka, S.	98	90	85	90	95	92	92	642	92
Foster, C.	85	85	90	85	80	85	88	598	85
Gonzales, E.	73	60	70	75	70	75	82	505	72
Grodsky, F.	65	65	60	55	60	75	75	455	65
Martin, J.	85	70	85	85	85	75	85	570	81
Picardi, O.	78	85	75	85	80	85	82	570	81
Ross, O.	83	90	90	95	95	95	92	640	91
Sachar, S.	83	75	80	60	80	88	85	551	79
Saja, J.	78	85	85	70	80	85	88	571	82
Stamos, G.	65	75	85	70	70	82	85	532	76
Whalem, W.	70	50	60	80	70	82	82	494	71
Yeh, T.	98	95	95	95	95	95	92	665	95

assessments because they are similar in format, given to the same group of pupils, cover topics taught in instruction, and are scored in the same way. Under these conditions, the spread of scores on different assessments will usually be close enough so that adjustments need not be made. Table 10.7 shows that the difference between the highest and lowest score on each of the seven assessments is 33 for the quiz score; 45, 35, 40, and 35 for the four unit tests; and 23 and 22 for the two projects. These ranges are similar enough to permit the seven components to be added and averaged to determine an overall pupil score.

Table 10.7 shows the final average of each pupil after each piece of assessment information was weighted in the way Ms. Fogarty chose. Consider P. Avadis's scores in the table. This pupil received a total quiz score of 88, based on the average of two quizzes rounded off to a whole number. The four test scores—with 20 points added to the unit 3 score—are as shown in the table. The two project grades are expressed in terms of the numerical equivalents Ms. Fogarty selected. Adding these scores gives a total score of 576, which, when divided by 7 (for the seven pieces of information that were combined), gives an average performance of 82. The average for each pupil gives an indication of the proportion of social studies objectives each pupil achieved in the marking period. Notice that this interpretation is only appropriate if Ms. Fogarty's various assessments are scored in terms of percentage mastery and if they are a fair and representative assessment of the things that were taught. Ms. Fogarty can now apply her performance standards to award pupils' grades.

TWO APPROACHES TO ASSIGNING GRADES

Here we return again to our basic distinction between norm- and criterion-referenced grading.

A Criterion-Referenced Example

Ms. Fogarty decided to assign grades based on a criterion-referenced approach because she felt that this approach gave each pupil a chance to get a good grade if he or she mastered what was taught. The performance standards Ms. Fogarty adopted for her social studies grades follow:

A = 94 or higher	C = 74 to 76
A− = 90 to 93	C− = 70 to 73
B+ = 87 to 89	D+ = 67 to 69
B = 84 to 86	D = 64 to 66
B− = 80 to 83	D− = 60 to 63
C+ = 77 to 79	F = less than 60

This is a widely used criterion-referenced grading standard.

Looking at the overall semester averages as shown in Table 10.7, Ms. Fogarty can apply her performance standards to award grades. At this juncture she is likely to consider pupils' nonacademic characteristics. For example, she may say to herself, this pupil has worked so hard this term despite an unsettled home situation that it's amazing she was able to focus on her schoolwork at all, or there is so little positive reinforcement in this kid's life right now that a failing grade would absolutely crush him, even though his performance has been very poor. In short, Ms. Fogarty, like most teachers, is aware of her responsibility to grade pupils primarily on their academic performance, but allows herself some room for small individual adjustments. Opinions will always differ about making such grading adjustments, as the following excerpts show.

> I grade strictly by the numbers. I calculate each pupil's average and assign grades based strictly on that average. A 79.4 average is not an 80 average, and thus will get a C+. This is the only way I can be fair to all pupils.

> I calculate the averages based on tests and assignments just like the books say to. But when it comes time to assign the grade, I know I'm not grading an average, I'm grading a kid I know and spend time with every day. I know how the kid has behaved, how much effort has been put into my class, and what effect a high or low grade will have on him or her. I know about the pressure the kid gets from parents and what reaction they will have to a particular grade. If I didn't know about these things, grading would be much easier.

When Ms. Fogarty applied her performance standards to her class averages, the grades awarded to each pupil were as follows:

Name	Average	Grade	Name	Average	Grade
Avadis, P.	82	B–	Picardi, O.	81	B–
Babcock, W.	84	B	Ross, O.	91	A–
Cannata, T.	71	C–	Sachar, S.	79	C+
Miarka, S.	92	A–	Saja, J.	82	B–
Foster, C.	85	B	Stamos, G.	76	C
Gonzales, E.	72	C–	Whalem, W.	71	C–
Grodsky, F.	65	D	Yeh, T.	95	A
Martin, J.	81	B–			

Teachers' judgments about nonacademic characteristics often enter into grading when the student is close to reaching the next higher grade level.

Notice that pupils Sachar and Stamos are within one point of the performance standard for the next higher grade. It is for pupils who are close to reaching the next higher grade that teacher judgments about nonacademic characteristics usually enter into grading.

To summarize, Ms. Fogarty had to make many decisions to arrive at these grades. She had to decide whether to use a norm-referenced or a criterion-referenced grading approach. Having selected the criterion-referenced approach, she had to decide on performance standards for

> ### Key Assessment Tools 10.1
>
> ## STEPS IN THE GRADING PROCESS
>
> 1. Select a standard of comparison (norm-referenced or criterion-referenced).
> 2. Select types of performances (tests, projects, etc.).
> 3. Assign weights for each type of performance.
> 4. Record the number of points earned out of the total possible points for *each individual performance* graded.
> 5. Total the points earned for *each type of performance* and divide this by the total number of possible points. This gives a percentage for each type of performance.
> 6. Multiply each of these percentages by the weights assigned.
> 7. Sum the totals and apply the chosen standard of comparison to the totals.
> 8. Review the grades and make adjustments if necessary.

awarding grades. Next she had to decide upon the kinds of assessment information that would be included in her grades and how to weight each kind. Ms. Fogarty then had to decide how to put all assessment scores on the same scale because some information was expressed in percentage scores and other information as letter grades. Then she had to decide whether to adjust any scores because of faulty instruments. Finally, she had to decide whether to base her grades solely on the pupils' average academic performance or to alter them slightly because of affective or personal characteristics (Borich, 2003; Tombari and Borich, 1999). Teachers with different classes and in different schools likely would have made different decisions than Ms. Fogarty, but all would have had to confront the same issues. Key Assessment Tools 10.1 summarizes the steps in the grading process.

A Norm-Referenced Example

To complete this example, consider how Ms. Fogarty would have assigned grades if she had chosen a norm-referenced grading approach. In this case, she would have decided in advance upon a grading curve that identified the percentage of pupils that she wanted to receive each grade. Suppose she used a norm-referenced curve that gave the top 20 percent of the pupils an A, the next 20 percent a B, the next 40 percent a C, and the last 20 percent a D.

To assign grades using this norm-referenced curve, Ms. Fogarty must first arrange the pupils from highest to lowest average score. The norm-referenced ordering for Ms. Fogarty's class follows.

In norm-referenced grading, a teacher decides in advance the percentage of pupils receiving each grade.

Name	Score	Name	Score
Yeh, T.	95	Saja, J.	82
Miarka, S.	92	Sachar, S.	79
Ross, O.	91	Stamos, G.	76
Foster, C.	85	Gonzales, E.	72
Babcock, W.	84	Cannata, T.	71
Avadis, P.	82	Whalem, W.	71
Martin, J.	81	Grodsky, F.	65
Picardi, O.	81		

In norm-referenced grading, two pupils who achieve the same score must receive the same grade, regardless of the curve used.

Because there are 15 pupils in the class, 20 percent of the class is three pupils. Thus, Yeh, Miarka and Ross, the three highest-scoring pupils, received A grades. The next 20 percent of the pupils—Foster, Babcock, and Avadis—got B grades. The next 40 percent of the class (six pupils) got C grades. Finally, the last 20 percent of the class—Cannata, Whalem, and Grodsky—received D grades. In assigning grades by the norm-referenced approach it is important to bear in mind that two pupils who attain the same score must receive the same grade, regardless of the curve being used. Notice the differences in the grade distributions under the norm-referenced and the criterion-referenced approaches. Remember that these differences are mainly the result of decisions made about the grading curve or performance standards that are used. Regardless of the method of grading adopted, it is extremely important for the teacher to be able to explain the grading process to pupils, parents, and administrators. Key Assessment Tools 10.2 lists the guidelines for grading.

Software can help teachers keep rank books, calculate grades, and store and organize test items.

Key Assessment Tools 10.2

GUIDELINES FOR GRADING

- ◆ The chosen grading system is consistent with the purpose of grading.
- ◆ Data for grading is gathered throughout the grading period.
- ◆ Varied pieces of data are collected (tests, projects, quizzes, etc.).
- ◆ Students are informed about the system used to grade them.
- ◆ The grading system separates subject matter achievements from nonacademic performance (effort, motivation, etc.). Nonacademic performance is evaluated independently of subject matter performance.
- ◆ Grading is based on valid and reliable assessment evidence.
- ◆ Important evidence of achievement is weighted more than less important evidence (e.g., tests weighted more than quizzes).
- ◆ The grading system is applied consistently across all pupils.

OTHER METHODS OF REPORTING
PUPIL PROGRESS

Report card grades are the most common way that pupils and their parents are kept informed of how things are going in the classroom. But the functionality of grades is limited because they are usually provided infrequently, provide little *specific* information about how a pupil is performing, and rarely include information about the teacher's perceptions of a pupil's effort, motivation, cooperation, and classroom demeanor. Moreover, since report card grades usually reflect pupil performance on a variety of assessment tasks, it is quite possible for two pupils to receive the same grade but have performed very differently on the assessments used to determine the grade. Because of these limitations, other approaches for reporting pupils' school progress also are needed and used by teachers. Key Assessment Tools 10.3 lists the many ways teachers can communicate and interact with parents. Each of these forms of communication can provide important supplementary information that rounds out the picture of a pupil's life at school.

Grades are the most common device by which students and parents are kept informed about how things are going in the classroom.

To have a complete and specific picture of their child's school performance, parents must receive more than the report card.

Parent-Teacher Conferences

Parent-teacher conferences allow flexible, two-way communication, unlike the one-way communication that grades provide. The nature of the communication differs as well. Conferences permit discussion, elaboration, and explanation of pupil performance. The teacher can get information from

Unlike grades, parent-teacher conferences provide flexible, two-way communication.

Key Assessment Tools 10.3

OPTIONS FOR PARENT-TEACHER COMMUNICATION

- ◆ Report cards
- ◆ Weekly or monthly progress reports
- ◆ Parents' nights
- ◆ School visitation days
- ◆ Parent-teacher conferences
- ◆ Phone calls
- ◆ Letters
- ◆ Class or school newsletter
- ◆ Papers and work products

the parents about their concerns and perceptions of their child's school experience. Information can also be obtained about special problems the pupil is having, from physical and emotional problems to problems of classroom adjustment. Parents can inform the teacher of their concerns and ask questions about their child's classroom behavior and about the curriculum being taught. Preschool teachers or those who teach the last grade of elementary or middle school will often be asked by parents to recommend the type of school, teacher, or academic program that is most suitable for their child. Certainly a parent-teacher conference can address a broader range of issues and concerns than a report card grade can.

Moreover, parents learn a great deal about their children's performance from parent-teacher conferences. A study by Shepard and Bliem (1995) on a sample of elementary school parents examined the usefulness of report cards, parent-teacher discussions, standardized tests, and graded examples of pupils' schoolwork for parents' understanding of their child's progress in school. Ninety-four percent of the parents indicated that discussions with teachers were useful or very useful in understanding their child's progress, and 90 percent also said that receiving graded examples of their child's work was useful or very useful. Only 76 percent of the parents felt that report cards were useful or very useful for informing them about their child's school progress. Thirty-six percent cited standardized tests as useful or very useful for informing them about progress. Parents look for information beyond report cards to indicate how their children are performing in school.

It is natural for teachers to feel somewhat uneasy at the prospect of a conference with parents. Teachers will want to be respected by the parents, will not want a confrontational experience, and may have to tell parents some unpleasant things about their child. Because teachers will have certain things they want the parents to know and because there is always an element of uncertainty about the way the conference will go, it is recommended that teachers prepare an agenda of the things they want to cover. Parents will probably do this also. For example, most teachers will want to provide a description of the pupil's academic and social classroom performance. They will also want to ask the parents questions such as "Does your child act this way at home?" "What does he say about the workload in school?" Certainly teachers will want to give parents the opportunity to ask questions. Parents are most likely to ask questions such as "What are my child's current levels in reading and math?" "How is my child's behavior in class?" "Does she get along with her classmates?" or "Why did my son get a C– in math?" Finally, teachers, in conjunction with the parents, may want to plan a course of action to help the pupil. The course agreed upon should contain actions on the part of teachers, parents, and pupil. Teachers may want a counselor or administrator to attend the conference if it is likely to be confrontational.

Planning conferences is necessary to accomplish such agendas. The individual teacher will want to gather samples of the pupil's work—perhaps in a portfolio—and identify (with examples) particular behavioral or attitudinal issues that should be raised. If there is a major existing or potential problem, the teacher ought to look over the pupil's permanent record file in the school office to see whether the problem surfaced in other grades. All of this preparation should be done before the conference.

Finally, the teacher will want to locate a comfortable, private spot to hold the conference. Usually this means before or after school in the teacher's classroom, when pupils are not present. If this is the case, provide suitable, adult-sized chairs for the parents. The author is a veteran of many elementary school conferences in which the teacher sat comfortably behind his or her desk and the author was scrunched down in a primary-sized pupil chair, knees near his chin, trying to act dignified and carry on a productive conference. Conferences work better when they are private and undisturbed, and when all parties are comfortably situated.

Tips for a Successful Parent-Teacher Conference

The following tips can help the actual parent-teacher conference proceed successfully.

1. *Set a proper tone.* This means making parents feel welcome, maintaining a positive attitude, and remembering that a pupil is not "their" concern or "your" concern, but a mutual concern. If possible, find out what parents want to know before the conference so that you can prepare for their questions. Don't do all the talking; be a good listener and use the conference to find out parents' perceptions and concerns. Talk in terms parents will understand; avoid educational jargon, such as "discovery learning," "rubrics," "higher-order thinking skills," or "prosocial behavior," that confuses rather than clarifies discussion. Providing examples of pupil work from portfolios, performance assessments, and scoring rubrics can help parents understand classroom expectations and pupil performance.

   Conferences should be private, undisturbed, and well planned.

2. *Be frank with parents, but convey both the pupil's strengths and weaknesses.* Do not hold back unpleasant information because you think the parents will become confrontational. The aim of parent-teacher conferences is for each party to understand and help the pupil. It is the teacher's responsibility to raise issues with parents that will help the pupil, even though discussion of those issues might be unpleasant. If you do not know the answer to a question, do not bluff. Tell the parents you do not know the answer, then research it after the conference and follow up by relaying it to the parents.

   Teachers must maintain their professional demeanor during parent-teacher conferences.

3. *Do not talk about other pupils or colleagues by name or by implication.* Never belittle colleagues or the principal in front of parents, no matter what your feelings. Saying things like "last year's teacher did not prepare Rosalie well in math" or "teachers get so little support for their ideas from the principal" is inappropriate. True or not, it is not

professional to discuss such issues with parents. Do not compare a child to other pupils by name or show parents other pupils' work, test scores, or grades. Teachers are professionals and they have an obligation to act professionally. This means being truthful with parents, not demeaning colleagues in front of parents, concentrating discussion only on the parents' child, and not discussing information from the conference with other teachers. This caution is appropriate for all forms of parent-teacher interaction.

4. *If a course of remedial action for the pupil seems appropriate, plan the action jointly with the parents.* Make both parties responsible for implementing the plan: "I will try to do these things with Janessa in class, and you will try to do these other things with her at home."

5. *Finally, summarize the conference before the parents leave.* Review the main points and any decisions or courses of action that have been agreed upon.

Parent-teacher conferences can be very useful to both teachers and parents if planned and conducted successfully. They allow the teacher to supplement his or her information about the pupil and the parents to obtain a broader understanding of their child's school performance. The main drawback to parent-teacher conferences is that they are time-consuming, although many school districts are beginning to set aside a day or two in the school calendar specifically for parent conferencing. Key Assessment Tools 10.4 supplements these guidelines with other useful suggestions.

Additional Reporting Methods

A common method of informing parents about their child's school performance is to either send examples of schoolwork home or to collect it in a portfolio to be examined during a parent-teacher conference or school open house. Periodic newsletters, often written and assembled by pupils, can be sent home. If a teacher has developed or selected a scoring rubric, a copy of the rubric with the pupil's level of performance circled can be used to provide information about an area of the pupil's learning.

Letters and phone calls to parents are used mainly to inform parents of a special problem that has occurred and, as such, should be used infrequently by teachers. Regular written or phone communication between a teacher and a parent is very rare and occurs only if the parent specifically requests frequent written progress reports and the teacher agrees to provide them. Certainly, from a time-efficiency viewpoint, phone calls are better than writing letters to parents. If you do write to parents, it is extremely important that your letter be free of spelling and grammatical errors. Few things can create a poorer impression in a parent's mind than a misspelled, grammatically incorrect letter from their child's teacher.

Key Assessment Tools 10.4

PARENT-TEACHER CONFERENCES

1. Plan in advance of the conference by gathering samples of the pupil's work and identifying issues to discuss with parents; if possible, find out what parents want to know before the conference.

2. Identify a private, comfortable place for the conference.

3. Set a proper tone by:

   a. Remembering that the pupil is of mutual concern to you and the parents.

   b. Listening to the parents' perspectives and concerns.

   c. Avoiding educational jargon, yet giving concrete examples.

   d. Being frank with parents when conveying the pupil's strengths and weaknesses.

4. Admit to not knowing the answer to a question and be willing to find out; do not try to bluff parents.

5. Do not talk about or belittle other colleagues or pupils by name or implication; do not compare one pupil to another by name.

6. If a remedial action is agreed upon, plan the action jointly with parents and make each party responsible for part of the plan.

7. Orally review and summarize decisions and planned actions at the end of the conference.

8. Write summary notes of the conference.

CHAPTER SUMMARY

♦ The process of judging the quality of a pupil's performance is called grading. The single most important characteristic of the grading process is its dependence on teacher judgment, which is always subjective to some degree.

♦ Grading is a difficult task for teachers because they have had little formal instruction in grading; they have to make judgments based on incomplete evidence; they have conflicting classroom roles; they must not allow pupils' personal characteristics and circumstances to distort subject matter judgments; and there is no single, universally accepted grading strategy.

♦ In grading, the teacher's prime aims are to be fair to all pupils and to reflect pupils' learning of the subject matter.

♦ The main purpose of report card grades is to communicate information about pupil achievement. Grades serve administrative, informational, motivational, and guidance functions.

CHAPTER REVIEW

Visit Chapter 10 of the Online Learning Center at **www.mhhe.com/ airasian5e** to take chapter quizzes, link to related websites, read PowerWeb articles and news feed updates, and access study tools, including the case study referenced in the chapter.

♦ All grades represent a comparison of pupil performance to some standard of excellence or quality.

♦ Norm-referenced grades compare a pupil's performance to that of other pupils in the class. Pupils with the highest scores receive the designated number of high grades as defined by the grading curve.

♦ Criterion-referenced grades compare a pupil's performance to a predefined standard of mastery. There is no limit on the number of pupils who can receive a particular grade.

♦ Basing grades on comparisons of a pupil's performance to the pupil's ability or record of improvement is not recommended.

♦ After selecting the comparative basis for grading, the teacher next must decide which pupil performances will be considered in awarding grades. For subject matter grades it is recommended that pupil performances that demonstrate mastery of the subject matter be included in the grade. Effort, motivation, participation, and behavior should not be major parts of subject mastery grades.

♦ Grading requires teachers to summarize many different types of information into a single score. More important types of pupil performance such as tests and projects should be weighted most heavily in arriving at a grade.

♦ To summarize various types of information, each type must be expressed in the same way and on the same scale, usually a percentage scale.

♦ Before combining information into a grade, the quality of each piece of selected assessment information should be reviewed and adjustments made if invalid assessments are found. Grades will be only as valid as the assessment information on which they are based.

♦ Grading information should be expanded and supplemented by other means of parent-teacher communication, such as conferences, open houses, progress reports, and papers and projects sent home.

QUESTIONS FOR DISCUSSION

1. What are the purposes of giving grades to pupils? How well do different grading formats meet these purposes?

2. What are a teacher's responsibilities to pupils when assigning grades on a paper, test, or project? What additional responsibilities to pupils do teachers have when they assign report card grades?

3. Is the task of assigning report card grades the same for elementary and high school teachers? How might the process of assigning grades differ at the two levels?

4. How can the information on report cards be supplemented and made more informative for parents and pupils?

5. What are possible ways, both good and bad, that grades can impact pupils? What can be done to lessen the detrimental impact of grades?

ACTIVITY

Table 10A contains information that a teacher accumulated about her pupils during a marking period. Use this information to assign a report card grade to each pupil. Answer the questions that follow the table.

								Quizzes		**Pupil's**
		Test				**Class**	**General**	**and**		**Ability**
Student	**1**	**2**	**3**	**4**	**Project**	**Participation**	**Effort**	**Homework**	**Behavior**	**(Estimate)**
Malcolm	40	60	55	100	A–	Good	G	G	G	M
Tiffany	90	95	45	85	A	Excellent	Ex	Ex	Ex	H
Jason	70	65	20	30	C	Excellent	G	P	P	M
Thomas	85	80	50	85	B–	Poor	P	G	P	H
Gretta	70	70	15	65	D	Good	Ex	P	Ex	L
Susan	45	75	45	100	C	Excellent	Ex	G	G	M
Maya	75	80	45	75	B–	Good	G	G	G	M
Maria	70	75	30	70	A	Excellent	G	G	G	M
Oscar	80	90	45	85	C	Poor	P	P	P	M
Angelina	30	40	10	40	D–	Poor	Ex	P	Ex	L
James	60	60	15	45	D	Poor	P	P	P	H

TABLE 10A   GRADING ACTIVITY

1. Will you use a norm-referenced or a criterion-referenced grading approach? Why?
2. Will you include all the information in the table in determining a grade or only some of the information? State what you will and will not include and explain why.
3. Will all the pieces of information you have decided to include count equally, or will some things count more than others?
4. How will you take into account the different representation of pupil performance on different pieces of information (e.g., percentages, letter grades, excellent-good-poor, high-middle-low)?
5. What, if anything, will you do about test 3?
6. How will you summarize the different pieces of information into a single score or rating?
7. What will be your grading curve (norm-referenced) or performance standards (criterion-referenced) for awarding grades?
8. What grade would each pupil receive?
9. In what ways is this exercise artificial? That is, would there be a difference between the way you graded these pupils and the way a teacher who had actually taught them for the marking period would grade them?

10. If you graded the pupils in a norm-referenced way, go back and regrade using a criterion-referenced approach. If you graded the pupils in a criterion-referenced approach, go back and regrade using a norm-referenced approach.

11. What are the strengths and weaknesses of the grading system you have developed?

REVIEW QUESTIONS

1. What are grades and why are they important? Why do schools and teachers give grades?

2. What questions must a teacher answer in order to carry out the grading process? What teacher judgments must be made in the grading process? Why is there no single best way to assign grades to pupils?

3. In what way is all grading based on comparison? What common methods of comparison are used in grading and how do they differ? What is the difference between norm- and criterion-referenced grading? Which method would you use and why?

4. What are advantages and disadvantages of norm- and criterion-referenced grading? What are the advantages and disadvantages of grading accommodations made for pupils with disabilities?

5. Why should grades be determined mostly by the academic performances of pupils, rather than other information a teacher has about pupils?

6. What information should a teacher provide students about the grading process?

7. What other methods exist for reporting pupil progress?

REFERENCES

Borich, G. D. (2003). *Effective teaching methods,* 5th edition. Englewood Cliffs, NJ: Prentice Hall.

Brookhart, S. M. (1992). *Teachers' grading practices: Meaning and values.* Paper presented at the annual meeting of the American Educational Research Association, San Francisco.

Brookhart, S. M. (1999). Teaching about communicating assessment results and grading. *Educational Measurement: Issues and Practice, 18*(1), 5–13.

Bursuck, W. D., Polloway, E. A., Plante, L., Epstein, M. H., Jayanthi, M., & McConeghy, J. (1996). Report card grading adaptations: A national survey of classroom practices. *Exceptional Children, 62*(4), 301–318.

Friedman, S. J., & Frisbie, D. A. (1993). *The validity of report cards as indicators of student performance.* Paper presented at the annual meeting of the National Council on Measurement in Education, Atlanta.

Frisbie, D. A., & Waltman, K. K. (1992). Developing a personal grading plan. *Educational Measurement: Issues and Practice, 11*(3), 35–42.

Gardner, H. (1995). *Frames of mind: The theory of multiple intelligence.* New York: Basic Books.

Griswold, P. A., & Griswold, M. M. (1992). *The grading contingency: Graders' beliefs and expectations and the assessment ingredients.* Paper presented at the annual meeting of the American Educational Research Association, San Francisco.

Guskey, T. R., & Bailey, J. M. (2001). *Developing grading and reporting systems for student learning.* Thousand Oaks, CA: Corwin Press.

Hubelbank, J. H. (1994). *Meaning of elementary school teachers' grades.* Unpublished dissertation, Boston College, Chestnut Hill, MA.

Kubiszyn, T., & Borich, G. (2003). *Educational testing and measurement, 7th edition.* New York: John Wiley & Sons, Inc.

Munk, D. D., & Bursuck, W. D. (2003). Grading students with disabilities. *Educational Leadership,* (61) 2, 38–43.

Nava, F. J., & Loyd, B. (1992). *The effect of student characteristics on the grading process.* Paper presented at the annual meeting of the National Council on Measurement in Education, San Francisco.

Polloway, E. A., Epstein, M. H., Bursuck, W. D., Roderique, T. W., McConeghy, J. L., & Jayanthi, M. (1994). Classroom grading: A national survey of politics. *Remedial and Special Education, 15*(3), 162–170.

Salend, S. J. (2001). *Creating inclusive classrooms: Effective and reflective practices,* 4th edition, Upper Saddle River, NJ: Merrill Prentice-Hall.

Shepard, L., & Bliem, C. (1995). Parents' thinking about standardized tests and performance assessment. *Educational Researcher, 24,* 25–32.

Sternberg, R. (1997). What does it mean to be smart? *Educational Leadership, 54*(6), 20–24.

Tombari, M., & Borich, G. (1999). *Authentic assessment in the classroom.* Upper Saddle River, NJ: Prentice-Hall.

Valdes, K. A., Williamson, C. L., & Wagner, M. M. (1990). *The national longitudinal transition study of special education students,* Vol. 1. Menlo Park, CA: SRI International.

CHAPTER 11

COMMERCIAL STANDARDIZED ACHIEVEMENT TESTS

KEY TOPICS

- *How Commercial Achievement Tests Are Created*

- *Administering the Test*

- *Interpreting Scores*

- *Three Examples of Test Interpretation*

- *The Validity of Commercial Achievement Tests*

- *Reporting Results to Parents*

- *Classroom Assessment: Summing Up*

CHAPTER OBJECTIVES

After reading this chapter, you will be able to:

♦ Define terms related to standardized testing
♦ State differences between teacher-made, commercial, and statewide tests in terms of objectives, construction, and scoring
♦ Interpret commercial achievement test results
♦ Identify factors that influence the validity and reliability of commercial and statewide achievement tests

THINKING ABOUT TEACHING

Do you think that the information from commercial standardized tests is important in assessing pupils and teachers?

Teachers do not create or have the freedom to modify all of the assessments that their pupils are required to take. **Standardized assessments** are designed to be administered, scored, and interpreted in a standard way across many classrooms and schools. Statewide assessments (discussed in Chapter 4) are one example.

Another example, nationally published **commercial achievement tests**, are the focus of this chapter. Private testing companies construct and sell these tests to various school systems, and the classroom teacher has little or no say in the choice. Here are some of the most widely used:

California Achievement Tests

Comprehensive Tests of Basic Skills

TerraNova

Iowa Tests of Basic Skills

Metropolitan Achievement Tests

Sequential Tests of Educational Progress

SRA Achievement Series

Stanford Achievement Tests

School systems vary in their decisions about the use of these tests and the grades that are tested, but in general the tests have three main purposes: (1) to compare the performance of local pupils to that of similar pupils nationwide, (2) to provide developmental information about pupil achievement over time, and (3) to identify areas of pupil strengths and weaknesses.

Standardized tests are designed for use across many different classrooms and schools and therefore are administered, scored, and interpreted the same way no matter where or when given.

Commercial achievement tests are usually given each year. They provide information about pupil performance over time and identify strengths and weaknesses.

Commercial achievements tests compare the performance of local pupils to that of similar pupils from across the nation.

TABLE 11.1   COMPARISON OF TEACHER-MADE, STATE-MANDATED, AND COMMERCIAL ACHIEVEMENT TESTS

	Teacher-Made	State-Mandated	Commercial Achievement
Content and/or objectives	Specific to class instruction; picked or developed by the teacher; narrow range of content tested, usually one unit or chapter of instruction in a subject	Topics commonly taught or desired to be taught in schools of a state or district; broad range of content covered in a subject area, often covering many years of instruction in a subject	Topics commonly taught in many schools across the nation; broad range of content covering a year of instruction in a subject
Item construction	Written or selected by the classroom teacher	Professional item writers	Professional item writers
Item types	Various	Multiple-choice and performance	Mainly multiple-choice
Item selection	Teacher picks or writes items as needed for test	Many items written and then screened; best items chosen for test	Many items written and then screened and tried out on pupils before few best items chosen for test
Scoring	Teacher	Machine and scorers	Machine
Scores reported	Number correct, percent correct	Usually pass-fail for individuals; percent or proportion of mastery for groups	Percentile rank, stanine, grade-equivalent scores
Interpreting scores	Norm- or criterion-referenced, depending on classroom teacher's preference	Criterion-referenced	Norm-referenced and developmental

Table 11.1 compares these commercial tests with teacher-made and state-mandated tests.

We should begin by acknowledging that many teachers have mixed reactions to achievement tests. The following comments provide a sense of the main issues that concern them.

The commercial tests are inappropriate for my class because our curriculum doesn't cover some of the test content.

Many parents put more faith in a 50-item commercial standardized test than in my judgment based upon months of observing their child in school. These tests are treated like the Good Housekeeping Seal of Approval of a kid's learning. Too much emphasis is placed on these short, general, one-shot tests.

My principal puts a great deal of emphasis on our school's performance on the commercial tests. He's very concerned about how we do compared to neighboring schools when the results are published in the local paper.

It's hard to know what to do with the commercial test results. They give a sense of how pupils are doing, but they mainly corroborate what I already know about the pupils. Occasionally a pupil will perform very differently than I expected and this forces me to look more carefully at my initial impression of the pupil. But for the most part, I don't need a commercial standardized test to tell me how pupils are doing.

The reality is that these standardized tests aren't created to serve the immediate needs of the classroom teacher. They're more for the use of administrators and curriculum planners. But they do contribute to the quality of the school system and thus indirectly to the pupil's education. In addition, the information the tests provide about an individual pupil can be useful as a check on the teacher's own evaluation based on classroom assessment. Therefore, it is important that teachers and pupils take these standardized tests seriously.

Most teachers do not think standardized tests are important to the day-to-day functioning of their classrooms, but parents often view the results with great seriousness.

In this chapter we will mainly acquaint you with how such tests are constructed and standardized, equip you to administer them, and prepare you to interpret them for your own knowledge and for explaining them to parents. We will also discuss issues of validity. The chapter ends with a brief review of the major ideas of the book.

HOW COMMERCIAL ACHIEVEMENT TESTS ARE CREATED

There are two key points to remember about commercial achievement tests: (1) they are usually norm referenced and (2) their main function is to compare a pupil's performance to that of a national group of similar pupils. The tests make possible statements such as "John scored higher than 87 percent of seventh graders nationwide in math"; "Maria is in the third grade, but her grade equivalent score on the commercial test was sixth grade, third month"; "Kerry scored above average in science compared to eighth graders in the United States"; and "Compared to second graders across the country, Sam was in the bottom quarter in reading." In each case, a pupil's test performance was obtained by comparing it to a group of similar pupils across the country. Commercial achievement tests are used in schools mainly because they provide comparisons of pupil achievement beyond the confines of their classroom. Such comparisons are not possible based on teacher-made tests.

Commercial achievement tests are usually norm referenced.

The most commonly used commercial achievement tests are published in the form of test batteries. A **test battery** is a collection of tests in many different subject areas that are administered together. Rather than constructing one test for math, a totally separate test for reading, and yet another for science, most commercial test publishers construct a single test battery that contains many different subject area tests. For example, the Iowa Tests of Basic Skills battery for the fifth grade is made up of the following 13 subject tests, or, as they are commonly called, **subtests:**

Vocabulary
Reading comprehension
Spelling
Capitalization
Punctuation
Usage and expression
Maps and diagrams

Reference materials
Math concepts and estimation
Math problem solving and data interpretation
Math computation
Social studies
Science

A test battery provides a general picture of a pupil's school performance and compares performance across subject areas.

A pupil gets a separate score on each subtest. The entire battery consists of 458 items that take over 5 hours to complete. The main advantages of a test battery are that (1) its broad content coverage provides a general picture of a pupil's school performance and (2) a pupil's score on one subtest can be compared to his or her score on other subtests.

Test Construction

Since the information obtained from a commercial achievement test differs from that obtained from a teacher-made, textbook, or statewide test, it should not be surprising to learn that the commercial test is constructed differently as well. A well-constructed commercial achievement test has three characteristics: (1) it is carefully constructed, with item tryouts, analysis, and revision occurring before the final version of the test is completed; (2) there are written directions and procedures for administering and scoring the test; and (3) score interpretation is based on the test having been administered to a carefully selected sample of pupils from across the nation. The performance of this national sample, or **norm group,** is what local pupil performance is compared to. Figure 11.1 compares the steps in constructing a teacher-made achievement test with the steps in constructing a commercial achievement test.

Commercial tests try to assess objectives that are taught nationally in classrooms at a particular grade level. This has become greater with varied statewide testing.

Choosing Objectives

A teacher-made test and a national commercial standardized achievement test both start with educational objectives. In the teacher-made test, the objectives that have been emphasized during instruction are assessed. The commercial test constructor, on the other hand, seeks to assess only objec-

CONSTRUCTING ACHIEVEMENT TESTS

TEACHER-MADE

State educational
objectives

Write test items
(total number needed)

Administer test

COMMERCIAL

State educational
objectives

Write test items (three
times number needed)

Try out test items
on a national sample

Select items for final version

Administer final version to a
national sample of pupils

Develop test norms

Sell test for use
in schools

tives that are commonly taught across the nation in all classrooms at a particular grade level. These objectives are found by examining widely used textbooks and state curriculum guidelines. The objectives and skills that are *common* across textbooks and guidelines are selected for inclusion in the test. This means that some objectives a particular classroom teacher emphasizes may not be assessed by a commercial achievement test.

Writing and Reviewing Items

Once the objectives are identified, the commercial test publisher, like the classroom teacher, must construct or select test items. Unlike the classroom teacher, who writes just as many items as are needed for a test, the commercial test publisher generates two or three times more items than are needed on the final test. A staff of professional item writers, most of them experienced teachers, research and write items and passages to be tried out.

The selected items go through several cycles of review and revision before being accepted for use. Curriculum specialists study the items to be sure they assess the intended objectives. Test construction specialists review them to be sure they are well written, without ambiguity or clues to test items. Other groups review the items to determine whether they are biased in favor of particular pupil groups. At the end of this stage of test

Commercial test items are reviewed and edited for content, style, and validity, as well as for ethnic, cultural, racial, and gender bias.

construction, a large group of items that have been screened by many groups are available to the test publisher. Each item and subtest is reviewed and edited for content, style, and appropriateness for measuring the objective, as well as for ethnic, cultural, racial, and gender bias (The Psychological Corporation, 1984, 1-1).

Trying Out Items

All the test items are tried out and the more valid and reliable ones are selected for the final version of the test. Since no test constructor—classroom teacher or commercial test publisher—knows how well any item will work until it actually is tried on a group of pupils, the publisher tries out the items on a sample of pupils similar to those for whom the final test is intended. The communities chosen for these tryouts represent different sizes, geographical locations, and socioeconomic levels. The trial test forms look like the final test form and are administered by classroom teachers so that the administrative situation during the tryout is as similar as possible to the way that the final, published test will be administered.

After tests are tried out, commercial test items are statistically analyzed to ensure that they provide the spread among scores that are needed on norm-referenced tests.

There are two reasons for trying out test items before finalizing the test. First, the test constructor wants to make sure that all the items are clearly written and understood by pupils. By examining pupil responses after the tryout, unclear items can be identified, revised, or discarded. Second, test items that ensure a spread of test scores among the test takers must be selected. After the tryout, the statistical properties of each item are analyzed to make certain the final test contains items that differentiate among test takers. This permits the desired norm-referenced comparisons in the commercial achievement tests.

Item difficulty indicates the proportion of test takers who answered the item correctly.

Item discrimination compares overall test scores on a particular item.

Two important indices for judging test items are difficulty and discrimination. The **difficulty index** of a test item indicates the proportion of test takers who answered the item correctly. Thus, a difficulty of 90 means that 90 percent of the pupils answered the item correctly, while an item with a difficulty of 15 was answered correctly by only 15 percent of the test takers. The **discrimination index** indicates how well pupils who scored high on the test as a whole scored on a particular item. An item that discriminates well among test takers is one that high test scorers get correct, but low test scorers get incorrect. That is, the item discriminates between pupils in the same way as the whole test.

To differentiate among students, commercial tests contain many items that approximately one-half of the test takers get right and one-half get wrong.

The test constructor's purpose is to differentiate among pupils according to their levels of achievement. The test constructor is not likely to select final items for the test that all pupils got right or wrong in the tryout, because these items do not help differentiate high from low achievers. To accomplish the desired norm referencing among test takers, the test must consist of items that about half the pupils get correct and half get incorrect and that discriminate among pupils in the same way as the test as a whole. Only then does the test differentiate pupils across the possible scoring range and permit the desired norm-referenced comparisons among test takers. The item tryout provides the information needed to select items for the final test version.

The preceding steps accomplish three important aims: (1) they identify test objectives that reflect what most teachers across the nation are teaching; (2) they produce test items that assess these objectives; and (3) they identify a final group of items that will produce the desired norm-referenced comparisons among test takers. The final version of the test, including the selected test items, directions for administration, separate answer sheets, and established time limits, must then be "normed."

Norming the Test

In order to provide information that allows comparison of an individual pupil's performance to that of a national sample of similar pupils, the final version of the test must be given to a sample of pupils from across the nation. This process is called norming the test. **Test norms** describe how a national sample of pupils who took the test actually performed on it.

Test norms describe how a national sample of students who are representative of the general population perform on the test.

Suppose that a commercial test publisher wishes to norm the final version of an achievement test for fifth graders. To do this, the publisher needs to obtain information about how fifth graders across the nation perform on the test. The publisher (1) selects a representative sample of fifth graders from across the country, (2) administers the test to this sample, (3) scores the test, and (4) uses the scores of the sample to represent the performance of all fifth graders across the country. Assuming the sample of fifth graders was well chosen, the scores made by the sample are a good indication of how all fifth graders would perform on the test.

Obviously, the representativeness of the sample determines how much confidence a teacher can have in the comparisons made between individual pupils and the "national average." The development of norms is a critical aspect of constructing these tests. Commercial test publishers recognize this and strive to select samples that are representative of the group for whom a test is intended. As one commercial publisher noted:

> A test is standardized nationally by administering it under the same conditions to a national sample of students. The students tested become a norm or comparison group against which future individual scores can be compared . . . The sample should be carefully selected to be representative of the national population with respect to ability and achievement. The sample should be large enough to represent the many diverse elements in the population (Riverside Publishing Company, 1986, 11).

Four criteria are used to judge the adequacy of the test norms: sample size, representativeness, recentness, and description of procedures. (Popham, 2000). In general, a large sample of pupils in the norm group is preferable to a small sample; other things being equal, we would prefer a norming sample of 10,000 fifth graders to one of 1,000 fifth graders. But size alone does not guarantee representativeness. If the 10,000 pupils in the

If we assume a norming sample is representative of the general population, a large sample is preferred to a small one.

norming sample were all from private schools in the same state, the sample would not provide a good representation of the performance of pupils nationwide. There must be evidence that the norming sample is representative of the national group for whom the test is intended.

School curricula change over time. New topics are added and others are dropped. Thus, it is important to renorm commercial norm-referenced tests about every 7 to 9 years to keep up with these changes. It is unfair to compare today's pupils to a norm group that was taught a different curriculum.

The final criterion for judging the adequacy of standardized test norms is the clarity of the procedures used to produce them. The clearer and more detailed the description of the procedures followed in test construction, the better the test user can judge the appropriateness of the test for his or her needs. Publishers provide different kinds of manuals outlining procedures to accompany their tests. A *technical manual,* for example, provides information about the construction of the test, including objective selection, item writing and review, item tryout, and norming. A *teacher's manual* provides a description of the areas tested, as well as guidelines for interpreting and using the results of the test. These manuals ought to be accessible to classroom teachers to help them understand and use the test results. Another source of information about published tests is the *Mental Measurement Yearbooks* (Plake, Impara, and Spies, 2003), which provide reviews written by experts in the field.

Commercial test manuals provide information about test construction and interpretation.

ADMINISTERING THE TEST

Once a test is normed, it is ready to be sold to school systems. School systems usually base their selection of a particular test on the judgment of a district administrator or a joint administrator-teacher committee. Once the testing program is selected, other decisions have to be made. In what grades will pupils be tested? Will all subtests of the achievement battery be administered? What types of score reports are needed? Should pupils be tested at the start of the school year or at the end of the year? Different school systems answer these questions differently. Whatever the ultimate decisions, it is usually the classroom teacher who is given the task of administering the tests.

The Need for Consistent Administration

A commercial test is meant to be administered to all pupils under the same conditions whenever and wherever it is given. The reason for standardizing administrative conditions is to allow valid comparisons between local scores and those of the national norm group. If a pupil takes the test under conditions different than the national norm group, then comparisons of the pupil's performance to the norm group are misleading. It is not fair to compare the performance of a pupil who was given 40 minutes to complete a test to others who were given only 30 minutes. It is not fair to compare a pupil who received coaching during testing to pupils who did not. Thus, every national commercial test comes with very specific and detailed directions to follow during test administration.

The directions spell out in great detail how a teacher should prepare for testing, how the room should be set up, what to do while the pupils are taking the test, how to distribute the tests and answer sheets, and how to time the tests. In addition, the directions suggest ways to prepare pupils for taking the test. Finally, the directions provide a script for the teacher to read when administering the test.

Commercial tests must always be administered under the same conditions in order for there to be valid comparisons between local scores and those of the national norm group.

Every teacher who administers a commercial test is expected to use its accompanying script and not deviate from it. If the conditions of administration vary from the directions provided by the test publisher, comparisons with the norming sample and interpretations of pupils' performances may be invalid.

Accommodations for Disabilities

While standard administration is the rule, commercial achievement test publishers are required to grant accommodations for students with certain disabilities. The Americans with Disabilities Act (ADA) and similar federal legislation require that reasonable test accommodations be made for students with disabilities, unless:

1. The student refuses the accommodation.
2. Providing an accommodation would burden the testing agency with undue hardship.
3. The area of impairment is what is being measured.
4. Accommodation would fundamentally distort the measurement.

Reasonableness implies that cases need to be judged individually, but testing publishers do provide guidelines. If a teacher is uncertain about whether an accommodation is allowed, he or she should receive advice from school administrators or other responsible parties.

Accommodations can be made for learning disabled high school students taking the SAT or ACT as part of college admissions. Accommodations are also often allowed for tests given at lower grades. However, the nature and extent of accommodation is usually carefully specified, and teachers are not free to improvise outside the guidelines that the testing authority provides.

Like some universities where accommodations are made for students with disabilities taking a graduate record examination, it is often necessary to request permission to make an accommodation and to register pupils for whom the accommodation is granted. Permission to accommodate may also depend on professional diagnosis of a disability, the existence of an IEP, or official designation of the pupil as having limited English proficiency (LEP).

Students who genuinely need accommodation are almost certain to gain by it. However, there is one disadvantage. Typically, when the scores of students who receive accommodation are reported, they are flagged to indicate that some accommodation was made, and the flagging may cause some interpreter to discount the student's performance (Heaney and Pullin, 1998).

INTERPRETING SCORES

Four to eight weeks after test administration, results are returned to the school. It is important to remember that the tests usually are norm-referenced and compare a pupil's performance to those of a reference group of pupils. The most common comparisons are of a pupil against a national sample of pupils in the same grade or of a pupil against his or her own performance in different subtest areas. However, these are not the only comparisons that can be made from a commercial achievement test.

A school system may also compare its pupils to a narrower sample than pupils in the same grade nationwide. For example, suppose a school district is an urban sector and serves a large, multi-racial, multi-ethnic population. The information sought for this school is likely to be how pupils compare to a national sample drawn from similar urban sector school districts. Most commercial test publishers can provide such a comparison.

Suppose that a school district is in an affluent suburban area. Past experience has shown that when pupils in the district are compared to a representative national sample, they generally do very well. Here the information sought is likely to be how pupils in the district do in comparison to similar pupils in other affluent suburban districts. Once again, commercial test publishers can usually provide such a comparison.

A pupil's test result may appear quite different depending on the norm group to which he or she is compared.

Sometimes school districts are interested in comparing pupil performance within that district. Test publishers can provide this information. Norms that compare pupils in a single school district are called **local norms.** Although national norms are the most commonly reported and used, most commercial test publishers can provide more specific standardized test norms according to geographic location, type of community (rural, suburban, urban), type of school (public, private), and particular school system. A pupil's test performance may appear quite different depending on the choice of norm group to which he or she is compared: a representative national sample, a sample of pupils in urban schools, a sample of pupils in suburban schools, or a sample of pupils from his or her own school district.

Commercial achievement tests provide the classroom teacher with many different kinds of scores. In interpreting these tests, the number of items a pupil got correct, called the **raw score,** is not useful in itself. The teacher needs to know how that raw score compares to the chosen norm group, and special types of scores provide this information. Since there are so many types of scores available, discussion here is confined to the three most common types: percentile rank, stanine, and grade equivalent score. If there is a question about the meaning and interpretation of scores not discussed here, the teacher's manual that accompanies a test contains the desired explanation.

The raw score, which is the number of items a student answered correctly, does not provide a basis for comparing commercial test scores.

Percentile Rank Scores

Probably the most commonly used score is the **percentile rank.** Percentile ranks range from 1 to 99 and indicate what percentage of the norm group the pupil scored above. If Tawon, a seventh grader, has a percentile rank of 91 on a commercial science test, she scored higher on the test than 91 percent of the national sample of seventh grade pupils who made up the norm group. If Josh has a percentile rank of 23 in reading, he scored higher on the reading test than only 23 percent of the pupils in the norm group. Percentiles do not refer to the percentage of items a pupil answered correctly; they refer to the percentage of pupils in the norm group who scored *below* a given pupil.

The most commonly used score is the percentile rank, which indicates what percentage of the norm group a student scored above.

The composition of the norm group defines the comparison that can be made. Thus, Tawon's percentile rank of 91 based upon local norms means that she did better than 91 percent of the seventh graders in her own school district. This does not necessarily mean that she would have a percentile rank of 91 if compared to seventh graders nationally. A pupil's percentile rank can vary depending on the group to which he or she is compared.

One of the main advantages of commercial test batteries is that they are normed on a single group. This allows the teacher to compare a pupil's performance across the many subtests and to identify strengths and weaknesses. Thus, a teacher can make statements about how a given pupil performs in math compared to science, reading, vocabulary, and other tested areas.

Stanine Scores

The **stanine** is a second type of standardized test score. Stanines are a nine-point scale, with a stanine of 1 representing the lowest performance and a stanine of 9 the highest. These nine numbers are the only possible stanine scores a pupil can receive. Like a percentile rank, stanines are designed to indicate a pupil's performance in comparison to a larger norming sample. Table 11.2 shows the approximate relationship between percentile ranks and stanines.

Stanines are a nine-point scale with 1 representing the lowest category and 9 the highest.

TABLE 11.2   APPROXIMATE PERCENTILE RANKS CORRESPONDING
TO STANINE SCORES

Stanine Score	Approximate Percentile Rank
9	96 or higher
8	89–95
7	77–88
6	60–76
5	40–59
4	23–39
3	11–22
2	4–10
1	below 4

Although there is comparability between stanine scores and percentile rank scores, most teachers use stanines to represent general achievement categories, with stanine scores of 1, 2, and 3 considered below average, 4, 5, and 6 considered average, and 7, 8, and 9 considered above average. While stanines are not as precise as percentile ranks, they are easier to work with and interpret, which is a major reason for their popularity among teachers and test publishers. As with the percentile rank, a pupil's stanine score in one subject can be compared to his or her stanine performance in another subject on the same test battery to identify strong and weak areas of the pupil's achievement.

Grade Equivalent Scores

A grade equivalent score is an estimate of a pupil's development level but is not indicative of the grade in which a pupil should be placed.

While stanines and percentile ranks provide information about a pupil's performance compared to the norm group, other types of standardized test scores seek to identify a pupil's development across grade levels. They are intended to compare pupil performance to a series of reference groups that vary developmentally. The most common developmental scale is the **grade equivalent score,** which is intended to represent pupils' achievement in terms of a scale based upon grade and month in school. A grade equivalent score of 7.5 stands for seventh grade, fifth month of school. A grade equivalent score of 11.0 stands for the beginning of the eleventh grade. On some tests, the decimal point is omitted in grade equivalent scores, in which case a grade equivalent score of 43 stands for fourth grade, third month and a score of 108 stands for tenth grade, eighth month.

Grade equivalent scores are easily misinterpreted. A scoring scale that is organized in terms of grade and month in school is so familiar to most test users that it can seduce them into making incorrect interpretations of scores. Consider Luisa, who took a commercial achievement test battery at the start of the fifth grade. When her teacher received the results he saw that Luisa's grade equivalent score in mathematics was 7.5. What does this score indicate about Luisa's mathematics achievement?

If we asked 100 teachers to explain what they believed Luisa's grade equivalent score in math meant, the great majority of them would give one of the following *incorrect* interpretations.

◆ Luisa does as well in mathematics as a seventh grader in the fifth month of school.

◆ Luisa can do the mathematics work of a seventh grader.

◆ Luisa's score indicates that she can succeed in a seventh grade mathematics curriculum.

However, except under very rare conditions, each of these interpretations is incorrect or unsubstantiated. Remember, Luisa took a *fifth grade* mathematics test, which contains mathematics items commonly taught in the fifth grade. Luisa did not take a seventh grade mathematics test, so we have no way of knowing how she would do on seventh grade math material. Certainly she wouldn't have had the benefit of math normally taught in the sixth grade. All we know is how Luisa performed on a fifth grade test, and this tells us nothing about how she might perform on tests for a higher grade level. If a common test had been given to fifth and seventh grade pupils, we might be able to say how Luisa performed in comparison to seventh graders, but this is rarely done.

If all of the preceding interpretations are inappropriate, what is the correct interpretation of Luisa's grade equivalent score of 7.5? The most appropriate interpretation is that *compared to other fifth graders,* Luisa is well above the national average in fifth grade mathematics. Developmentally, she is ahead of the "typical" fifth grader in mathematics achievement. Caution must be exercised when interpreting grade equivalent scores more than one grade level above or below that of the test taker. Commercial test publishers warn against misinterpretations of grade equivalent scores in their manuals, but unfortunately, classroom teachers rarely have access to these manuals. One test publisher includes the following very appropriate and useful caution regarding grade equivalent scores in the Test Coordinator's Handbook.

> Grade equivalents are not appropriate for placing students in school grades corresponding to the test scores. A second grade student who scores above 4.0 in reading should not be advanced to the fourth grade reading class as a result of the test score alone. This score of 4.0 is a good indication that the student reads considerably better than the average second grade student. However, if this student had taken a reading test designed for the fourth grade, it is possible that he or she would not have scored at 4.0. Because misinterpretation can easily result if thorough explanation does not accompany the score, it is strongly recommended that grade equivalents not be used in reporting a student's scores to parents or other persons with no training in testing.

TABLE 11.3   COMPARISON OF THREE COMMON STANDARDIZED TEST SCORES

	Percentile Rank	Stanine	Grade Equivalent Score
Format of score	Percentage	Whole number	Grade and month in school
Possible scores	1 to 99 in whole numbers	1 to 9 in whole numbers	Prekindergarten to 12.9 in monthly increments
Interpretation	Percent of pupils a given pupil did better than	1 to 3 below average; 4 to 6 average; 7 to 9 above average	Above average, average, below average compared to pupils in the same grade
Special issues	Small differences often overinterpreted	General index of pupil achievement	Frequently misinterpreted and misunderstood

olc

CHAPTER CASE STUDY

Visit the text OLC to read the case of Melinda Grant, a first-year elementary school teacher who worries about being held accountable for her students' year-end standardized test scores.

Another use of the grade equivalent score is to assess a pupil's academic development over time. The change in a pupil's grade equivalent score over time is often used as an indication of whether the pupil is making "normal progress" in his or her learning. For example, if a pupil's grade equivalent score is 8.2 when tested in the eighth grade, one might expect the pupil's grade equivalent to be around 9.2 if tested at the same time in the ninth grade. However, it is important to recognize that development is an irregular process, which may jump ahead greatly at certain times but remain static at others. Thus, small deviations from so-called normal growth of one grade equivalent per year should not be interpreted as representing a problem. Table 11.3 compares the characteristics of percentile rank, stanine, and grade equivalent scores.

For more discussion of the terms and concepts in this section, see Appendix D, "Statistical Applications for Classroom Assessment."

THREE EXAMPLES OF TEST INTERPRETATION

Commercial tests usually report percentile rank, stanine, and grade equivalent scores.

Although many types of commercial test scores can be provided by test publishers, the percentile rank, stanine, and grade equivalent are most often used. The following three examples show how commercial achievement tests are reported to classroom teachers.

Example 1: Pupil Performance Report

Figure 11.2 shows Brian Elliott's test results on the Metropolitan Achievement Test battery. The extreme top of the report tells us that Brian was administered the Metropolitan Achievement Test. The top of the form also tells us that Brian's teacher's name is Smith, his school is Lakeside Elementary School, and the school is part of the Newtown school system.

The middle portion at the top of the form tells us that Brian is in the fourth grade and that he took the Metropolitan Achievement Tests in May 1993. This is near the end of the school year, which has an important bearing on the national norming group against which Brian's performance is compared. Suppose that Brian took the test in October, at the beginning of the school year. How would his performance in October probably compare to his performance in May? In October, Brian was just starting the fourth grade and had not had much instruction on fourth grade objectives. By May, Brian had 9 months of instruction on fourth grade objectives, so it is likely that he would test higher in May than he would have tested in October. The time of the year that a pupil takes a commercial achievement test makes a considerable difference in his or her performance level; the more instruction the pupil has had, the higher his or her scores should be.

Commercial achievement test constructors recognize this fact and take it into account when they norm their tests. They develop different norms for tests in the fall and the spring, so that pupils who are tested in the fall can be compared to the fall norming group and pupils who take the test in the spring can be compared to the spring norming group. At the top of Brian's report form under "Norms" is the entry "Spring," which means that Brian, who was tested in May, was compared to a national sample of fourth graders who were tested in the spring.

Finally, the top of the form describes the level and form of the test Brian took. This information usually is not critical to interpreting the test results. The **level** of a test describes the grade level for which the test is intended. On the Metropolitan Achievement Tests the level called "Elem 2" is intended for the fourth grade. The **form** of the test refers to the version of the test administered. Often standardized test constructors will produce two interchangeable versions of a test to allow schools that wish to test more than once a year to use a different but equivalent version of the test each time.

Below this general information are Brian's actual test results. First, marked by the circled *A*, is a list of all the subtests that make up the Metropolitan Achievement Tests battery and the number of items in each. The subtest list starts with total reading and ends with thinking skills. Each of these subtests assesses performance in a distinct curriculum area. Subtest results can be grouped to provide additional scores. For example, the total reading score of 85 is made up of the combined performance on the vocabulary and reading comprehension subtests. What three subtests are combined to make the total language score? The basic battery total includes all

FIGURE 11.2 *Standardized Test Report for an Individual Pupil.*

METROPOLITAN ACHIEVEMENT TESTS
SEVENTH EDITION

INDIVIDUAL REPORT
FOR
Brian Elliott

TEACHER: SMITH	2004 NORMS:	MAT/ NATIONAL
SCHOOL: LAKESIDE ELEMENTARY GRADE: 04	SPRING	ELEM 2 S
DISTRICT: NEWTOWN TEST DATE: 05/05	LEVEL: ELEM 2 FORM: S	OLSAT NATIONAL E 2
		AGE 09 YRS 10 MOS

TESTS	NO. OF ITEMS	RAW SCORE	SCALED SCORE	NATL PR-S	NATL NCE	GRADE EQUIV	ACC RANGE
Total reading	85	66	632	68–6	59.9	5.9	MIDDLE
Vocabulary	30	27	667	90–8	77.0	8.4	HIGH
Reading comprehension	55	39	618	53–5	51.6	5.0	MIDDLE
Total mathematics	64	43	602	55–5	52.6	5.1	MIDDLE
Concepts and problem solving	40	29	617	68–6	59.9	6.0	MIDDLE
Procedures	24	14	579	37–4	43.0	4.3	LOW
Language	54	33	609	51–5	50.5	4.8	MIDDLE
Prewriting	15	10	606	47–5	48.4	4.7	MIDDLE
Composing	15	8	602	43–5	46.3	4.5	LOW
Editing	24	15	614	56–5	53.2	5.3	LOW
Science	35	25	628	65–6	58.1	5.9	MIDDLE
Social studies	35	25	630	69–6	60.4	6.0	MIDDLE
Research skills	36	29	635	73–6	62.9	6.5	MIDDLE
Thinking skills	83	56	615	61–6	55.9	5.7	LOW
Basic battery	203	142	617	60–6	55.3	5.4	MIDDLE
Complete battery	273	192	619	62–6	56.4	5.5	MIDDLE

NATIONAL GRADE PERCENTILE BANDS

Scale: 1   10   30   50   70   90   99

OTIS-LENNON SCHOOL ABILITY TEST	RAW SCORE	SAI	AGE PR-S	AGE NCE	SCALED SCORE	NATL GRADE PR-S	NATL GRADE NCE
Total	72	49	112	77–7	65.6	632	81–7	68.5
Verbal	36	25	114	81–7	68.5	637	85–7	71.8
Nonverbal	36	24	109	71–6	61.7	627	76–6	64.9

Source: Metropolitan Achievement Tests: 7th edition. Copyright © 1992 by Harcourt Brace & Company. Reproduced by permission. All rights reserved. "Metropolitan Achievement Tests" is a registered trademark of The Psychological Corporation.

subtests except science and social studies, while the complete battery total includes these two subtests.

What kind of information is provided about Brian's performance on the Metropolitan subtests? The section marked with a circled *B* lists raw scores; scaled scores (a developmental score used to measure year-to-year growth in pupil performance); national percentile ranks and national stanines (NATL PR-S); national normal curve equivalents (NATL NCE), a score similar to the percentile rank, grade equivalent scores; and an achievement-ability comparison labeled ACC. The raw score tells how many items Brian got correct on each subtest. He got 27 of the 30 items on the vocabulary subtest and 29 of the 40 items on the concepts and problem solving subtest correct. Because different subtests have different numbers of test items, raw scores are *not* useful in interpreting or comparing pupil performance on the subtests. Also, since scaled scores are difficult to interpret and normal curve equivalents are replaceable by percentile ranks in most cases, we shall not describe them here. More detailed information about these and other standardized test scores can be found in the interpretive guides for teachers that are available for most commercial achievement tests.

The score column labeled "NATL PR-S" shows Brian's national percentile rank and corresponding stanine score on each subtest. How should Brian's performance of 56-5 on the editing subtest be interpreted? Brian's percentile rank of 56 means that he scored higher than 56 percent of the fourth grade national norm group on the editing subtest. His stanine score of 5 places him in the middle of the stanine scores and indicates that his performance is average compared to fourth graders nationwide. Interpret Brian's national percentile rank and stanine on the vocabulary subtest.

Compare Brian's performance in reading comprehension and composing. In terms of percentile rank, Brian did better in reading comprehension (53rd percentile rank) than in composing (43rd percentile rank), but in terms of stanines, Brian's performance on the two subtests was the same (stanine 5). The apparent difference in the percentile rank and stanine scores illustrates two points. First, the stanine score provides a more general indication of performance than the percentile rank. Second, and more important, fairly large differences in percentile ranks, especially near the middle of the percentile rank scale, are not different when expressed as stanines.

Many teachers and parents forget that all test scores contain some unreliability. No test score, not even one from a published commercial test, can be assumed to provide an exact, error-free assessment of a pupil's performance. Unfortunately, people who ignore this fact mistakenly treat small differences in percentile ranks (up to eight or so percentile ranks) as indicative of meaningful difference in performance. Sometimes answering only one or two more items correctly can change a pupil's score by 8 to 10 percentile ranks, yet not alter a pupil's stanine score. This should caution Brian's teacher to not read too much into the percentile rank differences in these two areas.

The achievement-ability comparison (ACC) shown in Figure 11.2 is provided by many test publishers when the school testing program includes both a commercial achievement test and a commercial ability test. In essence, the comparison tries to provide information about how a pupil performs on the achievement test compared to a national sample of pupils who have a similar ability level. Problems associated with interpreting and using the achievement-ability comparison in a meaningful way are similar to those raised in the discussion of grading pupils based on their ability:

1. There are problems in accurately assessing ability.
2. The error in the two tests used in the comparison increases the imprecision of the decision.
3. Information about an achievement-ability comparison is difficult to translate into meaningful, instructionally related practices.
4. The information may label a pupil or influence a teacher's expectations for the pupil.
5. There are many different types of ability that affect learning in addition to those that can be elicited with paper-and-pencil tests.

For these reasons, achievement-ability comparisons can be misleading and should be interpreted and used with extreme caution.

The area marked with a circled *C* in Figure 11.2 shows the national percentile bands for Brian's performance on each subtest. Presenting Brian's performance in this way is useful, not only because it provides a graphic contrast to the numerical scores, but also because it reminds the test user about the unreliability in all test scores. In essence, the **percentile bands** tell us that no score is error-free, so it is wrong to treat a score as if it were precise and infallible. It is best to think of a score not as a single number, but as a range of numbers, any one of which could be the pupil's true performance on an error-free test. Thus, looking at the percentile bands, it is more appropriate to say that Brian's true performance on the total reading subtest falls somewhere between about the 62nd and 80th percentile rank, not exactly and precisely the 68th percentile. His true performance on the math procedures subtest is best interpreted to be between a percentile rank of about 22 and 45, rather than exactly 37. Thinking of test performance in terms of a range of scores prevents overinterpretation of test results based on small score differences. Even if percentile bands are not provided, it is important to think of all types of test scores as representing a range of performance, not a single point.

What does all of this information tell about how Brian performs in his fourth grade classroom? By itself, it tells very little. However, in conjunction with the teacher's own classroom observations and assessments, commercial achievement test results can be useful. As we noted at the beginning of the chapter, commercial achievement tests provide information about (1) how a pupil compares to a national sample of pupils in the same grade, (2) the pupil's developmental level, and (3) the pupil's strengths and weaknesses in important subject areas. The tests do not tell how the pupil does in the day-to-day activities in his or her own classroom. If Brian is in a class of low achievers, he may perform very well in class, much better than would be expected on the basis of his standardized test scores. If he is in a class of high achievers, he may perform much lower than his commercial standardized test scores would suggest. In either case, commercial achievement tests scores should not be interpreted without also considering information about the pupil's daily classroom performance.

Sometimes commercial test publishers provide information on pupils' performance on specific skill areas within a subtest. For example, the vocabulary subtest can be broken down into smaller skills such as synonyms, antonyms, and hyphenation; or a science subtest could be broken down into life science, physical science, earth science, and research skills. The classroom teacher can use this information to identify more specific areas where a pupil or the class has difficulty.

However, one caution should be noted in using this skill area information. In most cases, any single skill area will be assessed by a small number of items. A small number of items cannot be relied upon to provide reliable enough information for curriculum planning or decision making. Rather, teachers should follow up the skill area information with additional information collected on their own.

Example 2: Class Performance Report

Figure 11.3 shows the overall class performance for Mr. or Ms. Ness's fourth grade on the Iowa Tests of Basic Skills. The subtests of the Iowa tests are listed across the second line of the figure, beginning with vocabulary and ending with math computation. Four different scores are reported: the standard score (SS), the average grade equivalent score (GE), the average normal curve equivalent (NCE), and the average national percentile rank (NPR). Mr. or Ms. Ness can obtain a general picture of the performance of the class as a whole by examining the national percentile ranks.

The percentile ranks indicate the combined class average on each of the subtests of the Iowa in comparison to the national fourth grade norm. The composite score at the far right of Figure 11.3 shows that class performance across all the subtests in the battery had a percentile rank of 82. This indicates that summing across all subtests, the typical pupil in the class did better than 82 percent of similar students across the nation. Overall, the average national percentile ranks indicate that the class is somewhat above the national average on the various subtests. In most cases the class performed better than 70 to 80 percent of similar fourth graders nationwide. Note that the grade equivalent scores across the many subtests are also higher than the 4.3 one would expect of fourth graders tested in the third month of the fourth grade. This indicates that the pupils in this class answered more

FIGURE 11.3 *Standardized Test Report for a Class.*

Iowa Tests of Basic Skills

Service 9:
Report of Class Averages

Class/Group: NESS	Grade: 4
Building: WEBER	Form: K
Building Code: 304	Test Date: 03/93
System: DALEN COMMUNITY	Page: 40
Norms: SPRING 1992	
Order No. 000-A33-76044-00-001	

AVERAGES ITBS:

	READING			LANGUAGE					MATHEMATICS			CORE TOTAL	SOCIAL STUD-IES	SCI-ENCE	SOURCES OF INFO.			COM-POSITE	MATH COMPU-TATION
	VOCAB-ULARY	COMPRE-HENSION	TOTAL	SPELL-ING	CAPITAL-IZATION	PUNC-TUATION	USAGE/ EXPRESS	TOTAL	CON-CEPTS/ ESTIM.	PROBS/ DATA INTERP.	TOTAL				MAPS & DIA-GRAMS	REF. MATLS	TOTAL		
N	24	24	24	24	24	24	24	24	24	24	24	24	24	24	24	24	24	24	24
SS	2030	224.3	213.6	214.5	255.7	249.2	227.8	236.9	214.5	21.64	21.55	221.9	221.3	228.5	219.0	227.0	223.0	223.0	213.9
GE OF AVG SS	5.0	6.5	5.8	5.9	9.3	8.7	6.9	7.6	6.1	6.0	6.0	6.4	6.2	6.9	6.1	6.8	6.3	6.4	5.9
NCE	54.2	67.1	62.5	62.8	78.7	76.6	65.4	75.4	65.5	61.8	63.8	68.8	66.4	69.2	61.8	71.2	67.1	69.8	66.0
PR OF AVG SS: NATL STUDENT NORMS	58	78	72	74	91	88	77	88	77	72	74	81	78	81	74	84	79	82	78

N TESTED= 27

SS–Standard Score, GE=Grade Equivalent, NCE=Normal Curve Equivalent, NPR=Nat'l%ile Rank

THE RIVERSIDE
PUBLISHING COMPANY
a Houghton Mifflin Company

Source: Copyright © 1996 by the University of Iowa. All rights reserved. Reproduced from the *Iowa Tests of Basic Skills Interpretive Guide for Teachers and Counselors,* with permission of the publisher.

items correctly on the fourth grade test than did their peers nationally. Remember, grade equivalent scores do not indicate the grade level a pupil is achieving at or the grade she should be placed in. Figure 11.3 also shows that compared to most other subject areas, the class is relatively weak in vocabulary. This is something the teacher may wish to investigate further.

Example 3: Summary Reports for Parents

Figure 11.4 shows a California Achievement Tests report that is sent home to parents after testing to help them understand their child's performance. All commercial achievement test publishers can provide similar forms. The section marked with a boxed *A* provides parents with a general introduction to the test and its purposes. The section marked *B* shows Ken Allen's percentile ranks on the total reading, total language, and total math tests, as well as his performance on the total battery. The areas labeled "below average," "average," and "above average" give parents a general indication of how Ken did compared to his national fifth grade peers.

The right third of the figure (labeled *C* and *D*) provides more detailed information about Ken's performance. The four boxes contain, respectively, percentile ranks for the subtests that made up the total reading, total language, total math, and remaining battery subtests. Thus, for example, Ken's percentile ranks in vocabulary and comprehension, the two subtests that make up total reading, were 47 and 68. He scored higher than 47 and 68 percent of fifth graders nationally on vocabulary and comprehension, respectively. The boxes also show areas of Ken's strength and weakness on the skills that make up the reading, language, and math tests. This information is similar to the skill area information described in the discussion of the Metropolitan Achievement Tests (see Figure 11.2) and should be treated with the same caution. Teachers should be prepared to answer parents' questions about the information contained in such home reports.

Figure 11.5 shows another home report, this one for a sixth grader, Mary Brown. Her national percentiles also are graphed, providing concise information for a number of subjects and serving as a basis for discussion between the teacher and Mary's parents. See whether you can interpret the report.

1. What subjects were assessed?
2. In your own words, interpret what the report is saying about Mary's performance in each subject.
3. What does the pattern of scores suggest about Mary?

Commercial test publishers can provide scores and information additional to that described in the preceding sections, but Figures 11.2 through 11.5 show the basic types of information that are returned to classroom

FIGURE 11.4 *Parent Report Form.*

CAT/5 Home Report

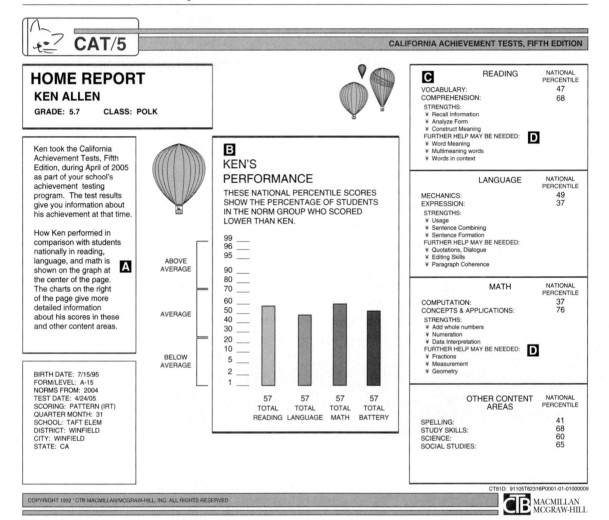

CAT/5

CALIFORNIA ACHIEVEMENT TESTS, FIFTH EDITION

HOME REPORT
KEN ALLEN
GRADE: 5.7   CLASS: POLK

Ken took the California Achievement Tests, Fifth Edition, during April of 2005 as part of your school's achievement testing program. The test results give you information about his achievement at that time.

How Ken performed in comparison with students nationally in reading, language, and math is shown on the graph at **A** the center of the page. The charts on the right of the page give you more detailed information about his scores in these and other content areas.

BIRTH DATE: 7/15/95
FORM/LEVEL: A-15
NORMS FROM: 2004
TEST DATE: 4/24/05
SCORING: PATTERN (IRT)
QUARTER MONTH: 31
SCHOOL: TAFT ELEM
DISTRICT: WINFIELD
CITY: WINFIELD
STATE: CA

B
KEN'S PERFORMANCE
THESE NATIONAL PERCENTILE SCORES SHOW THE PERCENTAGE OF STUDENTS IN THE NORM GROUP WHO SCORED LOWER THAN KEN.

ABOVE AVERAGE

AVERAGE

BELOW AVERAGE

99
96
95
90
80
70
60
50
40
30
20
10
5
2
1

57 TOTAL READING
57 TOTAL LANGUAGE
57 TOTAL MATH
57 TOTAL BATTERY

C
READING	NATIONAL PERCENTILE
VOCABULARY:	47
COMPREHENSION:	68

STRENGTHS:
¥ Recall Information
¥ Analyze Form
¥ Construct Meaning
FURTHER HELP MAY BE NEEDED: **D**
¥ Word Meaning
¥ Multimeaning words
¥ Words in context

LANGUAGE	NATIONAL PERCENTILE
MECHANICS:	49
EXPRESSION:	37

STRENGTHS:
¥ Usage
¥ Sentence Combining
¥ Sentence Formation
FURTHER HELP MAY BE NEEDED:
¥ Quotations, Dialogue
¥ Editing Skills
¥ Paragraph Coherence

MATH	NATIONAL PERCENTILE
COMPUTATION:	37
CONCEPTS & APPLICATIONS:	76

STRENGTHS:
¥ Add whole numbers
¥ Numeration
¥ Data Interpretation
FURTHER HELP MAY BE NEEDED: **D**
¥ Fractions
¥ Measurement
¥ Geometry

OTHER CONTENT AREAS	NATIONAL PERCENTILE
SPELLING:	41
STUDY SKILLS:	68
SCIENCE:	60
SOCIAL STUDIES:	65

CT81D: 91105T62316P0001-01-01000009

COPYRIGHT 1992 ' CTB MACMILLAN/MCGRAW-HILL, INC. ALL RIGHTS RESERVED

CTB MACMILLAN MCGRAW-HILL

Source: Reproduced from the California Achievement Tests, 5th Edition, by permission of the publisher, CTB/McGraw-Hill, a division of McGraw-Hill School Publishing Company. Copyright © 1992 by McGraw-Hill School Publishing Company. All rights reserved.

teachers and parents as part of a school district's commercial achievement testing program. Each test publisher presents the results in slightly different formats, but the basic information and its interpretation do not vary much from publisher to publisher. The variety of forms and pupil analyses that are available from a commercial test publisher can be found in the manual that accompanies the test.

FIGURE 11.5 *Example of a Computer-Prepared Narrative Report on an Individual Student's Standardized Test Performance. The Report is meant to be sent home to parents. Describe Mary's overall performance on TerraNova.*

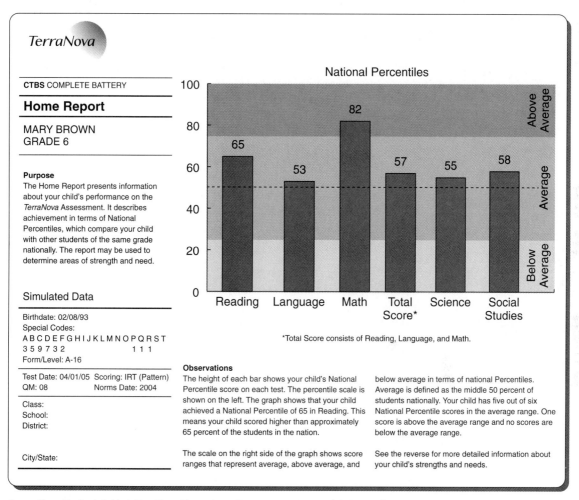

Source: From *Teacher's Guide to TerraNova,* Figure 3, p. 150. Monterey, CA: CTB/McGraw-Hill, 1997.

THE VALIDITY OF COMMERCIAL ACHIEVEMENT TESTS

A great deal of time, expertise, and expense are put into the construction of commercial achievement tests. The most widely used tests are technically strong, with well-written items, an attractive format, statistically sophisticated norms, and reliable, consistent pupil scores. More care, concern, and expertise are put into producing a standardized commercial achievement test than are typically put into constructing a teacher-prepared or textbook test.

It is still appropriate, however, to raise the question of whether a commercial achievement test provides the information needed to make valid decisions about pupil achievement. Teacher-prepared and textbook tests are judged mainly in terms of whether they provide a fair assessment of how well pupils have learned the things they were taught. Commercial achievement tests are judged on this basis too, but on other bases as well. Regardless of the test, if it does not provide the desired information about pupil achievement it is not valid and therefore not useful for decision making. For commercial achievement tests, four factors influence validity and reliability: (1) the appropriateness of the content and objectives tested, (2) the representativeness of the norming sample, (3) the conditions under which the test is administered, and (4) misinterpretations of test results. This section examines these issues and their potential effect on the validity of standardized achievement tests.

Appropriate Coverage

Commercial tests are designed to assess the core objectives that most classroom teachers at that grade level cover in their instruction.

Standardized tests are not constructed to assess every classroom teacher's unique instructional objectives. Rather they are designed to assess the core objectives that *most* classroom teachers cover in their instruction. By selecting a common set of objectives, commercial test constructors seek to ensure that most pupils have had exposure to the objectives tested. Of course, this does not mean that every commercial test is equally relevant to the curriculum in a given classroom where some of the topics taught are not included on standardized tests.

A commercial test cannot be valid for a particular class if it does not match the instruction given in that class.

While most classroom teachers find that the objectives tested on commercial achievement tests reflect their own instruction, few teachers find *all* of the topics they included in commercial tests. Teachers whose classroom instruction deviates greatly from the text or who consistently introduce unusual materials and concepts often find that the topics covered by the national tests are different from those they have been teaching. The time of year when testing takes place and the teacher's sequencing of topics also influence pupils' opportunities to learn the objectives being assessed.

Finally, virtually all commercial achievement tests rely heavily on multiple-choice test items. Restricting items to the multiple-choice format means that some topics or objectives may be tested differently than they were taught or tested in the classroom. For example, to assess spelling, most teachers give a weekly spelling test in which pupils have to spell each word correctly. In commercial achievement tests, spelling is assessed by presenting pupils with four or five words and asking them to identify the one that is spelled incorrectly. Most pupils are not taught spelling this way.

This and the preceding factors discussed can reduce the match between the content of a standardized achievement test and the content of classroom instruction, thus lowering validity.

It is the responsibility of each local school district to determine if the content of a commercial achievement test is valid for pupils in that district. If, after inspecting the test items and the publisher's description of what is tested, the test content appears to be different from what pupils were taught, judgments about pupils' achievement may not be valid and should be made with caution.

Each school or district must decide if the content of a commercial achievement test matches its own objectives.

Representative Norms

Commercial test publishers strive to obtain norming samples that are representative of national groups of pupils. However, there are some important factors that can undermine the appropriateness of test norms and thereby test validity: (1) norms go out of date; (2) the curriculum in a subject area changes; (3) textbooks are revised and new instructional materials appear; and (4) the same test is often administered in a school district over a number of years so teachers and pupils become familiar with its content and items. Inappropriate or out-of-date test norms reduce the validity of comparisons and decisions made from standardized achievement tests. While there is no hard-and-fast period within which standardized achievement test norms should be revised, 7 to 9 years is a generally accepted time period used by the publishers of the most widely used standardized tests. Obviously, the older the test norms, the less representative they are of instructional content and national pupil performance. Specific information about test norming procedures and the age of the norms should be provided in the publisher's test manual.

When commercial test norms do not match the characteristics of the local students, valid decisions cannot be made from the test results.

Conditions of Administration

It was emphasized earlier that valid interpretations of pupils' standardized test performance depend on pupils taking the test under the conditions recommended by the test publisher. Deviations from the test administration directions—allowing pupils more time than specified, helping pupils while they are taking the test, coaching pupils before the test on specific items they will be asked, and generally not following the directions provided—all reduce the validity of the test results and the decisions based on those results.

Deviating from test administration directions reduces the validity of test results.

Of course, pupils who require accommodations in testing should be provided with the appropriate resources as we noted earlier in the chapter. Typically, when the scores of pupils who receive accommodations are reported, they are flagged to indicate the test was not taken under standard conditions.

Potential Misinterpretations

There are two common problems in interpreting commercial standardized test scores: misinterpretation and overinterpretation. Because the types of scores that are used to describe pupil performance on standardized achievement tests are different from those teachers commonly use, the likelihood of misinterpretation is heightened. The most common misinterpretations involve the percentile rank, which is mistaken for the percentage of items a pupil answered correctly, and the grade equivalent score, which is mistakenly thought to indicate the curriculum level at which a pupil is performing in a subject area. Percentile ranks indicate the percentage of pupils in the norm group that a pupil scored above. Grade equivalent scores indicate how well a pupil performs on grade-level objectives compared to other pupils in that grade.

The main problem in interpreting commercial test scores is overinterpretation.

The main problem in interpreting commercial test scores is *over*interpretation, not misinterpretation. Because commercial standardized tests are constructed by professionals, tried out on nationwide samples of pupils, and provide numerical indices that describe a pupil's performance compared to pupils nationwide, there is a widespread belief that they give precise, accurate descriptions of pupil achievement. Certainly parents and the public at large put more faith in commercial test results than in teacher-made assessments gathered over time in the day-to-day classroom setting. But while the information provided by the 40 or so multiple-choice items found in a typical commercial subtest is useful, it can never match the information a teacher accumulates through daily instruction and assessment of pupils. As one publisher has stated:

Information gained from commercial tests may not be as revealing as information gathered through daily instruction and assessment by the classroom teacher.

> . . . test scores represent achievement in basic skills areas at only one particular time and must be reviewed together with the student's actual classroom work and other factors. Parents should also understand that the test measures the basic content skills that are most common to curricula throughout the country. It cannot possibly measure, nor should it attempt to measure, the full curriculum of a particular classroom, school, or district. (CTB/McGraw-Hill, 1986b, 100)

Teachers should guard against treating small differences in commercial test scores as if they were reliable indicators of real differences among pupils.

Even when there are no problems with test content, norms, and administration, standardized test scores still are overinterpreted. For example, it is common for teachers and parents to treat small differences in commercial test scores as if they are significant and indicate real performance differences. A percentile rank difference of 6 to 8 points or a 2- to 5-month grade equivalent difference between pupils rarely indicates important or meaningful differences in their achievement or development. There is sufficient unreliability in any test score, whether standardized or teacher-made, to make small scoring differences indicators of true differences among pupils. Commercial standardized test constructors try to defeat overinterpretation of small score differences by warning against them in their test manuals and by presenting scores as percentile or stanine bands (see Table 11.1), but they

---

TECHNOLOGY AND ASSESSMENT BOX

RESOURCES FOR COMMERCIAL STANDARDIZED TESTS

olc Visit Chapter 11 of the text website (www.mhhe.com/airasian5e) to link to the following Web-based resources on commercial standardized tests.

◆ Talking to Your High School Students about Standardized Tests
This article by Carolyn Boccella Bagin specifies some ways that teachers can help students prepare for standardized tests. Although the article was designed with secondary students in mind, many of the suggestions can easily be applied to elementary settings.

◆ Proficiency Test Materials and Sample Test Questions
These two sites provide sample standardized tests from several state-mandated testing programs. The items, or complete tests in some cases, are available free of charge in a downloadable format. The complete tests come from the Ohio Proficiency Testing Program, with individual sample items from the states of Illinois, Kentucky, and Missouri.

◆ Explaining Test Results to Parents
This brief article by Thomas Eissenberg and Larry Rudner provides very helpful suggestions for ways that teachers can communicate the purpose and results of standardized tests to parents. Specific suggestions are provided for ways to explain stanines, percentile ranks, and grade-equivalent scores.

◆ Integrating Testing with Teaching
Herbert Rudman discusses various ways in which the results of testing can be linked to teaching, as well as how testing can be used to help teachers and administrators.

are not always successful. In short, teachers should guard against treating small score differences as if they are meaningful.

Overinterpretation also occurs when teachers put too much faith in achievement-ability comparisons. These comparisons provide at best a general indication of how a pupil compares to other pupils of similar ability. Before a teacher acts on standardized test information of this type, he or she should reflect on personal knowledge of the pupil's work habits, personality, and achievement gained by daily exposure to the pupil in the classroom.

Finally, the smaller the number of items that make up a test, the less reliable its results and the less trustworthy its score. This can be a particular problem in commercial standardized achievement tests that include a few performance-based, open-ended items. While performance-based items can assess areas not tested by multiple-choice items, one must interpret performance-based items cautiously because there are relatively few such items. Normally, the subtest scores on standardized test batteries are quite reliable and consistent. However, when a subtest is further broken down into specific topics, skills, or objectives, with separate scores given for each, one must be cautious about how much one reads into the scores. Often such information is used to diagnose a pupil's strengths and weaknesses, and while such information may provide a basis for further exploration of pupil performance, it should be reviewed critically because of the very few items on which it is typically based.

Information from commercial achievement tests usually corroborates a teacher's perceptions of pupils.

While commercial achievement tests can give teachers useful assessment information that they cannot gather for themselves, such information should be used in conjunction with information gathered from their own assessments. For the most part, the information from commercial achievement tests corroborates perceptions the teacher has already formed about pupils. When the two types of evidence do not corroborate each other, the teacher should look again at his or her perceptions to be sure the pupil is not being misjudged.

REPORTING RESULTS TO PARENTS

Often teachers are expected to provide information to parents about pupils' performance on standardized tests. This may occur during a parent-teacher conference or by a written description sent to the parent. Explanation is easier done with a copy of the pupil's test results in hand or included in the mailing. Some useful guidelines for reporting to parents are contained in Key Assessment Tools 11.1.

To summarize, commercial achievement test batteries can be used to compare an individual pupil's performance to that of a larger group of pupils beyond the local classroom or district, usually a national sample of pupils in the same grade. They can also provide information about a pupil's areas of strength and weakness. Because such comparisons are sought, commercial achievement test constructors must go through a complicated test construction process to develop their tests. They must identify content and objectives that are commonly taught at a particular grade level in classrooms across the country. Then they must write and try out items that assess these common objectives. From this trial assessment a final set of items is selected based upon content appropriateness and a desired statistical range. The final version of the test, with its directions, answer sheets, and test booklets, is then administered to a large sample of pupils who are thought to represent pupils across the country. The purpose of this test "norming" is to provide information about the performance of a national sample of pupils against which the performance of future test takers can be compared.

Pupil performance on commercial achievement tests is described mainly through scores that indicate how a pupil compares to other pupils. The most commonly used scores are (1) percentile ranks which describe

---

Key Assessment Tools 11.1

REPORTING STANDARDIZED TEST RESULTS TO PARENTS

◆ Remember that the parent is not likely to be a testing expert and will basically want to know how the pupil performed.

◆ Start with some general information about the test and its purpose.

◆ Distinguish between a commercial standardized test and a classroom test or assessment.

◆ You do not need to tell parents all you know about standardized tests; your task is to get your message across in simple, understandable terms.

◆ Make your interpretations brief but accurate; you don't have to interpret every bit of information in the test report.

◆ Pick one or two subject areas such as math and reading, and one of the standardized scores (stanines or percentile ranks, but not grade equivalents because they are difficult to explain), and take the parent through the two subjects.

◆ Identify the pupil's strengths and weaknesses based on the test results; describe the pupil's overall performance.

◆ Do not patronize the parent; avoid comments like "You probably don't understand all of this" or "I understand that this is difficult for a parent."

◆ Be careful of stressing terms such as "error in testing," "flaws or imprecision in the tests," and "unreliability." Such remarks undermine the test information. It is better to say, "No single test can give an exact indication of performance" or "Although these tests are generally accurate, they can vary from time to time."

◆ Remember that standardized tests are "one-shot" assessments and should be interpreted in the context of the pupil's general classroom performance to fully understand the pupil's achievement.

---

what percentage of the norming sample the pupil scored above; (2) stanines which, scoring on a scale of 1 to 9, roughly divide pupils into below average, average, and above average categories; and (3) grade equivalent scores which are developmentally based scores indicating how well a pupil compares to a national sample of peers in his or her grade. Other kinds of scores are sometimes provided with commercial tests, but they are used less than these three.

Commercial achievement test results should be interpreted in conjunction with what teachers know about pupils from their own classroom assessments. Further, interpretations of commercial test results should be based on knowledge of the test objectives, the representativeness and age of the test norms, and the conditions under which the test was administered to pupils. A mismatch between test and classroom objectives, old or nonrepresentative norms, or not following prescribed administrative conditions can reduce the validity of decisions based on the test results.

Finally, test users must be cautious about assuming that commercial test scores are error-free. Small score differences should not be overinterpreted, because they rarely indicate meaningful performance differences.

CLASSROOM ASSESSMENT: SUMMING UP

As a way of summing up this book, let's revisit its central idea: that assessment is not an end in itself. It is a means to an end: classroom decision making. The decision-making process itself is made up of three steps: (1) collecting information, (2) interpreting information, and (3) making a decision based upon the interpretation. The validity of decisions depends upon both the quality of the information collected and the quality of the interpretation. Information is the raw material of classroom decision making, and meaning is added to this raw material when the teacher answers the question, "What is this information telling me?" Because the decisions that teachers make can affect both pupils and teachers in important ways, teachers are responsible for the quality of the assessment information they collect and the interpretations they make from that information.

Collecting Assessment Information

Good decisions are based upon good information, and three factors determine the quality of assessment information:

1. The conditions under which information is collected, including the physical and emotional context during assessment, the opportunity provided to pupils to show their typical behavior, and the quality of instruction provided prior to assessing achievement.
2. The quality of the instruments used to collect the information, including factors such as the clarity of test items or performance criteria, the relationship of an assessment procedure to the characteristic being assessed, and the appropriateness of the language level of items.
3. The objectivity of the information, including unbiased scoring.

If efforts are not made to minimize pitfalls, the assessment information that teachers rely on in their decision making will be seriously flawed. Consider, for example, the things that can lower the validity and reliability of the report card grades a teacher assigns.

♦ Portions of a teacher's achievement tests might assess things the pupils were not taught. (validity lowered)
♦ The items a teacher writes might be ambiguous, poorly written, or too complex for the pupils. (validity lowered)

◆ The sample of behavior observed might be too small to provide information about the pupils' typical behavior. (reliability lowered)

◆ Scoring of the assessment information might be careless and subjective. (validity and reliability lowered)

◆ Informal information about pupil interest, motivation, and attitude might be based on inappropriate indicators. (validity lowered)

Most teachers will interpret whatever information they have as if it were valid and reliable. If it is not, decisions will be faulty, and the grades will not be a valid indication of pupil learning. The same is true for all other teacher decisions.

Interpreting Assessment Information: Five Guidelines

The second step in decision making is interpreting the available assessment information. It is not until information is interpreted that decisions about classroom organization, discipline, planning, teaching, learning, and grading can be made. Although it is not reasonable to expect teachers to always interpret information correctly, it is reasonable to expect them to improve their interpretations as a result of conscientious practice.

Teachers are most likely to misinterpret assessment information early in the school year, when a pupil's behavior changes abruptly, or when new information about the pupil becomes available. In general, the less a teacher knows about a pupil, the more interpretation is required, and the more likely that subsequent interpretations will tend to be based upon earlier ones.

Key Assessment Tools 11.2 presents five general principles that should guide interpretation of classroom assessment information. These principles cut across all assessment purposes and types that have been discussed. The following describes these principles in greater detail.

Key Assessment Tools 11.2

PRINCIPLES FOR INTERPRETING ASSESSMENT INFORMATION

1. Assessment information describes pupils' learned behaviors and their present status.

2. Assessment information provides an estimate, not an exact indication, of pupil performance.

3. Single assessments are a poor basis for making important decisions about pupils.

4. Assessments do not always provide valid information.

5. Assessment information describes performance; it does not explain the reasons for it.

1. *Assessment information describes pupils' learned behaviors and their present status.* The behaviors and performances observed during assessment represent what pupils have learned to do, think, feel, and say. For a variety of reasons (e.g., cultural, societal, economic, familial), some pupils learn more, retain more, and have more opportunities to learn than others. Whatever the cause of these learning differences, the information provided by classroom assessment tells only about what pupils have learned to do.

Assessment also describes how pupils currently perform, not necessarily how they will perform in the future. Pupils can change. They can have sudden developmental spurts, become more interested in some things and less interested in others, and reach a point when they "bloom" academically after many years of poor performance or "hit the wall" and experience a decline in academic performance. Thus, when teachers or parents use words like *potential* and *capacity* to describe pupils, they are making assumptions that assessments do not always support. Discussion of a pupil's "capacity" suggests a fixed amount of ability, interest, or motivation that places a limit on a pupil's performance. Assessments cannot gauge such limits, and interpretations along these lines should be avoided. Interpretations focused on "potential" and "capacity" can be especially damaging to poor or disadvantaged pupils who often have had fewer opportunities to learn than other pupils, but who often perform quite well given proper opportunity and practice.

But isn't assessment information used to predict pupil success and adjustment? Aren't scores on the SAT and the ACT used by college admissions officers to predict pupils' performance in college? Don't the grades pupils receive in one school year often predict the grades they receive in future years? Aren't pupils in the lowest first grade reading group usually still in that group at the end of elementary school? Although these examples seem to suggest that assessments can provide information about pupils' potential or capacity, such a conclusion is faulty.

The chief reason that many pupils maintain the same subject grades or reading group placement over time has less to do with their "potential" or "capacity" than with the stability of their school and classroom environment. If we take a pupil at the start of first grade, place him or her in the lowest reading group, and provide objectives and instruction that are less challenging than those for other groups, we should not be surprised if the pupil fails to move out of that reading group by the end of the school year. This is an example of the self-fulfilling prophecy that was described in Chapter 2. It suggests that the reason assessments often remain stable over time has more to do with the nature of classroom expectations and instruction than with our ability to assess pupils' potential or capacity. Thus, assessment information should be interpreted as indicating a pupil's current level of performance, which can change.

2. *Assessment information provides an estimate, not an exact indication, of pupil performance.* Under no condition should assessment information be treated as if it were infallible or exact. There are always numerous sources of error that can influence pupils' performances. A single observation or test result has limited meaning and provides, at best, an approximation of a pupil's performance. Commercial achievement test publishers explicitly recognize this fact and use score bands to indicate the range of scores within which the pupil's true performance is likely to fall if tested many times. In all assessments, small differences or changes in pupils' performances should not be interpreted as real or significant. Placing Marcie in the top reading group and Jake in the middle reading group based upon a 3- or 4-point test score difference in reading performance is an over-interpretation of the assessment information.

Although informal assessments are rarely expressed numerically, they too are best treated as estimates of pupil performance. Individual assessments should always be interpreted with the above cautions in mind. The larger the sample of behavior obtained and the more varied the assessments used, the more confident a teacher can be when interpreting the information. In all cases, however, it is best to interpret assessments as if they provided an estimate of performance, not an exact indication of it.

3. *Single assessments are a poor basis for making important decisions about pupils.* Many teacher decisions can substantially affect the lives and opportunities of pupils. Consequently, such decisions should not be based on a single assessment. Also, a by-product of single-assessment decision making is the tendency to ignore additional information about pupils that might contribute to improving the validity of important decisions.

Unfortunately, in our fast-paced, bureaucratic world there is strong pressure to rely upon the results of a single assessment when making decisions. The growing use of scores from state-based tests to determine who will be promoted, receive a high school diploma, and require remedial education is one example of this pressure. Using a single score or rating seems objective and fair to people who do not understand the limitations of assessment information. Although reliance on single assessments makes decision making quicker and easier than collecting more broadly based information, it also increases the likelihood of making invalid decisions. Most teachers are sensitive to this danger and collect varied kinds of assessment information before making a grading, promotion, or placement decision about a pupil.

4. *Assessments do not always provide valid information.* Validity pertains to the interpretations made from assessment information. It deals with whether or not the information being collected is pertinent to the characteristics the teacher wishes to assess. Consequently, before interpreting assessment information, the classroom teacher should understand precisely what characteristic is being assessed. It is

important to know this because pupils are often described in terms of the general characteristics teachers think they have assessed, not in terms of the actual pupil behaviors observed. Thus, they describe a pupil as "unmotivated" as a result of receiving messy homework papers from that pupil; or they classify a pupil as a "poor learner" as a result of doing poorly on a classroom "achievement" test that was badly constructed and covered material not taught. Because the behavior actually observed is quickly replaced by more global labels like "unmotivated," "poor learner," "unintelligent," "self-confident," and "hard worker," it is very important that assessment information be a valid indicator of the desired pupil characteristic. Otherwise, improper interpretations and incorrect labeling will result.

5. *Assessment information describes performance; it does not explain the reasons for it.* An assessment describes pupil performance at a particular point in time: Jack was observed hitting Paul, Lisa performed poorly on the math test, Bart's oral speech was not well prepared, Ed acted up in class all day, Mary's astronomy project was the best in the class. When teachers observe pupils, they usually interpret their observations in terms of underlying causes they use to explain what they have seen. Jack hit Paul because he is aggressive. Lisa performed poorly on the math test because she is lazy. Bart has no interest in public speaking. Ed acted out because he is a defiant, spiteful child. Mary did the best work because she is the most motivated pupil in the astronomy class. Such interpretations of pupil behavior are typical, but often they are also incorrect and incomplete.

It is rarely possible to determine with reasonable certainty why pupils performed as they did just by examining the assessment itself. To explain pupil performance, teachers must look beyond the immediate assessment information. Did Paul provoke Jack into hitting him? Did Paul hit Jack first? Were they just horsing around? Was Lisa up all night working on a term paper? Did her grandmother recently die? The answers to these questions cannot be found in the original assessment information; new information must be collected to answer them. Teachers must be cautious when interpreting explanations of pupil performance because, more often than not, failure to look beyond the assessment information at hand leads to incorrect interpretations about pupils and their characteristics.

This caution is especially appropriate for minority pupils who have poor English fluency, limited out-of-school opportunities, or cultural behaviors different from those of the majority group. When a pupil is confronted by an unfamiliar language, new situations, or expectations that are alien to his or her culture, the underlying causes of that pupil's performance may be very different from those that underlie performance among majority group pupils. Teachers must be sensitive to such differences when interpreting pupils' performances. Key Assessment Tools 11.3 lists some specific do's and don'ts for interpreting assessment information.

> **Key Assessment Tools 11.3**
>
> ## GUIDELINES FOR INTERPRETING ASSESSMENT INFORMATION
>
> ◆ **Do** base interpretations on multiple sources of evidence.
>
> ◆ **Do** recognize the cultural and educational factors that influence and explain pupil performance.
>
> ◆ **Do** determine whether the information collected provides a valid description of a pupil's characteristics.
>
> ◆ **Do** recognize that any single assessment provides an estimate of a pupil's present status, which can change with changes in the environment.
>
> ◆ **Do** consider contextual factors that might provide alternative explanations for pupil behavior or performance.
>
> ◆ **Don't** use assessment results to draw conclusions about a pupil's capacity or potential.
>
> ◆ **Don't** treat small score or rating differences as if they were meaningful and important; scores and ratings that are similar, though not identical, should be treated the same.
>
> ◆ **Don't** rely upon a single assessment when making a decision that has important consequences for pupils.
>
> ◆ **Don't** confuse information provided by an assessment with explanations of what caused the performance; explanations must be sought outside the bounds of the original assessment information.
>
> ◆ **Don't** uncritically assume that an assessment procedure provides valid information about the desired characteristic.

Assessment: A Tool Used Wisely

Assessment is a chain of many links that imposes numerous responsibilities on teachers because it is such an integral part of what goes on in classrooms. It is not expected that teachers will always assess correctly, interpret information appropriately, and decide infallibly. However, it is expected that teachers will recognize their responsibilities in these areas and strive to carry them out as best they can. Remember, how teachers collect, interpret, and use assessment information has many important consequences for their pupils.

An analogy is an appropriate way to conclude. The automobile is a useful tool that enables us to accomplish a great many activities. When operated properly and with an understanding of its dangers and limitations, it saves much time and energy. However, if operated carelessly and improperly, the automobile also has the potential to inflict serious injury. When it was time for you to apply for your driver's license, your parents were apprehensive about the prospect of your driving. They knew the advantages of obtaining a license, but they also knew the dangers. They did not deny you the privilege of driving despite the dangers, but they probably explained to you both its benefits and its dangers. They also no doubt impressed on you the responsibility that accompanies being in control of an automobile. They said, "Get your license, drive, and take full advantage of the many benefits an automobile provides. But also be aware of the consequences of its misuse and of your responsibilities as a driver." The same advice is appropriate for your use of classroom assessment.

CHAPTER SUMMARY

CHAPTER REVIEW

Visit Chapter 11 of the Online Learning Center at **www.mhhe.com/ airasian5e** to take chapter quizzes, link to related websites, read PowerWeb articles and news feed updates, and access study tools, including the case study referenced in the chapter.

♦ Commercial standardized assessment instruments must be administered, scored, and interpreted in the same way no matter where or when they are used. Otherwise, valid interpretations of their scores are difficult.

♦ Although teachers have little voice in the selection and scoring of either type of commercial test, pressures are often exerted on them to ensure that their pupils do well on such tests.

♦ Commercial, norm-referenced tests are constructed and scored differently than teacher-made classroom assessments. The steps in construction are (1) identifying objectives that are common to most classrooms at a given grade level, (2) trying out many items to find ones that will spread out the scores of test takers for the final version of the test, (3) administering the final version to a large, national norm group of pupils, and (4) using the performance of the norm group as a basis for comparing the performance of pupils who subsequently take the test.

♦ Four criteria are used to judge the adequacy of commercial standardized test norms: sample size, representativeness, recency, and description of procedures.

♦ Commercial standardized achievement tests usually come in the form of a test battery containing subtests in a variety of subject areas. Scores are provided for each subtest and a composite score is provided for the overall test. The scores for a pupil or a class can be compared across subtests to identify strengths and weaknesses.

♦ To make valid interpretations from a commercial achievement test, you must follow its directions strictly.

♦ Special comparative and developmental scores are used to represent pupil performance on commercial achievement tests. The most commonly used scores are (1) the percentile rank, which indicates the percentage of similar pupils nationwide a given pupil scored above, (2) the stanine, which uses the scores 1 to 9 to indicate whether a pupil is below average (stanines 1, 2, and 3), average (stanines 4, 5, and 6), or above average (stanines 7, 8, and 9) compared to similar pupils nationwide, and (3) the grade equivalent score, which is a developmental score that indicates whether a pupil is above, below, or at the level of similar pupils in his or her grade nationwide.

◆ A pupil's test performance may appear quite different depending on the norm group (e.g., national, state, local, high or low achieving) to which he or she is being compared.

◆ Caution should be exercised when interpreting small differences in norm-referenced test scores, especially percentile ranks and grade equivalent scores. Since all tests have some degree of error in them, it is best to think of a score not as a single number, but as a range of numbers, any one of which indicates the pupil's true performance. Small differences in test scores are usually insignificant.

◆ Interpretation and use of commercial, norm-referenced achievement tests should be guided by a number of concerns: how well the tested content matches classroom instruction, how the information agrees or disagrees with the teacher's own perceptions of pupils, the recency of the test norms, the extent to which administrative directions were followed, and the understanding that no score is exact or infallible.

◆ Commercial achievement tests provide useful comparative and developmental information that teachers cannot get for themselves. However, teachers should always use such information in conjunction with their own assessments when making decisions about pupils. Usually, the two types of information corroborate each other.

QUESTIONS FOR DISCUSSION

1. Are standardized tests fair to all students? Why or why not? What personal characteristics could influence how a student does on a standardized test? Would these same characteristics influence how he or she performs on a teacher-prepared test? Why?

2. What can a teacher do to help make students less anxious about taking standardized tests? Would the same actions help students when they take teacher-prepared tests?

3. If you could select only one scoring format from a norm-referenced standardized test to explain to parents, which would you choose? Why? What are the limitations of your choice?

4. What factors should influence the use of commercial standardized test results for assessment by classroom teachers?

5. What are the differences in the information provided by a norm-referenced and a criterion-referenced standardized test?

6. What are some validity issues concerning commercial standardized tests?

7. How should results be communicated to parents?

ACTIVITY

Read the standardized test home report for Ken Allen, a fifth grade student in Figure 11.4. Your task is to write a one-page letter to Ken's parents explaining the results of his performance on the California Achievement Tests. The following suggestions should guide your letter.

◆ Ken's parents will receive a copy of the test report sheet.
◆ Ken's parents are not standardized testing experts and basically want to know how their son performed.
◆ You should start with some information about the test and its purpose.
◆ You should describe the information in the test report sheet.
◆ You should interpret the information about Ken's performance.
◆ What are Ken's overall strengths and weaknesses? How can the parents see these on the test report form?
◆ Describe Ken's overall performance to the parents.
◆ Indicate what the parents should do if they have questions.

Your letter will be judged on the accuracy of the information about Ken's performance you convey to the parents *and* the extent to which you make the information understandable to them. You do not have to convey every bit of information in the test report. You must identify the most important information and convey that in a way that parents can understand. A letter full of technical terms will not do. A letter full of technical terms will not do. Remember, parents can always arrange to visit you in school if more information is desired.

REVIEW QUESTIONS

1. What is a commercial standardized test? What information can such a test provide a teacher that a teacher-made or textbook test cannot? What is a test battery? What are subtests? How does the construction of a standardized achievement test differ from that of a teacher-made achievement test? Why are there these differences?

2. What are test norms? What information do they provide a teacher about a pupil's performance? How are the following norms interpreted: percentile rank, stanine, and grade equivalent score? How do test norms differ from raw scores? Why are norms used instead of raw scores?

3. What are fall and spring norms? Why do standardized tests provide them?

4. What factors should teachers consider when they try to interpret their pupils' standardized test scores? That is, what factors influence the results of standardized tests and thus should be thought about when interpreting scores?

REFERENCES

CTB/McGraw-Hill. (1986a). *California achievement tests forms E and F: Test coordinator's handbook.* Monterey, CA: CTB/McGraw-Hill.

CTB/McGraw-Hill. (1986b). *California achievement tests forms E and F: Class management guide.* Monterey, CA: CTB/McGraw-Hill.

Heaney, K. J., and Pullin, D. C. (1998). Accommodations and flags: Admission testing and the rights of individuals with disabilities. *Educational Assessment, 5* (2), 71–93.

Popham, W. J. (2000). *Modern educational measurement:* Practical guidelines for educational leaders, 3rd edition. Boston, MA: Allyn & Bacon. Englewood Cliffs, NJ: Prentice-Hall.

The Psychological Corporation. (1984). *Stanford Achievement Test technical review manual.* New York: The Psychological Corporation.

Riverside Publishing Co. (1986). *Iowa Tests of Basic Skills: Preliminary technical summary.* Chicago: Riverside.

APPENDIX A
Standards for Teacher Competence
in Educational Assessment of Students

The professional education associations began working in 1987 to develop standards for teacher competence in student assessment out of concern that the potential educational benefits of student assessments be fully realized. The Committee[1] appointed to this project completed its work in 1990 following reviews of earlier drafts by members of the measurement, teaching, and teacher preparation and certification communities. Parallel committees of affected associations are encouraged to develop similar statements of qualifications for school administrators, counselors, testing directors, supervisors, and other educators in the near future. These statements are intended to guide the preservice and in-service preparation of educators, the accreditation of preparation programs, and the future certification of all educators.[2]

A standard is defined here as a principle generally accepted by the professional associations responsible for this document. Assessment is defined as the process of obtaining information that is used to make educational decisions about students, to give feedback to the student about his or her progress, strengths, and weaknesses, to judge instructional effectiveness and curricular adequacy, and to inform policy. The various assessment techniques include, but are not limited to, formal and informal observation, qualitative analysis of pupil performance and products, paper-and-pencil tests, oral questioning, and analysis of student records. The assessment competencies included here are the knowledge and skills critical to a teacher's role as educator. It is understood that there are many competencies beyond assessment competencies which teachers must possess.

By establishing standards for teacher competence in student assessment, the associations subscribe to the view that student assessment is an essential

Standards developed by the American Federation of Teachers, the National Council on Measurement in Education, and the National Education Association. Copyright © 1990 by the National Council on Measurement in Education. Reprinted by permission of the publisher.

part of teaching and that good teaching cannot exist without good student assessment. Training to develop the competencies covered in the standards should be an integral part of preservice preparation. Further, such assessment training should be widely available to practicing teachers through staff development programs at the district and building levels.

The standards are intended for use as:

◆ A guide for teacher educators as they design and approve programs for teacher preparation

◆ A self-assessment guide for teachers in identifying their needs for professional development in student assessment

◆ A guide for workshop instructors as they design professional development experiences for in-service teachers

◆ An impetus for educational measurement specialists and teacher trainers to conceptualize student assessment and teacher training in student assessment more broadly than has been the case in the past

The standards should be incorporated into future teacher training and certification programs. Teachers who have not had the preparation these standards imply should have the opportunity and support to develop these competencies before the standards enter into the evaluation of these teachers.

Approach Used to Develop the Standards

The members of the associations that supported this work are professional educators involved in teaching, teacher education, and student assessment. Members of these associations are concerned about the inadequacy with which teachers are prepared for assessing the educational progress of their students, and thus sought to address this concern effectively. A committee named by the associations first met in September 1987 and affirmed its commitment to defining standards for teacher preparation in student assessment. The committee then undertook a review of the research literature to identify needs in student assessment, current levels of teacher training in student assessment, areas of teacher activities requiring competence in using student assessments, and current levels of teacher competence in student assessment.

The members of the committee used their collective experience and expertise to formulate and then revise statements of important assessment competencies. Drafts of these competencies went through several revisions by the committee before the standards were released for public review. Comments by reviewers from each of the associations were then used to prepare a final statement.

Scope of a Teacher's Professional Role and Responsibilities for Student Assessment

There are seven standards in this document. In recognizing the critical need to revitalize classroom assessment, some standards focus on classroom-based competencies. Because of teachers' growing roles in education and policy decisions beyond the classroom, other standards address assessment competencies underlying teacher participation in decisions related to assessment at the school, district, state, and national levels.

The scope of a teacher's professional role and responsibilities for student assessment may be described in terms of the following activities. These activities imply that teachers need competence in student assessment and sufficient time and resources to complete them in a professional manner:

♦ **Activities Occurring Prior to Instruction.** (a) Understanding students' cultural backgrounds, interests, skills, and abilities as they apply across a range of learning domains and/or subject areas; (b) understanding students' motivations and their interests in specific class content; (c) clarifying and articulating the performance outcomes expected of pupils; and (d) planning instruction for individuals or groups of students

♦ **Activities Occurring During Instruction.** (a) Monitoring pupil progress toward instructional goals; (b) identifying gains and difficulties pupils are experiencing in learning and performing; (c) adjusting instruction; (d) giving contingent, specific, and credible praise and feedback; (e) motivating students to learn; and (f) judging the extent of pupil attainment of instructional outcomes

♦ **Activities Occurring after the Appropriate Instructional Segment (e.g., Lesson, Class, Semester, Grade).** (a) Describing the extent to which each pupil has attained both short- and long-term instructional goals; (b) communicating strengths and weaknesses based on assessment results to students and parents or guardians; (c) recording and reverting assessment results for school-level analysis, evaluation, and decision making; (d) analyzing assessment information gathered before and during instruction to understand each student's progress to date and to inform future instructional planning; (e) evaluating the effectiveness of instruction; and (f) evaluating the effectiveness of the curriculum and materials in use

♦ **Activities Associated with a Teacher's Involvement in School Building and School District Decision Making.** (a) Serving on a school or district committee examining the school's and district's strengths and weaknesses in the development of its students; (b) working on the development or selection of assessment methods for school building or school district use; (c) evaluating school district curriculum; and (d) other related activities

◆ **Activities Associated with a Teacher's Involvement in a Wider Community of Educators.** (a) Serving on a state committee asked to develop learning goals and associated assessment methods; (b) participating in reviews of the appropriateness of district, state, or national student goals and associated assessment method; and (c) interpreting the results of state and national student assessment programs

Each standard that follows is an expectation for assessment knowledge or skill that a teacher should possess in order to perform well in the five areas just described. As a set, the standards call on teachers to demonstrate skill at selecting, developing, applying, using, communicating, and evaluating student assessment information and student assessment practices. A brief rationale and illustrative behaviors follow each standard.

The standards represent a conceptual framework or scaffolding from which specific skills can be derived. Work to make these standards operational will be needed even after they have been published. It is also expected that experience in the application of these standards should lead to their improvement and further development.

1. **Teachers should be skilled in choosing assessment methods appropriate for instructional decisions.** Skills in choosing appropriate, useful, administratively convenient, technically adequate, and fair assessment methods are prerequisite to good use of information to support instructional decisions. Teachers need to be well acquainted with the kinds of information provided by a broad range of assessment alternatives and their strengths and weaknesses. In particular, they should be familiar with criteria for evaluating and selecting assessment methods in light of instructional plans.

   Teachers who meet this standard will have the conceptual and application skills that follow. They will be able to use the concepts of assessment error and validity when developing or selecting their approaches to classroom assessment of students. They will understand how valid assessment data can support instructional activities such as providing appropriate feedback to students, diagnosing group and individual learning needs, planning for individualized educational programs, motivating students, and evaluating instructional procedures. They will understand how invalid information can affect instructional decisions about students. They will also be able to use and evaluate assessment options available to them, considering among other things, the cultural, social, economic, and language backgrounds of students. They will be aware that different assessment approaches can be incompatible with certain instructional goals and may impact quite differently on their teaching.

   Teachers will know, for each assessment approach they use, its appropriateness for making decisions about their pupils. Moreover, teachers will know where to find information about and/or reviews of various assessment methods. Assessment options are diverse and include text- and curriculum-embedded questions and tests, standardized criterion-referenced and norm-referenced tests, oral questioning, spontaneous and structured performance assessments, portfolios, exhibitions, demonstrations, rating scales, writing samples, paper-and-pencil tests, seatwork and homework, peer- and self-assessments, student records, observations, questionnaires, interviews, projects, products, and others' opinions.

2. **Teachers should be skilled in developing assessment methods appropriate for instructional decisions.** While teachers often use published or other external assessment tools, the bulk of the assessment information they use for decision making comes from approaches they create and implement. Indeed, the assessment demands of the classroom go well beyond readily available instruments.

   Teachers who meet this standard will have the conceptual and application skills that follow. Teachers will be skilled in planning the collection of information that facilitates the decisions they will make. They will know and follow appropriate, principles for developing and using assessment methods in their teaching, avoiding common pitfalls in student assessment. Such techniques may include several of the options listed at the end of the first standard. The teacher will select the techniques which are appropriate to the intent of the teacher's instruction.

   Teachers meeting this standard will also be skilled in using student data to analyze the quality of each assessment technique they use. Since most teachers do not have access to assessment specialists, they must be prepared to do these analyses themselves.

3. **Teachers should be skilled in administering, scoring, and interpreting the results of both externally produced and teacher-produced assessment methods.** It is not enough that teachers are able to select and develop good assessment methods; they must also be able to apply them properly. Teachers should be skilled in administering, scoring, and interpreting results from diverse assessment methods.

   Teachers who meet this standard will have the conceptual and application skills that follow. They will be skilled in interpreting informal and formal teacher-produced assessment results, including pupils' performances in class and on homework assignments. Teachers will be able to use guides for scoring essay questions and projects, stencils for scoring response-choice questions, and scales for rating performance assessments. They will be able to use these in ways that produce consistent results.

   Teachers will be able to administer standardized achievement tests and be able to interpret the commonly reported scores: percentile ranks, percentile band scores, standard scores, and grade equivalents. They will have a conceptual understanding of the summary indexes commonly reported with assessment results: measures of central tendency, dispersion, relationships, reliability, and errors of measurement.

Teachers will be able to apply these concepts of score and summary indexes in ways that enhance their use of the assessments that they develop. They will be able to analyze assessment results to identify pupils' strengths and errors. If they get inconsistent results, they will seek other explanations for the discrepancy or other data to attempt to resolve the uncertainty before arriving at a decision. They will be able to use assessment methods in ways that encourage students' educational development and that do not inappropriately increase students' anxiety levels.

4. **Teachers should be skilled in using assessment results when making decisions about individual students, planning teaching, developing curriculum, and school improvements.** Assessment results are used to make educational decisions at several levels: in the classroom about students, in the community about a school and a school district, and in society, generally, about the purposes and outcomes of the educational enterprise. Teachers play a vital role when participating in decision making at each of these levels and must be able to use assessment results effectively.

Teachers who meet this standard will have the conceptual and application skills that follow. They will be able to use accumulated assessment information to organize a sound instructional plan for facilitating students' educational development. When using assessment results to plan and/or evaluate instruction and curriculum, teachers will interpret the results correctly and avoid common misinterpretations, such as basing decisions on scores that lack curriculum validity. They will be informed about the results of local, regional, state, and national assessment and about their appropriate use for pupil, classroom, school, district, state, and national educational improvement.

5. **Teachers should be skilled in developing valid pupil grading procedures which use pupil assessments.** Grading students is an important part of professional practice for teachers. Grading is defined as indicating both a student's level of performance and a teacher's valuing of that performance. The principles for using assessments to obtain valid grades are known and teachers should employ them.

Teachers who meet this standard will have the conceptual and application skills that follow. They will be able to devise, implement, and explain a procedure for developing grades composed of marks from various assignments, projects, in-class activities, quizzes, tests, and/or other assessments that they may use. Teachers will understand and be able to articulate why the grades they assign are rational, justified, and fair, acknowledging that such grades reflect their preferences and judgments. Teachers will be able to recognize and to avoid faulty grading procedures such as using grades as punishment. They will be able to evaluate and to modify their grading procedures in order to improve the validity of the interpretations made from them about students' attainments.

6. **Teachers should be skilled in communicating assessment results to students, parents, other lay audiences, and other educators.** Teachers must routinely report assessment results to students and to parents or guardians. In addition, they are frequently asked to report or to discuss assessment results with other educators and with diverse lay audiences. If the results are not communicated effectively, they may be misused or not used. To communicate effectively with others on matters of student assessment, teachers must be able to use assessment terminology appropriately and must be able to articulate the meaning, limitations, and implications of assessment results. Furthermore, teachers will sometimes be in a position that will require them to defend their own assessment procedures and their interpretations of them. At other times, teachers may need to help the public to interpret assessment results appropriately.

Teachers who meet this standard will have the conceptual and application skills that follow. Teachers will understand and be able to give appropriate explanations of how the interpretation of student assessments must be moderated by the student's socioeconomic, cultural, language, and other background factors. Teachers will be able to explain that assessment results do not imply that such background factors limit a student's ultimate educational development. They will be able to communicate to students and to their parents or guardians how they may assess the student's educational progress. Teachers will understand and be able to explain the importance of taking measurement errors into account when using assessments to make decisions about individual students. Teachers will be able to explain the limitations of different informal and formal assessment methods. They will be able to explain printed reports of the results of pupil assessments at the classroom, school district, state, and national levels.

7. **Teachers should be skilled in recognizing unethical, illegal, and otherwise inappropriate assessment methods and uses of assessment information.** Fairness, the rights of all concerned, and professional ethical behavior must undergird all student assessment activities from the initial planning for and gathering of information to the interpretation, use, and communication of the results. Teachers must be well-versed in their own ethical and legal responsibilities in assessment. In addition, they should also attempt to have the inappropriate assessment practices of others discontinued whenever they are encountered. Teachers should also participate with the wider educational community in defining the limits of appropriate professional behavior in assessment.

Teachers who meet this standard will have the conceptual and application skills that follow. They will know those laws and case decisions which affect their classroom, school district, and state assessment practices. Teachers will be aware that various assessment procedures can be misused or overused resulting in harmful consequences such as embarrassing students, violating a student's right to confidentiality, and inappropriately using students' standardized achievement test scores to measure teaching effectiveness.

Notes

[1]The Committee that developed this statement was appointed by the collaborating professional associations. James R. Sanders (Western Michigan University) chaired the Committee and represented NCME along with John R. Hills (Florida State University) and Anthony J. Nitki (University of Pittsburgh). Jack C. Merwin (University of Minnesota) represented the American Association of Colleges for Teacher Education, Carolyn Trice represented the American Federation of Teachers, and Marcella Dianda and Jeffrey Schneider represented the National Education Association.

[2]The associations invite comments that may be used for improvement of this document. Comments may be sent to: Teacher Standards in Student Assessment, American Federation of Teachers, 555 New Jersey Avenue, NW, Washington, DC 20001; Teacher Standards in Student Assessment, National Council on Measurement in Education, 1230 Seventeenth Street, NW, Washington, DC 20036; or Teacher Standards in Student Assessment, Instruction and Professional Development, National Education Association, 1201 Sixteenth Street, NW, Washington, DC 20036.

Please note that this document is not copyrighted material and that reproduction and dissemination are encouraged.

APPENDIX B
Taxonomy of Educational Objectives: Major Categories

Major Categories in the Cognitive Domain[1]	Major Categories in the Affective Domain[2]	Major Categories in the Psychomotor Domain[3]
1. Knowledge	1. Receiving	1. Perception
2. Comprehension	2. Responding	2. Set
3. Application	3. Valuing	3. Guided Response
4. Analysis	4. Organization	4. Mechanism
5. Synthesis	5. Characterization by a Value or Value Complex	5. Complex Overt Response
6. Evaluation		6. Adaptation
		7. Origination

[1]From Benjamin S. Bloom et al., *Taxonomy of Educational Objectives: Book 1, Cognitive Domain*. Published by Allyn & Bacon, Boston, MA copyright © 1999 by Pearson Education.
[2]From David R. Krathwohl, Benjamin S. Bloom, & Bertram B. Masia, *Taxonomy of Educational Objectives: Book 2, Affective Domain*. Published by Allyn & Bacon, Boston, MA. Copyright © 1984 by Pearson Education.
[3]From *The Classification of Educational Objectives in the Psychomotor Domain*, by E. J. Simpson, 1972, Washington, DC: Gryphon House.

APPENDIX C
Sample Individual Education Plan

This is one example of an IEP form, used by a team of educators and a parent to plan the teaching of an individual pupil with a disability.

I. DEMOGRAPHIC INFORMATION

	Date (MM/DD/YY)	_____
Print Student's Name (Last) (First) (M.I.) _____	Student ID No.	_____

Address	Telephone	Date of Birth
Home School Name	Assigned School Name (Complete After Section X)	

II. CONFERENCE INFORMATION

Conference Date: _____   ☐ Interim Review Date: _____
(MM/DD/YY)   (MM/DD/YY)

Conference Type: ☐ Initial   ☐ Annual Review   ☐ Temporary Assignment   ☐ Reevaluation

(Check all that apply.)

☐ Consideration to/from Alternative Education Program   ☐ Region Staffing   ☐ District Placement Committee

Parent Notification:	Type	Date (MM/DD/YY)	Response
*Required	*(1) Written (Attach to IEP) *(2)		

Model/Language of Communication of Parent/Guardian _____

III. SIGNATURES AND POSITIONS OF PERSONS ATTENDING CONFERENCE

☐ Procedural Safeguards Available to Parents of Exceptional Students has been received by and was explained to the parent(s) or guardian(s) of the student.

☐ Parent was not in attendance.

_____ (LEA Representative)	_____ (_____)
_____ (Parent)	_____ (_____)
_____ (Parent)	_____ (_____)
_____ (Evaluation Specialist)	_____ (_____)
_____ (Teacher)	_____ (_____)
_____ (Student)	_____ (_____)

IV. EXCEPTIONAL STUDENT EDUCATION (ESE) PROGRAM ELIGIBILITY

The student has been determined eligible for the following ESE programs: _____

_____

_____

V. PRESENT PERFORMANCE LEVELS/NARRATIVE

(Do not complete if addressed on Individual Transition Plan insert.)

Area Assessed	Date (MM/YY)	Instrument	Level/Ability

Narrative: _____

_____

_____

_____

VI. DIPLOMA OPTION (Grades 8–12 only)

☐ Standard Diploma   ☐ Special Diploma

VII. PROGRAMS FOR LIMITED ENGLISH PROFICIENT (LEP) EXCEPTIONAL STUDENTS
(Complete this section only if the student is LEP.)

Home Language of Student _____

Language Dominance/Proficiency Assessment: _____ _____ _____
                                             (MM/DD/YY)   (Test Used)   (ESOL Level)

ESOL Entry Date _____   Test Used _____   Raw Score _____
             (MM/DD/YY)

ESOL Exit Date _____   Test Used _____   Raw Score _____
             (MM/DD/YY)

Results of Most Recent Standardized Achievement Test (if applicable): _____

Type and Location of LEP Services: (Check all that apply based upon present performance levels, behavioral observations, and the language dominance/proficiency assessment.)

	Regular Program*	ESE Program**
☐ English for Speakers of Other Languages (ESOL)	☐	☐
☐ Curriculum Content in English Using ESOL Strategies	☐	☐
☐ Curriculum Content in the Home Language (Elementary Schools)	☐	☐
☐ Bilingual Curriculum Content (Secondary Schools)	☐	☐
☐ Home Language Arts or ☐ Home Language Strategies	☐	☐
	*LEP Plan Required	**Attach Goals and Objectives.

Post Reclassification Monitoring (for exited students who continue to participate in an ESE program.)

Please Note: Monitoring procedures do not require parent notification or signature.

For use by IEP committee only:

1. Date: _____   ☐ No change in status   ☐ Refer to IEP committee
       (MM/DD/YY)
Signature:_____

☐ reclassify
Date:_____
       (MM/DD/YY)

2. Date: _____   ☐ No change in status   ☐ Refer to IEP committee
       (MM/DD/YY)
Signature:_____

☐ reclassify
Date:_____
       (MM/DD/YY)

3. Date: _____   ☐ No change in status   ☐ Refer to IEP committee
       (MM/DD/YY)
Signature:_____

☐ reclassify
Date:_____
       (MM/DD/YY)

VIII. EDUCATIONAL AND RELATED SERVICES

1. The committee has determined that the attached annual goals and short term objectives (K-8) or Individual Transition Plan (9–12 or earlier if appropriate) is necessary to provide appropriate education.

2. The committee has determined that the student be enrolled in:

   ☐ Regular Physical Education   ☐ ESE Physical Education   ☐ Not Applicable

   (Attach goals and objectives)

3. The committee has determined that the student requires the following related services to access an educational program:

   ☐ Physician's Request for In-School Nursing and/or Respiratory Therapy Services submitted. Implementation contingent upon review by the Office of Exceptional Student Education.

   ☐ Authorized   ☐ Not Authorized   ☐ Date: _____   Initial: _____

   ☐ Special Transportation: (specify)   ☐ Individual PickUp   ☐ Lift Bus   ☐ Safety Vest

   ☐ Other: _____

   ☐ No Related Services Required at this time.

IX. OTHER PERTINENT INFORMATION

☐ Medication(s): _____

☐ Other (e.g., allergies, restrictions): _____

☐ Board Approved Physical Restraint Procedures may be used if student presents a danger to self and/or others, or property.

☐ Student will participate in State Assessment Programs (e.g., Florida Writes, High School Competency Test). Modifications may include:

   ☐ Flexible Scheduling   ☐ Flexible Setting   ☐ Recording of Answers   ☐ Revised Format   ☐ Auditory Aids

☐ Student will participate in other assessment programs (e.g., Stanford Achievement Test, Scholastic Aptitude Test). Modifications may be requested prior to testing.

X. LEAST RESTRICTIVE ENVIRONMENT (LRE) PLACEMENT

Considerations: Some of the factors considered in selecting the student's placement and ensuring that it is in the least restrictive environment include the following: (Check all that apply.)

☐ Student frustration and stress

☐ Student self-esteem and worth

☐ Disruption of students in regular classes

☐ Disruption of students in special education classes

☐ Distractibility

☐ Need for lower pupil-to-teacher ratio

☐ Time required to master educational objectives

☐ Need for instructional technology

☐ Mobility problems in a large school setting

☐ Safety concerns due to physical conditions

☐ Health and safety concerns requiring adaptive equipment

☐ Emotional control causing harm to self and others

☐ Social skills causing increased isolation

☐ Difficulty completing tasks

☐ Other(s):_____

_____

Placement(s): The following placement decision is based upon a review and consideration of former placements, current performance levels, parent comments, behavioral observations, goals and objectives, previous educational modifications, the extent to which the student can participate in the regular education program, and/or other information delineated on this IEP. The committee believes that for each program listed below, the student requires special education from an ESE teacher for the specified amount of hours/periods per week.

Program	Hours/Periods per Week
_____	_____
_____	_____
_____	_____
_____	_____

* For Speech, Language, Occupational Therapy, and Physical Therapy, time may be expressed as a range of minutes within 30 minute blocks (e.g., 30–60 min./wk.).

(Check if applicable.) ☐ The student will be removed from the regular education program for more than 50% of the school day because this is the least restrictive environment.

Program Location:

Will the student be educated in the school he or she would attend if non-handicapped?   ☐ Yes   ☐ No

The goals and objectives of the IEP can be appropriately met at: _____

(Name of School)

XI. REGULAR EDUCATION PARTICIPATION

(Regular/vocational education teacher(s) should be included in, or informed of, results of IEP development.)

Description of participation (e.g., specific subjects, art, assemblies, yearbook, lunch, field trips, fund-raising, recess, etc.): _____

_____

_____

Modification required:

(select as appropriate)   ☐ Increase/decrease instructional time   ☐ Use of special communication system

☐ Vary instructional methodology   ☐ Modification of tests

☐ Consultation   ☐ Other(s): Specify below

Mainstream Cost Factor (specify):

(1) Services, aids and/or equipment   (2) Applicable subject(s)   (3) Amount of time per week

_____

_____

_____

XII. IEP IMPLEMENTATION

Persons responsible for the implementation of this IEP include:

☐ ESE Teacher   ☐ Occupational Therapist   ☐ Physical Therapist   ☐ Orientation and Mobility Specialist   ☐ Speech/Language Pathologist

☐ Other(s):_____

_____

XIII. INITIATION/DURATION DATES

Services delineated on the IEP, unless otherwise indicated:

• Will initiate _____.
          (MM/DD/YY)

• and have an anticipated duration through _____.
                (MM/DD/YY)

XIV. PARENT(S)/GUARDIAN(S) COMMENTS

Parent(s)/Guardian(s), if present, please indicate: ☐ Agreement   or   ☐ Disagreement

Comments: _____

_____

_____

_____

Notes: _____

_____

_____

_____

_____

_____

_____

_____

Source: Vaughn, S., Bos, C., Schumm, J. (2000). *Teaching Exceptional, Diverse, and At-Risk Students in the General Education Classroom,* 2nd edition. Boston, MA: Allyn & Bacon.

APPENDIX D
Statistical Applications for Classroom Assessment

This appendix describes some of the basic statistical information classroom teachers can use in scoring and interpreting their pupils' test performance. It contains a basic introduction to four areas: (1) raw scores and score distributions, (2) the mean and standard deviation, (3) item difficulty and discrimination, and (4) the normal distribution and standardized test scores.

Raw Scores and Score Distributions

A *raw score* indicates the number of points a pupil got on a test. For example, Joe took a 70-item multiple-choice test and got 42 items correct. If 1 point is given for each correct answer, his raw score is 42. Jemma took a 20-item short-answer test on which each item counted 5 points. She got 17 items correct and thus received a raw score of 85 (17 items × 5 points each). Most frequently, raw scores are converted to percentage scores using the formula: raw score/highest possible score × 100 = percentage score. Thus Joe's percentage score is 60 (42/70 × 100 = 60), and Jemma's percentage score is 85 (85/100 × 100 = 85).

Either raw or percentage scores can be arranged into a **test score distribution** that shows how the class as a whole performed. The raw and percentage scores for a class of 15 pupils who took a math test that had 10 problems worth 5 points each appear in Table D.1.

The performance of this class can be represented in a test score distribution by listing scores from highest to lowest. Test score distributions can be based on either raw scores or percentage scores. To construct a distribution, start by listing the possible scores pupils could have earned. For example, the class above took a 10-item test on which each item counted 5 points. Thus, the only raw scores possible ranged from 50 to 0 in 5-point increments (i.e., 50, 45, 40, 35, . . ., 15, 10, 5, 0). Similarly, since percentage scores are based on a 100-point scale, the only percentage scores possible on the 10-item test ranged from 100 to 0 in 10-point increments (i.e., 100, 90, 80, . . ., 20, 10, 0). The test score distributions in Table D.2 show how the class did. "Number" indicates the number of pupils who got a

TABLE D.1

Name	Raw Score (Number Right × 5)	Percentage Score (Raw Score/50 × 100)
Lloyd	25	50
Chris	35	70
Jennifer	50	100
Kristen	40	80
Gail	25	50
Marta	35	70
Marita	40	80
David	40	80
Juan	45	90
Mike	20	40
Ted	30	60
Charles	50	100
Christina	35	70
Heather	40	80
Sara	50	100

TABLE D.2

Raw Score Distribution		Percentage Score Distribution	
Raw Score	Number	Percentage Score	Number
50	3	100	3
45	1	90	1
40	4	80	4
35	3	70	3
30	1	60	1
25	2	50	2
20	1	40	1
15	0	30	0
10	0	20	0
5	0	10	0
0	0	0	0

particular score; for example, three pupils got a raw score of 50, four got 40, and none got 10.

The two test score distributions show the same information on two different scales. The raw score scale is based on the total number of points on the test, 50, while the percentage score scale is based on a test of 100 total points. Teachers often transform the raw score distribution into a percent-

TABLE D.3		
Name	**Raw Score**	**Percentage Score**
Lloyd	25	50
Chris	35	70
Jennifer	50	100
Kristen	40	80
Gail	25	50
Marta	35	70
Marita	40	80
David	40	80
Juan	45	90
Mike	20	40
Ted	30	60
Charles	50	100
Christina	35	70
Heather	40	80
Sara	50	100
Sum of scores	560	1120

age score distribution to keep all of their tests on a 100-point scale. Recall from Chapter 10 that Ms. Fogarty did this with her test, quiz, and project scores so there would be comparability across them.

Notice also that the above example is intended to be mathematically simple to convey the basic ideas of test score distributions. For practice, redo this example assuming that the pupils' raw scores remained the same but that the test had 12 items worth 5 points each.

Summarizing Test Scores

The Mean

Test score distributions are useful, but often teachers want to summarize the information they provide into a single score that represents the performance of the class. There are many ways to summarize scores, but the most common is the **mean.** The mean, also commonly called the **average,** is calculated by adding together each pupil's test score and dividing the total by the number of pupils. One can calculate the mean of either raw scores or percentage scores.

The original raw and percentage scores for our hypothetical class appear in Table D.3. The sums of the raw and percentage scores are shown at the bottom of the table. If these sums are divided by the total number of pupils, 15, the raw and percentage score means are 37.33 and 74.67, respectively.

TABLE D.4	
Raw Score	**Number**
50	3
45	1
40	4
35	3
30	1
25	2
20	1
15	0
10	0
5	0
0	0

These means provide a single-number description of the class's performance. The mean raw score for the class is 37.33 out of 50, and the mean percentage score is 74.67 out of 100.

Two additional, though less frequently used, indices of the average performance of a class are the median and the mode. The **median** is the middle score in the test score distribution, after the scores have been arranged in order from highest to lowest. The **mode** is the score that more pupils got than any other. Medians and modes are best determined after constructing a test score distribution. For example, consider the score distribution in Table D.4.

The median is the middle score in the distribution. Because there are 15 pupils who took the test, the middle score is the eighth from the top. Three pupils had raw scores of 50, one had a raw score of 45, and four had a score of 40. Thus, the eighth score from the top is a 40, and this is the median. Note that if there is an even number of scores in the distribution, the median would be determined by taking the average of the two middle scores. The mode is the score (or scores, as there can be more than one mode) that more pupil received than any other. The distribution shows that the score more pupils got than any other was 40, so the mode is 40. In this case, the median and the mode were the same, although this is not always the case.

The Standard Deviation

Suppose that two classes were tested with the same test and that the mean score in each class was 74. Could we conclude that performance in the two classes was identical? No, we could not, because the mean does not tell us how the scores of the two classes are distributed from high to low. Table D.5 compares the scores of pupils in two classes, each of which has a mean of 74.

TABLE D.5

Pupil	Class A	Class B
1	72	74
2	76	64
3	74	84
4	75	50
5	73	98
6	74	60
7	77	88
8	71	59
9	72	89
10	76	74
Sum	740	740
Mean	74	74

Construct two score distributions to compare the classes. Would you say that the performance in the two classes was identical?

Comparing the performance of the two classes indicates that the pupils in class A performed much more alike than the pupils in class B. The **range,** or the difference between the highest and lowest score, was 6 (77–71) in class A and 48 (98–50) in class B. In other words, pupils in class A were much more similar, or homogeneous, in their performance than pupils in class B, who were quite heterogeneous. The mean score for each class, though the same, does not indicate how similar or dissimilar the scores within the classes were. Note how a sense of the spread of scores could be obtained by examining the score distribution for each class.

When we describe a test score distribution, we also must consider the extent to which the scores are spread out around the mean. To find out about this characteristic of scores, we use another statistic called the **standard deviation.** The standard deviation provides information about score variability—that is, how similar or dissimilar a class's test scores are. Usually, test scores are described by both their mean and standard deviation. The mean tells about the average performance of a class, and the standard deviation tells about how homogeneous or heterogeneous scores were within the class.

Mathematically, the standard deviation (σ) is represented as:

$$\sigma \ (\text{Standard deviation}) = \sqrt{\frac{\text{sum of } (x^2)}{n}}$$

where x is the difference of a pupil's score from the mean (score minus the mean) and n is the number of pupils who were tested. Calculating the standard deviation for class A's scores would be done as shown in Table D.6,

TABLE D.6

Pupil	Class A	(Pupil's Score – Mean Score)^2
1	72	$(72 - 74)^2 = 4$
2	76	$(76 - 74)^2 = 4$
3	74	$(74 - 74)^2 = 0$
4	75	$(75 - 74)^2 = 1$
5	73	$(73 - 74)^2 = 1$
6	74	$(74 - 74)^2 = 0$
7	77	$(77 - 74)^2 = 9$
8	71	$(71 - 74)^2 = 9$
9	72	$(72 - 74)^2 = 4$
10	76	$(76 - 74)^2 = 4$

given that the mean score for class A was 74. Adding up the squared difference of each pupil's score from the mean equals 36. Thus, according to the formula, the standard deviation of the scores in class A is equal to the square root of 36 divided by 10 (the number of pupils who were tested), or 3.6. The square root of 3.6 is equal to 1.89, which is the standard deviation for class A. Calculate for yourself the standard deviation for class B, which also has a mean of 74. You should get a standard deviation of 14.81 [square root of (2194/10) = 14.81]. Notice that the larger the standard deviation, the more spread out the scores are around the mean. Although class A and class B had the same mean score, the standard deviation of class B was much larger than that of class A, indicating greater heterogeneity in class B.

Item Difficulty and Discrimination

As we noted in chapter 11, the difficulty index of a test item is indicated by the proportion or percentage of pupils who got the item correct. Thus, if 20 out of 25 pupils in a class answered an item correctly, the difficulty of that item would be $(20/25) \times 100 = 80$ percent. Thus, somewhat confusingly, the higher the "difficulty," the easier the item.

The difficulty of test items is related to the spread of test scores. If all items on a test are very easy, most pupils will get high scores and there will be few differences among pupils. The same is true if all the test items are very difficult, except that all pupils will get low scores. When the difficulty of test items is around 50 percent, meaning that about half the pupils pass and half fail each item, the resulting test scores will be maximally spread out from low to high. This is an important result for the construction of commercial standardized *norm-referenced* tests, which are intended to compare the relative achievement of pupils. The more pupils' scores differ, the better for making comparisons and distinctions among them. Thus, in standardized norm-referenced test construction, it is necessary to have items that have difficulties in the middle (35 to 65 percent) range to ensure a spread of scores.

In classroom assessment, which is generally *criterion-referenced* and focuses on individual pupil mastery (not differentiation among pupils), item difficulty is not a major concern. Classroom assessment items usually have higher difficulties (i.e., are easier) than standardized, norm-referenced test items. This would be expected as long as classroom tests reflect classroom instruction.

Also as we noted in Chapter 8, a test item's discrimination index compares the difference in performance of high and low test scores on an item. An item is said to have **positive discrimination** if more pupils who do well on the test as a whole answer it correctly than pupils who do poorly on the test as a whole. Thus, if 85 percent of the class with the highest overall test scores got an item correct compared to only 55 percent of those with the lowest overall test scores, the item discrimination would be 85 percent – 55 percent = 30 percent. In determining item discrimination, the lower group's percentage is always subtracted from that of the higher group. The higher the discrimination, the greater the difference between the high and low test scorers on that item. Notice that it is possible to get **negative discriminations.** For example, if 40 percent of the top scorers and 60 percent of the bottom scorers got the item correct, the discrimination index would be 40 percent – 60 percent = –20 percent. In such a case, one might want to check the scoring key or look at the options in the item to try to identify the ones that the top group is selecting incorrectly.

Item discrimination, like item difficulty, is important in the construction of commercial standardized tests. It is necessary that each item in such tests have high positive discrimination. While it is also desirable for classroom tests to have items with positive discrimination, it is less important than for commercial tests because classroom tests are usually scored in a criterion-referenced way and their higher item difficulties reduce the differences between high and low scorers.

Normal Distributions

The *normal distribution* is the familiar "bell-shaped" curve shown in Figure D.1. This curve is extremely important in commercial standardized achievement testing because norms such as the percentile rank and stanine are derived from it.

Normal distributions can be used to describe scores when a large group of people take a well-designed standardized test. As indicated along the bottom of the curve, the lowest possible scores correspond to the far left portion of the curve, while the highest possible scores correspond to the far right portion. Other scores fall at regular increments between the two extremes. The height of the distribution at any given point represents the

FIGURE D.1
*The Normal
Distribution and
Related Measures.*

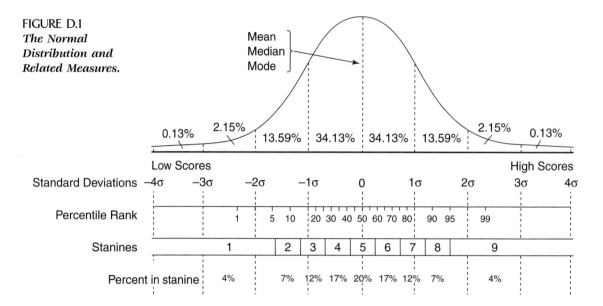

number of pupils who got the score that corresponds to that point. Notice that the distribution is highest in the middle and lowest at the two ends, indicating that most test takers score near the middle and very few score at either end.

As we noted, when a well-designed test with many items is given to a large number of pupils, the resulting scores tend to distribute themselves according to this "normal" pattern. As Figure D.1 shows, the normal distribution has three important properties:

♦ The mean score is exactly in the middle of the distribution, and half of all scores fall above it and half below it.

♦ The median and mode scores are the same as the mean.

♦ The standard deviation divides the normal distribution into sections as follows:

   1. About sixty-eight percent of all the pupils' scores fall between 1 standard deviation below the mean and 1 standard deviation above the mean.

   2. About ninety-five percent of all the pupils' scores fall between 2 standard deviations below the mean and 2 standard deviations above the mean.

   3. Almost 100 percent of all the pupils' scores fall between 3 standard deviations below the mean and 3 standard deviations above the mean.

The following is a concrete illustration of these properties and how they are used in obtaining norm-referenced scores on standardized achievement

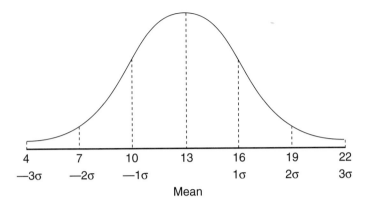

FIGURE D.2
Normal Distribution of Scores with Mean of 13 and Standard Deviation of 3.

tests. Assume you are a standardized test constructor who has produced a 30-item norm-referenced mathematics computation test for seventh graders. To do this, you followed the steps described in Chapter 11: select common objectives, write items to assess these objectives, and try the items out on many seventh graders to identify the items with moderate difficulties and high discriminations to include on the final test version. You have identified the 30 items for your test and have but one additional step to complete: administering the test to a representative sample of 10,000 seventh graders from across the country in order to develop test norms. These norms will be the comparative scores that will be used to interpret future test takers' performance.

You administer the test to the 10,000 seventh graders who are meant to represent all seventh graders across the country, and you score each pupil's test. You now have 10,000 scores. Because you selected items of moderate difficulty and high discrimination and because you tried out the final version of the test on a large number of seventh graders, the distribution of scores on your test will be similar to the normal curve; many pupils will score near the middle of the score range and few will score very low or very high. Because 10,000 individual scores is a large number to deal with, you decide to summarize them by calculating the mean and standard deviation, using the procedures described previously. Let's assume that when your computer finishes these calculations on the math computation test scores, the mean score is 13 and the standard deviation is 3. You have a normal distribution with a mean score of 13 and a standard deviation of 3. This distribution is shown in Figure D.2.

Notice that the score of 13, which is the mean score for the group, is at the center of the distribution. Note also how the standard deviation has been used to mark off other score points on the distribution. The scores that correspond to 1 standard deviation below the mean, 10 (13 − 3 = 10), and to 1 standard deviation above the mean, 16 (13 + 3 = 16), are shown, along with the scores corresponding to 2 standard deviations below (13 – 6 = 7) and above (13 + 6 = 19) the mean and 3 standard deviations below (13 – 9 = 4) and above (13 + 9 = 22) the mean.

Suppose a pupil got a raw score of 13 items correct on your test. What percent of the 10,000 pupils who represent all seventh graders did she perform better than? (Hint: Compare Figure D.2 with Figure D.1) If her score was 13, she was exactly at the mean of the norm group and, according to the first property of the normal curve, the mean divides the normal curve into two equal halves. Thus, she performed better than about 50 percent of seventh graders in the norm group. Notice how using the normal curve allows one to turn a raw score (13) into a percentile rank (50th) (see Chapter 11).

Suppose another pupil had a raw score of 16 items correct. What is that pupil's percentile rank? Look back at Figure D.2 for a clue. Remember that 68 percent of all the pupils are between the score corresponding to the mean minus 1 standard deviation (10) and the score corresponding to the mean plus 1 standard deviation (16). Because the mean (13) divides the normal curve in half, 34 percent of the students are between the mean (13) and 1 standard deviation below the mean (10), and 34 percent are between the mean (13) and 1 standard deviation above the mean (16). So, if a pupil had a score of 16, she was higher than all the 50 percent of pupils who were below the mean and also higher than just about all the 34 percent who were between the mean (13) and 1 standard deviation above the mean (16). Thus, a raw score of 16 on the math computation test corresponds to a percentile rank of 84 (50 + 34 = 84). The pupil scored higher on the test than 84 percent of the norm group. Now see if you can find the percentile rank that corresponds to a raw score of 10 and a raw score of 19.

The above example was designed to illustrate how the normal curve can be used to change raw scores into the comparative scores that can give meaning to standardized norm-referenced test performance. The example did not indicate how to change scores that are not exactly 1, 2, or 3 standard deviations above or below the mean into percentile ranks. Most introductory statistics books provide examples of how to do this, and you should refer to one if you wish further information.

GLOSSARY

Ability What one has learned over a period of time from both school and nonschool sources; one's general capability for performing tasks.

Achievement What one has learned from formal instruction, usually in school.

Affective behaviors Behaviors related to feelings, emotions, values, attitudes, interests, and personality; nonintellectual behaviors.

Analytic scoring Essay scoring method in which separate scores are given for specific aspects of the essay (e.g., organization, factual accuracy, and spelling).

Anecdotal record A short, written report of an individual's behavior in a specific situation or circumstance.

Aptitude One's capability for performing a particular task or skill; usually involves a narrower skill than ability (e.g., mathematics aptitude or foreign language aptitude).

Assessment The broad process of collecting, synthesizing, and interpreting information to aid classroom decision making; includes information gathered about pupils, instruction, and classroom climate.

Average The number derived by adding up all the test scores and dividing the total by the number of pupils who took the test.

B

Bias A situation in which assessment information produces results that give one group an advantage or disadvantage over other groups because of problems in the content, procedures, or interpretations of the assessment information; a distortion or misrepresentation of performance.

C

Checklist A written list of performance criteria associated with a particular activity or product on which an observer marks the pupil's performance on each criterion using a scale that has only two choices.

Commercial achievement tests Typically a norm-referenced test that compares a pupil's score to a national group of similar pupils.

Conceptual knowledge Knowledge that demonstrates understanding of general concepts.

Convergent question A question that has one correct answer.

Criterion-referenced grading Determining the quality of a pupil's performance by comparing it to preestablished standards of mastery.

Curriculum The skills, performances, attitudes, and values pupils are expected to learn from schooling; includes statements of desired pupil outcomes, descriptions of materials, and the planned sequence that will be used to teach pupils.

Cut score A predetermined score used to differentiate levels of pupil performance, given usually in statewide assessment.

D

Difficulty index Indicates the proportion or percentage of pupils who answered a test item correctly.

Direct indicators Information or perspectives provided by a firsthand observer or source.

Discrimination index Indicates the extent to which pupils who get a particular test item correct are also likely to get a high score on the entire test.

Distractor A wrong choice in a selection test item.

Divergent question A question that has more than one acceptable answer.

E

Early assessments Assessments used by teachers in the first weeks of school to get to know pupils so that they can be organized into a classroom society with rules, communication, and control.

Educate To change the behavior of pupils; to teach pupils to do things they could not previously do.

Educational objectives Statements that describe a pupil accomplishment that will result from instruction—specifically, the behavior the pupil will learn to perform and the content on which it will be performed.

Evaluation Process of judging the quality or value of a performance or a course of action.

F

Form The particular version of a commercial test that has more than one equivalent version.

Formative assessment The process of collecting, synthesizing, and interpreting information for the purpose of improving student learning while instruction is taking place; assessment for improvement, not grading.

G

Global objectives Very broad statements of intended learning that require years to accomplish.

Grade equivalent score A standardized test score that describes a pupil's performance on a scale based upon grade in school and month in grade; most commonly misinterpreted score; indicates pupil's level of performance relative to pupils in his/her own grade.

Grades Symbols or numbers used by teachers to represent a pupil's achievement in a subject area.

Grading The process of judging the quality of a pupil's performance.

Grading system The process by which a teacher arrives at the symbol or number that is used to represent a pupil's achievement in a subject area.

H

Holistic scoring Essay scoring method in which a single score is given to represent the overall quality of the essay across all dimensions.

I

Individual Education Program (IEP) A special education plan developed for a pupil after extensive assessment of the pupil's special educational needs.

Instruction The methods and processes by which pupils' behaviors are changed.

Instructional assessment The collection, synthesis, and interpretation of information needed to make decisions about planning or carrying out instruction.

Instructional objectives Specific objectives used to plan daily lessons.

Interpretive exercise A test situation that contains a chart, passage, poem, or other material that the pupil must interpret in order to answer the questions posed.

Items Questions or problems on an assessment instrument.

K

Key A list of correct answers for a test.

L

Level The grade level(s) at which a particular commercial test should be administered to pupils.

Levels of tolerance The extent to which a teacher can tolerate different noise levels, activities, and pupil behavior.

Local norms Norms that are confined to pupils in a specific school district.

Logical error The use of invalid or irrelevant assessment information to judge a pupil's status or performance.

M

Mean The average of a group of scores.

Measurement The process of assigning numbers or categories to performance according to rules and standards (e.g., scoring a test).

Median The middle score of when all scores are listed from lowest to highest.

Mode The score that is obtained by more pupils in a group than any other; there can be more than one mode in group of scores.

N

Negative discrimination When a test item is answered incorrectly more frequently for high scorers on the test than for low scorers; the item discriminates in a different direction than the total score of the test.

Nonstandardized assessment An assessment approach intended to assess a single group of pupils, such as a class.

Norm group The group of pupils who were tested to produce the norms for a test.

Norm-referenced grading Determining the quality of a pupil's performance by comparing it to the performance of other pupils.

Norms A set of scores that describes the performance of a specific group of pupils, usually a national sample at a particular grade level, on a task or test; these scores are used to interpret scores of other pupils who perform the same task or take the same test.

Numerical summarization Use of numbers to describe performance on an assessment.

O

Objective Agreement among independent judges, scorers, or observers.

Official assessments Assessments, such as grading, grouping, placing, and promoting pupils, that teachers are required to carry out because of their official responsibilities.

Options Choices available to select from when answering a multiple-choice test item.

P

Percentile bands The range of percentile ranks in which a pupil is expected to fall on repeated testing; a way to indicate the error in scores to avoid overinterpretation of results.

Percentile rank A standardized test score that describes the percentage of pupils a given pupil scored higher than (e.g., an 89th percentile rank means that a pupil scored higher than 89 percent of the pupils in the norm group).

Performance assessment Observing and judging a pupil's skill in actually carrying out a physical activity (e.g., giving a speech) or producing a product (e.g., building a birdhouse).

Performance criteria The aspects of a performance or product that are observed and judged in performance assessment.

Performance standards The levels of achievement pupils must reach to receive particular grades in a criterion-referenced grading system (e.g., higher than 90 receives an A, between 80 and 90 receives a B, etc.).

Portfolio A well-defined collection of pupil products or performances that shows pupil achievement of particular skills over time.

Positive discrimination When a test item is answered correctly more frequently for high scorers on the test than for low scorers; the item discriminates in the same direction of the total score of the test.

Practical knowledge The beliefs, prior experiences, and strategies that enable a teacher to carry out classroom duties and activities.

Prejudgment Inability to make a fair and objective assessment of another person because of interfering prior knowledge, first impressions, or stereotypes.

Premise The stem or question part of a matching item.

Psychomotor domain Physical and manipulative activities such as holding a pencil, buttoning buttons, serving a tennis ball, playing the piano, and cutting with scissors.

R

Range The difference between the highest and lowest test scores in a group; obtained by subtracting the highest test score from the lowest test score.

Rating scale A written list of performance criteria associated with a particular activity or product on which an observer marks a pupil's performance on each criterion in terms of its quality using a scale that has more than two choices.

Raw score The number of items correct or the total score a pupil obtained on an assessment.

Reliability The extent to which an assessment consistently assesses whatever it is assessing; if an assessment is reliable, it will yield the same or nearly the same information on retesting.

Response The answer choices given for a matching item.

S

Scoring rubric A rating scale based upon written descriptions of varied levels of achievement in a performance assessment; also called a descriptive rating scale.

Selection item A test item to which the pupil responds by selecting the answer from choices given; multiple-choice, true-false, and matching items.

Self-fulfilling prophecy The process in which teachers form perceptions about pupil characteristics, treat pupils as if the perceptions are correct, and pupils respond as if they actually have the characteristics, even though they might not have originally had them; an expectation becomes a reality.

Specific determiners Words that give clues to true-false items; *all, always, never,* and *none* indicate false statements, while *some, sometimes,* and *may* indicate true statements.

Standard deviation A measure of the variability or spread of scores for a group of test takers.

Standardized assessment An assessment that is administered, scored, and interpreted the same for all pupils taking the test, no matter when and where it is used.

Stanine A standardized test score that describes pupil performance on a 9-point scale. Scores of 1, 2, and 3 are often interpreted as being below average; 4, 5, and 6 as being average; and 7, 8, and 9 as being above average.

Stem The part of a multiple-choice item that states the question to be answered.

Subjective Lack of agreement among judges, scorers, or observers.

Subtests Sets of items administered and scored as a separate portion of a longer, more comprehensive test.

Summative assessment The process of collecting, synthesizing, and interpreting information for the purposes of determining pupil learning and assigning grades; assessments made at the end of instruction or teaching.

Supply item A test item to which the pupil responds by writing or constructing his/her own answer; short answer, completion, essay.

Supply question A test item requiring the pupil to write or construct an answer: short answer, completion, essay.

T

Test A formal, systematic, usually paper-and-pencil procedure for obtaining a sample of pupils' behavior; the results of a test are used to make generalizations about how pupils would perform on similar but untested behaviors.

Test battery A group of subtests, each assessing a different subject area but all normed on the same sample; designed to be administered to the same group of test takers.

Test score distribution The listing of test scores from lowest to highest; the spread of pupils' scores.

Testwise skills The test taker's ability to identify flaws in test questions that give away the correct answers; used during tests to outwit poor item writers.

V

Validity The extent to which assessment information is appropriate for making the desired decision about pupils, instruction, or classroom climate; the degree to which assessment information permits correct interpretations of the desired kind; the most important characteristic of assessment information.

CREDITS

Chapter opener 1: © Elizabeth Crews

Chapter opener 2: © Elizabeth Crews

Chapter opener 3: © Mary Kate Denny/PhotoEdit

Chapter opener 4: © Charles Gupton/Corbis

Chapter opener 5: © David Young Wolff/PhotoEdit

Chapter opener 6: © Elizabeth Crews

Chapter opener 7: © Mary Kate Denny/PhotoEdit

Chapter opener 8: © Elizabeth Crews

Chapter opener 9: © Elizabeth Crews

Chapter opener 10: © Elizabeth Crews

Chapter opener 11: © Tony Freeman/PhotoEdit

NAME INDEX

SUBJECT INDEX